T3-BOH-508

SOCIAL PROBLEMS

SOCIAL PROBLEMS

Dennis E. Poplin
Murray State University

Scott, Foresman and Company
Glenview, Illinois
Dallas, Tex. Oakland, N.J. Palo Alto, Cal. Tucker, Ga. London, England

Library of Congress Cataloging in Publication Data

Poplin, Dennis E.
Social problems.

Bibliography: p.
Includes index.
1. United States—Social conditions—1960–
2. Social problems. 3. Deviant behavior. 4. Social institutions—United States. I. Title.
HN59.P663 309.1'73'092 77-10100
ISBN 0-673-07973-2

Printed in the United States of America.

1 2 3 4 5 6 7 8—RRC—82 81 80 79 78 77

To Kay Brandon Poplin and John H. Watson

Acknowledgments

Chapter 2

Saab Motor Company Advertisement cited in MODERN SOCIAL REFORMS: SOLVING TODAY'S SOCIAL PROBLEMS by Arthur B. Shostak, published by Macmillan Publishing Co., Inc. Reprinted by permission of Saab-Scania of America, Inc.

Table 2.1, "Modes of Individual Adaptation to Materialism," from *Social Theory and Social Structure*, Rev. and Enl. Edition, The Free Press, 1957, p. 140. Reprinted by permission of the publisher.

Chapter 3

Selection from ABNORMAL PSYCHOLOGY AND MODERN LIFE by James C. Coleman. Copyright © 1976 Scott, Foresman and Company.

Chapter 4

Selection from "Alcoholism: New Victims, New Treatment," reprinted by permission from TIME, The Weekly Newsmagazine; Copyright Time Inc., 1974.

Figure 4.1, "Behavioral Pattern of Employee with Drinking Problem," from *Counseling on Alcoholism and Related Disorders*, Robert T. Dorris and Doyle F. Lindley, Glencoe, 1968, p. 59.

Table 4.7, "Alcohol-Related Health Hazards," from *Alcohol and Health: Report from the Secretary of Health, Education, and Welfare*, Charles Scribner's Sons, 1973, p. 111. Reprinted by permission of the publisher.

Chapter 5

Selection from "Drug Users Vs. Drug Abusers: How Students Control Their Drug Crisis," by Daniel Yankelovich. Reprinted by permission of *Psychology Today* Magazine, Copyright © 1975 Ziff-Davis Publishing Company.

Chapter 6

Excerpts from "The Porno Plague" reprinted by permission from TIME, The Weekly Newsmagazine; Copyright Time Inc. 1976.

Table 6.1, "Percentage With Premarital Coital Experience," from "Changing Sex Norms in America and Scandinavia," *Journal of Marriage and the Family*, 32, November, 1970, Table 3 by Harold T. Christensen and Christina F. Gregg. Copyright 1970 by the National Council on Family Relations. Reprinted by permission.

Chapter 7

Selection from "All Kinds of Crime—Growing . . . Growing . . . Growing" from U.S. NEWS & WORLD REPORT, December 16, 1974. Copyright © 1974.

Chapter 8

Selection from "Economic Crime: Portrait of an Arrogant Crook," by Jack Horn. Reprinted by permission of *Psychology Today* Magazine, Copyright © 1976 Ziff-Davis Publishing Company.

Table 8.2, "Costs of Index Crimes, 1971," from *The Geography of Crime and Justice*, by Keith D. Harries, McGraw-Hill Book Company, 1974, p. 10. Reprinted by permission.

Chapter 9

Selection from "Those 26 Million 'Poor' " reprinted by permission from TIME, The Weekly Newsmagazine; Copyright Time Inc. 1976.

Figure 9.1, "How the Negative Income Tax Would Work," from "A Way Out of the Welfare Mess," by Edmund K. Faltermeyer, *Fortune*, LXXVIII (July 1968), p. 134. Reprinted by permission from *Fortune*, Copyright Time Inc., 1968.

Table 9.1, "Table of Poverty Lines, 1974," from *The World Almanac and Book of Facts: 1976*, p. 206, Copyright 1975. Reprinted by permission of Newspaper Enterprise Association.

Chapter 10

Selection from James A. Banks, "The Role of the School in a Democratic Society." *Educational Leadership* 32 (3): pp. 163–66, December 1974. (Taken from a condensation of his article which appeared in *Education Digest*, XL, April 1975.) Reprinted with permission of the Association for Supervision and Curriculum Development and James A. Banks. Copyright © 1974 by the Association for Supervision and Curriculum Development.

Figure 10.1, "Annual Unemployment Rates for Whites and Nonwhites, 1954–1973," from *Still a Dream: The Changing Status of Blacks Since 1960* by Sar A. Levitan, William B. Johnston, and Robert Taggart, published by Harvard University Press, 1975.

Table 10.1, "Years of Education Completed by Persons 25 Years of Age and Over, 1972." Adapted from Sar A. Levitan, William B. Johnston, and Robert Taggart, *Still a Dream: The Changing Status of Blacks Since 1960*, 1975, Harvard University Press, Cambridge, Mass.

Table 10.2, "Housing Characteristics of Black Americans." Adapted from Sar A. Levitan, William B. Johnston, and Robert Taggart, *Still a Dream: The Changing Status of Blacks Since 1960*, 1975, Harvard University Press, Cambridge, Mass.

Chapter 11

Selection from "Girls, Boys and Books" by Thomas P. Hanaway and Gordon M. Burghardt. Reprinted by permission of *Psychology Today* Magazine, Copyright © 1976 Ziff-Davis Publishing Company.

Chapter 12

Selection from ABNORMAL PSYCHOLOGY AND MODERN LIFE by James C. Coleman. Copyright © 1976 Scott, Foresman and Company.

Chapter 13

Selection from "Looking to the ZPGeneration" reprinted by permission from TIME, The Weekly Newsmagazine; Copyright Time Inc. 1977.

Figure 13.3, "Schematic Drawing of the Theory of Demographic Transition," from "The History of the Human Population," by Ansley J. Coale. Copyright 1974 by Scientific American, Inc. All rights reserved.

Figure 13.4, "Grain Needed to Produce Other Foods," from "The World Food Crisis," TIME (November 11, 1974, p. 75). Reprinted by permission from TIME, The Weekly News Magazine; Copyright Time Inc., 1974.

Table 13.1, "Doubling Times Under Various Rates of Natural Increase, the World and Its Major Regions: 1977," from *1977 World Population Data Sheet*. Reprinted by permission of the Population Reference Bureau, Inc.

Table 13.2, "Examples of Proposed Measures to Reduce U.S. Fertility." Adapted from Robin Elliot, Lynn C. Landman, Richard Lincoln, and Theodore Tsuoreka, "U.S. Population Growth and Family Planning: A Review of the Literature," *Family Planning Perspectives*, 2 (October 1970), p. ix. By courtesy of the Planned Parenthood Federation of America.

Chapter 14

Selection from "Recreating Family Life: The Means Are in Our Hands," by Bruno Bettelheim as reprinted in *Parents' Magazine*, October 1976. Reprinted by permission of the author.

Table 14.2, "Marital Complaints Among 600 Couples Applying for Divorce, Classified by Sex and Social Position of Respondents." Source: George Levinger, "Sources of Marital Dissatisfaction Among Applicants for Divorce," from *American Journal of Orthopsychiatry*, vol. 36, no. 5. Reprinted by permission.

Table 14.3, "Percentages of Marriages Ending in Divorce or Separation, by Religious Category." Source: Clark E. Vincent, "Interfaith Marriages: Problem or Symptom?" in Ruth E. Albrecht and E. Wilbur Bock (eds.), *Encounter: Love, Marriage, and Family*, Holbrook Press, 1972, p. 222. Reprinted by permission of the author.

Chapter 15

Selection from "How Much Must a Student Master?" reprinted by permission from TIME, The Weekly Newsmagazine; Copyright Time Inc. 1977.

Chapter 16

Selection from "Let the Punishment Fit the Crime" by Philip Brickman. Reprinted by permission of *Psychology Today* Magazine, Copyright © 1977 Ziff-Davis Publishing Company.

Preface

Since there are so many college-level social problems textbooks now on the market, the question might be raised, Why publish yet another textbook on social problems? I will answer this question by pointing out some of the distinctive features of this new book.

First, I have tried to make the book comprehensive. As the table of contents indicates, a large number of social problems and issues are covered—fourteen to be exact. There are, of course, some other social problems which could have been considered; but the most important social problems have been covered, and they have been covered in proper depth.

Second, I have tried to write a book that introduces students to the major concepts, theories, and research findings that pertain to particular social problems. To the greatest extent possible, each problem is analyzed from the standpoints of its extent and severity and its correlates and causes. The end of each chapter explores some of the things that are currently being done or potentially could be done to ameliorate the problem. Each chapter discusses the most significant theories and latest research which bear on the particular problem under discussion.

Finally and most importantly, I have tried to produce a textbook that students will *want* to read. This has been a very challenging task. Every teacher and every author knows the difficulty of presenting concepts and ideas to a sometimes unresponsive student audience. Every attempt has been made to catch and to hold the student reader's interest by using simple but not fatuous language, an informal but not condescending style, and a straightforward but not dull organization.

As in most projects of this kind, the end result has been influenced by many minds and assisted by many hands. First, I must express my appreciation to the personnel of Scott, Foresman and Company for their help and encouragement, especially Robert Runck, Mary Útt, Ralph Croston, John Nolan, and Walter Dinteman. Second, I would like to acknowledge the contributions of several of my colleagues, Professors John H. Watson, Miles E. Simpson, Ed Armstrong, and K. M. George. Furthermore, I would like to thank two of my students, Cynthia Laws and Steven DeVoss, for reading the manuscript and asking helpful questions.

I wish to extend special notes of thanks to Professor Robert Ellis of Amarillo College and Professor Walter J. Cartwright of Texas Tech University. Without the help of Professor Ellis, there would probably not be a chapter on problems in contemporary American education in this book. Professor Cartwright continuously spurred me on and provided me with many ideas.

I also wish to thank Murray State University for providing me with a summer professional leave so that I could work on the manuscript. In particular, I would like to thank Dean Kenneth E. Harrell for his support and encouragement.

Finally, this book could not have been completed without the support and assistance of my wife.

Dennis E. Poplin

Contents

SOCIAL PROBLEMS

PART I

UNDERSTANDING SOCIAL PROBLEMS

Introduction

The Social Setting for Social Problems

Chapter 1
Introduction

When we hear the term *social problem*, most of us immediately think of the murder that occurred last night, of the pollution and traffic congestion in our cities, of people going hungry, of discrimination. We also think of the increasing rates of alcoholism, narcotics addiction, mental illness, and illegitimacy. This catalogue of social problems, of course, is only a very partial list. Given the variety and scope of these different kinds of problems, is it even possible to fashion a working definition of the general term *social problem*?

A Definition of a Social Problem

We will define a social problem as *a pattern of behavior that constitutes a threat to society or to those groups and institutions of which society is composed.* Let us look at this definition phrase by phrase.

"A Pattern of Behavior"

People face many problems, not all of which are *social* problems. For example, earthquakes and tornadoes often destroy lives and property and disrupt regular patterns of social behavior. Earthquakes and tornadoes, however, are not *social* problems because they do not involve a pattern of behavior and because they do not grow out of social interaction; they cannot be eliminated by changing the ways in which people behave. For a problem to be a *social* problem, it must involve a pattern of behavior that is susceptible to human intervention. We should point out, however, that natural disasters such as earthquakes and tornadoes can lead to social problems. In the wake of a serious earthquake, for example, rates of looting and burglary may soar, con men may invade the devastated area in search of the perfect opportunity to make a quick dollar while supposedly helping people to recover from the damages they have suffered, and so on. Geologists and meteorologists, not sociologists, are equipped to examine the causes of earthquakes and tornadoes and the natural patterns they assume.

Crime is an obvious social problem because it involves a pattern of behavior on the part of an individual or group which threatens and infringes on the rights of other individuals or groups and which could lead to a breakdown of social order. Similarly, the practice of forcibly retiring older people from the labor force wastes the talents and abilities of older people and infringes on their right to lead self-sufficient lives. It is the sociologist who is equipped to examine such things as the causes of crime and compulsory retirement and the human patterns they assume.

"That Constitutes a Threat"

All societies have rules and regulations that prohibit such actions as murder, rape, incest, and robbery. These rules and regulations are called *social norms.* The reason that societies have norms prohibiting certain behaviors is simple—if certain behaviors became commonplace, social life would become chaotic and impossible. Can you imagine a society, for example, in which individuals were free to murder those who, in their judgment, had done them wrong? In such a society many marriages would not endure because even a moderately serious family quarrel could result in the death of one or more family members. Likewise, you would be afraid to go to work or to school for fear of losing your life.

Not all social problems, however, grow out of violations of social norms. Indeed, many social problems are directly attributable to behavior that is in accord with social norms. For example, through what we say and what we do, most of us to some extent help to propagate racism and sexism. Likewise, one of the greatest threats to the world is the population explosion.[1] If the world's population continues to grow at its present rate, standards of living will eventually plummet to the point where not a person on the face of the earth will be exempt from the effects of famine and starvation. One of the reasons that the world's population continues to grow rapidly, of course, is that couples around the world continue to have large families. These couples are not acting contrary to the norms and values of their societies; rather, they are clinging to norms and values pertaining to family size that were appropriate in centuries past but which are inappropriate today.

◀ Natural disasters such as earthquakes and tornadoes can lead to social problems. In the wake of a serious earthquake, for example, rates of looting and burglary may soar.

"To Society"

The third important phrase in our definition of a social problem is "to society or to those groups and institutions of which society is composed." No society has ever suffered total collapse because some people became mentally ill, some became addicted to narcotics, or some could not control their consumption of alcoholic beverages. Rather, these patterns of behavior are social problems because they have become common enough to be costly for those groups and institutions of which society is composed. Our point can be illustrated by reference to alcoholism. Rates of job absenteeism seem to be substantially higher among alcoholic employees than among nonalcoholic employees: as the employee's drinking problem becomes more acute, there is a substantial decrease in work efficiency.[2] Likewise, alcoholism can lead to marital disruption and automobile accidents. Given these facts, it is not surprising that alcoholism is considered a serious social problem. Essentially the same comments could be made about mental illness, narcotics addiction, and similar types of behavior.

Social problems, as we have already pointed out, involve patterns of behavior that represent a threat to society or to the groups and institutions of which it is composed. However, what people *perceive* as a threat to society, its groups and/or its institutions varies from time to time and from place to place. What is defined as a serious social problem at one time may not be so defined at another, and what the members of one society perceive as a serious threat to their society may not be so perceived by the members of another society. Earl Rubington and Martin S. Weinberg put the case well when they say:

> Some of the long list of items that have been considered social problems were not so considered in earlier times, places, and circumstances. And similarly some events now being ignored will, in the future, come to have bona fide status as social problems. And finally, some events, regardless of their troublesome nature, never have and never will be considered social problems.[3]

We can cite several examples to illustrate the relativity of social problems. For instance, the use of addictive drugs—mainly opium and its derivatives—for pleasure and relaxation as well as to treat illness has been going on for centuries. Yet narcotics addiction is not regarded as a social problem in many societies and did not become defined as one in the Western world until about one hundred years ago. Today, narcotics addiction is considered by many to be one of the most serious social problems facing our society. Likewise, it has recently been suggested that there is widespread discrimination against pregnant women in the areas of employment, the receipt of unemployment compensation, and education.[4] Although most people do not consider this to be a serious social problem at the present time, it may become so defined in the future.

This brings us to a crucial question: Who identifies and defines social problems for the rest of society? The best answer to this question is, "It depends." Sometimes social problems are defined for the rest of society by those who are most directly affected by them. A case in point is sexism. It has only been in recent years that women's groups have fully brought the inequalities heaped on women to public attention, and it has only been in recent years that sexism has come to be defined by large segments of the public as a serious social problem. Sometimes scientists play a key role in defining social problems. It is doubtful, for example, that environmental decay would be considered a social problem if scientists had not provided a steady stream of information about pollution, resource depletion, and so on. Sometimes the government plays a key role in identifying and defining social problems. The government can pass a law against a certain behavior or create a bureaucracy to regulate that behavior. Sometimes the government can overestimate the seriousness of a problem. For example, through its actions the government has fostered the notion that the use of marijuana is an extremely serious social problem. In this book, however, we shall argue that the use of marijuana is not even a social problem.

We have stressed the idea that social problems involve patterns of behavior that people *perceive* as problems. This being the case, what happens when different groups in a society define the same problem in radically different ways? What happens if a pattern of behavior is hidden from public view and therefore cannot be perceived as a threat to society or to the groups and institutions of which it is composed?

To be more specific, it should be obvious that what one defines as a social problem depends a great deal on one's race, age, education, place of residence, sex, socioeconomic status, and religion. Most Americans would agree, for example, that we still have serious race relations problems in the United States. However, the racist's definition of the problem differs radically from that of the civil libertarian. To the racist, the race problem in the United States involves the breakdown of social order and the destruction of a system of "racial etiquette" that worked "well" for years. To the civil libertarian, the problem is that racial prejudice violates the founding ideas of our democracy—freedom, equality, and the right of all to develop to their fullest capacities. To whom do we listen?

Furthermore, many patterns of behavior are hidden from view and therefore cannot be defined as social problems. For instance, has racial discrimination always been a social problem in the United States? Or did it become a problem in the middle of the twentieth century when millions of Americans began waking up to its social, economic, and psychological costs? Has the use of addictive drugs always been a social problem in the United States? Or did it become a social problem in 1914 when Congress brought narcotics addiction to public attention by making the sale, transfer, or possession of narcotics illegal?[5] We could cite other examples of social problems that were not considered as such in the past because people were not aware of them. In the future, social problems that we do not recognize today will be brought to public attention.

Because of these difficulties, the sociologist must have the freedom to participate in the process of identifying and defining social problems. In deciding what constitutes a social problem, sociologists are not arbitrary and capricious. Rather, they base their decision on their understanding of American values.[6] The sociologist argues that racial discrimination is a social problem in the United States partly because it flies in the face of deeply rooted values, such as our belief in freedom, equality, and the right of each person to realize his or her full potential. Similarly, the sociologist argues that poverty has always been a basic social problem in the United States, even though poverty in America has only recently been rediscovered.[7] One reason is that poverty condemns people to a sometimes permanently inferior status, a fact that clashes with some highly cherished American values.

Perspectives on Social Problems

A variety of concepts and theories have been developed to explain each of the social problems we will discuss in this book. The concepts and theories that are used to explain one problem are going to differ from the concepts and theories that are used to explain another. Nevertheless, there are several overall perspectives that help us to see what certain social problems have in common. These perspectives also allow us to categorize social problems in some consistent way. In this book we will analyze and categorize social problems from the standpoints of deviant behavior, problems of structure, and institutional crises.

Deviant Behavior

Generally speaking, the term *deviant behavior* refers to a situation in which a person cannot or does not act in ways considered acceptable by most members of society. To be more specific, deviant behavior can take two forms. The first form involves an outright violation of social norms: criminals and juvenile delinquents are considered deviants because they purposefully violate important social rules and regulations. The second form of deviant behavior includes those people who adopt socially unacceptable ways of dealing with their environment. Most contemporary books on social problems, for instance, consider the mentally ill, alcoholic individuals, and those who abuse drugs and narcotics to be deviants. These people are considered deviants not only because they violate the norms of society but also because mental illness, alcoholism, drug abuse, and narcotics addiction interfere with their ability to play their social roles.

There is one extremely important fact that must be noted about the term *deviant:* it does *not* imply a moral judgment or moral disapproval on the part of the sociologist. Rather, it is a neutral value term that simply refers to a person who cannot or does not adhere to the norms of society—nothing more and nothing less. As we shall see, there are many causes of deviant behavior, only one of which is the purposeful, willful violation of social norms. Among the other reasons for deviant behavior are that certain people are unaware of some societal norms and that some others are literally unable to meet social expectations.

Explanations of Deviant Behavior

The causes of deviant behavior are many and varied. In Part II of this book we shall examine in great detail specific theories about the causes of mental illness, alcoholism, drug abuse and narcotics addiction, sexual deviance, juvenile delinquency, and crime. Now, however, we will look at three general explanations of deviant behavior.

Ignorance From time to time all of us unintentionally violate norms either because we are ignorant of their very existence or because we do not know that we are violating them. Most of us are appalled, for example, when we find out that we have been systematically violating a law that we did not know even existed. It is a rare person who has not at one time or another unintentionally done something that is highly embarrassing. We do not, of course, consider deviant acts performed out of sheer ignorance or temporary carelessness to be very serious—punishment may consist of a small fine, teasing, ridicule, or gossip.

The Desire to Achieve The idea that deviant behavior represents an illegitimate means to attain a legitimate end has been popular in sociology.[8] To cite a common example, almost from birth the American child, regardless of social class, is taught that

▲ Almost from birth, the American child, regardless of social class, is taught that the possession of a wealth of material goods is a highly desirable goal. Furthermore, the middle- or upper-class child acquires the ability to obtain these goods through legitimate channels.

the possession of a wealth of material goods is a highly desirable goal. Furthermore, the middle- or upper-class child acquires the ability to obtain these goods through legitimate channels. When the middle-class child is young, his or her parents provide the best of everything, including a quality education. After graduation, the middle-class child is most likely to be equipped to compete in a world that measures success in materialistic terms.

On the other hand, the lower-class child often lacks the opportunity to realize success in legitimate ways. As a result, the lower-class youth may resort to shoplifting, burglary, or gambling as a means of achieving the goal. Likewise, if environmental factors preclude achieving the goal, the youth may simply give up and not even try to reach the goal. In short, he or she may become a retreatist.[9] Retreatists may be particularly likely to find their niche in a subculture which is marked by the excessive use of drugs and alcohol.

Labeling Recently, much has been written about labeling as a source of deviance. According to labeling theory,

> forms of deviance *per se* do not differentiate deviants from non-deviants; it is the responses of the conventional and conforming members of the society who identify and interpret behavior which sociologically transforms persons into deviants.[10]

Put most simply, labeling theory maintains that people become deviants when society evaluates a pattern of behavior negatively and attaches the label *deviant* to it. Sometimes this is done on a formal basis—by passing a law that says, for example, "If you use heroin, you are a deviant." Sometimes the labeling process occurs on a more informal basis, such as when acquaintances say, "We do not understand your behavior, and therefore you must have a mental problem." Labeling theory maintains that there is nothing inherent in patterns of behavior themselves which makes them deviant. Rather, deviant behavior is a result of society's decisions as to which types of behavior are acceptable and which are not.

Labeling theory maintains that people become deviants when society evaluates a pattern of behavior negatively and attaches the label *deviant* to it.
▼

Once someone is considered deviant, the label alone may serve as a stimulus for that person to engage in further deviant activities. As Ritchie P. Lowry puts it, "If someone is continually treated as inferior, dangerous, and deviant, the chances are great that he will come to see himself in this way and act accordingly."[11] This is simply an extension of the old sociological principle

that people tend to act as others expect them to act and is well illustrated by reference to the ex-convict. Many people consider ex-convicts to still be criminals; hence they are not fully accepted into the law-abiding community. Likewise, because they have the label *criminal* or *con*, they are often unable to find jobs. Given the general society's reaction to the convict, it is not surprising that many ex-convicts commit further crimes.

Deviant Behavior and Social Issues

In our preceding discussion of deviant behavior, the reader may have noticed that we have not referred to marijuana use, homosexuality, prostitution, and the consumption of pornography as social problems. The reason is that these patterns of behavior are not, strictly speaking, social problems. Rather, they are best thought of as *social issues.*

To be more specific, we have defined a social problem as a pattern of behavior that constitutes a threat to society or to those groups and institutions of which society is composed. At the present time, not one of the patterns of behavior just mentioned constitutes such a threat. Contrary to what many people think, marijuana use does not lead to crime and the marijuana user does not necessarily develop a deviant life-style. Likewise, our birth rate is not affected in any significant way by the small percentage of Americans who prefer homosexual over heterosexual relationships. And, if anything, prostitution is becoming less and less important as a sexual outlet. Finally, it simply is not true that pornography leads to sex crimes and other disruptive patterns of behavior. Thus, it is more accurate to say that marijuana use, homosexuality, prostitution, the consumption of pornographic materials, and so on are social issues rather than social problems.

Social issues frequently arise when a group of people engage in a pattern of behavior which is not, objectively speaking, a threat to society but that is nonetheless the object of widespread and sometimes vigorous social disapproval. Sometimes this disapproval can in itself create problems. Because the public holds the marijuana user, the homosexual, the prostitute, and even the person who consumes pornographic materials in such low esteem, these people are thrown into the deviant category and suffer all of the negative consequences of being labeled as such. This brings us to a basic question that might well guide our discussion of these patterns of behavior: Given the fact that marijuana use and sexual deviance do not at present constitute a threat to society and the groups and institutions of which it is composed, should we discontinue referring to these patterns of behavior as deviant and instead recognize that human beings can be shaped and formed in a wide variety of different ways? Many marijuana users, homosexuals, and prostitutes are now demanding an affirmative answer to this question. On the other hand, society in general continues to define these alternative ways of behaving as evil, immoral, and illegal. Because the right of the individual to engage in these patterns of behavior as opposed to society's right to exercise control over them will continue to be a controversial issue in the years ahead, we will discuss the social issues of marijuana use, homosexuality, prostitution, and the consumption of pornographic materials in Part II.

Problems of Structure

Most sociologists would agree with Jonathan H. Turner's contention that "major social problems are created, maintained, and exacerbated by prominent features of American social structure."[12] In Part III of this book we will look closely at problems of structure—problems of poverty, prejudice and discrimination, sexism, aging, and population growth. But in the next few sections, we will try to briefly sketch how our social structure creates, maintains, and exacerbates social problems. We will look at the concepts of structured inequality, social disorganization, and value conflict respectively.

Structured Inequality

There is a growing recognition that many structural social problems are created and maintained by the inequalities that are built into our society. All societies have systems of social stratification. Among other things, this means that some people are more highly rewarded than others. Some people have a great deal of money and a great deal of power. Other people have little or no money and power. There are reasons why societies have systems of stratification, but they need not concern us here.[13]

One consequence of structured inequality is that some people get locked into their disadvantaged positions. A case in point are the poor. Because of their lack of money, the poor are usually forced to live in neighborhoods where schools are bad. As a result, poor children receive an inferior education or become school dropouts at an early age. In addition, because their families are often isolated from the middle and upper classes, poor children do not always learn how to cope with employers and may not learn middle-class norms relating to punctuality and good workmanship. The end result is that the children of poor families reach adulthood ill equipped to function in and contribute to a highly technological society. They inherit the same poverty and economic deprivation that characterized their fathers and mothers. Among the other social problems that can be fruitfully analyzed in terms of structured inequality are racism, sexism, and the problems of aging.

Social Disorganization

The term *social disorganization* draws our attention to the fact that many social problems grow out of faults and inconsistencies in the structure of society itself. Human societies can change with breathtaking rapidity, but not all the elements in a society change at the same rate. The result is that there may be a lack of coordination between the various elements which, in turn, can give rise to social problems.

The concept of social disorganization can help us analyze the problems of older Americans. When we were a predominately rural nation and most Americans lived on farms, the needs of older people were met partly because they maintained control over the purse strings and held the deeds to the family farm. Quite often, young and middle-aged adults were dependent on their parents for housing and it was not uncommon for three or even four generations to live under the same roof. In short, old people could be reasonably sure that their children would be around and would help them when they became sick or disabled.

Today, however, we live in a highly urbanized society. In an urban society, the typical young or middle-aged adult is financially independent of his or her parents, is geographically mobile, and is ill equipped to house and care for aging parents. In sum, because of rapid urbanization, conditions have changed to the point where the family can no longer be expected to completely meet the needs of older people. Yet we have failed to develop alternative community resources to meet the financial, health, nutritional, housing, and other needs of old people. Besides the problem of aging, the concept of social disorganization is often used to analyze poverty, divorce, sexism, and racism.

The concept of social disorganization is valuable because it reminds us that many social problems are a direct result of social change. As Rubington and Weinberg put it, "The root cause of social disorganization is, broadly speaking, social change. Parts of the system become out of tune with other parts as changes occur."[14] Indeed, whenever we analyze a social problem, we can profitably ask at least three questions: (1) To what extent is the problem a product of change? (2) What, if any, changes helped to

Many structural social problems are created and maintained by the inequalities that are built into our society. Among other things, this means that some people are more highly rewarded than others.

AUTO SALES
EX

create the problem? (3) What changes are required to alleviate the problem?

Value Conflict

Another useful concept for analyzing the origin of structural social problems is value conflict. The term *value,* of course, refers to anything that the members of a society consider worthwhile to pursue and attain—it can be a desirable object, state, or condition. There are some value orientations that are shared by almost everyone. Most of us, for example, value freedom, democracy, and individualism.[15]

At the same time, in our complex, heterogeneous society it is inevitable that different groups will occasionally hold different value orientations. Sometimes these differing value orientations can and do come into conflict. When conflict occurs, a social problem can emerge. For example, we have been socialized to believe that males must take the primary responsibility for supporting their families. This value orientation, in turn, led to the belief that males should be paid more than females, that males should have first claim on available jobs, and so on. As long as women accepted this definition of the male role, sexism was not identified and defined as a social problem. However, many women have now come to realize that the value that we place on male dominance of the labor market conflicts with the desire that women also have to be economically successful. The value conflict (competing interests) perspective can also help us understand racial and ethnic discrimination, poverty, and a number of other social problems.

Two facts should be noted about value conflict. First, conflict between different interest groups is not inevitably bad for society.[16] Rather, when value conflicts are successfully resolved, the result may be a society that is more just for all its members. For example, we are slowly taking steps to tone down and perhaps even eliminate blatantly sexist practices in our society. As a result, someday both men and women may enjoy more freedom and variety in the way that they conduct their lives. Second, it should be obvious that there is a close relationship between value conflict and structured inequality. Thus, very often the advantaged members of society create social structures which prevent disadvantaged groups from competing with them. Over the course of our history, for example, institutional structures have emerged that keep black Americans and other minority groups in a subservient position. Similarly, our society is structured in such a way that the poor find it difficult to climb out of their disadvantaged economic position.

Institutional Crises

The term *institution* refers to "a formal and stable way of carrying out an activity or function that is important to society."[17] All societies have institutions which socialize the young, produce needed goods and services, help people through times of crisis, and maintain social order. When institutions do not function properly, social problems can arise.

In Part IV of this book we shall look at three social institutions that are not functioning adequately. First, we shall look at the family as a social institution and its attendant problems. Second, we shall examine the many crises that beset our educational institution. Third, we shall look at the failure of our legal institution to dispense equal justice to all and to rehabilitate criminals.

Of the three institutions we shall be looking at in Part IV, the family is far and away the most important sociologically and has produced the greatest amount of intense controversy and debate. The family is a critically important institution because it both reproduces, socializes, and nurtures the young and it provides people with much needed primary group ties. It is therefore essential that the student of social problems keep a close eye on increasing rates of divorce and illegitimacy and on emerging forms of marriage and family life. If we are unable to develop and sustain patterns of marriage and family life that meet the needs of both the individual and society as we approach the twenty-first century, the very survival of our society will be placed in jeopardy.

Discussion Questions

1. Can the weather ever be considered a social problem? Could a severe and prolonged heat or cold wave be a social problem? If not, could it create or exacerbate other social problems? If so, which ones?

2. If the public is not aware of a pattern of behavior that constitutes a threat to society or to those groups and institutions of which society is composed, is it a social problem anyhow? What role do the media, particularly television, play in bringing social problems to public attention?

3. Who should decide what constitutes a social problem? Is this something that should be decided by the general public, by pollsters, by political leaders, by sociologists? Explain and justify your answer.

4. Is cigarette smoking, objectively speaking, a social problem? Do Americans currently consider cigarette smoking to be a social problem? If not, do you think that they will at some time in the future?

5. What is a social norm? Have you personally ever violated any norms? If so, why? To what extent can we all, in a certain sense, be considered deviants?

6. What is meant by the labeling perspective on deviant behavior? Can you think of any undesirable patterns of behavior that you display simply because other people expect you to display them?

7. What is meant by structured inequality? Are ghetto children really locked into their disadvantaged social position? Do ghetto children have a reasonable amount of opportunity to escape from the ghetto if they try hard to do so?

8. Are the ultimate consequences of conflict between different groups inevitably bad? What are some of the good things that might eventually grow out of intergroup conflict?

9. By using the concept of social disorganization, analyze the phenomenon of divorce as it occurs in our society. Might our high divorce rate be due to rapid social change? What are some of the social and cultural changes occurring in our society that might influence our divorce rate?

Glossary

deviant behavior Conduct considered unacceptable by most members of society. Deviant behavior can take two forms—the outright violation of social norms and the adoption of socially unacceptable ways of dealing with one's environment.

institution A formal and stable way of carrying out an activity or function that is important to a society. All societies have several basic social institutions—familial, religious, economic, political, and educational.

labeling theory A perspective on deviant behavior which maintains that there is nothing inherent in patterns of behavior themselves which makes them deviant. Rather, people are likely to behave deviantly when society evaluates their behavior negatively and attaches the label *deviant* to it.

norms (or social norms) Shared rules and expectations that govern our conduct in social situations, for example, it is against social norms to appear naked in public, to get drunk on the job, to commit murder, and so on.

social disorganization A situation in which social problems stem from faults and inconsistencies in the structure of society itself. Social disorganization is often the direct result of rapid social change.

social issue A pattern of behavior which is not, objectively speaking, a threat to society but which is nonetheless the object of widespread and sometimes vigorous social disapproval, for example, homosexuality and prostitution are social issues.

social problem A pattern of behavior that constitutes a threat to society or to those groups and institutions of which society is composed.

structured inequality Inequalities which are built into society itself. Structured inequalities often lock people into their disadvantaged social positions.

value Anything that the members of a society consider worthwhile to pursue and attain—a desirable object, state, or condition.

value conflict A situation in which two or more value systems clash with one another, for example, the belief in neighborhood schooling versus the belief in school busing to achieve equal educational opportunity.

Suggestions for Further Reading

Becker, Howard S., *Outsiders: Studies in the Sociology of Deviance* (New York: Free Press, 1963). An extremely important contribution to the labeling perspective on deviance. Becker illustrates his concepts with studies of marijuana users and dance musicians, which he refers to as a "deviant occupational group."

Eitzen, D. Stanley, *Social Structure and Social Problems in America* (Boston: Allyn and Bacon, 1974). An insightful analysis of the interaction between social problems, social institutions, and social values in America. The author relies heavily on a conflict approach to the study of social problems.

Erikson, Kai T., *Wayward Puritans: A Study in the Sociology of Deviance* (New York: Wiley, 1966). An impressive book which uses historical data on the Puritans of Massachusetts Bay Colony to develop insight into the sociology of deviance.

Glaser, Daniel, *Social Deviance* (Chicago: Markham, 1971). A short but penetrating discussion of deviance and social control in the United States.

Lowry, Ritchie P., *Social Problems: A Critical Analysis of Theories and Public Policy* (Lexington, Mass.: Heath, 1973). Probably the best introduction to social problems paradigms that is available. Through analysis and the use of numerous examples, Lowry sheds much light on deviant behavior, social and cultural disorganization, and social problems as functions of the social system.

Mills, C. Wright, "The Promise," in Frank Lindenfeld, ed., *Radical Perspectives on Social Problems* (New York: Macmillan, 1968), pp. 13–21.

In this excerpt taken from his classic work, *The Sociological Imagination*, Mills draws a distinction between private troubles and public issues. It is the sociologist's task to study public issues for it is in them that the clues to understanding private troubles are to be found.

Rubington, Earl, and Martin S. Weinberg, eds., *The Study of Social Problems: Five Perspectives* (New York: Oxford, 1971). This helpful volume provides clear summaries of five different perspectives on social problems, three of which are deviant behavior, social disorganization, and value conflict. It also contains reprints of some of the most significant articles and writings pertaining to each of these perspectives.

Turner, Jonathan H., *American Society: Problems of Structure*, 2nd Ed. (New York: Harper & Row, 1976). This volume shows how some of the most pressing social problems of our time are the direct result of the way in which our society is structured.

Notes

[1]For a popular account of the world population explosion, see Paul R. Erlich, *The Population Bomb*, New Rev. Ed. (New York: Ballantine, 1976). A more sophisticated and advanced discussion of world and national population problems is to be found in Philip M. Hauser, *The Population Dilemma*, 2nd Ed. (Englewood Cliffs, N.J.: Prentice-Hall, 1970).

[2]See Harrison M. Trice, "The Job Behavior of Problem Drinkers," in David J. Pittman and Charles R. Synder, eds., *Society, Culture, and Drinking Patterns* (New York: Wiley, 1962), pp. 493–510. See also H. M. Trice, "Alcoholic Employees: A Comparison with Psychotic, Neurotic, and 'Normal' Personnel," *Journal of Occupational Medicine*, 7 (March, 1965), pp. 94–98.

[3]Earl Rubington and Martin S. Weinberg, eds., *The Study of Social Problems: Five Perspectives* (New York: Oxford, 1971), p. 5.

[4]See Eve Cary, "Pregnancy Without Penalty," *The Civil Liberties Review*, 1 (Fall, 1973), pp. 31–48.

[5]For a history of narcotics legislation in the United States see Rufus King, *The Drug Hang-up; America's Fifty-Year Folly* (New York: Norton, 1972). See also Alfred R. Lindesmith, *The Addict and the Law* (Bloomington, Ind.: Indiana, 1965), pp. 3–34.

[6]Here we are not saying that sociologists ought to decide what values Americans *should* hold in high esteem. Rather, we are simply suggesting that because he or she is a student of society, the sociologist is in a particularly strategic position to tell us what values and beliefs Americans *do* hold in high esteem.

[7]This rediscovery is due chiefly to the work of Michael Harrington. See Michael Harrington, *The Other America* (New York: Macmillan, 1962).

[8]See Robert K. Merton, *Social Theory and Social Structure*, Rev. Ed. (New York: Free Press, 1957), pp. 131–60.

[9]*Ibid.*, pp. 153–55.

[10]John I. Kitsuse, "Societal Reaction to Deviant Behavior: Problems of Theory and Method," *Social Problems*, 9 (Winter, 1962), p. 253.

[11]Ritchie P. Lowry, *Social Problems: A Critical Analysis of Theories and Public Policy* (Lexington, Mass.: Heath, 1973), p. 118. See also Daniel Glaser, *Social Deviance* (Chicago: Markham, 1971), p. 42.

[12]Jonathan H. Turner, *American Society: Problems of Structure* (New York: Harper & Row, 1972), pp. 1–2.

[13]A classical analysis of why all societies have a system of social stratification has been offered by Kingsley Davis and W. E. Moore, "Some Principles of Stratification," *American Sociological Review*, 10 (April, 1945), pp. 242–49.

[14]Rubington and Weinberg, *The Study of Social Problems*, p. 53.

[15]For a more thorough discussion of major value orientations in America, see Robin M. Williams, Jr., *American Society: A Sociological Interpretation*, 3rd Ed. (New York: Knopf, 1970), pp. 452–500.

[16]See Lewis A. Coser, *The Functions of Social Conflict* (New York: Free Press, 1956).

[17]David Popenoe, *Sociology*, 2nd Ed. (Englewood Cliffs, N.J.: Prentice-Hall, 1974), p. 112.

Chapter 2
The Social Setting for Social Problems

Values and Social Problems
- Material Success
  - *Conformists*
  - *Innovators*
  - *Ritualists*
  - *Retreatists*
  - *Rebels*
  - *A Final Note*
- Individualism
- Work
  - *Blue-Collar Problems*
  - *White-Collar Problems*
- Violence
  - *What Is Violence?*
  - *The Tools of Violence*

Urbanism and Social Problems
- Large Population Size
- High Population Density
- Heterogeneity

The Amelioration of Social Problems
- Individual Treatment
- Law
- Government Action

Summary

"We wouldn't have any social problems if people would just straighten up and act like decent, hard-working, law-abiding, God-fearing Americans!" How often we have heard this old bromide or words to the same effect—the sentiment has been around since cherry pie. Many of us still believe that social problems are an abnormal, malignant growth on an otherwise healthy society. If this cancer could only be cut out, some of us like to think, all would be right with our world.

In fact, however, most, if not all, of our social problems are deeply rooted in the structure of our complex society. They are both natural and predictable and can be traced to those very values that we define as good, just, or desirable. Yet another cause of some of our most pressing problems is the rapid pace at which our society is becoming urbanized. In less than a century the United States has become one of the most highly urbanized nations on the face of the earth.

Values and Social Problems

In order to clarify just how social problems are a natural, predictable outcome of our complex society, in this section we will

We define success in materialistic terms, and people who do not achieve success in these terms are generally considered failures by both themselves and other people.
▼

examine some basic American values and the problems that they create. We will explore four aspects of our value system—material success, individualism, work, and violence.

Material Success

Americans place profound emphasis on material success.[1] The array of things we want seems limitless—split-level homes, luxurious cars, clothes for every occasion, and the latest gimmicks, gadgets, and appliances. We also want enough money to travel widely and entertain extravagantly. In short, we define success in materialistic terms, and people who do not achieve success in these terms are generally considered failures by both themselves and other people.

A noted sociologist, Robert K. Merton, has developed a method of analyzing the relationship between materialism and social problems.[2] His basic theory is that the achievement of wealth and material success is a highly esteemed goal in our society but that different individuals, because of their circumstances, adopt different orientations to this goal. As shown in Table 2.1, individuals can be classified as conformists, innovators, ritualists, retreatists, or rebels.

Table 2.1
Modes of Individual Adaptation to Materialism

Modes of Adaptation	Acceptance of Goal	Acceptance of Approved Means of Achieving Goal
Conformity	Yes	Yes
Innovation	Yes	No
Ritualism	No	Yes
Retreatism	No	No
Rebellion	No	No

Adapted from Robert K. Merton, *Social Theory and Social Structure*, Rev. Ed. (New York: Free Press, 1957), p. 140.

Conformists

Conformists have two basic characteristics. First, they accept the positive value we place on materialism and believe that it is good to be affluent and materially successful. Second, they achieve material success using the means that society considers legitimate—hard work, wise investments, prudent savings. In sum, conformists accept materialism as a goal and use socially acceptable means to achieve it.

Fortunately, most of us are conformists. Otherwise our rates of deviant behavior would be much higher. However, the pursuit of material success through hard work can be carried to destructive extremes. Workaholics, for example, are people who, while pursuing material success, become so addicted to their work that their family and social relationships deteriorate; eventually their physical and mental health may suffer.[3]

Innovators

Innovators accept the positive value we place on material success but reject working hard, investing, and saving as the means to achieve it. They devise instead their own means of realizing material success, including robbery, extortion, fraud, or income tax evasion. Innovators use deviant means to achieve legitimate ends.

Clearly, innovators are the cause of some of our most serious social problems. For example, to professional robbers a crime is a means of livelihood. During any year the robber may make four or five "big scores." The gain is usually more than $500 in a robbery, sometimes going up to more than $10,000.[4]

Others who pursue material success through the use of illegitimate means are *some* kidnappers, prostitutes, shoplifters, and gamblers. The word *some* must be emphasized because deviant behavior has many causes. In some cases, for example, kidnappers do not seek money for personal gain but use kidnapping as a means of drawing attention to a cause or putting pressure on political authorities.

Ritualists

Ritualists are people who have given up hope of achieving wealth and material success but nonetheless continue to engage ritualistically in conformistlike behavior. Examples of ritualists include disenchanted blue-collar workers, migrant laborers, and older persons who continue to slave away at their jobs even though they have come to believe that work doesn't really pay off. Ritualists often sum up their attitudes in such statements as, "I'll never get anywhere. It's just my lot in life to work hard."

We normally give little thought to ritualists as either having or creating social problems. Since they go through the motions of conforming to social expectations, their problems are not immediately apparent. Nonetheless, if large numbers of people begin to feel that their situation is essentially hopeless, the potential problems are great. Indeed, the breakdown of ritualism seems to have been a major factor contributing to racial unrest during the 1960s when many blacks concluded that no matter how hard they tried they could not achieve success through the traditional system of getting a good education and a job with a future.[5] If in spite of their best efforts individuals repeatedly fail to realize material success, they are likely to adopt some other mode of orientation toward materialism.

Retreatists

Retreatists are similar to ritualists in that they also give up achieving wealth and material success. Retreatists, however, no longer engage in goal-oriented behavior—they are true social dropouts.

Retreatists not only give up achieving wealth and material success, they do not even engage in goal-oriented behavior—they are true social dropouts.

There are many examples of retreatism: "In this category fall some of the adaptive activities of psychotics, autists, pariahs, outcasts, vagrants, vagabonds, tramps, chronic drunkards, and drug addicts."[6] Some unemployed persons also become retreatists.

These persons sometimes try repeatedly to obtain employment and, after failing time and again, eventually drop out of the labor market. As a result of their inability to play expected roles, they may abandon their families and never be heard from again.

Retreatism is a problem for society for two reasons. First, people who retreat from supporting their families place great burdens on their spouses and children and on the taxpayers who must often assume the cost of supporting their families. Second, retreatists participate only marginally, if at all, in the production of goods and services so they contribute little if anything to society. At the same time, their behavior may make costly demands, in terms of time and money, on police, courts, and welfare and rehabilitative agencies. Retreatism may be the only way some people can orient themselves to society's goal of material success, but it is not functional for society itself. Our society would not last long if retreatism occurred on a massive scale.

Rebels

Rebels, like retreatists, reject both the emphasis our society puts on material success and the socially approved means of achieving this success. There is, however, a basic difference between rebels and retreatists—retreatists simply give up and stop trying whereas rebels openly challenge our materialistic values. To rebels, materialistic values are negative values that are not worth pursuing.

Perhaps the best example of rebels were the hippies of the 1960s who maintained that wealth and material success were not worth pursuing and that there were better things in life.[7]

> [T]he hippies repudiated the values of conventional society, particularly as these related to work and commerce. They decried consumption mania—the ethic and passions which compel people to buy more and more. They grieved that so many people are locked into the system, making or selling things which other people do not need and buying from them equally useless things.[8]

Regrettably, the hippie movement became entangled with drug abuse and sexual exploitation (perhaps a by-product of the "do-your-own-thing" ethic and the desire to escape the constraints of middle-class morality). Many of the hippies' core values were essentially positive. Some segments of the hippie movement believed in sharing possessions, called for love and equality between the sexes, and advocated the development of individual creative potential. Indeed, there was enough of value in the hippie movement that it has been suggested that "we may all be hippies someday."[9]

Some people feel that rebels are a threat to our society because they question its values and goals and they reject material wealth and hard work. This is undoubtedly a reason why society in general was so hostile to the hippie movement. However, from another perspective rebels can be thought of as making a positive contribution. If nothing else, they force other people to reexamine and rethink their own values and they suggest alternate life-styles. Hippies and other rebels have raised a number of important questions: Have we become so enamored with the pursuit of wealth that we have sacrificed our humanity? Is it more important to achieve material success than to enjoy family and friends?

A Final Note

Perhaps, after reading the preceding sections on materialism, you may find yourself agreeing with the rebels that materialism is a bad value and ought to be rejected. But we should caution you now not to overreact; do not ignore the very positive effects materialism can have. The emphasis we place on material success undoubtedly accounts for the growing, dynamic quality of our society. And, if America is to grow and prosper, we will have to continue to work hard; and most of us will continue to be motivated to work hard by the promise of monetary reward. We can only hope that we will eventually temper our emphasis on material success so that there are fewer costly failures in both human and material terms.[10]

Individualism

Our society believes strongly in the individual and in individualism: "The cult of individual personality . . . sets a high value on the unique development of each individual personality and is correspondingly adverse to invasion of individual integrity: to be a person is to be independent, responsible, and self-respecting, and thereby to be worthy of concern and respect in one's own right."[11] The component of individualism that seems most closely linked to social problems is the belief that individuals should be free to be what they want to be and to do what they want to do. We have traditionally given individuals a tremendous amount of freedom and we have expected them to use their freedom wisely.

Our belief in rugged individualism has probably not created social problems so much as it has hindered efforts to solve social problems. Our emphasis on individual personality can lead us to misinterpret the causes of social problems and thus lead us to the wrong answers. We often blame such diverse social problems as mental illness, crime, alcoholism, and poverty on faults and weaknesses in the individual; and we further argue that we can only solve these problems by better moral training, "teaching the individual a lesson," or punishment. In short, social problems are assumed to be caused by bad people who choose not to use their freedom wisely.

Our strong belief in individualism may also account for the generally poor quality of our aid and rehabilitation services; our country has provided fewer welfare services for disadvantaged people than many other countries have.[12] Furthermore, our solution to many social problems such as crime, juvenile delinquency, and narcotics addiction has been severe punishment. We have made little effort to reclaim deviant individuals and to reintegrate them into the larger society.

This picture of poor rehabilitation services combined with an emphasis on punishment can be traced back to our faith in the individual. We reason that individuals can solve their problems if they want to—the poor can lift themselves out of poverty if they only work more diligently, and with a little self-discipline alcoholic individuals and the mentally ill can overcome their problems. And if some individuals stray too far and commit a crime or violate a basic moral code, punishment is needed to "straighten them out." We continually fail to realize that most social problems are not due to human faults and weaknesses at all but have their roots in the structure of our society itself.

Work

Traditionally, the profound significance we attach to hard and diligent work has been explained in terms of the Protestant Ethic; that is, the belief that hard work leads to success and that success is a sign of being among God's elect.[13] More recently, however, it has been suggested that neither the desire to please God nor the fear of physical hunger accounts for our dedication to work:

> [T]here is a new hunger. The candied carrot, the desire for goods, has replaced the stick; the standard of living has become a built-in automatic drive. . . . If the American worker has been "tamed," it has not been through the discipline of the machine but by the "consumption society," by the possibility of a better living which his wage, the second income of his working wife, and easy credit all allow.[14]

Thus, we may not be dedicated to work as an end in itself, but most of us see work as a means for buying a higher standard of living. And despite the dedication we express toward our work, many of us have problems with our jobs. Going to work is often a hateful experience; and many workers, both blue-collar and white-collar, seem to live only for the weekend. However, blue-collar factory and unskilled workers and white-collar workers face quite different sets of problems.

Blue-Collar Problems

Several studies have found fairly high levels of job dissatisfaction among laborers, especially factory workers.[15] Much of this dissatisfaction stems from the very nature of factory work.

The earliest critics of the factory system, among them Karl Marx, saw the meaninglessness of factory work as the chief source of worker discontent. The modern factory is "a place of order in which stimulus and response, the rhythms of work, derive from a mechanically imposed sense of time and pace."[16] Much factory work is routine and repetitive and the pace of work is regulated by the conveyor belt; the worker, in Marx's words, is "a mere living appendage" of the machine.[17] So we shouldn't be surprised that people who work forty or more hours a week on an assembly line view their work "as an irksome chore to be shirked, or to be finished as fast as possible."[18]

Much factory work is routine and repetitive; the worker, in Marx's words, is "a mere living appendage" of the machine.

The frustrations of factory workers are increased by the fact that they are, for the most part, locked into their occupational roles. Despite popular notions about advancement, few manual workers are able to cross the gap in the skills hierarchy which separates people who work with their hands from those who work with their minds. Within the factory system even lower-level white-collar jobs are not filled by people from the line but by college-educated personnel. Furthermore, the factory worker's dream "of having a mechanic's shop, a turkey farm, a gas station, of 'owning a small business of one's own' is little more than an escapist fantasy."[19] Most factory workers cannot raise the capital to launch a commercial venture; and even if they can, they usually lack the skills to succeed, particularly in today's economy. The only way out of the factory for most workers is retirement.

Not surprisingly, some factory workers try to escape the meaninglessness of their lives through drugs and alcohol (forms of retreatism); others spend their hard-earned wages trying to buy happiness. Many factory workers look for satisfaction in the consumption ethic that characterizes our society, and sometimes they compound their problems with huge debts.

As long as factory workers view their work as tedious, worker discontent cannot be eliminated. However, steps can be taken to boost employee morale and make work more pleasant. Profit-sharing plans seem promising; when workers are rewarded above their normal wages, they are likely to become more concerned with what they are doing and how well they do it. Much can also be done to humanize the factory setting. Workers, for example, can be given the responsibility for governing themselves, producing an acceptable quantity of work and organizing their own work routines. And in many industries the tedium of the assembly line can be at least partially eliminated, as this Saab Motor Company advertisement points out:

> Bored people build bad cars. That's why we're doing away with the assembly line.
>
> Working on an assembly line is monotonous. And boring. And after a while, some people begin not to care about their jobs anymore. So the quality of the product often suffers.
>
> That's why, at Saab, we're replacing the assembly line with assembly teams—Groups of just three or four people who are responsible for a particular assembly process from start to finish. . . .
>
> It's a slower, more costly system, but we realize that the best machines and materials in the world don't mean a thing, if the person building the car doesn't care.[20]

Finally, companies should make every effort to open channels of upward mobility. For example, they could offer educational programs for their employees and advance workers, as their skills increase, into more rewarding jobs. It seems paradoxical that we make educational programs available in prisons, as we should, but not in factories. We must begin to realize that the economy would collapse without the blue-collar worker.[21] We should thus try to make factory work as rewarding as possible.

What about the many other nonfactory blue-collar workers, such as waitresses, janitors, letter carriers, fire fighters, police, truck drivers, and small farmers? On the whole, the work-related problems of these people seem to be less severe than those of factory workers. Their work is more diversified, their time schedules are more flexible, and they have a wider range and variety of contacts with other people. Their greatest concern at present is to keep up with the steadily increasing cost of living—a 5 percent pay hike means little when inflation raises the cost of living 10 percent. It's tremendously demoralizing for a worker to discover that he or she works harder, earns more, but has less.

White-Collar Problems

Compared to the problems of the blue-collar worker, the problems of the white-collar worker may seem less important—after all, white-collar workers are generally supposed to be well paid for work that is challenging. But white-collar workers also have their serious work-related problems.

Job dissatisfaction is not uncommon.[22] Much white-collar work is essentially routine and boring, such as the work of a bank teller, a secretary, or a salesperson in a large department store. Middle- and upper-echelon white-collar employees are often overworked. Contrary to what some students may think, only one-quarter of all professors work less than forty-five hours a week.[23] Some professional men and women work sixty and seventy hours per week.[24] These long hours can hurt both their family lives and their physical and mental health.

Finally, white-collar workers often suffer severe disillusionment when they realize that they will not reach the top of some highly competitive profession. In addition, young people entering white-collar jobs often find that more of their time must be spent in impressing fellow workers and cultivating the right contacts than in developing professional skills. Indeed, "when white-collar people get jobs they sell not only their time and energy but their personalities as well."[25]

Violence

Some may object to our classifying violence as a basic American value. Nonetheless, violence not only underlies some of our gravest social problems, it is also one of our ways of dealing with problems. Both our history and our contemporary behavior strongly suggest that we consider violence a solution to individual and collective problems. And this is in itself a serious problem. Was H. Rap Brown right when he said, "Violence is as American as cherry pie"?[26]

What Is Violence?

By *violence* we mean "the intentional use of force to injure, to kill, or to destroy property."[27] Violence can take many forms. Violence can be the act of an individual or it can be the work of an organized collective. In either case it can be "official," sanctioned by some legitimate authority, or it can be "unofficial," outside the framework of the law.

Some types of violence are culturally approved. We clearly approve of some wars, for example, such as World War II. The recent call for law and order indicates that many Americans feel that crime rates can be reduced only through rigid—and violent—enforcement of the laws, including police brutality, the third degree, and the death penalty.[28] On the other hand, we clearly do not approve of individually propagated, unofficial violence such as murder, rape, or assassination. But a very few of us do consider unofficial, collective violence—rioting—a way of improving society.

The Tools of Violence

Even unarmed, we are a violent people; but, in addition, "Americans own 30 million handguns, or one for every household, and about 100 million shotguns and rifles."[29] Senator Edward Kennedy calls this "the largest and most deadly civilian arsenal in the history of mankind."[30] More people are killed by guns in the United States than in any other country, and nearly 900,000 Americans have died as a result of gun wounds in this country.

The widespread availability of deadly, portable weapons greatly facilitates robberies, kidnappings, hijackings, and other crimes.

This figure can be compared to the 647,000 who have perished in all of our wars.[31] But loss of life is not the only danger with firearms. The widespread availability of deadly, portable weapons greatly facilitates robberies, kidnappings, hijackings, and other crimes.

Despite these figures, there is resistance to gun-control legislation. To date, one of the most powerful lobbying groups, the National Rifle Association, has successfully blocked the passage of control laws. The National Rifle Association bases its argument against gun control on several grounds, including the argument that "guns don't kill, people do." The Association also claims that gun control would interfere with the activities of people who use guns to hunt or for sport, and that it is unconstitutional.[32] Serious and responsible gun users and collectors, as well as gun manufacturers, seem to have unintentionally used their influence to allow conditions that make it easy for irresponsible people such as children, irate spouses, and those intent on killing to obtain guns. Most advocates of gun-control legislation do not propose to stop hunting and target shooting; what they do propose is that we strip a very violent society of one of its chief tools of violence.

Urbanism and Social Problems

One of the most striking features about the United States is the rapid pace at which it has become urbanized. As Table 2.2 indicates, in 1790 only 5.1 percent of the population lived in places classified as urban by the U.S. Bureau of the Census. Today, 73.5 percent of the population do so. Even more impressive is the fact that 68.6 percent of the population lives in metropolitan areas—that is, cities of 50,000 or more.[33]

Sociologist Louis Wirth has suggested that three variables are associated with urbanism—large population size, high population density, and heterogeneity.[34] Among other things, large population size gives rise to the fragmentation of human relationships, rationality, and formal mechanisms of social control.[35] Second, urbanism implies high population density, or a concentration of population in a relatively small geographic area. Finally, cities are heterogeneous, made up of people of all races, religions, social classes, ethnic backgrounds, and national origins.

Large Population Size

The rapid and largely unplanned growth of our cities has created numerous problems. The problem of transporting people from where they live to where they shop, work, and play is one of the most critical.[36] And the problem is not being solved—we con-

Table 2.2

Percentage of the Total U.S. Population Living in Urban (over 2,500 population) and Rural (under 2,500) Places, 1790–1970

Year	Urban	Rural
1790	5.1	94.9
1800	6.1	93.9
1810	7.3	92.7
1820	7.2	92.8
1830	8.8	91.2
1840	10.8	89.2
1850	15.3	84.7
1860	19.8	80.2
1870	25.7	74.3
1880	28.2	71.8
1890	35.1	64.9
1900	39.7	60.3
1910	45.7	54.3
1920	51.2	48.8
1930	56.2	43.8
1940	56.5	43.5
1950[a]	64.0	36.0
1960	69.9	30.1
1970	73.5	26.5

[a]In 1950 the U.S. Bureau of the Census modified its definition of urban. This accounts for 5 percent of the increase that occurred between 1940 and 1950.

SOURCE: U.S. Bureau of the Census, *Census of Population, 1970*, Vol. I, *Characteristics of the Population: U.S. Summary* (Washington, D.C.: U.S. Government Printing Office, 1973), Table 3.

tinue to rely on private cars and, as we do, the quality of urban life deteriorates. Streets and highways become more and more congested and dangerous, and the air becomes dirtier and dirtier because cars are among our leading polluters.[37] In addition, the continuing heavy migration of people from farms to cities has created a shortage of *adequate* urban housing, especially for low-income families.[38]

The large populations in our cities have also brought definite changes in mechanisms of social control. In rural communities most social control occurs on a primary-group basis—individuals are constantly under the watchful eyes of their friends and relatives and, if they violate social norms, they risk being gossiped about, ridiculed, or even ostracized. In cities, however, these informal pressures are much weaker and sometimes entirely absent. Urban populations rely on formal secondary mechanisms, such as the police, courts, and other regulatory bodies, to deal with people who violate social norms.[39]

Very probably, the need to rely on secondary mechanisms of social control in urban areas accounts for the hostility some

Americans feel toward the police.[40] In small rural communities the police play a small role in people's daily lives, intervening only when a serious crime is committed. In a large city, however, the police must involve themselves in the activities of essentially law-abiding citizens. In a typical day, urban police write out traffic tickets, break up domestic disputes, take neglected children away from their parents, and deal with young people who misbehave. When the authorities intervene in what many would consider none of their business, the potential for police-community conflict is great.

The large size of cities may also contribute to feelings of alienation. Certain segments of the urban population—such as migrants, old people, singles, the divorced and widowed—are especially likely to be isolated from meaningful relationships with other people. Whether isolation and alienation lead to high rates of deviant behavior is unclear. On the one hand, "little evidence exists to support the contention that migrants exhibit more deviant behavior than do non-migrants."[41] In addition, old people, the widowed, and the divorced do not have high rates of deviant behavior. On the other hand, rates of deviant behavior are highest in city areas with large numbers of alienated people. However, these high rates are not necessarily attributable to alienation itself. Some alienated groups, like old people, display low rates, suggesting that other factors, such as socioeconomic status, influence whether alienated people engage in deviant behavior.[42]

High Population Density

Among animals, high population density and overcrowding seem to lead to increased rates of abnormal behavior. For example, under extremely crowded conditions rats display increased rates of sexual misconduct and tend to become either extremely passive or extremely violent.[43] Under the same conditions, baboons tend to become extemely violent or aggressive and often engage in bloody fighting.[44]

It is tempting to generalize these findings to human beings: rates of deviant behavior do tend to be highest in the densely settled, overcrowded sections of large cities. Similarly, overcrowded ghettos were the setting for the violent riots and demonstrations of the mid-1960s. However, the question again arises: Is socially deviant or disruptive behavior a product of overcrowding itself, or can the high rates of deviant behavior found in overcrowded areas be traced to other factors? The socioeconomic status of people living in overcrowded slums and ghettos tends to be low. In many ways these people have the least to gain by adhering to middle-class norms—they might easily become innovators, retreatists, or rebels. Furthermore, they live under the constant scrutiny of the police and other representatives of the larger society (for example, welfare officials) and therefore the risk that they will be identified and labeled as deviant is high. The overcrowded urban slum or ghetto may also attract persons already prone to deviant behavior. Here they can interact with other people who have similar inclinations in the anonymity of the large, overcrowded central city.

Heterogeneity

Cities are characterized by an extreme diversity of people and institutions. There is an array of different economic levels, racial and ethnic groups, political persuasions, and religious orientations. As fascinating as this array might be, it can create problems.

First, heterogeneity implies inequality. For example, the poor are constantly aware of the affluence of middle-class Americans who live in comfortable homes, travel in plush cars, eat well, and receive good, private medical care. Consequently, it is not surprising that people on the lower end of the economic scale frequently resort to innovative behavior to obtain at least some middle-class luxuries.[45] The carrot is dangled in front of everyone but not everyone can reach it legitimately. In general, when gross inequalities exist and the disadvantaged are aware of them, the potential for conflict is high.

In a heterogeneous urban setting, an individual can easily get caught between two worlds. On the simplest level this may involve role conflict. For example, some Southern white racists who migrate North may find that many of their fellow employees as well as some of their new supervisors are black. They must decide how to behave. They have been taught that blacks are inferior, yet they are now the ones in the inferior position. Serious role conflicts are likely to occur in a heterogeneous urban setting, and a prolonged conflict could have a disorganizing effect on the individual.

Urban heterogeneity can also give rise to *marginal people*—people who stand on the borders of two social groups. Black police officers, for example, might not be fully accepted by their fellow officers because of their race and might be rejected by their families and friends as well because hostility toward police runs high in black communities. Double-bind situations of this type have tremendously disruptive effects on individuals.

Finally, the heterogeneity that is characteristic of urban slum neighborhoods can give rise to problems. For example, very often lower-class juvenile gangs are organized along racial and ethnic lines. Given the hostility and prejudice that sometimes exists between gangs, a considerable amount of tension and conflict—and sometimes even bloodshed—can be generated.

The Amelioration of Social Problems

As we have already seen in this chapter, our social problems are natural consequences of our complex society—of our values and our rapid urbanization. At the same time, we must understand that our values also affect whether and how social problems are solved.

How can we solve our social problems? We could take the easy way out and answer, "We can't solve our social problems unless we are willing to abandon many of our democratic values and create a totalitarian state." It is probably true that a free, open, and democratic society will always have more social problems than a rigid, repressed society that lacks respect for individuals and their rights. However, we can take steps to reduce the extent, severity, and consequences of social problems. In this section we will look at individual treatment, law, and government as tools of amelioration (improvement).

Individual Treatment

Americans have always assumed that social problems are caused by misguided or ill-intentioned individuals, so we have always put a great deal of faith in rehabilitating the individual as one way of solving social problems. Rehabilitation can take many different forms. It can be therapeutic or punitive: therapeutic procedures include psychotherapy and casework; imprisonment is a punitive procedure. Rehabilitation can also take place on a one-to-one basis or in a group context. Many therapists assume that the goal of rehabilitating the individual can best be achieved through an intensive, one-to-one relationship. In recent years, however, the value of group therapy has achieved much wider recognition, largely because of the fairly high success rate of Alcoholics Anonymous. Finally, rehabilitation may be voluntary or forced. People go to psychiatrists, join Alcoholics Anonymous, and use most casework and group work services voluntarily. But they do not go to prison or pay fines voluntarily. People who seek treatment on their own probably have a greater chance of being rehabilitated than people undergoing forced treatment.

Efforts to treat and rehabilitate the individuals caught up in our social problems must continue. Indeed, one of the greatest challenges we face is to improve the services provided by mental hospitals, juvenile correctional facilities, and prisons. However, the individualized treatment approach is only a partial solution for two reasons. First, overall rates of success are rather low: Alcoholics Anonymous, which is often praised for its effectiveness, has about a 50 percent success rate in rehabilitating alcoholic individuals.[46] Programs aimed at rehabilitating criminals, juvenile delinquents, and narcotic addicts generally have even lower success rates. Second, even if these rates of success could be increased dramatically, individual treatment is still something of a futile approach: the cases simply keep coming and coming because individual treatment does not deal with the fundamental social and cultural causes of the problem behavior. Most people who create or get caught up in social problems are simply responding to the pressures that society places on them to succeed.

Law

Even though the United States is crime-ridden, Americans profess a deep and abiding faith in law. Quoting John Adams, we say that ours is "a government of laws and not of men." We consider the courts the proper arena for settling interpersonal and intergroup conflicts.

The law can be used in two ways to try to ameliorate social problems. First, legal force represents one control on certain types of deviant behavior, such as crime, the abuse of dangerous drugs and narcotics, and sexual deviancy. The presence of law enforcement officers and the fear of being apprehended does seem to reduce the likelihood that certain types of crime will be committed. For example, the general crime rate in Denmark rose immediately after German occupation forces arrested the entire police force in 1944 and assigned police duties to an "ineffective unarmed watch corps."[47] This suggests that the presence of law enforcement officers helps to keep the lid on certain types of crime. Whether it actually reduces the incidence of crime is an open question.

The second way law can be used to try to ameliorate social problems is to help change social conditions that give rise to social problems. The power of the law to change social conditions is highly controversial. Many believe that if people are not ready to accept a change, all the laws and court decisions in the world will not bring that change about. They cite the failure of prohibition as an example. Nonetheless, in 1954 the Supreme Court used law to try to change the character of race relations in the United States with its *Brown* v. *Board of Education* decision banning segregation in the schools. Although much still remains to be done before blacks achieve full equality, more positive social change has occurred as a result of this decision than could have been imagined in 1954.[48]

Law, however, is limited in its ability to deal with social problems. The vigorous enforcement of some laws, for example, those against homosexuality, prostitution, and the sale or possession of narcotics, often seems to do more harm than good. Law enforcement can become arbitrary, can lead to undesirable police practices, and can result in criminal subcultures (see Chapters 5 and 6). There is also a danger that overzealous enforcement will result in violations of civil liberties. In 1973, narcotics agents forced their way late at night into a couple's home in Collinsville, Illinois, destroying much of their property in a search for drugs while holding them at gunpoint and refusing to let them dress; the woman subsequently suffered a nervous breakdown and the agents subsequently discovered they had the wrong house. But probably the chief limitation of law as a means of social change is that its effects are felt only very slowly. It has been over twenty years since the Supreme Court declared school segregation unconstitutional, yet segregated school systems still operate in many parts of the country and busing continues to be a major issue.

Government Action

Despite our dislike of big government, we have responded to increasing world tensions and domestic problems by creating bigger and bigger government bureaucracies at all levels—local, state, and national. Complaining bitterly about the excesses of big government, we nonetheless look increasingly to the government to solve our problems.

Can government solve social problems? Potentially it can. Only government can marshall the money and energy required to renovate cities, achieve racial equality, reduce poverty, and launch population control programs. In addition, government clearly will have to play a leading role in improving our educational and health systems.

Unfortunately, however, government easily gets bogged down in its efforts to ameliorate social problems. For one thing, government bureaucracies sometimes become so large and cumbersome that more money is spent in maintaining the bureaucracy than in rendering needed services. Furthermore, the problems government is called on to solve—urban decay, poverty, rapid population growth—are tremendously expensive to solve. Some people feel that federal money is potentially available only if we are willing to spend less on national defense—in 1975 an $85.3 billion item, or 27.2 percent of the total budget.[49] At state and local levels, money for new programs often does not exist and tax increases are unpopular. So far, federal revenue sharing has had little impact on the financial crisis of our cities and states.

▲ The problems government is called on to solve—urban decay, poverty, rapid population growth—are tremendously expensive to solve.

In addition, proposed government programs to help solve social problems have often been blocked by vested interest groups. As previously mentioned, the National Rifle Association has blocked effective gun-control legislation. The American Medical Association has opposed plans for national health insurance, industry has hindered stringent antipollution laws, and landlords have opposed public-housing programs. Until the American public demands that the government be run for them and not for powerful vested interest groups, government is not likely to be a particularly effective force in solving social problems.

Summary

Social problems are a natural, predictable outcome of our complex society; some of the most bothersome contemporary social problems can be directly traced to what we value as good or just or desirable.

Four basic American values that are linked to social problems are material success, individualism, hard work, and violence. In order to come to terms with our society's emphasis on materialism, a person might become a conformist, innovator, ritualist, retreatist, or rebel. Materialism is not a bad value in itself—it undoubtedly accounts for the growing, dynamic quality of our society. But the best values can have the worst consequences.

Our belief in individualism has hindered efforts to solve social problems. Emphasis on individualism can lead us to misinterpret the causes of social problems and thus lead to the wrong answers. Our belief in individualism may also account for the poor quality of services to help and rehabilitate the individual. Our answer to many social problems such as crime, juvenile delinquency, and narcotics addiction has been severe punishment. Little effort has been made to reclaim deviant individuals and reintegrate them into the larger society.

Although we attach profound significance to hard work, many of us, both white-collar and blue-collar, have problems with our jobs. For blue-collar workers, factory work can be boring, the pace of work can be regulated by the conveyor belt, workers can become locked into their occupational roles. To escape, some factory workers turn to drugs and alcohol; others try to buy happiness. However, steps can be taken to improve the lot of the factory worker through profit sharing, humanizing factory conditions, and opening channels of upward mobility.

Much white-collar work can also be routine and boring, and white-collar employees are frequently overworked and underpaid. Often, they suffer severe disillusionment when they realize that their aspiration to be the top man or woman in their profession will never be achieved. In addition, white-collar workers must often spend more time impressing fellow workers and cultivating the right contacts than in developing professional skills.

Both our history and our contemporary behavior strongly suggest that we consider violence a solution to problems. Violence can be collective or individual, official or unofficial. Violence in America is particularly destructive because we are armed to the hilt. But the National Rifle Association and gun manufacturers have blocked gun-control laws and thus helped create conditions that make deadly weapons available to irresponsible people. Gun control would not stop hunting and target shooting, but it would help strip a very violent society of a chief tool of violence.

One of the most striking features about the United States is its rapid rate of urbanization. Three variables are associated with urbanism: large population size, high population density, and heterogeneity. The large size of the modern city has led to definite changes in mechanisms of social control. It may also contribute to feelings of alienation.

High population density appears to lead to increased rates of abnormal behavior among animals, and it is tempting to generalize these findings to human beings. Is socially deviant or disruptive behavior a product of overcrowding or can it be traced to other factors? In overcrowded slums and ghettos, socioeconomic status is typically low, there is the risk of being labeled deviant, and such areas often attract people already prone to deviance. Heterogeneity implies inequality, and an individual can easily get caught between two worlds in a role conflict or as a marginal person who stands on the borders of two social groups.

Our values affect whether and how social problems are solved. Americans believe that social problems originate with the individual and put a lot of faith in "individual treatment" to solve social problems. Such treatment must be continued, but it is only a partial solution. Individual treatment has rather low overall rates of success and it is futile because it does not deal with basic social causes.

Two other tools, law and government, can potentially be used to solve social problems. The law can help control certain types of deviant behavior and can be used as a tool to induce social change. Potentially, government can marshall the vast resources needed to eliminate poverty, renovate our cities, and attack other social problems. Unfortunately, however, the government often gets bogged down in its efforts to solve social problems because of the tremendous expense involved and because of opposition from powerful vested interest groups.

Discussion Questions

1. Discuss the following statement: "Young people today are less concerned with wealth and material success than their parents and grandparents." Do you personally agree with this statement? Why or why not?

2. Discuss the hippie movement of the '60s. What were the positive values of the hippie movement? Why do you think that the hippie movement has virtually disappeared from the American scene?

3. Given rapid population growth and our growing shortages of natural resources, is it feasible for us to continue to define success in materialistic terms? Can we adjust to a world in which material goods may be less available and abundant?

4. It has been said that people who work wish they didn't and that people who don't work wish they did. Do you think that this statement has any truth to it? Why?

5. In what ways, if any, does violence or the fear of violence affect your life? Is violence a basic American value? Explain and justify your answer.

6. It has been argued that "guns don't kill, people do." Is this a legitimate argument against gun-control legislation? Would there be fewer violent crimes in our society if we did not possess "the largest and most deadly civilian arsenal in the history of mankind"?

7. We know that among certain animals, high population density and overcrowding leads to increased rates of sexual misconduct, violence, and other types of deviant behavior. Do you think that the same thing is true of human beings? Is it safe to draw generalizations about human beings from observations of animals such as mice and baboons? Explain and justify your answer.

8. Discuss individual treatment, law, and governmental action as approaches to the amelioration of social problems. Why do we place such faith in rehabilitating the individual as an approach to the solution of social problems? Can law be used to change those social conditions that give rise to social problems? Has our government been successful in solving any social problems? If so, which ones?

9. The basic thesis of this chapter is that social problems are a natural, predictable outcome of the complex society in which we live. What do we mean by this statement? Do you agree with it? Why or why not?

10. What do you see as the three most important social problems in your community? Develop some concrete, specific suggestions for solving these problems.

Glossary

alienation The feeling of being cut off from meaningful group ties. The alienated person may feel isolated, lonely, afraid, powerless, and meaningless.

conformist A person who fully accepts the values or goals of a society (usually material success) and who uses socially approved means to achieve these values or goals.

individualism The belief that individuals should be free to be what they want to be and to do what they want to do.

innovator A person who accepts the values and goals of a society but who does not use socially approved means of achieving them. Innovators, for example, devise their own deviant means of achieving material success such as robbery, extortion, or income tax evasion.

marginal people People who belong to two (or more) social groups but who are not fully accepted by either group. A black police officer might be a marginal person.

materialism The belief that it is important to possess a wealth of goods, including split-level homes, luxurious cars, and so forth.

population density The number of persons per square mile of land. The population density of urban areas is much higher than that of rural areas.

Protestant Ethic A group of beliefs, ideas, and norms which emphasizes the value of frugality and hard work. Practitioners believe that frugality and hard work lead to success and that success is a sign of being among God's elect.

rebel A person who replaces conventional goals and means with new ones. For example, a rebel may reject the pursuit of wealth and material success in favor of participation in a social movement.

retreatist A person who rejects conventional values and goals and the accepted means of achieving them. Retreatists abandon materialistic success and become true social dropouts.

ritualist A person who rejects conventional values and goals but nevertheless follows the means for achieving them. For example, a ritualist may have given up hope of achieving material success but continues to behave in a manner that supposedly leads to material success.

role (or social role) The behavior that individuals are expected to display because of the position that they occupy in a group or in society. For example, the role of a professor as opposed to that of a student.

role conflict A situation in which people have two or more roles that make contradictory demands on them. If they play one role adequately, they may not be able to function effectively in the other role.

vested interest group A group organized to influence decision making which puts pressure on the government (or other institutions) to adopt a particular policy or program.

violence The intentional use of force to injure, to kill, or to destroy property. Some people mistakenly see violence as a solution to personal or social problems.

Suggestions for Further Reading

"Does TV Violence Affect Our Society?" *TV Guide,* 23 (June 14, 1975). There has been a tremendous amount of debate on whether television affects our behavior. This special issue of *TV Guide* takes a surprisingly sophisticated and balanced look at televised violence.

"The Life and Death of the Hippie Movement," in John R. Howard, *The Cutting Edge: Social Movements and Social Change in America* (Philadelphia: Lippincott, 1974), Ch. 8. A fascinating account of the hippie movement. This reading illustrates the nature of rebellion as a mode of adjustment of materialism.

Merton, Robert K., *Social Theory and Social Structure*, Rev. Ed. (New York: Free Press, 1957), pp. 131–60. Merton discusses conformity and the other modes of adaptation to materialism and other values that our society holds in high esteem. Very worthwhile reading for the more advanced student.

Shostak, Arthur B., *Modern Social Welfare Reforms: Solving Today's Social Problems* (New York: Macmillan, 1974). This book provides a great deal of insight into potential solutions for many of our most pressing social problems. Of particular relevance are the sections on workplace reforms and gun-control legislation.

Terkel, Studs, *Working* (New York: Pantheon, 1974). Through interviews with people in dozens of different occupations, Terkel gives the reader valuable insight into people's jobs and how they feel about them.

Weinberg, Martin S., and Earl Rubington, *The Solution of Social Problems: Five Perspectives* (New York: Oxford, 1973). A collection of twenty readings that discuss various approaches to the solution of social problems.

Williams, Robin M., Jr., *American Society: A Sociological Interpretation*, 3rd Ed. (New York: Knopf, 1970). Probably the most sophisticated analysis of American society that is available today. Although Williams does not deal directly with social problems, his discussion of American values and beliefs provides the reader with the tools needed to understand the relationship between culture and social problems. For the more advanced reader.

Notes

[1]See Robin M. Williams, Jr., *American Society: A Sociological Interpretation*, 3rd Ed. (New York: Knopf, 1970), pp. 469–72.

[2]Robert K. Merton, *Social Theory and Social Structure*, Rev. Ed. (New York: Free Press, 1957), pp. 131–60.

[3]See "Hooked on Work," *Time*, 98 (July 5, 1972), p. 42. See also Wayne E. Oates, *Confessions of a Workaholic* (Nashville, Tenn.: Abington, 1972).

[4]John E. Conklin, *Robbery and the Criminal Justice System* (Philadelphia: Lippincott, 1972), p. 64.

[5]See *Report of the National Advisory Commission on Civil Disorders* (Washington, D.C.: U.S. Government Printing Office, 1968), esp. Ch. 4.

[6]Merton, *Social Theory and Social Structure*, .p. 153.

[7]For an absorbing discussion of the hippie movement see John R. Howard, *The Cutting Edge: Social Movements and Social Change in America* (Philadelphia: Lippincott, 1974), pp. 181–96; and Bennett M. Berger, *Looking for America* (Englewood Cliffs, N.J.: Prentice-Hall, 1971), pp. 118–30.

[8]Howard, *The Cutting Edge*, p. 191.

[9]Fred Davis, "Why All of Us May Be Hippies Some Day," *Transaction*, 5 (1967), pp. 10–18.

[10]For an excellent discussion and case studies of the costs and casualties of an acquisitive society, see Harry C. Bredmeier and Jackson Toby, *Social Problems in America: Costs and Casualties* (New York: Wiley, 1960).

[11]Williams, *American Society*, p. 495.

[12]Harold L. Wilensky and Charles N. Lebeaux, *Industrial Society and Social Welfare* (New York: Free Press, 1965), esp. p. 157.

[13]See Max Weber, *The Protestant Ethic and the Spirit of Capitalism* (London: Allen & Unwin, 1930).

[14]Daniel Bell, *The End of Ideology: The Exhaustion of Political Ideas in the Fifties*, Rev. Ed. (New York: Free Press, 1962), p. 254. This quotation and much of the material that follows is taken from Chapter 11 in Bell's book, appropriately entitled "Work and Its Discontents."

[15]For example, see Harold L. Sheppard and Neal Q. Herrick, *Where Have All the Robots Gone? Worker Dissatisfaction in the '70s* (New York: Free Press, 1972), esp. Part I; and George Strauss, "Workers: Attitudes and Adjustments," in *The Worker and the Job*, ed. Jerome M. Rosow (Englewood Cliffs, N.J.: Prentice-Hall, 1974), pp. 73–98.

[16]Bell, *The End of Ideology*, p. 229.

[17]Karl Marx, *Capital* (New York: Modern Library, 1936), p. 462.

[18]Bell, *The End of Ideology*, p. 391.

[19]*Ibid.*, p. 255.

[20]Cited in Arthur B. Shostak, *Modern Social Welfare Reforms: Solving Today's Social Problems* (New York: Macmillan, 1974), p. 193.

[21]For a more extended discussion of workplace reforms see *Ibid.*, pp. 187–215.

[22]See Strauss, "Workers: Attitudes and Adjustments," esp. p. 75.

[23]Harold L. Wilensky, "The Uneven Distribution of Leisure: The Impact of Economic Growth on 'Free Time,' " in *Work and Leisure*, ed. Erwin O. Smigel (New Haven, Conn.: College and University Press, 1963), p. 117.

[24]See William H. Whyte, Jr., "How Hard Do Executives Work?" in *Organizations and Human Behavior*, ed. Gerald D. Bell (Englewood Cliffs, N.J.: Prentice-Hall, 1967), pp. 172–82.

[25]C. Wright Mills, *White Collar* (New York: Oxford, 1951), p. xvii.

[26]Cited in St. Clair Drake, "What Is 'Natural' Today Need Not Be Natural Tomorrow," *The New York Times Magazine* (April 28, 1968), p. 24.

[27]Jerome H. Skolnick, *The Politics of Protest* (New York: Simon & Schuster, 1969), p. 6.

[28]For further discussion of the law-and-order ideology, see *The Scales of Justice*, ed. Abraham Blumberg (Chicago: Aldine, 1970), pp. 1–31.

[29]Shostak, *Modern Social Welfare Reforms,* p. 287.

[30]Cited in *Ibid.,* p. 287.

[31]Ronald P. Kriss, "Gun Control: A Missed Target," *Saturday Review,* LV (August 26, 1972), p. 26.

[32]*Ibid.,* p. 26; and Shostak, *Modern Social Welfare Reforms,* p. 288.

[33]U.S. Bureau of the Census, *Statistical Abstract of the United States: 1974* (Washington, D.C.: U.S. Government Printing Office, 1974), Tables 17, 18.

[34]Louis Wirth, "Urbanism as a Way of Life," *American Journal of Sociology,* 44 (July, 1938), pp. 1–24.

[35]For a discussion of these traits, see Dennis E. Poplin, *Communities: A Survey of Theories and Methods of Research* (New York: Macmillan, 1972), pp. 37–38.

[36]See John W. Dyckman, "Transportation in Cities," in *Urban Studies: An Introductory Reader,* ed. Louis K. Loewenstein (New York: Free Press, 1971), pp. 424–31.

[37]See Senator Fred R. Harris and Mayor John V. Lindsay, Cochairmen, *The State of the Cities: Report of the Commission on the Cities in the '70s* (New York: Praeger, 1972), pp. 63–64.

[38]See The President's Committee on Urban Housing, "The Shape of the Nation's Housing Problems," in Loewenstein, *Urban Studies,* pp. 346–64.

[39]Poplin, *Communities,* p. 48.

[40]See The President's Commission on Law Enforcement and Administration of Justice, *Task Force Report: Police* (Washington, D.C.: U.S. Government Printing Office, 1967), pp. 144–49.

[41]Ralph Thomlinson, *Population Dynamics* (New York: Random House, 1965), p. 229.

[42]Thus, in our society young single males are, within limits, expected to be "wild" and "raise a little hell" whereas old people are not.

[43]John B. Calhoun, "Population Density and Social Pathology," *Scientific American,* 206 (February, 1963), pp. 139–48.

[44]S. Zuckerman, *The Social Life of Monkeys and Apes* (London: Kegan Paul, 1932).

[45]Merton, *Social Theory and Social Structure,* pp. 141–49.

[46]This figure must be regarded as tentative and is cited in Paul B. Horton and Gerald R. Leslie, *The Sociology of Social Problems,* 3rd Ed. (New York: Appleton-Century-Crofts, 1970), p. 503.

[47]Johannes Andenaes, "The General Preventive Effects of Punishment," in *Law and Change in Modern America,* ed. Joel B. Grossman and Mary H. Grossman (Pacific Palisades, Calif.: Goodyear, 1971), p. 84.

[48]See "20 Years of Civil Rights," *Chicago Sun-Times* (May 12, 1974), Sec. 1–A.

[49]U.S. Bureau of the Census, *Statistical Abstract of the United States: 1975* (Washington, D.C.: U.S. Government Printing Office, 1975), Table 372. It should be noted that the percentage of the federal budget spent on defense would be much higher if one discounted payments made under social security and similar insurance programs which have, in effect, been paid for by the beneficiaries themselves and which are not financed out of general revenues.

PART II

DEVIANT BEHAVIOR

Mental Disorders

Deviant Sexual Behavior

Alcoholism

Juvenile Delinquency

Drug Abuse and Narcotics Addiction

Crime

Chapter 3
Mental Disorders

Extent and Costs of Mental Illness

What Is Mental Illness?

- Signs of Mental Health and Illness
- Labeling

Types of Mental Illness

- Neuroses
- Psychosomatic Disorders
- Functional Psychoses
- Organic Brain Syndrome

Explanations for Mental Illness

- Individual Factors
  - *Heredity and Psychosis*
  - *Biochemistry and Psychosis*
  - *Life Experiences*
- Sociological Factors
  - *The Labeling Perspective*
  - *Societal Pressures*

Treatment

- Facilities and Personnel
  - *Private Practice Therapists*
  - *The Mental Hospital*
  - *Outpatient Mental Health Clinics*
- Approaches to Treatment
  - *Biological or Organic Therapies*
  - *Psychotherapy and Related Therapies*

Summary

If you suddenly found yourself—right now, just as you are—in a South Sea island village, you would no doubt seem pretty strange to the islanders. Your dress, attitudes, and behavior would all be very different from theirs. According to the norms of South Sea society, you would be classified as a *deviant*. You would not be right or wrong, good or bad; you simply would not conform. If, during your South Sea stay, you persistently behaved as though you were on an American college campus, you would most likely be called crazy.

Although our example is admittedly rather farfetched, perhaps it will help you understand the dilemma of those people who suffer from mental disorders in our own society. Mentally ill people are deviants in that they do not, perhaps cannot, behave in ways that are appropriate and acceptable to the majority of other people. Mentally ill people are in many ways strangers in their own society.

Some evidence suggests that, in this country, at least one in eight people needs some type of treatment for a mental disorder.[1] That estimate puts the total at about twenty-six million people, and this number may be increasing. Mental illness is a serious social problem and it can be studied from many perspectives. Anthropologists, biologists, psychologists, psychiatrists, and other professionals have all contributed to our understanding of mental illness. In this chapter we will refer to the research findings of many disciplines, but we will be primarily concerned with the research findings of sociology. We will attempt to answer these kinds of questions: How can sociology improve our understanding of mental disorders? What are the sociological factors in mental illness?

Extent and Costs of Mental Illness

Every year mental illness directly affects large numbers of people. In 1971 a total of 1,269,029 persons were admitted to inpatient mental health care facilities in the United States.[2] As shown in Table 3.1, most of these people were between the ages of 18 and 64, the age group in which people normally play such important social roles as husband, wife, parent, or employee. As in the case of any hospital, most of the people admitted for care were not hospitalized for prolonged treatment. So in spite of the total number of people admitted to mental health care facilities, only 433,786 were actually in mental hospitals at the end of 1970.[3]

Many more people, while they do not require inpatient care, are impaired in their ability to perform their social roles. In 1971, 1,378,822 persons were admitted for outpatient care in psychiatric facilities.[4] In addition, it has also been estimated that between

Table 3.1
Percent Distribution of Admissions to Psychiatric Inpatient Services by Sex and Age, United States, 1971.

Age	Males	Females
Under 18	6.7	7.7
18–24	19.4	14.2
25–44	38.9	41.7
45–64	28.3	27.5
65+	6.7	8.9

SOURCE: National Institute of Mental Health, *Utilization of Mental Health Facilities: 1971*, DHEW Publication No. NIH-74-657 (Washington, D.C.: U.S. Government Printing Office, 1973), p. 21.

750,000 and 1,200,000 persons receive treatment from private psychiatrists each year.[5]

These figures provide only a crude estimate of the extent of mental illness in the United States because only a small percentage of all people who need help with their emotional problems actually seek it out. It is estimated that in Baltimore, for example, approximately 12.5 percent of the population (or 1 in 8 persons) suffer from "a more or less serious mental disorder at any given point in time."[6] A study of midtown Manhattan found even higher rates of impairment due to mental illness.[7]

Many more people are affected by mental illness than those who are themselves ill. Untold numbers of spouses, children, parents, friends, fellow workers, and others suffer in some way as a result of another's mental disorder.

Mental illness also places a burden on the economy. In 1968, mental illness cost the American public approximately $21 billion.[8] This estimate includes both the costs of treatment and prevention and the cost of lost productive capacity (earnings lost by people who cannot work due to their mental condition). The figure is undoubtedly much higher today, given the increased costs of patient care, higher wage scales, and so on. The highest costs of mental illness, however, are tallied in human suffering and unhappiness.

Finally, mental illness may contribute to various other social problems. Some alcoholic individuals, drug users, and narcotics addicts are dependent and anxiety ridden. Moreover, we can only speculate as to whether mental disorders are important contributing factors to our high rates of crime, delinquency, and family problems. The word *contributing* must be emphasized—certainly not all deviant behavior stems from emotional disturbances. But if mental disorders do play a significant role in creating these problems, we are indeed dealing with an extremely serious social problem.

What Is Mental Illness?

Mental health and mental illness can be thought of as the end points on a continuum. Most of us have known people who were emotionally mature and stable. These people can work productively; they can fully relax; they can play with real enjoyment. In addition, they know when and where each of these activities is appropriate. In short, they have the capacity for realizing their emotional potential most of the time.

At the other end of the continuum are the people whose patterns of thought and emotion are so disturbed that they cannot work or relax or play. Most of us, naturally, fall somewhere between these two extremes.

How can we recognize mental illness? The task of defining mental illness is not an easy one, and few experts entirely agree on a definition. But researchers have compiled lists of traits that typically characterize the mentally ill person.

Signs of Mental Health and Illness

Mental health and mental illness are complex concepts that involve many dimensions of a person's behavior and personality. Thus, a "multidimensional view of the well-functioning personality is in order."[9] Of the many variables involved, five traits have been suggested as characterizing the mentally healthy individual:

1. Can adapt and be flexible.
2. Can love, work effectively, and play.
3. Can understand his or her own feelings.
4. Experiences a certain degree of self-realization, that is, some relationship exists between actual achievements and temperament, talents, and goals.
5. Has a positive ego identity, which means satisfaction with self, position in life, and relationships with other people.[10]

Such a person will almost certainly lead a happy, rewarding life.

In contrast, the mentally ill person is handicapped in life by the opposite characteristics. The following traits are associated in some degree with the ill or disordered personality:

1. Lacks adaptability and flexibility. Minor events turn into major catastrophes; major events, such as a job layoff or loss of a loved one, call for readjustments that are extremely difficult for the individual to make.
2. Has difficulty building meaningful, tension-free relationships with other people, enjoying work that must be done, and making use of leisure time in a personally satisfying manner.

3. Lacks insight into personal feelings and motivations—is often baffled by and anxious about his or her drives, emotions, and behavior.

4. Sees life as burdensome and full of dashed hopes. Both employment and marriage may be major disappointments. Other people appear not to appreciate the person's "fine qualities."

5. Lacks a positive ego identity. Has a negative self-image and a negative view of his or her position in life and relationships with other people.

Labeling

Not all people who display the symptoms associated with mental illness, however, are defined by themselves or by society at large as mentally ill. Rather, to a great extent "mentally ill" is a label which is initially given to a person by his or her family, friends, and associates. (Later we will consider whether the mere act of labeling itself contributes to mental illness.) One authority on the sociology of mental illness states:

> The early definitions of mental illness, especially in middle-class populations, are likely to take place in groups within which the person primarily operates; evaluations are made by family, fellow employees, friends, and employers. If symptoms appear and are not recognized as such by members of the individual's more primary groups, it is unlikely that he will become accessible to psychiatric personnel unless his symptoms become visible, and disturbing enough to lead to his commitment to some treatment center by external authorities.[11]

What behavioral patterns might lead one person to define another person as mentally ill? A study conducted among the wives of men admitted to mental hospitals found that they defined their husbands as mentally ill on the basis of a variety of problem behaviors. Among the most commonly cited behaviors were deviations from routine; expressions of inadequacy or hopelessness; nervousness, irritability, and worried withdrawal; aggressive or assaultive and suicidal behavior; and strange or bizarre thoughts, delusions, and hallucinations.[12]

Clearly, not all the people who display these problem behaviors are patients in mental hospitals. However, if a person is hospitalized, he or she almost automatically becomes defined as mentally ill: "persons are brought to the hospital on the basis of lay definitions, and once they arrive, their appearance alone is usually regarded as sufficient evidence of 'illness.' "[13] Thus, people in effect "become" mentally ill if others so label them. Even though labeling theory does not provide us with clinical definitions of mental illness, it does help us understand why some disturbed people are considered mentally ill and others are not. The difference between the mentally ill person and the mentally healthy person is not only, or perhaps even primarily, a matter of difference in behavior.

Types of Mental Illness

Mental illness can take various forms. By examining some of the major forms of mental problems, we can increase our understanding of mentally disordered behavior.

Neuroses

Neuroses are incapacitating forms of behavior which stem from anxiety but in which the afflicted person remains oriented to social reality.[14] We all worry at times, but the neurotic person carries worry to an extreme and may suffer from a state of continual inner panic. The hallmarks of neurosis seem to be either chronic (long-term and continual) anxiety or sporadic attacks of acute anxiety. The anxiety and fear that the neurotic person experiences is irrational. A person who worries about having lost a job and source of income is not neurotic; he or she has good cause to worry. However, if a competent, tenured employee constantly worries about losing his or her job, the anxiety is not realistic and there is reason to suspect that he or she may be neurotic. Because neurotic people are conflict ridden, they are often a source of irritation to others. They constantly look to other people for support and approval, yet are so wrapped up in their own anxieties that they are often unable to respond to other people with genuine warmth and interest.

Neurosis is one of the most common types of mental illness in the United States. But, since people suffering from neurosis are rarely hospitalized, it is extremely difficult to estimate the prevalence of this disorder. One study found that "there are at least 20 million individuals in the United States that might be classified as neurotic."[15] Another study found that over half the population of a rural Pennsylvania county had at one time or another displayed neurotic symptoms.[16] Obviously, only a handful of these people were so neurotic that they required professional treatment.

Psychosomatic Disorders

We have all experienced occasional physical discomfort because of emotional tension and anxiety. However, when a person develops a chronic physical disorder that can be traced to emotional stress, the disorder is psychosomatic or psychophysiological. Common physical disorders which frequently have emotional roots are peptic ulcers, migraine headaches, high blood pressure, and some types of asthma. However, even though the psychoso-

▲ The neurotic person carries worry to an extreme and may suffer from a state of continual inner panic. The hallmarks of neurosis seem to be either chronic anxiety or sporadic attacks of acute anxiety.

matic disorders are the products of emotional stress, they are very real, and the person needs competent medical as well as psychological care.

Functional Psychoses

The *functional psychoses* are among the most serious mental disorders. Although much research is still being carried on, these disorders do not appear to be inherited nor have they been persuasively explained in terms of brain damage or the biochemical makeup of the individual. Rather, these disorders seem to be a function of the individual's life experiences. The two most common categories of functional psychoses are schizophrenia and the affective disorders.

The term *schizophrenia* refers to a collection of closely related disorders.[17] Basically, the schizophrenic person may suffer from delusions and hallucinations and "tends to withdraw temporarily from interactions with others and to become preoccupied with his own world of experiencing."[18] The schizophrenic person has disorganized patterns of thought and speech and reacts to various

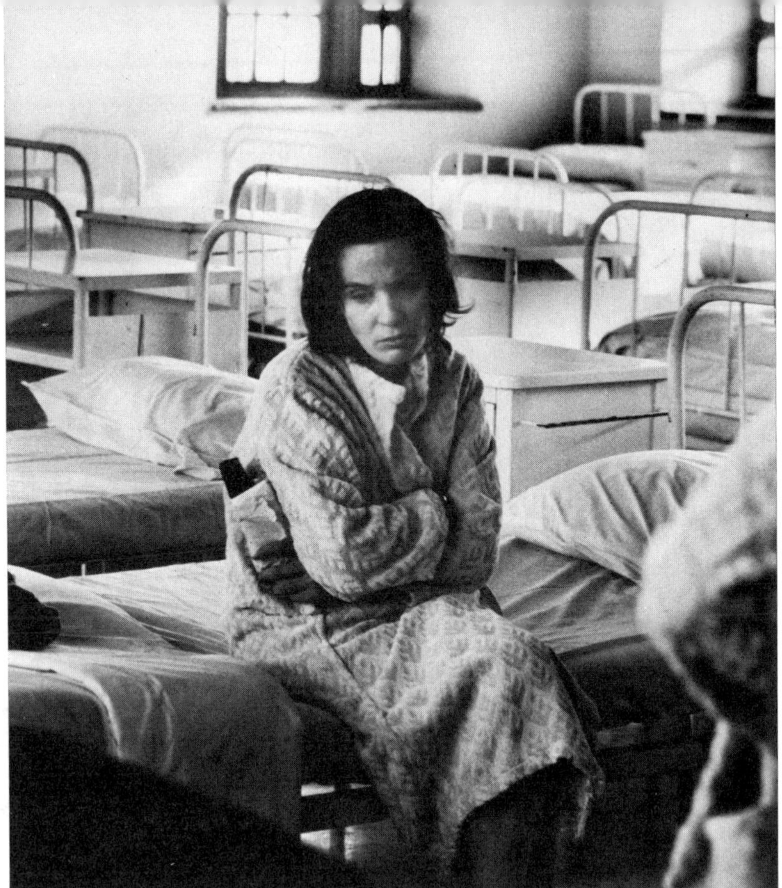

Schizophrenic people ▸ tend to withdraw temporarily from interactions with others and to become preoccupied with their own world of experiencing.

situations with apathetic, inappropriate, or inconsistent behavior. Paranoid schizophrenia, one of the most common types, is marked by extreme suspiciousness and delusions of persecution or grandeur.

Obviously, few schizophrenics can handle everyday routines and responsibilities, and most are hospitalized. Indeed, more people who enter mental hospitals suffer from schizophrenia than from any other type of disorder. In 1971, 27 percent of all persons admitted to inpatient treatment facilities were diagnosed as schizophrenic.[19] Since recovery from this disorder is usually a long, slow process, at any given time about half the mental hospital population consists of people diagnosed as schizophrenic.

The *affective disorders* entail gross alterations in mood—fluctuations between extreme excitement and severe depression. The most common affective disorder is manic-depressive psychosis.[20] In the manic syndrome, an individual experiences irrational euphoria and elation, and displays extreme hyperactivity. It is sometimes very difficult for other people to cope with a manic individual because of his or her short attention span, impulsiveness, and extreme talkativeness. In the depressive syndrome, on the other hand, an individual experiences strong feelings of hopelessness, despair, and loneliness. Not surprisingly, "about 75 percent of depressed cases have suicidal thoughts and some 10 to 15 percent attempt suicide."[21]

The manic-depressive disorders remind us better than most disorders that the line between mental health and mental illness is indeed a thin one. We all have moments, hours, or perhaps even days when our feelings of euphoria or of hopelessness reach irrational proportions. The big difference, however, is that we regain our equilibrium and carry on.

Organic Brain Syndrome

Organic brain syndrome is an umbrella term that covers all the mental disorders with known organic or physiological causes. This category includes some of the mental disorders associated with old age. Considerable evidence now suggests that old people often become forgetful, disoriented, quarrelsome, etc., because of hardening of the arteries around the brain and/or other organic changes associated with aging. Other mental disorders that fall under the umbrella of organic brain syndrome include those due to syphilis of the brain, brain tumors, and the overingestion of certain metals, gases, and drugs.

Explanations for Mental Illness

Why does one person suffer from mental disorders while another person, in a similar situation, is happy and healthy? The causes of mental illness are obscure, but students of mental illness have proposed at least two general hypotheses. The first hypothesis is that the cause lies within the individual, that mental illness is rooted in factors intrinsic to the individual. These factors include hereditary or organic defects and damaging childhood experiences.

The second hypothesis is that the cause lies outside the individual, that mental illness is rooted in factors extrinsic to the individual. The proponents of this second hypothesis—the sociological hypothesis—find the causes of mental illness in society itself. For example, some sociologists have argued that mental illness is a social role into which some individuals are cast. Thus, *schizophrenia* would refer to a certain type of behavior that is labeled as such and not to a specific illness. Moreover, some sociologists think that certain forms of mental illness may be caused by the hectic pace of modern life.

In this section, we will first discuss the arguments and evidence supporting the first hypothesis—that mental illness is caused by factors intrinsic to the individual. Next we will discuss the sociological hypothesis—that the causes of mental illness can be found in society. Our emphasis, of course, will be on the sociological hypothesis because we firmly believe that sociologists can help illuminate the causes of mental illness.

Individual Factors

Biologists are among those studying individually related factors in mental illness. While it is unlikely that biologists can shed much light on neurotic disorders, they have been very actively looking at the question, Do the functional psychoses, and especially schizophrenia, have a hereditary or organic cause? Scientists have long hoped to find a concrete explanation of the functional psychoses that would relieve them from having to struggle with "the intangibles of feeling and emotion"[22] that mental illness involves. If psychoses could be traced to individual biological abnormalities, serious social problems might be solved with pills, injections, or surgery—clean and simple biomedical solutions.

Heredity and Psychosis

Some data seem to indicate that psychosis might be hereditary, passed on from one generation to the next. For example, one study found that 68.1 percent of the children of two schizophrenic parents and 16.4 percent of the children of one schizophrenic parent became schizophrenic themselves.[23] These data are significant because the expected incidence rate for psychosis in the general population is about 1.0 percent.[24] Thus, the children of schizophrenic parents more commonly become schizophrenic than do the children of nonschizophrenic parents.

The hypothesis that psychosis might be hereditary looks even better when we examine rates of concordance for schizophrenia among blood relatives. A rate of concordance answers the question, If person *A* develops a certain trait, in what percentage of cases will person *B* develop the same trait? For schizophrenia, one investigator found a rate of concordance of 86.2 percent for identical twins, 14.5 percent for fraternal twins, and 14.2 percent for siblings. For unrelated persons, the rate of concordance is only 0.9 percent.[25] Other investigators have reported similar rates of concordance.[26]

While these studies appear to support the hypothesis that schizophrenia is inherited, there may still be better explanations for the high rates of concordance. For example, merely the experience of growing up in a home dominated by schizophrenic parents might increase the likelihood that a child will become schizophrenic. And although no two children are socialized in exactly the same way, children who grow up in the same home and share the same parents will tend to develop some common personality traits. This tendency might be particularly true of twins.

Biochemistry and Psychosis

Dozens of biochemical abnormalities have been investigated in connection with schizophrenia. For example, in the 1950s a substance called taraxein was isolated in the bloodstreams of schizophrenics. When taraxein was injected into the bloodstream of nonpsychotic persons, they temporarily developed schizophreniclike behavior patterns.[27] More recently, interest has centered on serotonin, a substance that appears to influence rates of brain metabolism. Excessively high levels of serotonin "lead to behavioral signs such as excitement and hallucinations whereas deficiencies result in lethargy, depression, and stupor."[28] Since all of these behavioral traits, to some degree, characterize the psychotic individual, the hypothesis was advanced that schizophrenic patients suffer from an oversupply or an undersupply of serotonin. This hypothesis has been discredited, however, by "studies that show that the average level of serotonin in the brains of schizophrenics does not differ from that of normals."[29] Numerous other biochemical and neurophysiological explanations of schizophrenia have been put forth.

Research into possible biochemical bases for schizophrenia and the other psychoses is extremely important for the potential rehabilitation of the mentally ill. If organic bases for mental disturbance exist, modern medicine surely could treat the disease by altering the patient's chemical makeup. However, the research accomplished to date must be viewed with extreme skepticism. For example, in some cases the altered physiological state of the psychotic patient can be traced to factors which are unique to the mental hospital itself. Most research on the mentally ill focuses on patients in mental hospitals; and hospitalized people lead unique lives in that their diets are controlled and they may be given drugs on a prolonged basis. These factors, in turn, could influence the chemical composition of their blood, urine, or spinal fluid. Furthermore, mental disorders may cause imbalances in biochemical makeup rather than vice versa. Just as adrenaline is secreted into the bloodstream when an individual is in a tight situation, other glands may secrete excessive amounts of taraxein or serotonin into the bloodstream when an individual is under severe emotional stress. Essentially, there is a long history of inconclusive research into possible physiological causes of mental disorders. As one critic of this research reports:

> Year after year, papers appear which purport to distinguish between the state of schizophrenia and that of normalcy. The sum total of the differences reported make the schizophrenic patient a sorry physical specimen indeed: his liver, brain, kidney, and circulatory functions are impaired; he is deficient in practically every vitamin; his hormones are out of balance, and his enzymes are askew. Fortunately many of these claims of metabolic abnormality are forgotten in time with a minimum of polemic, but it seems that each new generation of biologists has to be indoctrinated—or disillusioned—without the benefit of the experience of its predecessors.[30]

This does not mean that the search for a biochemical explanation for psychoses should be abandoned. Finding a physiological base for mental disorders could potentially be a major breakthrough in the treatment of mental illness.

Life Experiences

Many authorities believe most mental illness is rooted in the social and psychological history of the individual. According to this view, "the most important etiological factor in the development of the functioning psychic apparatus is Human Experience, however we may look at it or describe it—be it childhood trauma, intrafamilial psychodynamics, the competitive struggle for dominance, or the complex, ever changing culture of our society."[31]

The hypothesis that neuroses spring from the social and psychological history of the individual is widely accepted. One expert maintains that a nagging fear that one's subconscious hostilities will come bubbling to the surface at some inopportune moment lies at the heart of the anxiety that plagues the neurotic person.[32] This subconscious hostility could have many origins, including parental rejection in early childhood. Generally it seems neurotic people fear, for unknown reasons, losing control of their emotions, their environment, or both.

The hypothesis that psychoses, especially schizophrenia, spring from the unique life experiences of the individual is not as widely accepted as the same hypothesis about neuroses because of the doubtful and complex nature of psychoses themselves. Nonetheless, one theory maintains that preschizophrenic individuals are caught in a double-bind relationship with their mothers.[33] This simply means that the mother of a schizophrenic, perhaps less than healthy herself, insists that the child be affectionate and loving toward her. But, when the child does express affection toward her, she subtly recoils in horror, a severe form of psychological punishment for the child. As a result, the child withholds affection from the mother. Yet when this occurs, the mother again raises the question, in some equally painful way,

Many authorities believe most mental illness is rooted in the social and psychological history of the individual.

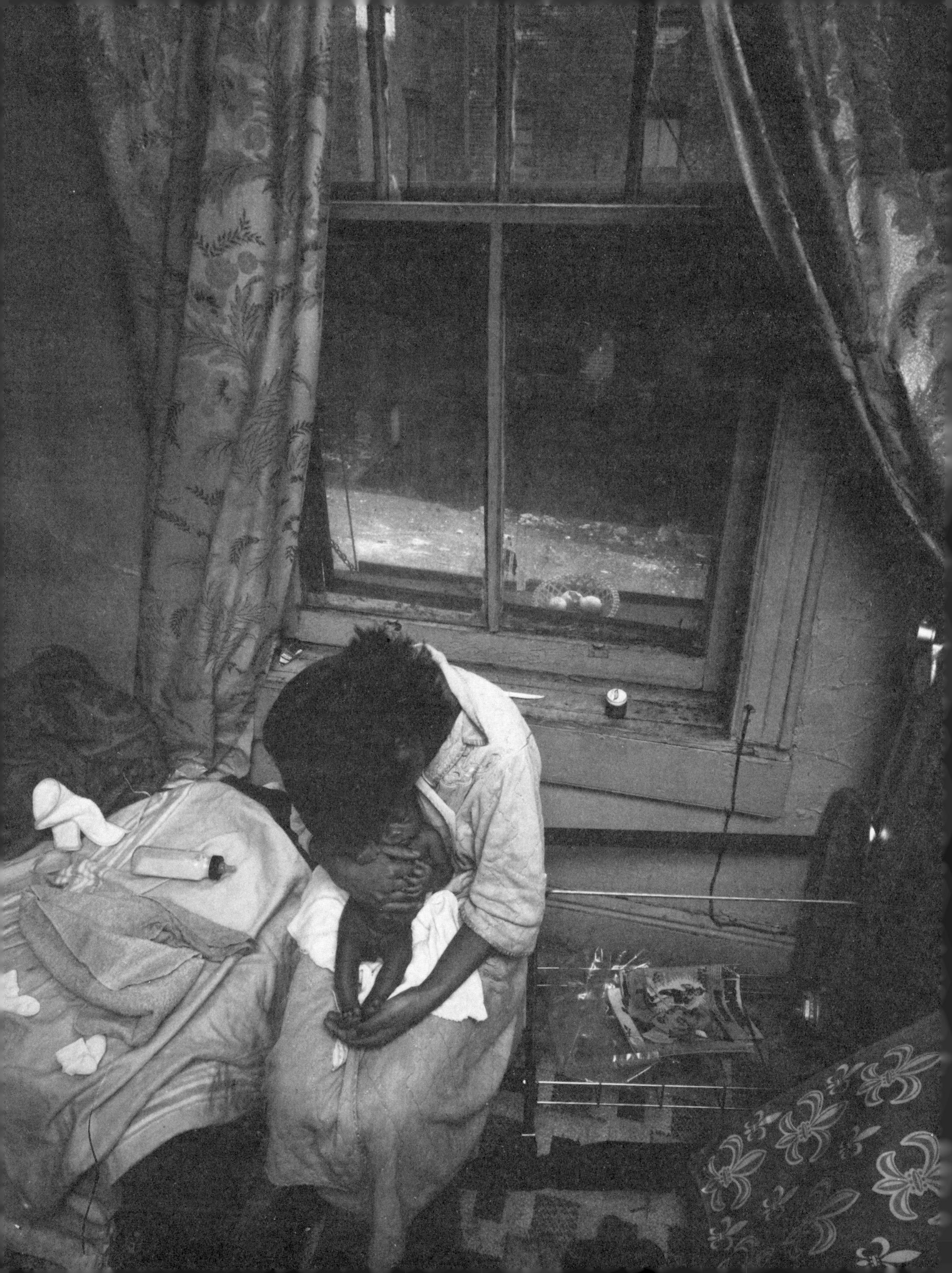

Don't you love me anymore? The child is punished for expressing affection toward the mother and punished for not doing so.

As a result of these formative experiences, the child's ability to interpret the actions and motivations of others becomes totally warped. "If a person said to [a schizophrenic], 'What would you like to do today?' he would be unable to judge accurately by the context or by the tone of voice or gesture whether he was being condemned for what he did yesterday, or being offered a sexual invitation, or just what was meant."[34] The schizophrenic child might come to read a hidden and malicious meaning into every statement, or give up trying to figure out what other people mean, or completely withdraw from interpersonal communication.[35] All three of these coping mechanisms characterize schizophrenia.

Clearly, it is difficult to trace mental illness to the unique social and psychological history of an individual. Pinpointing exactly the type of family relationship most likely to contribute to the psychoses, particularly to schizophrenia, is extremely difficult. And once such a relationship is identified, it is even more difficult to convert this descriptive data into a theoretical statement about the causes of this disorder. For example, the nature of the double-bind relationship is clear, but why this particular mother-child relationship might contribute to schizophrenia is fuzzy.

Sociological Factors

The theories of mental illness outlined in the preceding section all have one element in common—they assume that disorder *within the individual* causes mental illness. This disorder might be a hereditary defect, a chemical imbalance, or injurious life experiences. Sociologists, on the other hand, look to society, rather than to the individual, for the basic causes of mental illness.

The Labeling Perspective

In his book *Being Mentally Ill*, Thomas J. Scheff argues that the causes of mental illness lie in society's reaction to the individual.[36] At one time or another, most of us act in a socially unacceptable manner—we snap at other people, we become depressed, we let our thoughts wander, or we withdraw from social interaction. Our behavior may be due to many factors, including organic stress (such as fatigue), psychological stress, or external pressures.[37] In most cases, though, our rule breaking is overlooked and soon forgotten by other people. However, if we persistently break rules or if the rule breaking is serious enough, other people may label us "mentally ill." Once tagged with this label, we may begin to act the way other people expect us to act. In short, being mentally ill becomes our social role.

Once we step into the mentally ill role, the chances are greatly increased that we will engage in the behaviors associated with mental illness. In other words, "the more the rule-breaker enters the role of the mentally ill, the more he is defined by others as mentally ill; but the more he is defined as mentally ill, the more fully he enters the role, and so on."[38] Mentally disordered behavior, then, becomes a self-fulfilling prophecy—if other people consider me mentally ill, then I must be mentally ill.

Our society provides plenty of opportunities to learn the behaviors associated with mental illness. The mass media constantly dramatize how crazy, deranged, or insane people supposedly act. Scheff thus speaks of the "institution of insanity"—our stereotyped ideas about how insane people act. If certain people expect us to act insane, we have role models to follow at our disposal.

Scheff also maintains that once labeled mentally ill, there are rewards for playing the stereotyped role of the mentally ill and punishments for attempting to return to conventional roles. For example, if patients in a mental hospital "correctly" play the role assigned to them, they are rewarded with attention from therapists and are insulated by the hospital from their troubles in the outside world. They are also accepted by other patients in the institution. On the other hand, a person labeled mentally ill attempting to return to a more conventional role "usually finds himself discriminated against in seeking to return to his old status, and on trying to find a new one in the occupational, marital, social, and other spheres."[39] As a result, the patient simply adopts "being mentally ill" as his or her role in life. Thus, other people define an individual as mentally ill, that individual eventually identifies with the role of the mentally ill, and being mentally ill becomes that individual's mode of adjustment to life.

Theories of mental illness like Scheff's appeal to sociologists because they trace mental illness to society's reactions to the individual. The causes of mental illness are extrinsic to the person; the person is, in effect, forced into the mentally ill role.

However, labeling is not alone the cause of mental illness. If it were, how would we account for people who manifest continuing symptoms of mental illness, even though they are never labeled "mentally ill"? Or, if a person recovers from mental illness, does this mean that society has changed its evaluation of and label for that person? Scheff does not explain why many people recover from mental illness, even after carrying the label "mentally ill." In sum, the labeling perspective leaves many questions unanswered. We can correctly conclude, however, that labeling contributes to and helps propagate mental illness. Certainly people do tend to behave as other people expect them to behave. But we cannot definitively conclude that labeling is a direct cause of mental illness.[40]

Societal Pressures

Every day each one of us is subjected to a tremendous amount of pressure, strain, tension, and anxiety. We live in a world where we can be fired, flunked, overworked, rejected, and hassled. Considering the extent of mental illness, might it not in part be attributable to the daily stress of modern life?

Several studies suggest an inverse relationship between social class and rates of psychosis; that is, as social class goes up, rates of psychosis, particularly schizophrenia, go down, and vice versa.[41] Perhaps this tendency is due to the stresses and strains of occupying a position at the bottom of the status heap. The lower-class person experiences a great deal of job insecurity, financial difficulty, family disruption, and so on. However, there are other, and perhaps better, explanations for the inverse relationship between social class and rates of mental illness.

For example, lower-class people are more likely than middle- or upper-class people to come into contact with the courts, welfare officials, and other authorities who are in a position to label them "mentally ill." They are thus more likely to be so labeled and committed to public mental hospitals.[42] Furthermore, mentally ill people may tend to drift into lower-class positions. Some researchers report that the "psychiatric condition of the patient appears to determine his social class rather than his social class determining or influencing his disorder."[43]

But, we must point out, the lower classes do not have a monopoly on mental illness. Middle-class people also experience a tremendous amount of strain and frustration, much of it associated with their strong desire to be upwardly mobile and their corresponding fear of sliding down in social status. Again, some evidence suggests that both the upwardly mobile and the downwardly mobile are somewhat more likely to become mentally ill than those who do not experience significant shifts in their class position.[44] Perhaps the desire for success and the fear of failure that pervade our society contribute to mental illness, but the case is by no means clear.

In addition, the relationship between societal pressures and mental illness can also be examined by looking at rural-urban differentials in rates of mental illness. Many assume that the urban population lives at a busy, hectic, fast pace while the rural population leads a much more stable, serene, slow life. But we have no definitive evidence that rates of mental disorder in rural areas are lower than in urban areas. In fact, one study concluded that "urban living per se is not more conducive to mental illness than rural living."[45]

Another study looked at the Hutterites, an extremely isolated, rural religious group living in Canada, Montana, and the Dakotas. The study found rates of mental disorder among the Hutterites almost as high as the rates in New York State.[46] If mental illness is a product of life in modern society, why do the Hutterites, who are isolated from many of the pressures and tensions that the average American experiences, display typically high rates of mental illness?

What can we conclude, then, about the relationship between mental illness and our hectic pace of life? On the whole, the evidence does not tend to support a cause-and-effect relationship.[47] Until further research accumulates, we should perhaps assume that a hectic, fast-paced life may contribute to—but not really cause—high rates of mental illness.

Treatment

We have established the seriously disruptive nature of mental illness to both the individual and society. The costs of mental disorders are high, both financially and socially. Mental illness disrupts families and ruins careers. It may also contribute to high rates of crime, delinquency, alcoholism, and other social problems. But mental illness also has sociological aspects. While labeling, for example, is probably not the cause of all mental illness, it does contribute to the development of symptoms of mental illness in some individuals. It also propagates mental illness by locking an individual into the social role of the mentally ill. Similarly, high rates of mental illness may not be caused by the hectic pace of modern life, but the pressures and tensions in our society may contribute to the development of mental disorders in persons already predisposed to mental illness by hereditary or biochemical factors or by their life experiences. How, then, can we solve this complex, multifaceted problem? What are some of the different approaches to treating the mentally ill?

Facilities and Personnel

People with mental disorders may seek help from various sources. Family physicians and ministers are among the most frequently consulted.[48] Professional treatment of mental illness is available from private practitioners such as psychiatrists, clinical psychologists, and social workers; from public and private mental hospitals; and from outpatient community mental health clinics.

Social Problems and You

Mental Illness: Some Popular Misconceptions

Throughout most of history . . . beliefs about mental disorders have been generally characterized by superstition, ignorance, and fear. Although successive advances in the scientific understanding of abnormal behavior have dispelled many false ideas, there remain a number of popular misconceptions that merit brief discussion.

The belief that abnormal behavior is bizarre. The instances of abnormal behavior reported in the mass media, like those recorded in history and literature, are likely to be extreme ones involving murder, sexual assault, airplane hijacking, or other striking deviations from accepted social norms. Patients in mental hospitals and clinics are often pictured as a weird lot who spend their time ranting and raving, posing as Napoleon, or engaging in other bizarre behavior. In fact, most hospitalized patients are quite aware of what is going on around them, and only a small percentage exhibit behavior that might be labeled as bizarre. The behavior of most mental patients, whether in a clinical setting or not, is indistinguishable in many respects from that of "normal" people.

Actually, the term "abnormal" covers a wide range of behaviors. Some types of abnormal behavior are bizarre; but in the great majority of cases, abnormal behavior is so labeled because it is self-defeating and maladaptive. Such self-defeating patterns are a cause of concern, but they are well within the bounds of ordinary, understandable human experience. Included here would be the college student who for no apparent reason is so anxious that she can't concentrate on her studies and has to drop out of school, or the youth who creates serious difficulties in his social relationships by telling trivial lies. . . .

Finally, there are behaviors that are recognized generally as severely abnormal—the adolescent who pours gasoline over an old man and sets him on fire; the indignant youth who insists that his enemies have set up an electronic device that "pours filth into his mind." . . .

Cases like these are unusual, however, and not typical of abnormal behavior in general.

The view that "normal" and "abnormal" behavior are different in kind. Clearly, a sharp dividing line between "normal" and "abnormal" behavior simply does not exist. There are not "normal" people on the one hand and "abnormal" people on the other—two different and distinct kinds of beings. Rather, adjustment seems to follow what is called a normal distribution, with most people clustering around a central point or average, and the rest spreading out toward the two extremes. Most people are moderately well adjusted, with minor maladaptive patterns; a few at one extreme enter mental hospitals or clinics; and a few at the other extreme lead unusually satisfying and effective lives.

We have probably all known and sympathized with someone who became severely depressed after an unhappy love affair, or someone who began to drink excessively following a serious business failure. These people were showing behavior that differed only in degree from that of patients in mental hospitals or clinics, on the one hand, and from that of "normal, well-adjusted" people on the other.

Not only does the behavior of different individuals range by imperceptible degrees from normal to abnormal, but most of us shift our position somewhat along the continuum from time to time. For example, we may be coping adequately with our problems when some change in our life—perhaps a hurtful divorce, a prolonged illness, a serious financial loss, or several problems at once—may increase the severity of the demands made on us to the point where we can no longer cope with them satisfactorily. . . .

The view of former mental patients as

SOURCE: James C. Coleman, *Abnormal Psychology and Modern Life* (Glenview, Ill.: Scott, Foresman, 1976), pp. 10–13.

unstable and dangerous. The common misconception persists that mental disorders are essentially "incurable." As a consequence, persons who have been discharged from mental hospitals or clinics are often viewed with suspicion as being unstable and possibly dangerous. Commonly they are discriminated against in employment or job advancement as well as in the political arena. While it is true that persons with certain forms of mental disorders—such as those associated with severe senile brain damage—will never recover completely, most mental patients respond well to treatment and later meet their responsibilities satisfactorily. Indeed, many achieve a higher level of personality adjustment than before their breakdowns.

Moreover, the great majority of persons who recover from serious mental disorders do not engage in violent or socially disruptive behavior after completing treatment. While it is apparent that care should be taken in releasing patients with a history of violence, less than 1 percent of all patients released from mental hospitals or clinics can be regarded as dangerous, and they are much more likely to be a threat to themselves than to others. . . .

The belief that mental disorder is something to be ashamed of. Many people who do not hesitate to consult a dentist, a lawyer, or other professional person for assistance with various types of problems are reluctant to go to a psychologist or a psychiatrist with their emotional problems. Actually, a mental disorder should be considered no more disgraceful than a physical disorder. Both are adaptive failures.

Nevertheless, there is still a tendency in our society to reject the emotionally disturbed. Whereas most people are sympathetic toward a crippled child or an adult with cancer, they may turn away from the person suffering from an incapacitating mental disorder. Even many psychologists and medical personnel are both uninformed and unsympathetic when they are confronted with persons evidencing mental disorders. . . . Yet the great majority of persons suffering mental disorders are doing the best they know how and desperately need understanding and help.

Fortunately, treatment of mental disorders is becoming an integral part of total social and community health programs. But the stigma that has traditionally been attached to mental disorders still lingers in the minds of many people in our society.

An exaggerated fear of one's own susceptibility to mental disorder. Fears of possible mental disorder are quite common and cause much needless unhappiness. "Other people seem so self-assured and capable. They cannot possibly have the irrational impulses and fantasies I do, or feel the hostility or anxiety or despair that plagues me." Probably most people feel anxious and discouraged during difficult periods in their lives, and may notice with alarm that they are irritable, have difficulty in concentrating or remembering, or even feel that they are "going to pieces." In one study, a representative sample of Americans were asked if they had ever felt they were going to have a "nervous breakdown." Almost one out of five people interviewed replied "yes." . . .

We should not be misled by the apparent self-confidence and competence of other people into thinking that we alone are unhappy and having difficulty with life's problems. Often we are surprised, when we are going through a particularly difficult period, to find that other people do not notice our distress. By the same token, we often fail to recognize the unhappiness of others. . . .

Of course, any of us may experience serious emotional difficulties, especially when problems seem to pile up. In such instances we can avoid unnecessary mistakes and suffering by obtaining competent psychological assistance instead of worrying it out alone. However, a realization that our difficulties are not unique and that most people have many "loose ends" does help reduce the feelings of isolation and of being different that often play a large part in personal fears of mental disorder. . . . By gaining a better understanding of abnormal behavior and of the factors that can interfere with or foster mental health, students can become increasingly confident of their own ability to function effectively.

Private Practice Therapists

Mental health professionals in private practice can consider a client's problems at length and in depth. But private therapy has two limitations. First, since the therapist can only treat a small number of patients per week, the cost is high; private therapy is for the affluent or for those with insurance. Second, most techniques used in various psychotherapies are fully effective only with clients skilled in expressing themselves—the client must be able to communicate ideas and feelings to the therapist and also be able to assimilate ideas that the therapist suggests. As a result, private therapy is usually most successful with middle- or upper-class people since they are "usually in the same social class as the therapist and can readily communicate with him [or her]."[49] However, if we are to really attack mental illness as a social problem, we must also make high quality treatment programs available to the lower classes—those less affluent and less able to communicate with therapists.

The Mental Hospital

The most important treatment facility for the severely disturbed is the public, particularly the state, mental hospital.[50] Until relatively recently, mental hospitals were "holding pens" with little to offer in the way of help and rehabilitation.[51] Today, however, mental hospitals perform three essential functions:[52]

1. They protect both the public and the patient. "The hospital excels in its function of segregating psychotic persons, a minority of whom are harmful, from conventional society. Relatively few persons escape from the hospital, and, as far as can be determined, few patients commit suicide or homicide."[53]

2. Mental hospitals provide care and custodial services for their patients. Some patients do need a protective environment. Disturbingly, however, mental hospitals are to some extent used as dumping grounds for old people who could function in a family situation if their children were willing to let them.

3. The mental hospital renders treatment. On the surface, it appears that each year mental hospitals do a little better in this regard. For instance: "Since 1955, each year has seen a decline in the number of resident patients, despite the fact that the number of new admissions to long-term hospitals has continued to rise. The decline has resulted from the fact that newly admitted patients are, on the average, not staying as long as before."[54] Unfortunately, however, the decline in resident patients probably has little to do with better quality rehabilitation or therapy in mental hospitals. Rather, the decline is due partly to the development of drugs that permit many patients who previously required hospitalization to return to their home communities. In addition, attitudes toward mental patients have changed in recent years. Most people have come to see mental patients as less of a threat to themselves and to others and have become less reluctant to have them discharged from the hospital. Mental health professionals now recognize the importance of quickly reintegrating patients into their home communities.

Despite their positive functions, mental hospitals are problem-ridden and, to some extent, problem-creating institutions. For example, in 1973 the average nonfederal psychiatric hospital spent $26.83 per day on its patients. During the same year, the average nonfederal, short-term general hospital spent $114.69 per day on its patients.[55] Because of their lack of financial resources, most mental hospitals are seriously understaffed both in terms of the quantity and quality of their staff members. Under such conditions, a mental hospital simply cannot give its patients the kind of rehabilitative services that they need and deserve.

Furthermore, the large mental hospital may have an undesirable influence on the patient. It can strengthen and perpetuate the images patients have of themselves as sick, incompetent, and inadequate—the very self-images that must be overcome if patients are to be rehabilitated. Similarly, hospitalization often deprives patients of everyday opportunities to acquire the personal and social skills needed for self-sufficiency in the community. J. K. Wing describes this problem of "total institutions":

> Even the smallest detail, such as when an inmate shall bathe or cut his nails, may be decided for him. Social experience is reduced to a uniform dullness. The inmate is no longer looked upon as a father, or an employee, or a customer, or as a member of numerous specialized social groups, and his ability to play everyday social roles may atrophy from disuse. He does not practice travelling on buses, or spending money, or choosing food or clothes. His relationships with the outside world are reduced to a minimum.[56]

While mental patients may need the therapeutic treatment and other services which mental hospitals can provide, they also need to see themselves as competent and adequate, as able to handle normal interpersonal relations, and as able to play appropriate social roles. Since hospitalized mental patients are largely denied the opportunity to fulfill these latter needs, the mental hospital may do some patients more harm than good.

Outpatient Mental Health Clinics

One of the most encouraging developments in the treatment of mental illness has been the rapid growth of outpatient mental health clinics within communities. Before World War II, fewer than 350 such clinics were in operation.[57] By January 1972, though, 2,279 U.S. mental health facilities provided outpatient services.[58] During 1971, these outpatient facilities cared for 2,316,754 people.[59] However, if all individuals in all U.S. communities are to have reasonable access to mental health services, still more clinics offering more services are very much needed.

Outpatient mental health clinics have been developed in response to several factors, including increased awareness that mental illness is a widespread social problem and that therapeutic services must be made available to individuals who do not require hospitalization and who cannot pay for long-term individual therapy. Significantly, services at community facilities are usually provided free of charge or on a sliding scale according to each person's ability to pay.

Properly staffed, community mental health clinics can be a great help to many people. First, they can aid the many people in any community who are unhappy, ill at ease, and ineffective but who can still function to some degree in the community. Such people may not require or benefit from hospitalization. Further, given the high cost of private therapy, outpatient mental health clinics may be the only source of professional treatment and care within the reach of many people.

Second, outpatient mental health facilities can help locate people who are a threat to themselves or to others. Sometimes the outpatient facility staff can directly treat the disturbed individuals they locate. In other cases, the staff may refer people to another appropriate treatment facility such as a mental hospital.

Finally, outpatient mental health facilities can help mental patients who are discharged from hospitals to reintegrate themselves into community life. Without encouragement, emotional support, and help in finding a job and readjusting to the demands of family life, these people have high probabilities of relapse.

Approaches to Treatment

Any one of several approaches to treating mental illness may be taken by personnel in mental health facilities or in private practice. In this section we will discuss two broad approaches to therapy—biological types of treatment and psychotherapy.

Biological or Organic Therapies

In 1932, Polish psychiatrist Manfred Sakel found that introducing insulin into the bloodstreams of psychotic patients decreased some of their symptoms. While it is not clear why this decrease occurs, we do know that the patient experiences a chemical shock and slips into a comalike state. Following Sakel's discovery, a variety of other shock or convulsion-inducing agents were "used on every imaginable category of emotional disorder."[60] Chemical shock was used particularly to treat people suffering from severe depression. To some extent, it is still used in treating certain types of psychosis when other forms of therapy prove ineffective.

However, there are dangers in the use of shock-inducing drugs—principally that the physician administering the chemical cannot always determine the appropriate dosage. Probably a safer way to induce convulsions is through electrotherapy (electric, rather than chemical, shock). Electrotherapy is used to treat certain types of psychosis, particularly severe depression. As with shock-inducing drugs, the reason electrotherapy alleviates some psychotic symptoms is not well understood.

Electrotherapy is used to treat certain types of psychosis, particularly severe depression.
▼

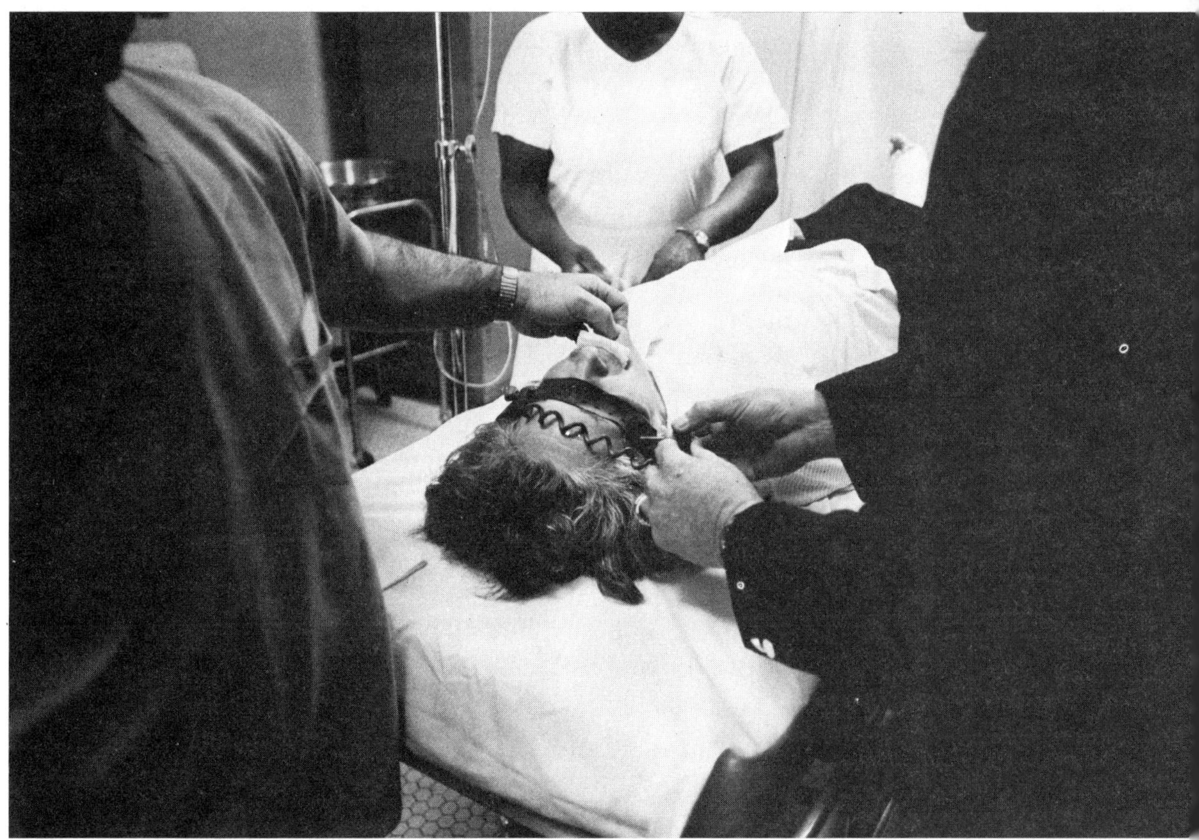

The 1950s saw a revolution in the treatment of mental disorders with the development of psychoactive drugs. Basically, these drugs fall into three categories. The antipsychotic drugs, such as Thorazine and Stelazine, are powerful tranquilizers which help calm psychotic patients who suffer from emotional tension, disordered thought processes, or hyperactivity. They also seem to minimize and sometimes even eliminate hallucinations and delusions.[61]

The second category of psychoactive drugs includes the minor tranquilizers, or antianxiety drugs—for example, Librium, Valium, and Miltown. These drugs are widely used to help alleviate some of the symptoms (such as anxiety) associated with neurotic and psychosomatic disorders. One study, however, reports that "there is no reliable evidence that these minor tranquilizers are any better than the harmless sugar coated placebos."[62]

The third category of drugs used in treating mental disorders are the antidepressants, such as Benzedrine and Dexedrine. These drugs serve as mood elevators for people who suffer from depression, and, as such, they can often substitute for electrotherapy.

The psychoactive drugs have sometimes been enormously helpful to people suffering from certain types of mental disorder. The tranquilizers and antidepressants make it possible for many patients who previously required hospitalization to live at home. The drugs also help alleviate severe depression and clear up disordered thought processes so that individuals can be reached with other therapeutic tools.

However, we must stress the point that none of these drugs cure mental illness. At best, they can control the symptoms of mental illness. For the most part, mental illness does not seem to be biologically or organically based. Rather, the causes of mental disturbance seem to lie largely in the social and psychological history of individuals and in their relationships with society. If we actually want to rehabilitate the mentally ill, we must turn to psychotherapy and other nonorganic approaches that work with the individual on an interpersonal level.

Psychotherapy and Related Therapies

Although psychotherapists vary widely in their assumptions about human behavior and in the methods they use to treat disturbed people, any kind of psychotherapy usually involves a relatively long-term and intense relationship between client and therapist.[63] Some psychotherapists assume that memories of bad childhood experiences, stored away in the subconscious mind, crop up to distort an individual's perceptions and feelings. The key to rehabilitation for these psychotherapists, then, is to deal with the unresolved feelings and conflicts that lie behind the client's present difficulties and problems. Other psychotherapists assume that the person's difficulties are rooted in current situations and inadequate ways of dealing with them. These therapists put more emphasis on helping clients understand how their own behavior may be contributing to their difficulties. Resocialization, supportive therapy, and a variety of other techniques are also available.

Psychotherapy does have several limitations and drawbacks as an approach to treating mental illness. As already mentioned, psychotherapy can be a long, tedious, and costly process; the low-income individual is effectively priced out of the psychotherapy market. In addition, psychotherapy is not particularly well suited for use in mental hospitals where there are severe shortages of qualified personnel. Furthermore, most psychotherapy depends upon a high level of communication between the therapist and the patient; people who lack highly developed communication skills may not benefit much. Finally, traditional psychotherapy is not effective with people who have completely withdrawn from reality or whose patterns of thought and emotion are so severely disturbed that they cannot relate to the therapist. Indeed, one researcher questions whether psychotherapy is of help even to neurotic patients.[64] Nonetheless, different forms of psychotherapy have been used successfully for the treatment of various problems, and it remains today the cornerstone of the mental health professions.

In recent years, behavior therapy has seriously challenged psychotherapy.[65] Behavior therapists assume that mental disorders and related problems are a product of faulty learning; that is, mental patients have learned inappropriate and unsuccessful ways of dealing with stresses and strains and with other people. Like Henry Higgins in *My Fair Lady*, behavior therapists attempt to eliminate undesirable patterns of behavior and to replace them with desirable ones. Once people learn, or are conditioned, to respond in appropriate ways, then their opportunities to develop healthy personalities are enhanced. Inappropriate behavior is assumed to cause emotional distress and malfunctioning rather than vice versa. Behavior therapy has clearly had some success, but it has also been criticized on the grounds that it deals with the symptoms rather than the causes of mental illness. The debate raises the question, Are mental disorders the products of faulty learning, or do they result from deep-seated personality disturbances?

Because much of individual psychotherapy is expensive and time-consuming, various forms of group therapy have recently emerged. These include psychodrama, analytic group psychotherapy, and client-centered group therapy.[66] The basic goal of these three therapies is to help people learn and change through interaction with other people. The interaction is guided by a trained therapist.

▲
Because individual psychotherapy is expensive and time-consuming, various forms of group therapy have recently emerged. The basic goal of group therapy is to help people learn and change through interaction with other people.

One type of group therapy that has become especially popular lately is transactional analysis.[67] Basically, transactional analysis assumes that there are three components to a personality—the child, the adult, and the parent. If the child component dominates, then the individual gets by only as long as other people, particularly a spouse, play the complementary roles of parent or adult. However, if other people cease playing the complementary roles, the individual experiences conflict and frustration. The goals of transactional analysis include helping people *(a)* to see through the games they play with each other, *(b)* to develop more meaningful interpersonal relationships, and *(c)* to gain increased insight into their own behavior and that of others.

Summary

Mental illness is a serious social problem in American society. Its human, social, and financial costs are high.

Despite intensive research within many of the social sciences and medical specialties, there are huge gaps in our knowledge about mental illness. Even the seemingly simple task of defining mental illness is difficult. Many people manifest the signs and symptoms of mental illness, but whether specific individuals are labeled mentally ill depends a great deal on the people around them.

The causes of mental and emotional disturbance are complex and poorly understood. The root cause may lie in an individual's unique life experiences, and some sociologists maintain that the mere practice of labeling some persons as mentally ill may actually contribute to and propagate mentally disordered behavior. Being mentally ill may become an individual's social role. The hectic pace of life in modern society does not seem to play a major role in causing mental disorders, although it may contribute to mental illness in persons who, because of constitutional or sociopsychological factors, already have a predisposition to mental illness.

At the present time no plausible hypothesis concerning the causes of mental illness can be abandoned. For example, even though hereditary or biochemical factors probably do not play a large role in causing mental illness, research along these lines must be pursued because the identification of a hereditary or biochemical basis for mental illness could constitute a significant breakthrough in the rehabilitation of mental patients.

Much more attention should be devoted to the treatment of mental illness. Private treatment is limited in that, for all practical purposes, it is available only to the affluent. And some believe that mental hospitals may do many patients more harm than good. Outpatient mental health clinics probably offer our best hope; but if they are to make a dent in our high rates of mental illness, they will have to be expanded, strengthened, and, in some cases, upgraded.

Discussion Questions

1. Do you think that most deviant behavior stems from emotional disturbances? Why or why not? Explain and justify your answer.

2. Would you consider a 20-year-old football star who constantly worries that he might have a heart attack to be mentally healthy? What about a football star who sometimes worries that he might pull a leg muscle during an important game? Do you think that he is neurotic? Why or why not?

3. How would you explain the fact that a high percentage of children who are reared by schizophrenic parents become schizophrenic themselves? Does this, in effect, prove that schizophrenia is inherited?

4. Discuss the labeling perspective on mental illness. Does labeling cause mental illness? Does labeling contribute to and help propagate mental illness? Explain your answers.

5. What are some of the positive functions that are performed by mental hospitals? Do you think that mental hospitals do some patients more harm than good? In what sense might this be the case?
6. Do the psychoactive drugs cure mental illness? Explain and justify your answer.

Glossary

affective disorders Mental disorders which entail gross alterations in mood, either in the direction of irrational excitement and euphoria or in the direction of severe depression.

behavior therapy An approach to the treatment of mental disorders that assumes that mental disorders are a product of faulty learning and behavior. The behavior therapist attempts to eliminate undesirable patterns of behavior and replace them with desirable ones.

electrotherapy The use of electrical shocks to treat certain types of psychosis, particularly severe depression.

functional psychoses Severe mental disorders which are characterized by several traits, including a loss of contact with reality. Functional psychoses are attributable to the individual's life experiences rather than to organic, physical causes.

group therapy Any form of psychotherapy practiced in a group setting under the guidance of a trained therapist. The goal of group therapy is to help people learn and change through interaction with other people.

labeling perspective (on mental illness) A way of viewing mental illness which maintains that the causes of mental illness lie in society's reaction to the individual. If people define an individual as mentally ill, he or she may adopt mental illness as his or her social role.

mental health A condition in which the individual is emotionally mature and stable. Among other things, mentally healthy people are flexible, effective in their activities, and understand their own feelings.

mental illness A condition in which the individual's thoughts and emotions are disturbed. The mentally ill person, to a greater or lesser degree, is inflexible and has difficulty in effectively playing his or her social roles.

neuroses Emotional disorders in which an individual remains oriented to reality but suffers from either chronic anxiety or sporadic attacks of acute anxiety.

organic brain syndrome An umbrella term that includes all the mental disorders with known organic or physical causes.

psychosomatic disorders Emotional disorders characterized by physical manifestations, often including actual tissue damage.

psychotherapy The treatment of mental disorders through a relatively long-term and intense relationship between client and therapist. Psychotherapists use a variety of different methods to treat mentally disturbed persons.

rate of concordance A statistic which answers the question: If person *A* develops a certain trait, in what percentage of cases will person *B* develop the same trait?

schizophrenia A type of psychosis which involves, among other symptoms, severely disorganized patterns of thought and speech, delusions and hallucinations, and temporary withdrawal from reality.

total institutions Residential treatment institutions in which an effort is made to modify the behavior of the residents, patients, or inmates. Examples include mental hospitals, prisons, and juvenile correctional facilities.

transactional analysis A type of group therapy which attempts to help people to understand the games they play with each other, to develop more meaningful interpersonal relationships, and to gain increased insight into their own behavior and that of others.

Suggestions for Further Reading

Ausubel, David P., "Personality Disorder Is Disease," *The American Psychologist,* 16 (February, 1961), pp. 69–74. Ausubel argues that the concept of mental illness is still useful. He also draws some significant parallels between physical illness and mental illness. This article should be read in conjunction with that by Thomas Szasz which is cited below.

Bateson, Gregory, et al., "Toward a Theory of Schizophrenia," *Behavioral Science,* 1 (October, 1956), pp. 251–64. This is one of the most significant attempts to link schizophrenia to a particular type of family constellation; that is, it is argued that schizophrenic individuals are victims of double-bind relationships with their mothers.

Coleman, James C., *Abnormal Psychology and Modern Life,* 5th Ed. (Glenview, Ill.: Scott, Foresman, 1976). Although this basic textbook is intended for use in psychology courses, it provides an excellent introduction to the many facets of mentally disordered behavior. This book offers the reader all the basic knowledge that is needed to understand mental illness.

Kesey, Ken, *One Flew Over the Cuckoo's Nest* (New York: Viking, 1962). In this novel the reader is given an in-depth and sometimes chilling look at the inside workings of a mental hospital ward. Perhaps more than anything else, this book vividly portrays how a mental hospital can dehumanize both its patients and its staff.

Lemert, Edwin M., "Paranoia and the Dynamics of Exclusion," in Edwin M. Lemert, ed., *Human Deviance, Social Problems, and Social Control,* 2nd Ed. (Englewood Cliffs, N.J.: Prentice-Hall, 1972), pp. 246–64. In this extremely influential, sociologically oriented article, the author argues that paranoia, in large measure, represents a realistic reaction to the situation in which paranoiac individuals find themselves.

Mechanic, David, *Mental Health and Social Policy* (Englewood Cliffs, N.J.: Prentice-Hall, 1969). A relatively short but informative discussion of the nature of mental health and of policies and programs for dealing with mental disorders in the United States.

Scheff, Thomas J., *Being Mentally Ill: A Sociological Theory* (Chicago: Aldine, 1966). This is perhaps the most significant statement on the labeling approach to the analysis and understanding of mental illness.

Srole, Leo, et al., *Mental Health in the Metropolis: The Midtown Manhattan Study,* Rev. Ed. (New York: Harper & Row, 1975). One of the most ambitious and influential studies of the incidence of mental illness among a highly urbanized population.

Szasz, Thomas S., "The Myth of Mental Illness," *The American Psychologist,* (February, 1960), pp. 113–18. In this article Szasz points out that at one time we used to refer to people who had problems in living as being possessed by demons, devils, and witches; today we say that they are "possessed" by mental illness. Szasz advocates abandoning the term *mental illness* because it implies that the person suffers from a specific illness or disease.

Vonnegut, Mark, *The Eden Express: A Personal Account of Schizophrenia* (New York: Praeger, 1975). In this book the author gives a firsthand account of his experiences with schizophrenia. There is reason to think that Vonnegut's disorder is entirely the product of abnormal body chemistry.

Weinberg, S. Kirson, ed., *The Sociology of Mental Disorders: Analyses and Readings in Psychiatric Sociology* (Chicago: Aldine, 1967). This important collection of articles deals with almost every aspect of the sociology of mental disorders.

Notes

[1]Extrapolation of findings in Baltimore, Maryland, by Benjamin Pasamanick, "A Survey of Mental Disease in an Urban Population," *Archives of General Psychiatry,* 5 (August, 1961), p. 154.

[2]National Institute of Mental Health, *Utilization of Mental Health Facilities: 1971,* DHEW Publication No. NIH-74-657 (Washington, D.C.: U.S. Government Printing Office, 1973), p. 19.

[3]*Ibid.,* p. 20.

[4]*Ibid.,* p. 19.

[5]*Ibid.,* p. 2.

[6]Pasamanick, "A Survey of Mental Disease in an Urban Population."

[7]See Leo Srole et al., *Mental Health in the Metropolis* (New York: McGraw-Hill, 1962).

[8]National Institute of Mental Health, *The Cost of Mental Illness: 1968*, Statistical Note 30 (Washington, D.C.: National Clearinghouse for Mental Health Information, 1970), p. 3. The techniques and problems involved in estimating the cost of mental illness are discussed in Rashi Fein, *Economics of Mental Illness* (New York: Basic Books, 1958).

[9]Eric Pfeiffer, *Disordered Behavior: Basic Concepts in Clinical Psychiatry* (New York: Oxford, 1968), p. 197.

[10]*Ibid.*, pp. 196–201.

[11]David Mechanic, "Some Factors in Identifying and Defining Mental Illness," *Mental Hygiene*, 46 (January, 1962), p. 67.

[12]Marian Radke Yarrow et al., "The Psychological Meaning of Mental Illness in the Family," *Journal of Social Issues*, XI (1955), p. 17.

[13]Mechanic, "Some Factors in Identifying and Defining Mental Illness," p. 69.

[14]S. Kirson Weinberg, *Social Problems in Modern Urban Society*, 2nd Ed. (Englewood Cliffs, N.J.: Prentice-Hall, 1970), p. 386.

[15]James C. Coleman, *Abnormal Psychology and Modern Life*, 5th Ed. (Glenview, Ill.: Scott, Foresman, 1976), p. 217.

[16]Dorothea C. Leighton et al., *The Character of Danger* (New York: Basic Books, 1964), p. 310.

[17]For a discussion of the various types of schizophrenia see Coleman, *Abnormal Psychology*, pp. 297–308.

[18]*Ibid.*, p. 297.

[19]National Institute of Mental Health, *Utilization of Mental Health Facilities*, p. 23.

[20]Contrary to popular opinion, the manic and the depressive syndromes infrequently appear in the same individual. In one early study of 208 patients, Rennie found that less than 25 percent manifested both the manic and the depressive reaction. See Thomas A. C. Rennie, "Prognosis in Manic-Depressive Psychosis," *The American Journal of Psychiatry*, 98 (May, 1942), pp. 801–14. There are, of course, other affective disorders, one of which is involutional melancholia. This disorder appears for the most part in women 40 to 55 years of age. However, involutional melancholia does not appear to be due to endocrine or other organic disturbances that are associated with menopause. Rather, involutional melancholia seems to have its roots in psychological and interpersonal factors. See Coleman, *Abnormal Psychology*, p. 363.

[21]Coleman, *Abnormal Psychology*, p. 341.

[22]Elton B. McNeil, *The Psychoses* (Englewood Cliffs, N.J.: Prentice-Hall, 1970), p. 50.

[23]Franz J. Kallman, *Heredity in Health and Mental Disorder* (New York: Norton, 1953), pp. 145–46.

[24]McNeil, *The Psychoses*, p. 51.

[25]Kallman, *Heredity in Health and Mental Disorder*, pp. 144–46.

[26]See James Shields, "Concepts of Heredity for Schizophrenia," in Robert Cancro, ed., *Annual Review of the Schizophrenic Syndrome: 1972* (New York: Brunner/Mazel, 1972), pp. 319–34.

[27]See G. G. Heath et al., "Behavioral Changes in Nonpsychotic Volunteers Following the Administration of Taraxein, the Substance Extracted from Serum of Schizophrenic Patients," *American Journal of Psychiatry*, 114 (1958), pp. 917–20.

[28]Theodore Millon, *Modern Psychopathology: A Biosocial Approach to Maladaptive Learning and Functioning* (Philadelphia: Saunders, 1969), p. 154.

[29]*Ibid.*, p. 154.

[30]M. K. Horwitt, "Fact and Artifact in the Biology of Schizophrenia," *Science*, 124 (September, 1956), p. 429.

[31]Joseph H. Merin, "Conclusion," in Joseph H. Merin, ed., *The Etiology of the Neuroses* (Palo Alto, Cal.: Science and Behavior, 1966), p. 163.

[32]See S. Kirson Weinberg, *The Sociology of Mental Disorders: Analyses and Readings in Psychiatric Sociology* (Chicago: Aldine, 1967), p. 144. The view that repressed hostilities lie at the root of anxiety is shared by psychiatrist Karen Horney. See her classic work, *The Neurotic Personality of Our Time* (New York: Norton, 1937), esp. p. 63.

[33]See Gregory Bateson et al., "Toward a Theory of Schizophrenia," *Behavioral Science*, 1 (October, 1956), pp. 251–64.

[34]*Ibid.*, p. 255.

[35]*Ibid.*, p. 256.

[36]See Thomas J. Scheff, *Being Mentally Ill: A Sociological Theory* (Chicago: Aldine, 1966).

[37]*Ibid.*, p. 40.

[38]*Ibid.*, pp. 97–98.

[39]*Ibid.*, p. 87.

[40]See Walter R. Gove, "Societal Reactions as an Explanation of Mental Illness: An Evaluation," *American Sociological Review*, 35 (October, 1970), pp. 873–883.

[41]For example, see E. L. Faris and H. Warren Dunham, *Mental Disorders in Urban Areas* (Chicago: University of Chicago, 1938); August B. Hollingshead and Frederick C. Redlich, *Social Class and Mental Illness: A Community Study* (New York: Wiley, 1958); Srole et al., *Mental Health in the Metropolis*; and William Rushing, "Two Patterns in the Relationship Between Social Class and Mental Hospitalization," *American Sociological Review*, 34 (August, 1969), pp. 533–41.

[42]Rushing, "Two Patterns in the Relationship Between Social Class and Mental Hospitalization," p. 539.

[43]H. Warren Dunham, "Social Class and Schizophrenia," *American Journal of Orthopsychiatry*, 34 (July, 1964), p. 641.

[44]See A. B. Hollingshead, R. Ellis, and E. Kirby, "Social Mobility and Mental Illness," *American Sociological Review*, 19 (October, 1954), pp. 577–84.

[45]Eleanor Leacock, "Three Social Variables and the Occurrence of Mental Disorder," in Alexander H. Leighton, John A. Clausen, and Robert N. Wilson, eds., *Explorations in Social Psychiatry* (New York: Basic Books, 1957), p. 336.

[46]Joseph W. Eaton and Robert J. Weil, *Culture and Mental Disorders* (New York: Free Press, 1955).

[47]Other writers doubt that urban living and the pace of life in modern society have much influence on rates of mental disorder. See David Mechanic, *Mental Health and Social Policy* (Englewood Cliffs, N.J.: Prentice-Hall, 1969), p. 44; and Karl Menninger et al., *The Vital Balance: The Life Process in Mental Health and Illness* (New York: Viking, 1963), esp. p. 150.

[48]See Gerald Gurin, Joseph Veroff, and Sheila Feld, *Americans View Their Mental Health* (New York: Basic Books, 1960), pp. 302–15.

[49]Weinberg, *Social Problems in Modern Urban Society*, p. 431.

[50]There have been numerous studies of mental hospitals. See Erving Goffman, *Asylums* (New York: Doubleday, 1961); Ivan Belknap, *Human Problems of a State Mental Hospital* (New York: McGraw-Hill, 1956); William Caudill, *The Mental Hospital as a Small Society* (Cambridge, Mass.: Harvard, 1958); H. Warren Dunham and S. Kirson Weinberg, *The Culture of a State Mental Hospital* (Detroit: Wayne State, 1960); and Alfred Stanton and Morris Schwartz, *The Mental Hospital* (New York: Basic Books, 1954).

[51]Histories of the care that the U.S. has extended to the mentally ill are contained in Albert Deutsch, *The Mentally Ill in America* (New York: Columbia, 1949); and in Gerald N. Grob, *The State and the Mentally Ill* (Chapel Hill, N.C.: University of North Carolina, 1966).

[52]See S. Kirson Weinberg, *Society and Personality Disorders* (Englewood Cliffs, N.J.: Prentice-Hall, 1952), pp. 376–86.

[53]*Ibid.*, p. 377.

[54]John A. Clausen, "Mental Disorders," in Robert K. Merton and Robert Nisbet, eds., *Contemporary Social Problems*, 3rd Ed. (New York: Harcourt Brace Jovanovich, 1971), p. 79.

[55]U.S. Bureau of the Census, *Statistical Abstract of the United States: 1975*, 96th Ed. (Washington, D.C.: U.S. Government Printing Office, 1975), p. 81.

[56]J. K. Wing, "Institutionalism in Mental Hospitals," in Thomas J. Scheff, ed., *Mental Illness and Social Processes* (New York: Harper & Row, 1967), pp. 220–21.

[57]Clausen, "Mental Disorders," p. 75.

[58]National Institute of Mental Health, *Utilization of Mental Health Facilities*, p. 18.

[59]*Ibid.*, p. 15.

[60]McNeil, *The Psychoses*, p. 139.

[61]Coleman, *Abnormal Psychology*, p. 675.

[62]McNeil, *The Psychoses*, p. 145.

[63]Psychotherapy should not be confused with psychoanalysis. Psychoanalysis is based on classical Freudian concepts of personality and assumes that mental disorder has its roots in conflicts between the id, the ego, and the superego. In order to discover these conflicts, the psychoanalyst makes use of free association, dream analysis, and other methods of uncovering subconscious materials. Psychoanalysis is infrequently used because it is costly and time-consuming. Its effectiveness has also been questioned. Psychotherapy, on the other hand, is much more eclectic and makes use of a wide variety of tools in treating the disturbed person.

[64]H. J. Eysenck, "The Effects of Psychotherapy: An Evaluation," *Journal of Consulting Psychology*, 16 (1952), pp. 319–24.

[65]For further discussion of behavior therapy see Albert Bandura, *Principles of Behavior Modification* (New York: Holt, Rinehart & Winston, 1969). See also Albert Bandura, "Behavioral Psychotherapy," *Scientific American*, 216 (March, 1967), pp. 78–86.

[66]The different approaches to group therapy are discussed in Robert A. Harper, *Psychoanalysis and Psychotherapy: 36 Systems* (New York: Aronson, 1974), pp. 129–42.

[67]Transactional analysis has been pioneered by Eric Berne. See Eric Berne, *Games People Play: The Psychology of Human Relationships* (New York: Grove, 1964).

Chapter 4
Alcoholism

A 100-year-old gentleman, when asked the secret of his longevity, replied, "A fifth a day keeps the doctor away!" In 1973 alcohol dependence was labeled "without question, the most serious drug problem" in the United States.[1] In addition, alcohol may be the most popular drug in our highly drugged society. For temporary relief from emotional aches and pains, alcohol is often less costly and more readily available than tranquilizers, antidepressants, or barbiturates. In moderate amounts, alcohol helps "obtain feelings of pleasure as well as relief from fears and tensions."[2] The problem, of course, is that some people come to rely too heavily on alcohol. Some people gradually become problem drinkers or alcoholic individuals.

Most of us are aware of the suffering caused by alcoholism in the lives of both the alcoholic individuals themselves and the people with whom they are involved—family, friends, office workers, etc. Problem drinking seriously disrupts careers, marriages, families, and social relationships. Furthermore, alcoholism contributes to a variety of other social problems. For example, alcoholic individuals burden social institutions: a fairly high percentage of people admitted to general hospitals suffer from alcohol-related disorders; and drunken persons, including drunken drivers, account for about one-third of the arrests in this country. Clearly alcoholic individuals place a burden on police departments, courts, and correctional agencies. Excessive drinking and alcoholism affect so many people in so many ways.

What Is Alcoholism?

There is no easy definition of alcoholism. However, one of the most widely accepted was developed by the Cooperative Commission on the Study of Alcoholism and defines alcoholism as a "condition in which the individual has lost control over his alcohol intake in the sense that he is consistently unable to refrain from drinking or to stop drinking before getting intoxicated."[3] As this definition implies, the loss of control associated with drinking can take two forms. First, an individual may have a continuing need for alcohol and may be unable to abstain from its use for very long, perhaps because it helps the individual manage tension. Second, an individual may lose control and not be able to stop drinking until totally intoxicated. Both forms of loss of control may appear in the same individual.

Most of us are aware of the suffering caused by alcoholism in the lives of both the alcoholic individuals themselves and the people with whom they are involved.

Although alcoholism is generally attributed to psychological and social factors, some people who drink heavily for many years become physiologically addicted to alcohol and experience a

"RIGHTEOUSNESS
EXALTETH A NATION"

withdrawal syndrome when they cease drinking. This withdrawal syndrome includes "rapid heartbeat, profuse sweating, severe nausea, uncontrollable tremors, and, in a more extreme form, disorientation, hallucinations, and the classic seizures known as delirium tremens."[4] According to one estimate, a maximum of 1 percent of all alcohol users become physically addicted to alcohol.[5]

In the past, people who suffered from alcoholism were called *alcoholics*. Today, though, many writers prefer the terms *alcoholic person* and *alcoholic individual*. These terms remind us that alcoholism is not the person's only characteristic: the alcoholic individual plays a variety of roles and possesses a complete set of strengths and weaknesses. He or she is not qualitatively different from the rest of us. Rather, the alcoholic individual is a person who has a problem with drinking alcohol, just as the obese person has a problem with eating food. Calling the former an *alcoholic* is as stigmatizing as calling the latter an *overeater*.

Problem Drinking

Alcoholic individuals are not the only people who have problems with alcohol. The Cooperative Commission on the Study of Alcoholism distinguishes problem drinking from alcoholism and defines problem drinking as the "repetitive use of beverage alcohol causing physical, psychological, or social harm to the drinker or to others."[6] This very broad definition includes almost all alcoholic individuals since they harm both themselves and others. However, the definition also includes the factory worker who has a few beers at lunch and then operates dangerous equipment or the head of a poverty-stricken family who, even though always sober, consistently spends money on alcohol which could be better used to pay the family's bills. Clearly, alcohol abuse is a many-sided problem.

Alcoholism as a Disease

For over one hundred years, alcoholism has been called a disease. Unquestionably, the people who developed the disease concept of alcoholism had good intentions. During recent years, however, many experts have hotly debated the advantages and the disadvantages of the disease concept of alcoholism.[7] Since the now common practice of referring to alcoholism as a disease has a profound impact on our attitudes toward the alcoholic individual, on how the alcoholic individual is treated, and even on how the alcoholic individual perceives his or her own situation, we need to briefly examine the issues in this debate.

On the positive side, the disease concept of alcoholism has encouraged both the public and the medical community to regard the alcoholic individual as a person with a very real but treatable problem. In the past, alcoholic individuals were most often viewed as weak, morally spineless people who could solve their drinking problems if they only had the will. The disease concept of alcoholism, however, has helped us realize that the alcoholic individual needs professional treatment and care. The alcoholism-as-a-disease concept has also helped stimulate research on alcoholism in hopes of finding a cure and has led to the establishment of treatment facilities for alcoholic individuals. Because of the disease concept of alcoholism, some physicians are now willing to try to help the alcoholic individual.

On the negative side, the practice of referring to alcoholism as a disease has several major drawbacks. First, it may serve as an alibi for alcoholic individuals who refuse to try to improve their own condition or to seek help from other sources. They may reason that, if alcoholism is really an irreversible disease, nothing can be done about it.[8] Second, "the disease 'alcoholism' has not been defined and there is no specific treatment for it. Physicians can hardly be expected to apply a nonexistent treatment to an undefined disease in a population that denies the disease and rejects the treatment."[9] Third, the concept of alcoholism as a disease is confusing to the general public.[10] Fourth and finally, the disease concept of alcoholism probably encourages simplistic and naive thinking about the nature, causes, and treatment of alcoholism. It may foster the notion that something is physiologically wrong with the person that must be treated or removed before the alcoholism can be cured.

What, then, can we conclude about the disease concept of alcoholism? Certainly it has served some useful purposes. But it may have outlived its usefulness. Rather than continuing to apply an inaccurate concept that may do more harm than good, we should begin to view alcoholism as a serious but treatable personal and social problem.

How Much Alcoholism?

Estimating the number of alcoholic individuals is not easy. For one thing, where is the line drawn between heavy social drinking and alcoholism? Mrs. Fred Tooze, head of the National Women's Christian Temperance Union, defines an alcoholic individual as "anyone who drinks alcohol."[11] In her estimation, then, approximately 100 million individuals are alcoholic—the approximate number of Americans who use alcoholic beverages.[12] More realistically, governmental agencies estimate that there are about 10 million alcoholic individuals and/or problem drinkers in the United States.[13] This represents about 7 percent of the adult population (aged 18 and over). Further, about 5 percent of America's alcoholic individuals are not adults; they are minors between the ages of 10 and 19.[14]

Who Is Alcoholic?

Television advertisements tell us that no one is exempt from alcoholism. The alcoholic individual may be young or old, black or white, male or female, rich or poor, in any occupation—factory worker, doctor, lawyer, minister, teacher, or housewife. But, by correlating a number of different studies we can form a tentative picture of who is most likely to suffer from alcoholism.

Age

It takes time to become dependent on alcohol. So it is no surprise that several surveys and studies have found that rates of problem drinking and alcoholism reach their peak in groups aged 35 to 64.[15] However, one of the most discouraging aspects of the alcohol problem is the apparent upswing in rates of alcoholism among young people in their twenties and thirties.[16] This upswing could

The 1970s have seen a dramatic increase in alcoholism among teenagers. An estimated 450,000 grade-school children and teenagers are alcoholic individuals. ▼

be an illusion, however. We are more aware today that anyone can develop a drinking problem and we are more willing to seek help with our problems. If young people are now more likely to seek treatment, their rates of problem drinking and alcoholism may appear to be increasing. Most public treatment facilities not only render treatment, they also compile statistics on their patients as well.

Although the trend is not yet thoroughly documented, the 1970s have seen a dramatic increase in alcoholism among teenagers. An estimated 450,000 grade-school children and teenagers are alcoholic individuals.[17] Corresponding to this trend, the number of young people arrested for intoxication has multiplied. During the past decade, the number of girls aged 18 and younger arrested on this charge increased 300 percent, and the number of boys arrested increased 250 percent.[18] Very likely, young people are abandoning drugs such as marijuana and speed, and turning to alcohol instead. They are safer, legally, using alcohol than using illicit drugs; and in most communities alcohol is more readily available. Finally, since alcohol is one of America's favorite medications, it should not be surprising that young people are turning to the drug used so extensively by their parents.

Sex

Male alcoholic individuals far outnumber female alcoholic individuals. Between 1910 and 1956, the ratio of male to female alcoholic persons fluctuated between 5 to 1 and 6 to 1.[19] However, the percentage of females in the alcoholic population is increasing: "In the '50s . . . one of every five or six alcoholics was a woman; the ratio is now one woman for every four men."[20]

Why are more women now turning to alcohol? Beyond our greater acceptance of women drinking, both at home and in public, this recent phenomenon may be due in part to the fact that sex roles are changing in our society. More women are working now and, like men, feel the stresses and strains of holding a job. Some women may feel threatened by the changes, while others may be growing resentful of the tedium of minding the children and keeping the house. Such tensions may be driving more women to the bottle.

Race and Ethnicity

Little is known about the association between race and alcoholism. However, rates of excessive drinking in this country appear higher among blacks than among whites.[21] High rates of alcoholism also characterize other disadvantaged minority groups, but—and this must be emphasized—these high rates cannot be traced to biological predispositions. Rather, the excessive use of alcohol among American minorities probably serves as an escape from lives marked by poverty and discrimination. In addition, definitions of what constitutes problem drinking and/or alcoholism vary from group to group. "Problem drinking" in the white-collar world may be "alcoholism" in the ghetto.

Socioeconomic Status

Data indicate that the relationship between occupational status and the likelihood that a person will drink heavily is by no means clear-cut.

A study of Maryland psychiatric facilities found that poorly educated persons are overrepresented among persons treated for alcoholism.[22] This overrepresentation, however, could stem entirely from the greater tendency of lower-class people to use mental health facilities; middle- and upper-class persons more often seek

help from family physicians or from private-practice psychiatrists and psychologists, and data are not readily available from these sources (see Chapter 3). As a matter of fact, data collected in 1964–65 indicated that the relationship between occupational status and the likelihood that a person will drink heavily is by no means clear-cut. Lower-class persons are not necessarily more likely to have problems with alcohol than middle- or upper-class persons.[23]

Size of Community

Size of community and rates of problem drinking and/or alcoholism are directly related—as community size increases, problem drinking and alcoholism also rise.[24] Alcoholism may be somewhat less common in rural areas because a certain amount of prohibitionist sentiment still survives and many rural counties are dry. It is more likely, however, that alcoholism is less frequent because the excessive drinker is more visible in small rural communities and thus more likely to be pressured by family and friends to exercise control.

Alcoholism: Its Costs and Consequences

The high costs associated with alcoholism are tallied not only in terms of human suffering, but in terms of family disorganization, loss of productivity, and danger to health and safety as well.

On Family

Like the rest of the adult population, most alcoholic individuals are married. However, the alcoholic individual's ability to play social roles may become impaired to the point where he or she is unable to play such roles as spouse, parent, and wage earner in a satisfactory manner. The alcoholic individual can also be very difficult to live with: at times jovial, loving, and outgoing, but on other occasions moody, depressed, and even abusive. Families of alcoholic individuals are thus much more likely to be broken through divorce or separation than families in the general population.[25]

Several studies have been conducted on how alcoholism affects family life.[26] As the individual's alcoholism worsens, his or her family attempts to cope with the problem in a series of stages, first in the direction of family disorganization, later in the direction of reorganization. For example, as her husband's drinking problem begins to emerge, the wife first denies that a problem exists and then attempts to cope with the problem herself. Initial attempts to deal with the problem may involve discussions with him, trying to control the availability of liquor, and setting up norms: "She may agree to drink with him, both of them stopping at a certain point."[27] However, as the drinking problem grows worse and the wife's attempt to solve it fails, the quality of the husband-wife relationship can completely deteriorate. Quite often the husband totally ceases to play his roles, and the wife reestablishes some equilibrium in the family by assuming the roles of breadwinner, disciplinarian, handyman, and so on. At this point, the wife may well decide to simply terminate the marriage. Finally, if the husband does get help and overcomes his problem, provisions must be made for re-admitting him into the family. Although re-establishing healthy family life is clearly desirable, it takes time to rebuild rewarding role relationships and to overcome the nagging fear of relapse.

Alcoholism's impact on the family is tragic: "The life of the family revolves around the bottle as does the life of the alcoholic."[28] A wife, for example, may resent the fact that her husband's behavior sometimes forces her to be a nurse rather than a wife, or she may feel responsible for her husband's problem, which is probably not the case. The alcoholic father may be inconsistent and unpredictable. As a result, his children may be anxious and confused and in some cases "a youngster may find himself in the position of the responsible member of the household, thereby reversing the parent-child relationship."[29] In addition, unemployment and the high cost of alcoholic beverages may create financial difficulties for families.

Obviously, no two alcoholic individuals are alike and no two families react to a member's emerging drinking problem in the same way. The alcoholic individual who goes on drinking sprees will affect his or her family much differently than the person who maintains a constant state of intoxication. And an affluent upper-class family will attempt to cope with problem drinking in a different manner from a disadvantaged lower-class family. Furthermore, there can be a two-way relationship between drinking and family problems. Certainly alcoholism puts a tremendous strain on marriage and family life. At the same time, however, marital strife and conflict may be one of the factors that cause alcohol abuse.

On Work

Just as the quality of his or her family life may deteriorate, so too the alcoholic individual's job performance may deteriorate from about 90 percent to 50 percent effectiveness during the early and middle stages of alcoholism. During this period the employee is reprimanded more and more frequently by superiors and no longer advances in pay or position. Eventually, the alcoholic individual's job performance becomes so erratic that dismissal is inevitable.

The tragedy is that the majority of alcoholic individuals are between the ages of 35 and 50—the age group for which employment is most important, central to their lives.[30] So alcoholism is also a major—and costly—problem for industry. Alcoholic employees tend to have high rates of job absenteeism, and the quality of their work is poor. Indeed, "supervisors of alcoholic employ-

Figure 4.1 **Behavioral Pattern of Employee With Drinking Problem**

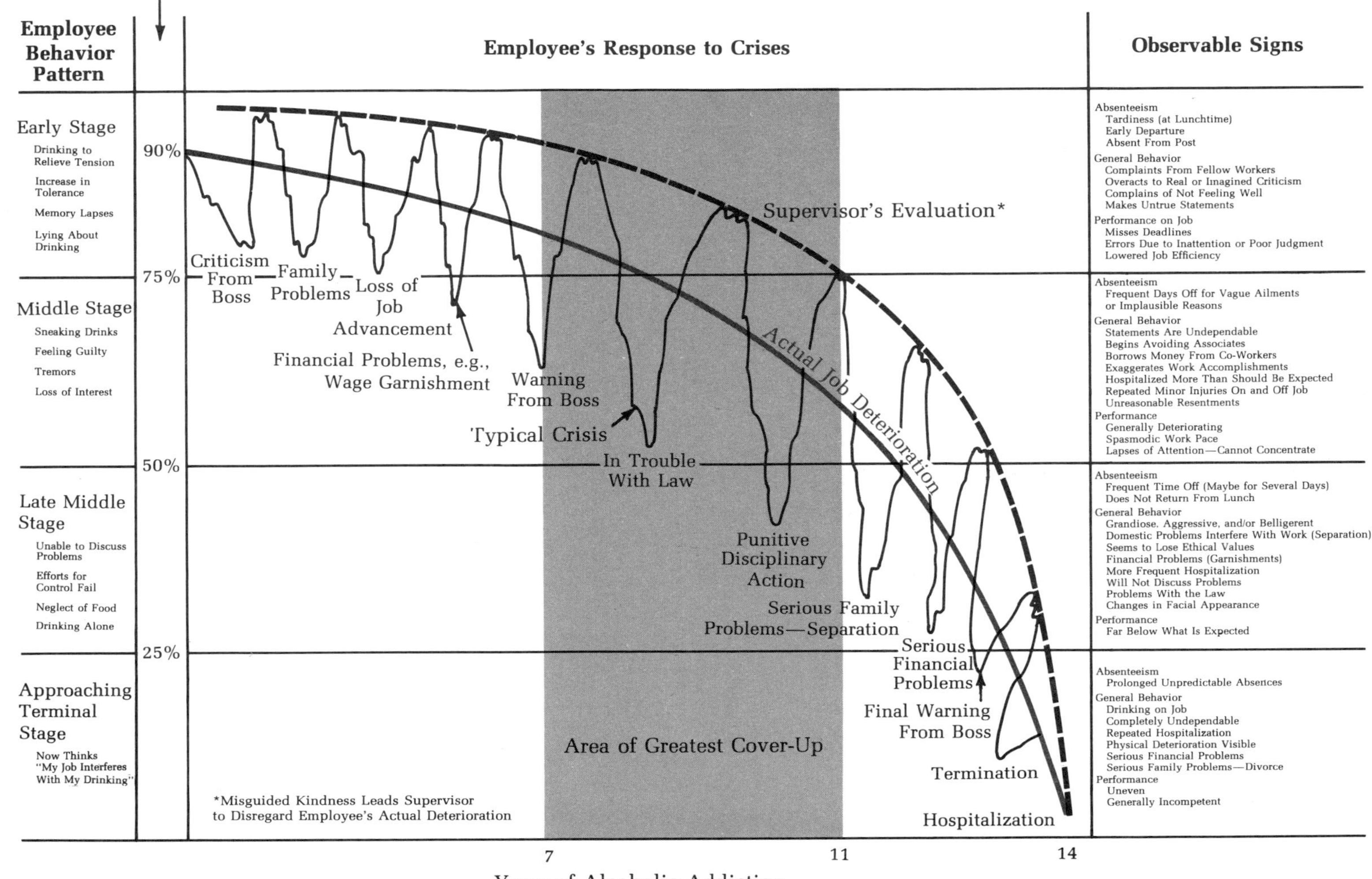

SOURCE: Robert T. Dorris and Doyle F. Lindley, *Counseling on Alcoholism and Related Disorders* (Beverly Hills, Calif.: Glencoe, 1968), p. 59.

ees . . . consistently saw them as closer to their worst employees than to their best."[31]

To combat alcoholism, some industries and individual companies now have rehabilitation programs for employees with drinking problems. The company benefits can be rather sizeable when these programs are successful. An employee "earning $10,000 a year will cost his firm an additional $5,000 each year if he is an alcoholic."[32] The cost to the company may be even greater if the alcoholic employee is an executive. An alcoholic executive is responsible for making important decisions, draws a high sal-

Table 4.1

Alcohol-Related Health Hazards

Gastrointestinal
- Esophagitis
- Esophageal carcinoma
- Gastritis
- Malabsorption
- Chronic diarrhea
- Pancreatitis
- Fatty liver
- Alcoholic hepatitis
- Cirrhosis (may lead to cancer of liver)

Cardiac
- Alcoholic cardiomyopathy
- Beriberi

Skin
- Rosacea
- Telangiectasia
- Rhinophyma
- Cutaneous ulcers

Neurologic and psychiatric
- Peripheral neuropathy
- Convulsive disorders
- Alcoholic hallucinosis
- Delirium tremens
- Werniche's syndrome
- Korsakoff's psychosis
- Marchiafava's syndrome

Muscle
- Alcoholic myopathy

Hematologic
- Megaloblastic anemia

Vitamin-deficiency disease
- Beriberi
- Pellagra
- Scurvy

Metabolic
- Alcoholic hyperglycemia
- Alcoholic hyperlipemia

SOURCE: *Alcohol and Health: Report from the Secretary of Health, Education, and Welfare* (New York: Scribner's, 1973), p. 111.

ary, has talents that the company needs, and would be costly to replace. These facts all add up: it is definitely in a firm's interest to offer rehabilitation programs for employees who have problems with alcohol.

On Health and Safety

There is convincing evidence that excessive use of alcohol is harmful to an individual's health. For example, alcohol abuse is directly related to cirrhosis of the liver, a disorder responsible for 29,866 deaths in the United States during 1969.[33] Some of the other alcohol-related health hazards are shown in Table 4.1. As already mentioned, a fairly high percentage of hospital admissions are alcohol-related, and excessive use of alcohol is also thought to contribute to cancer.[34] One government report indicates that the person who abuses alcohol may shorten his or her life span by as much as ten to twelve years.[35]

Most of us are aware of the association between alcohol and traffic accidents. In 1973, for example, drunk drivers were responsible for half of the 54,700 traffic deaths that occurred in the United States.[36] They are also responsible for a large percentage of the nearly two million motor vehicle injuries that occur each year. In the interest of public safety, governmental and public-service agencies have tried to get across the message: "Don't drink when you drive. Don't drive when you drink." But so far, it is apparent that strong and effective norms have not been established in this direction. Unfortunately, the relationship between alcoholism and accidents goes far beyond the car; it has been estimated that "alcohol is a contributing factor in about 20 percent of accidental asphyxiations in the home, 20 percent of falls, 25 percent of all deaths attributed to choking on food, 20 percent of all drownings, and *all* deaths caused by freezing."[37] In sum, the excessive use of alcohol can only endanger health and safety.

On Other Social Problems

Although most research has been focused on the relationships between alcoholism and family problems, alcoholism and job performance, and alcoholism and health and safety, alcoholism has been linked to other social problems as well. In 1973, for example, approximately 31 percent of all arrests in this country involved an alcohol-related offense such as drunkenness, drunken driving, and the violation of liquor laws.[38] Many arrests for vagrancy and disorderly conduct involve problem drinkers. Alcohol-related offenses place a tremendous burden on our law enforcement and judicial agencies.

Little more is known about the relationship between the excessive use of alcohol and other social problems. A study of 588 murders in Philadelphia found that in 63.6 percent of the cases either the victim, the perpetrator, or both had been drinking.[39] But this does not mean that a cause-and-effect relationship exists between alcohol and murder because other variables come into play—whether a weapon is available, whether a quarrel occurs, and so on. Alcoholism also seems to contribute to a significant number of suicides; alcoholic individuals are more likely to commit suicide than nonalcoholic individuals.[40] Whether the excessive use of alcohol makes a significant contribution to other social problems is unclear.

The Causes of Alcoholism

As we have seen, alcoholism is a major problem for both the alcoholic individual and society. But what causes alcoholism? As we did when examining the causes of mental illness in Chapter 3, we must look at three variables: the biological, the psychological, and the social or cultural.

Biological Factors

Despite some promising leads, research has yet to conclusively demonstrate that alcoholism has a physiological basis.[41] However, speculation persists as to whether alcoholism might be inherited and whether some people might be allergic to alcohol and therefore might be particularly susceptible to alcoholism.

Is Alcoholism Inherited?

Many alcoholic persons have parents who were also alcoholic: "In a study of 259 hospitalized alcoholics, . . . slightly over 40 percent had parents—usually the father—who were alcoholics. . . . [A] review of earlier studies . . . reported a higher incidence—finding that more than half the individuals who became alcoholics have an alcoholic parent."[42] These findings, however, do not prove that alcoholism is inherited. In fact, in a study of 36 children of alcoholic parents who were removed from their homes and placed in foster homes, none showed signs of alcoholism during their adult years and only 7 percent used alcoholic beverages regularly.[43] These results suggest that excessive use of alcohol may be a form of learned behavior; that is, some children who grow up in homes dominated by an alcoholic parent or parents may learn to abuse alcohol.

Are Some People Allergic to Alcohol?

The allergy theory of alcoholism is popular with laymen, some members of Alcoholics Anonymous, and even some physicians because, on the surface, it seems to explain why some people cannot "hold their liquor."[44] However, one study concludes that "there is no valid evidence for a true allergy to alcohol."[45] Other theories attempting to trace alcoholism to glandular or biochemical abnormalities have, so far, not withstood rigorous scientific scrutiny.

Psychological Factors

To understand the psychology of alcoholism, we must first understand how alcohol affects a drinker's emotional state. Alcohol "is mainly a sedative and sedatives, in general, are tranquilizers."[46] So, when intoxicated, a person may experience a sense of warmth and well-being. Unpleasant realities and nagging worries are left behind, at least temporarily, and "the drinker's feelings of self-esteem and adequacy rise."[47] Since the consumption of alcohol can for a while make individuals feel better about themselves and their situations, we might ask: (1) Is alcoholism a way for some individuals to prop up their essentially inadequate personalities? (2) Is alcoholism a learned way for some individuals to deal with stress?

Is There an Alcoholic Personality?

Because alcohol can change a person's feelings about himself or herself, attempts have been made to trace alcoholism to various personality inadequacies. Alcoholic individuals have been described as suffering from repressed homosexual tendencies, sex-role conflict, anxiety, guilt, emotional immaturity, maternal deprivation, poor self-images, a low tolerance for frustration, the inability to express anger effectively, etc. In fact, the alcoholic person has been described in so many different ways that we cannot possibly list them all.[48] But implied in all these various descriptions is that drinking helps the person cope with his or her personal inadequacies.

The search for a particular alcoholism-prone personality type has not been fully successful. So far, we have only established that "alcoholics as a group suffer more frequently from personality aberrations of one kind or another than do (nondeviant) nonalcoholics."[49] Beyond this, descriptions of the alcoholism-prone personality could, at one time or another, fit nearly all of us—but we aren't all alcoholic. Further, the personality trait approach does not adequately explain why rates of alcoholism vary radically from group to group, even within the same social setting. For example, in the United States, alcoholism is much more prevalent among males than among females. But we cannot thus conclude that males on the average have less adequate personalities than females. A much more satisfactory explanation perhaps can be made in terms of social and cultural variables.

Is Alcoholism Learned?

Psychologist Albert Bandura sees alcoholism as a learned means of coping with environmental stress.[50] That is, since alcohol can temporarily relieve worry, anxiety, self-consciousness, etc., people who feel environmental stress may find the use of alcohol rewarding. By drinking, an individual experiences a reward (the reduction of stress), and the drinking behavior is reinforced.

If a person continues to drink heavily and continually, he or she may become addicted to alcohol. According to Bandura, addiction provides "the basis for a second maintaining mechanism [for alcohol consumption] that is quite independent of the original functional value of alcohol."[51] Specifically, a person addicted to alcohol experiences tremulousness, nausea, vomiting, diarrhea, and a variety of other unpleasant symptoms when drinking ceases. These symptoms can be relieved by large quantities of alcohol, so the drinking behavior is again reinforced. Now, the person experiences a reduction in both environmental stress and physiological stress.

On the surface, Bandura's theory seems deficient. First, while excessive consumption of alcohol may have short-term rewards, certainly over the long run it holds devastating consequences for the drinker, including enormous personal, social, economic, and health problems. Because excessive consumption of alcoholic beverages eventually leads to punishment rather than to reward, Bandura's theory is discounted by some critics. However, Bandura counters such criticism by pointing out that "behavior is more powerfully controlled by its immediate, rather than delayed, consequences and it is precisely for this reason that persons may persistently engage in immediately reinforcing, but potentially self-destructive, behavior."[52] In other words, the rewards of excessive drinking are immediate. The adverse effects lie off somewhere in the future and are difficult to perceive.

Bandura's theory also does not seem to account for the fact that not all persons who experience environmental stress develop problems with alcohol. However, Bandura recognizes that cultural and subcultural norms influence whether or not a person drinks excessively, if at all. In addition, he realizes that, through family and peer groups, an individual learns patterns of drinking behavior and may acquire attitudes conducive to total abstinence, moderate drinking, or excessive drinking.

Is Alcoholism a Game?

Transactional analysis can be considered a third psychological approach to alcoholism.[53] Its advocates view alcoholism as a game in which the alcoholic individual seeks certain rewards. For example, "the 'Drunk and Proud' game is often played by salesmen and executives with their wives, the purpose of the game being to punish the wife for her domineering and possessive attitudes."[54] In other words, by "playing" alcoholic, the individual finds an excuse for inflicting punishment on other people or demanding attention or whatever. The other players also gain certain rewards. For example, the wife of an alcoholic individual may find it gratifying to mother and care for her husband. At the same time, she has a perfect excuse for her inability to relate to her husband in a healthy, mature way.

The view that alcoholism is a game in which one or more of the players gains certain rewards may have its merits. But it may also apply to only a relatively few people. For all alcoholic individuals and their families, the penalties associated with alcoholism far outweigh its rewards. If alcoholism is a game, it is certainly a game without a winner.

Sociological Factors

Both the biological and the psychological theories of alcoholism hypothesize that the causes of alcoholism lie within the individual—alcoholism can be traced to heredity, to an allergy, or to personality inadequacies. Now we are going to turn our attention to the sociological explanations of alcoholism and the behavior of drunken individuals. Even though there are many sociological theories of alcoholism, they all have one thing in common—they assume that alcoholism, and drunken behavior patterns in general, can be traced to the ways in which people experience their society and culture.

Drunken Comportment

In their book, *Drunken Comportment: A Social Explanation*, Craig MacAndrew and Robert B. Edgerton do not investigate the causes of alcoholism as such.[55] Rather, they attempt to answer the question: Why do we behave as we do when we are under the influence of alcohol? They question the conventional view that alcohol consumption leads to a loss of inhibitions and that this, in turn, causes our behavior to undergo changes for the worse; that is, in the direction of quarrelsomeness, surliness, violence, sexual excess.

To build their argument, MacAndrew and Edgerton cite a wealth of data from primitive societies. For example, in some societies, drunkenness leads to genuine goodwill and merriment among the drinkers; in others, drunkards comport themselves in a silent and unobtrusive manner. Apparently, individuals can react to alcohol in dozens if not hundreds of different ways, and how individuals act when they are drunk depends partly on the society in which they live.

MacAndrew and Edgerton not only present evidence which suggests that the way in which people act when they are drunk is culturally patterned, but also seek to explain why:

> Over the course of socialization, people learn about drunkenness what their society "knows" about drunkenness; and, accepting and acting upon the understandings thus imparted to them, they become the living confirmation of their society's teachings.[56]

In other words, we are socialized to act in a certain way when we are drunk. If we are socialized to believe that drunkenness leads to meanness and quarrelsomeness, we will be mean and quarrelsome when we are drunk. If we are socialized to believe that drunkenness leads to somberness and pensiveness, we will be somber and pensive when we are drunk.

MacAndrew and Edgerton's thesis seems to be at least partially substantiated. Their evidence does suggest that how people comport themselves when they are drunk may in part be culturally patterned. However, their claim that alcohol does not have disinhibiting effects on behavior is weak. In the societies that they studied, people's behavior did change when they were drunk. All that is in question is the direction of the change; the disinhibiting effects of alcohol do not necessarily have to manifest themselves in changes for the worse. The impairment of judgment associated with drunkenness can manifest itself in many ways—meanness and quarrelsomeness, goodwill and merriment, somberness and unobtrusiveness. The word *disinhibiting* thus means only that drunken people are less inhibited than sober people; they are not necessarily worse behaved than sober people. And there is ample evidence to suggest that disinhibition is due to the toxic effects of alcohol on the brain.

Sociocultural Factors

Alcohol abuse would not be a major problem if the excessive consumption of alcoholic beverages did not have some immediate rewards. It does, and these rewards might attract almost anyone. There are times when alcohol could relieve the excessive tension and environmental stress we all experience; alcohol could also allow us to fulfill our occasional need to punish other people. What with these and other potential rewards of intoxication, the question arises again: Why aren't we all alcoholics?

Social Problems and You

Some Facts About Alcoholism

In the U.S., the age-old problem of excessive drinking is taking a disturbing new turn and affecting new kinds of victims. On a New York subway train, a school-bound 15-year-old holds his books in one hand, a brown paper bag containing a beer bottle in the other. He takes a swig, then passes bag and bottle to a classmate. In a San Francisco suburb, several high school freshmen show up for class drunk every morning, while others sneak off for a nip or two of whisky during the lunch recess. On the campuses the beer bash is fashionable once again, and lowered drinking ages have made liquor the high without the hassle. . . .

The upsurge of problem drinking among the young is only part of a more disturbing nationwide and even worldwide problem. In the past few years alcoholism—among youths and adults alike—has at last been recognized as a plague. From 1960 to 1970, per capita consumption of alcohol in the U.S. increased 26%—to the equivalent of 2.6 gal. of straight alcohol per adult per year. It is now at an all-time high, probably surpassing the levels during such notoriously wet eras as the pre–Civil War and pre-Prohibition years. Moreover, according to the NIAAA (National Institute on Alcohol Abuse and Alcoholism), about one in ten of the 95 million Americans who drink is now either a full-fledged alcoholic or at least a problem drinker (defined by NIAAA as one who drinks enough to cause trouble for himself and society). Uncounted thousands of the problem drinkers are under 21. . . .

The facts gathered by NIAAA about alcohol abuse are as depressing as they are impressive:

- After heart disease and cancer, alcoholism is the country's biggest health problem. Most deaths attributable to alcoholism are caused by cirrhosis of the liver (13,000 per year). An alcoholic's life span is shortened by ten to twelve years. Recently, medical researchers have found evidence suggesting that excessive use of alcohol may also quietly contribute to certain kinds of heart disease, and that it eventually damages the brain.
- In half of all murders in the U.S., either the killer or the victim—or both—have been drinking. A fourth of all suicides are found to have significant amounts of alcohol in their bloodstreams. People who abuse alcohol are seven times more likely to be separated or divorced than the general population.
- The dollar cost of alcoholism may be as much as $15 billion a year, much of it from lost work time in business, industry and the Government.
- At least half of each year's 55,500 automobile deaths and half of the 1 million major injuries suffered in auto accidents can be traced directly to a driver or a pedestrian "under the influence."

Many of the deaths and injuries are caused by the under-21 age group, and arrests of young people for drunken driving have skyrocketed since states began lowering the drinking age from 21. In the year following its lowering of the drinking age, for example, Michigan reported a 141% increase in such arrests. . . .

The National Council on Alcoholism, a voluntary health organization, has drawn up a checklist of 26 questions for drinkers. In its view, a yes answer to any one of them warns of possible alcoholism. Some of the Council's questions: Do you drink heavily after a disappointment or a quarrel? Did you ever wake up on the morning after and discover you could not remember part of the evening before, even though you did not pass out? Do you try to have a few extra drinks when others will not know it? Are you secretly irritated when your family or friends discuss your drinking? Have you often failed to keep the promises you have made to yourself about controlling or cutting down on your drinking?

SOURCE: "Alcoholism: New Victims, New Treatments," *Time*, 103 (April 22, 1974), pp. 75–76.

Sociologist Robert F. Bales has suggested that the answer to this question may lie in the fact that each one of us experiences our society and culture in a somewhat different way.[57] Specifically, our group affiliations influence, in several ways, whether we are likely to engage in excessive consumption of alcohol.

Some groups, for example, are cast into roles that are highly stress-provoking, others are not. In our society, the lower-class black male, in part because he has traditionally been denied a good education, has difficulty finding a good job. This, in turn, makes it extremely difficult for him to feel adequate in his roles as husband and father. When these socially induced stresses bear down on a person who, psychologically speaking, is already vulnerable, the chances that that person will seek escape through alcohol or drugs are potentially enhanced. In fact, it appears that higher rates of alcoholism are found among lower-class black males and similarly situated groups than among groups (for example, middle-class white females) that receive better treatment by society in general.[58]

However, most lower-class black males do not become alcoholic individuals whereas some middle-class white females do. Thus, another variable that influences whether a person drinks excessively is the degree to which family, peer groups, and others in his or her environment condone the use of alcoholic beverages for tension-relieving purposes. For example, some groups favor having a drink to unwind after a hectic day at the office or as a means of bracing up for a trying event. Others do not. If a person who occupies a stress-producing position *also* functions in groups and social settings that encourage the use of alcohol to relieve tensions, that person has a rather high chance of developing a drinking problem.

Finally, whether a person consumes alcohol in excessive amounts depends to a certain extent on the degree to which his or her peer groups and cultural environment provide alternative means of dealing with socially induced tension. Almost all of us experience stress, but we find different ways of coping with it. Not all of these ways are harmful. One researcher, for example, maintains that "alcoholism is a pseudoreligion, an attempt to deal with existential anxiety."[59] In other words, rates of alcoholism may be lower among groups, for example, practicing Jews, who still find religion a meaningful, integral part of everyday life than among individuals for whom religion has become largely irrelevant. Another study suggests that the high rates of problem drinking found among lower socioeconomic groups can in part be traced to their lack of recreational and other opportunities to release tension.[60]

Many of sociology's other hypotheses, theories, and research findings about alcoholism fit into Robert F. Bales's group framework. Bales's theoretical statements can incorporate, directly or indirectly, most of the *sociological* elements which appear repeatedly in the literature.[61] For example, as already pointed out, Bales's formulation helps account for high rates of alcoholism among black males. He also helps explain why, even though a high percentage of Jews drink alcoholic beverages, their rates of alcoholism are low.[62]

Sociological variables influence rates of alcoholism in a number of other ways. For example, in the process of growing up, people acquire a variety of attitudes toward the use of alcohol. By observing their parents, some children learn to associate alcohol with sociability and may conclude that they cannot have a good time at a party or other social gathering without imbibing heartily. Indeed, to some men, being able to "hold their liquor" and to drink their companions "under the table" are signs of masculinity.

In summary, millions of people in our society occupy stress-provoking positions within peer groups who approve of alcohol, and many of us have learned attitudes that could easily lead to the harmful use of alcoholic beverages.

A Final Note

It would be a major breakthrough in the social sciences if we could conclude this section with a tight, all-inclusive statement about the causes of alcoholism. But, as we have already indicated, the causes are multiple, complex, and only partly understood.

From one point of view, the causes of alcoholism lie in the effects alcohol has on the drinker. Alcohol can temporarily make drinkers feel better about themselves and their relationships with society. Albert Bandura's contention that the consumption of alcoholic beverages has immediate rewards, at least for some people, is beyond dispute. However, not all people who gain rewards from drinking become alcoholic individuals.

Rather, the probability of people who drink becoming alcoholic is influenced by several social structural variables, including: (1) whether an individual occupies positions that are consistently stressful, (2) whether an individual's peer groups encourage the use of alcohol to relieve tensions, and (3) whether an individual functions in groups and social settings which provide alternative outlets for environmental as well as psychological stress. However, an individual may still not be destined for alcoholism if he or she does experience rewards from drinking and sociocultural factors do point in that direction. This important fact reminds us again of the complexities surrounding the causes of alcoholism.

Alcoholism may be treated on an individual basis or in a group context. In individual therapy an attempt is made to help the alcoholic individual cope with stress.

Treating Alcoholism

Alcoholism wastes people and talent; it breaks up families and friends; it endangers health and safety, even lives. We should thus take a look at current methods of treating alcoholism and rehabilitating alcoholic individuals.

Prerequisites to Treatment

Three prerequisites must be met if the alcoholic individual is to be successfully rehabilitated. First, most experts agree that the individual must accept the idea that he or she can never drink again, even on a social basis.[63] The individual became dependent on alcohol before, and there is the chance that it will happen again.

Second, the alcoholic individual must be motivated to stop drinking. Treatment seems to be most successful when it is coupled with a serious crisis in an individual's life which was precipitated by the excessive use of alcohol.[64] This crisis might involve the threatened or actual loss of spouse or job, arrest for drunken driving, an accident, etc. Crises such as these serve to motivate alcoholic individuals to do something about their drinking problem, and they are thus receptive to therapy.

Finally, a treatment program is most likely to succeed when it includes the alcoholic individual's family, especially the spouse.[65] For example, as we have pointed out, the wife who derives psychological rewards from nursing and mothering an alcoholic husband reinforces her husband's drinking problem. If she joins her husband's treatment program, she may not only gain an understanding of her husband's problem but also learn to understand and modify her own behavior as well.

Specific Approaches

Alcoholism may be treated on an individual basis or in a group context. In individual psychotherapy an attempt is made to help the alcoholic individual cope with stress. Sometimes the person is helped to grow up emotionally.[66] To date, psychiatric treatment has not been particularly successful, possibly because of the high cost of psychiatric care and the extraordinary amount of time required for rehabilitation. Individual psychotherapy is unquestionably a slow, tedious process. In addition, psychiatric treatment benefits only people who are highly motivated to change their behavior; often, this high motivation is absent in the alcoholic individual. During recent years considerable interest has been shown in aversion, or conditioned-reflex, therapy as an approach to treating alcoholism.[67] Aversion therapy attempts to create an association in the alcoholic individual's mind between the consumption of alcohol and the experience of severe pain. When the person drinks, pain is induced by drugs that cause

◄ Aversion therapy attempts to create an association in the alcoholic individual's mind between the consumption of alcohol and the experience of severe pain. When the person drinks, pain can be induced by administering electrical shocks.

severe vomiting or by administering electrical shocks. In theory, if the person's experience with alcohol is painful enough, he or she will lose the desire to drink. Some investigators have reported fairly high success rates in using aversion therapy.[68]

Alcoholics Anonymous has developed one of the most successful treatment approaches. Alcoholics Anonymous is a voluntary association of alcoholic and "ex-alcoholic" individuals found in most major cities.[69] It is important to note that Alcoholics Anonymous takes a nonprofessional approach in the sense that it does not employ trained, professional therapists and does not render treatment in the strictest sense of the word.

Alcoholics Anonymous appears to help its members in three ways. First, it represents a group in which the alcoholic individual can find acceptance and security: "Here is one place where the individual, all too often rejected by society, finds acceptance and tolerance for a while."[70] Second, although Alcoholics Anonymous is not affiliated with any religious organization, sect, or denomination, it strongly emphasizes that alcoholic individuals must make peace with God and their fellow human beings. One of the Twelve Steps to recovery suggests that the alcoholic individual turn his or her life over to the care of God as he or she understands Him. Still another step suggests that the person list all the people he or she has harmed or injured by being an alcoholic individual and make "direct amends to such people whenever possible, except when to do so would injure them or others."[71] Finally, and perhaps most important, Alcoholics Anonymous teaches norms that discourage drinking while helping the individual over the crises in his or her life. Essentially, Alcoholics Anonymous is a self-help organization whose members support each other in their efforts to remain sober.

Summary

Alcoholism is a serious and costly social problem that is also complex and not clearly understood. Alcoholism has been defined many ways; an authoritative and popular definition calls it a "condition in which the individual has lost control over his alcohol intake in the sense that he is consistently unable to refrain from drinking or to stop drinking before getting intoxicated."

Alcoholism almost invariably leads to marital disruption and poor job performance. The alcoholic individual also places his own health in jeopardy and threatens the safety of others. The extent to which alcoholism contributes to other social problems is difficult to determine.

The alcoholic individual may occupy any social and economic status, but is typically a married, employed, middle-aged male. Today, unfortunately, the rates of alcoholism among women and young people (including children) appear to be increasing. Much more research is needed among these groups.

The causes of alcoholism are extremely complex. It does not appear to be inherited and the idea that some people are allergic to alcohol has been discounted. The immediate causes of alcoholism may lie in the rewarding effects alcohol has on the drinker. Alcohol can temporarily make drinkers feel better about themselves and their relationships with society. However, not everyone who experiences rewards from drinking becomes alcoholic. Rather, becoming alcoholic depends on several factors: (1) whether the person occupies positions that are consistently stress-provoking, (2) whether the person's peer groups encourage the use of alcohol to relieve tensions, and (3) whether the person functions in groups and social settings which provide alternative outlets for environmental as well as psychological stress. Clearly though, a person is not destined to become an alcoholic individual even if he or she experiences rewards from drinking and sociocultural factors point in that direction.

Alcoholic individuals have been successfully rehabilitated through aversion therapy, Alcoholics Anonymous, and other treatment programs. For treatment to be successful, however, the alcoholic individual must want to stop drinking. Treatment programs are usually more successful when they involve the individual's family.

Discussion Questions

1. Alcoholism has recently been called our nation's number one health problem. Do you agree? Why or why not?
2. Discuss the differences between alcoholism and problem drinking. Are all alcoholic individuals problem drinkers? Are all problem drinkers alcoholic individuals? Explain your answers.
3. Is the excessive use of alcoholic beverages a problem in your community or on your campus? If so, describe and discuss some of the problems it creates. If not, why not?
4. What are some of the advantages of referring to alcoholism as a disease? Has the disease concept of alcoholism outlived its usefulness? Explain your answers.
5. How do you account for the fact that the '70s have witnessed a dramatic increase in alcoholism among teenagers? Why do you suppose the percentage of females in the alcoholic population is increasing?

6. How would you account for the fact that many alcoholic individuals have parents who were also alcoholic individuals? Does this prove that alcoholism is inherited? Why or why not?
7. It is widely agreed that the consumption of alcoholic beverages does have some immediate rewards. Using the framework developed by Robert F. Bales, answer the question: Why aren't we all alcoholic individuals?

Glossary

alcohol addiction A condition in which an individual experiences a physiologically caused withdrawal syndrome when he or she ceases drinking. It is estimated that a maximum of 1 percent of all alcohol users become physically addicted to alcohol.

alcoholism A condition in which individuals have lost control over their alcohol intake in the sense that they are consistently unable to refrain from drinking or to stop drinking before getting intoxicated.

Alcoholics Anonymous A voluntary association of alcoholic and ex-alcoholic individuals whose members support each other in their efforts to stop drinking and remain sober. A chapter of Alcoholics Anonymous is found in most communities of moderate or large size.

aversion (or conditioned-reflex) therapy An approach to the treatment of alcoholism that attempts to create an association in the alcoholic individual's mind between the consumption of alcohol and the experience of severe pain.

disease concept of alcoholism A perspective on alcoholism which views the alcoholic individual as a person who has a very real but treatable problem.

drunken comportment Conduct of individuals when they are intoxicated.

game theory of alcoholism A psychological explanation of alcoholism which views alcoholism as a game in which the alcoholic individual seeks certain rewards. By "playing" alcoholic, the individual finds an excuse for inflicting punishment on other people, for demanding attention, and so forth.

learning theory of alcoholism A psychological explanation of alcoholism that sees alcoholism as a learned means of coping with environmental stress.

problem drinking The repetitive use of alcohol to the point that it causes physical, psychological, or social harm to the drinker or to other people.

Suggestions for Further Reading

"Alcoholism: New Victims, New Treatments," *Time*, 103 (April 22, 1974), pp. 75–81. An informative article on alcoholism in America, its victims, and its treatment. Of special interest are five case histories that show the price of alcoholism for the alcoholic individual and his or her family.

Bales, Robert Freed, "Cultural Differences in Rates of Alcoholism," *Quarterly Journal of Studies on Alcohol*, 6 (March, 1946), pp. 480–99. In this classic analysis, the author develops a theoretical framework for studying intergroup and cross-cultural variations in rates of alcoholism. Almost all of the research data on alcoholism collected by sociologists can be incorporated into Bales's framework.

Cahalan, Don, *Problem Drinkers: A National Survey* (San Francisco: Jossey-Bass, 1970). This book describes the drinking problems that people have and attempts to identify those subgroups which are most likely to have problems associated with drinking.

Cahalan, Don, and Ira H. Cisin, "American Drinking Practices: Summary of Findings from a National Probability Sample," *Quarterly Journal of Studies on Alcohol*, 29 (March, 1968), pp. 657–84. This article summarizes the results of a national survey of drinking practices in the United States. Data are presented on rates of problem drinking by age, sex, race, place of residence, and so forth.

MacAndrew, Craig, and Robert B. Edgerton, *Drunken Comportment: A Social Explanation* (Chicago: Aldine, 1969). In this book the authors argue that the way in which people act when they are drunk is culturally patterned. Some fascinating and insightful descriptions of drunkenness in various societies are presented.

Roebuck, Julian B., and Raymond G. Kessler, *The Etiology of Alcoholism: Constitutional, Psychological, and Sociological Approaches* (Springfield, Ill.: Thomas, 1972). A thorough and detailed review of a multitude of theories pertaining to alcoholism. Recommended for the advanced, serious reader.

Steiner, Claude, *Games Alcoholics Play* (New York: Grove, 1971). A statement of how transactional analysis can help us understand the alcoholic individual. Among the alcoholic games that Steiner describes are "Drunk and Proud," "Lush," and "Wino."

Notes

[1]*Drug Use in America: Problem in Perspective*, Report of the National Commission on Marijuana and Drug Abuse (Washington, D.C.: U.S. Government Printing Office, 1973), p. 143.

[2]*Alcohol and Health: Report from the Secretary of Health, Education, and Welfare* (New York: Scribner's, 1973), p. 89.

[3]Cooperative Commission on the Study of Alcoholism, *Alcohol Problems* (New York: Oxford, 1967), p. 39.

[4]Robert Straus, "Alcoholism and Problem Drinking," in Robert K. Merton and Robert Nisbet, eds., *Contemporary Social Problems*, 4th Ed. (New York: Harcourt Brace Jovanovich, 1976), pp. 194–95.

[5]Cooperative Commission, *Alcohol Problems*, p. 44.

[6]*Ibid.*, p. 38.

[7]The pros and cons of referring to alcoholism as a disease are summarized in Don Cahalan, *Problem Drinkers: A National Survey* (San Francisco: Jossey-Bass, 1970), pp. 3–10.

[8]A number of authorities have contended that the "sick" role which is assigned to alcoholic individuals does more harm than good. *Ibid.*, p. 6.

[9]*Ibid.*, p. 8.

[10]See H. A. Mulford and D. E. Miller, "Public Definitions of the Alcoholic," *Quarterly Journal of Studies on Alcohol*, 22 (June, 1961), p. 320; and P. W. Haberman and J. Sheinberg, "Public Attitudes Toward Alcoholism As an Illness," *American Journal of Public Health*, 59 (July, 1969), pp. 1209–1216.

[11]Cited in "Alcoholism: New Victims, New Treatments," *Time*, 103 (April 22, 1974), p. 76.

[12]The estimate of 100 million is taken from Straus, "Alcoholism and Problem Drinking," p. 189.

[13]*Ibid.*, p. 183.

[14]"Rising Toll of Alcoholism: New Steps to Combat It, " *U.S. News & World Report*, 75 (October 29, 1973), p. 45.

[15]For example, see National Institute of Mental Health, *Utilization of Mental Health Facilities: 1971*, DHEW Publication No. NIH-74-657 (Washington, D.C.: U.S. Government Printing Office, 1973), Table 19; and Kurt Gorwitz, Anita Bahn, Frances J. Warthen, and Myles Cooper, "Some Epidemiological Data on Alcoholism in Maryland," *Quarterly Journal of Studies on Alcohol*, 31 (June, 1970), p. 433.

[16]"Alcoholism: New Victims, New Treatments," p. 76.

[17]See August Gribbin, "Alcoholic Children," *The National Observer*, 13 (May 11, 1974), p. 1.

[18]"Rising Toll of Alcoholism," p. 46.

[19]S. Kirson Weinberg, *Social Problems in Modern Urban Society*, 2nd Ed. (Englewood Cliffs, N.J.: Prentice-Hall, 1970), p. 454.

[20]"Alcoholism: New Victims, New Treatments," p. 76.

[21]For example, see Lee N. Robins, George E. Murphy, and Mary B. Breckenridge, "Drinking Behavior of Young Urban Negro Men," *Quarterly Journal of Studies on Alcohol*, 29 (September, 1968), pp. 657–84.

[22]Gorwitz et al., "Some Epidemiological Data on Alcoholism in Maryland," p. 438.

[23]*Alcohol and Health*, p. 66.

[24]See Harold A. Mulford, "Drinking and Deviant Drinking, U.S.A., 1963," *Quarterly Journal of Studies on Alcohol*, 25 (December, 1964), p. 640; Don Cahalan and Ira H. Cisin, "American Drinking Practices: Summary of Findings from a National Probability Sample," *Quarterly Journal of Studies on Alcohol*, 29 (March, 1968), pp. 140–41; and Weinberg, *Social Problems in Modern Urban Society*, pp. 454–55.

[25]Thus, Straus reports that "alcoholics are more frequently divorced or separated than nonalcoholics, and the wives, husbands, and children of alcoholics have relatively high rates of physical, emotional, and psychosomatic illnesses." Straus, "Alcoholism and Problem Drinking," p. 210. See also Margaret B. Bailey, "Alcoholism and Marriage," *Quarterly Journal of Studies on Alcohol*, 22 (March, 1961), pp. 80–94.

[26]For example, see Joan Jackson, "The Adjustment of the Family to the Crisis of Alcoholism," *Quarterly Journal of Studies on Alcohol*, 15 (December, 1954), pp. 562–86; and Edwin M. Lemert, "The Occurrence and Sequence of Events in the Adjustment of Families to Alcohol-

ism," *Quarterly Journal of Studies on Alcohol,* 21 (December, 1960), pp. 679–97. To date, most studies have assumed that the alcoholic individual will be a male and hence a husband and a father. There is a need for more studies of wives and mothers who also happen to be alcoholic individuals.

[27]Harrison M. Trice, *Alcoholism in America* (New York: McGraw-Hill, 1966), p. 65.

[28]Robert T. Dorris and Doyle F. Lindley, *Counseling on Alcoholism and Related Disorders* (Beverly Hills, Calif.: Glencoe, 1968), p. 42.

[29]*Ibid.*, p. 42.

[30]Trice, *Alcoholism in America*, p. 69.

[31]*Ibid.*, p. 70.

[32]Dorris and Lindley, *Counseling on Alcoholism and Related Disorders*, p. 42.

[33]U.S. Public Health Service, *Vital Statistics of the United States: 1969*, Vol. II, *Mortality* (Washington, D.C.: U.S. Government Printing Office, 1973), Table 7–9.

[34]See Mary Leonard, "Liquor: Hazard—and Boon?" *The National Observer,* 13 (July 20, 1974), p. 18.

[35]*Alcohol and Health,* p. 112.

[36]Ruth Moose, "One Woman's War Against Drunk Driving," *Good Housekeeping,* 178 (February, 1974), p. 54.

[37]Dorris and Lindley, *Counseling on Alcoholism and Related Disorders,* pp. 44–45.

[38]Computed from data contained in Federal Bureau of Investigation, *Crime in the United States: 1973* (Washington, D.C.: U.S. Government Printing Office, 1974), p. 131.

[39]Marvin E. Wolfgang, "Victim-Precipitated Criminal Homicide," *Journal of Criminal Law, Criminology, and Police Science,* 48 (May–June, 1957), p. 5.

[40]See William A. Rushing, "Individual Behavior and Suicide," in Jack P. Gibbs, ed., *Suicide* (New York: Harper & Row, 1968), pp. 104–105.

[41]See Barry A. Kinsey, *The Female Alcoholic: A Social Psychological Study* (Springfield, Ill.: Thomas, 1966), pp. 35–37.

[42]James C. Coleman, *Abnormal Psychology and Modern Life*, 4th Ed. (Glenview, Ill.: Scott, Foresman, 1972), p. 414.

[43]Anne Roe, "The Adult Adjustment of Children of Alcoholic Parents Raised in Foster Homes," *Quarterly Journal of Studies on Alcohol,* 5 (December, 1944), p. 382. Roe reported that 9 percent of a control group were regular users of alcoholic beverages.

[44]Howard W. Haggard, "Critique of the Concept of the Nature of Alcohol Addiction," *Quarterly Journal of Studies on Alcohol,* 5 (September, 1944), p. 240.

[45]Kinsey, *The Female Alcoholic,* p. 35.

[46]Leon A. Greenberg, "Alcohol and Emotional Behavior," in Salvatore P. Lucia, ed., *Alcohol and Civilization* (New York: McGraw-Hill, 1963), p. 112.

[47]Coleman, *Abnormal Psychology and Modern Life,* p. 407.

[48]For a review and discussion of many of the studies that attempt to trace alcoholism to personality inadequacies see Julian B. Roebuck and Raymond G. Kessler, *The Etiology of Alcoholism: Constitutional, Psychological, and Sociological Approaches* (Springfield, Ill.: Thomas, 1972), esp. pp. 86–94, 99–116.

[49]*Ibid.,* pp. 122–23.

[50]See Albert Bandura, *Principles of Behavior Modification* (New York: Holt, Rinehart and Winston, 1969), pp. 528–37.

[51]*Ibid.,* p. 533.

[52]*Ibid.,* p. 530.

[53]For a detailed explanation of transactional analysis, see Claude Steiner, *Games Alcoholics Play* (New York: Grove, 1971).

[54]*Ibid.*, p. 72.

[55]See Craig MacAndrew and Robert B. Edgerton, *Drunken Comportment: A Social Explanation* (Chicago: Aldine, 1969).

[56]*Ibid.*, p. 88.

[57]See Robert Freed Bales, "Cultural Differences in Rates of Alcoholism," *Quarterly Journal of Studies on Alcohol*, 6 (March, 1946), pp. 480–99. The following discussion leans heavily on Bales's work.

[58]For example, see Robins, Murphy, and Breckenridge, "Drinking Behavior of Young Urban Negro Men," pp. 657–84.

[59]See Roebuck and Kessler, *The Etiology of Alcoholism*, p. 151.

[60]*Ibid.*, p. 221.

[61]*Ibid.*, p. 219.

[62]See Charles R. Snyder, *Alcohol and the Jews* (New York: Free Press, 1958).

[63]Trice, *Alcoholism in America*, p. 107. In fairness, it must be pointed out that a recent Rand Corporation study has suggested that some rehabilitated alcoholic individuals can safely resume drinking on a social basis. The findings of this study have given rise to considerable

controversy and have been called "premature" and "dangerous" by the National Council on Alcoholism. See "Can Alcoholics Drink?" *Newsweek*, 87 (June 21, 1976), p. 58.

[64]*Ibid.*, p. 108.

[65]*Ibid.*, p. 111.

[66]*Ibid.*, p. 95.

[67]For example, see W. L. Voegtlin, "The Treatment of Alcoholism by Establishing a Conditioned Reflex," *American Journal of the Medical Sciences*, 199 (1940), pp. 802–809; Ernest C. Miller, B. Anthony Dvorak, and Don W. Turner, "A Method of Creating Aversion to Alcohol by Reflex Conditioning in a Group Setting," *Quarterly Journal of Studies on Alcohol*, 21 (September, 1960), pp. 424–31; and Roger E. Vogler et al., "Electrical Aversion Conditioning with Chronic Alcoholics," *Journal of Consulting and Clinical Psychology*, 34 (June, 1970), pp. 302–307.

[68]See Albert Bandura, *Principles of Behavior Modification*, Table 8–1.

[69]In reference to Alcoholics Anonymous, the term "*ex-alcoholic*" must be used in quotation marks since Alcoholics Anonymous believes that once a person becomes an alcoholic individual, he or she will always be an alcoholic individual. Perhaps the term *nondrinking alcoholic* would be better.

[70]Marvin A. Block, *Alcoholism: Its Facets and Phases* (New York: Day, 1965), p. 149.

[71]Anonymous, *Twelve Steps and Twelve Traditions* (New York: Alcoholics Anonymous, 1953), p. 85.

Chapter 5
Drug Abuse and Narcotics Addiction

Around the end of the last century, traveling medicine shows brought patent medicines—guaranteed to cure all your aches, pains, and ailments—to innumerable respectable, God-fearing, American families. In many households, dear old auntie just couldn't get along without her patent medicine for her "rheumatiz."

This quaint little scene seems far removed from our current notion of pushers and junkies; but, in fact, many of those patent medicines contained narcotics like cocaine and morphine. And many aunties who took them for rheumatism were really addicts.

In Chapter 1 we stressed the idea that social problems are a matter of definition: what is considered a serious social problem in one society at one time may not be so considered in another society or at another time. So auntie, the traveling salesman, and the patent medicine weren't considered manifestations of a social problem at least partly because they weren't defined as such.

Today, public definitions of what constitutes dangerous drug abuse do not seem to match the realities of the situation. Further, many of the problems associated with drug use seem to arise because of the public's reaction to users and its insistence on calling them deviants. This chapter, then, will examine some of the current ideas about and patterns of drug use in this country.

What Is Drug Abuse?

We are a nation of heavy drug users. Every year we consume billions of aspirins, sleeping tablets, liver pills, and other medications. At what point does drug use become drug *ab*use? This question is hard to answer because it is difficult to define precisely what is meant by the term *drug abuse*. Basically, there are two ways to go about defining *drug abuse*.

The first way of defining *drug abuse* is to use scientific terms This is more challenging than it might seem; most of the books and articles on drug abuse do not define the term. One scientific expert, however, tells us that "in general, . . . [he] would define drug 'abuse' or 'misuse' as (regular, excessive) use of a drug to the extent that it is damaging to a person's social or vocational adjustment, or to his health, or is otherwise specifically detrimental to society."[1]

At first glance, this definition seems sound. Most of us would agree that use becomes abuse when a drug becomes damaging to a person's health, social relationships, or job status, or to society in general. However, this definition and others like it hold little

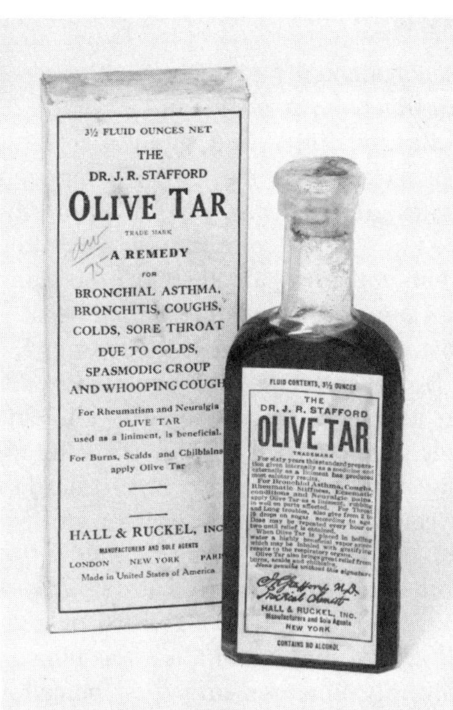

Around the end of the last century, traveling medicine shows brought patent medicines—guaranteed to cure all your aches, pains, and ailments—to innumerable American families. ◀

practical value. For example, a person who smokes two or three packs of cigarettes a day clearly damages his or her health, but most of us do not think of that person as a drug abuser. In fact, most of us do not think of nicotine as a drug at all. The same applies to the person who drinks alcohol to the point where it interferes with his or her health, marriage, or job performance. In short, "one man's beverage is another man's drug, one country's drug is another country's medication, and one agency's subsidized crop is another bureau's focus for criminal law enforcement."[2]

The second way of defining *drug abuse* is to use social terms. Out of the innumerable drugs potentially available to us, we select a few and define them as dangerous or as lending themselves to abuse. For example, marijuana has, at least until recently, been defined as a dangerous drug at least partly because many people (including lawmakers) have been taught to believe that it is a dangerous drug, and people who smoke marijuana are considered drug abusers because the public has been taught that they are. On the other hand, we do not generally think of nicotine or alcohol as dangerous drugs because nobody has taught us to believe that they are.[3]

Extent of Drug Abuse

Not counting excessive use of alcohol and nicotine, the most widespread drug problem in this country may well be the use of substances like diet pills, sleeping pills, and tranquilizers for other than their intended purposes. "[I]n any one year enough amphetamines and barbiturates are medically prescribed to provide every man, woman, and child in the country with a month's supply."[4] According to recent statistics, "35,000,000 Americans use sedatives, stimulants, or tranquilizers, mostly obtained legally through their doctors."[5] Most of these people use their drugs for legitimate medical reasons. However, others intentionally use the drugs to get high. Still others unintentionally become psychologically dependent on the drugs, sometimes without even realizing it. Indeed, possibly most drug abuse in our society can be traced to the willingness of the medical profession to prescribe a pill for virtually every human problem.[6]

Whether drug abuse of this type is necessarily bad is partly a philosophical question. It can be argued that if a given drug enables its users to cope with life, then they should use it as long as their performance is not severely impaired and their behavior does not become overly disruptive to society. Unfortunately, however, very few drugs can be considered totally safe. For example, in small quantities barbiturates do have a relaxing, calming effect on an individual; heavy use can cause a person to feel depressed and quarrelsome, and experience a rather severe withdrawal reaction when taken off the drug. Similarly, small doses of amphetamines can improve performance on relatively simple tasks that require alertness; heavy, repeated use of amphetamines, though, can lead to weight loss, sleeplessness, and even paranoid delusions.

Moreover, a person's heavy use of barbiturates, amphetamines, or even tranquilizers suggests some maladjustment to social roles. It would be difficult, for example, to argue that the student who relies on amphetamines to get through examination week has really learned to handle and enjoy the challenges of academic life.

People abuse drugs for many reasons, but one of the main reasons is simply that we live in a drug-oriented culture. One evening viewing television amply demonstrates that drug use is part of our culture. A constant barrage of advertisements for drugs lures us with promises of giving us that extra lift, calming our nerves, or even cheering us up. The viewer may well reason that if relatively inexpensive patent medicines can make life worth living, surely more potent prescription drugs do it that much better!

Similarly, widespread drug abuse among the young probably stems from the pervasiveness of drugs in our society. Every day, young people see their parents and other adults "enjoying" life with drugs or, perhaps more accurately, needing drugs to cope with life. So the young learn to use drugs the same way that they learn any other pattern of culture—through the process of socialization.

In sum, we live in a pill-popping culture, one that teaches and approves drug-abusive behavior with socially approved drugs. Many problems of drug abuse arise because of society's definitions of what drugs are not socially approved and its insistence that users of those drugs are deviant. Perhaps the best illustration is the "great marijuana debate."

Marijuana

In the late '60s and early '70s, few issues came closer to ripping the generations apart than the great marijuana debate. To millions of adults the use of marijuana by their children symbolized the things in our society that they feared most and understood

Widespread drug abuse among the young probably stems from the pervasiveness of drugs in our society.

least—the hippie movement, political protest, communal living, and, more generally, dropping out.

On the other hand, to young people the reaction of adult society to marijuana use stood as a monument to the ignorance and hypocrisy that they felt characteristic of the older generation. Since marijuana use illustrates so well the concept of a social problem as a matter of definition, we will examine the great marijuana debate in more detail. Our chief task will be to distinguish fact from fantasy in order to answer the question: Is the use of marijuana really a threat to society or to those groups and institutions of which society is composed? If the answer is negative, then marijuana use should not be considered a social problem.

We actually know a lot about marijuana and its users. We also know quite a bit about how marijuana affects the individual and society.

The Marijuana User

Three facts can be stated with certainty. First, the marijuana user tends to be young. A 1972 national survey sponsored by the National Commission on Marijuana and Drug Abuse found that approximately 24 million people over the age of 11 had tried marijuana at least once.[7] The study also found that approximately 27 percent of 16- and 17-year-olds, 40 percent of 18- to 21-year-olds, and 38 percent of 22- to 25-year-olds had tried marijuana. On the other hand, only 6 percent of the over-50 age group had ever used marijuana.[8]

Second, only about 8 or 9 percent of the people who have ever tried marijuana use it more than once a week. Most Americans who try marijuana seem either to use it for a while and then stop or use it once a month or less.[9]

Third, and perhaps most important, marijuana use is a form of social behavior: "Knowing other people who use marijuana predisposes the individual to use marijuana, and having marijuana-using friends provides the social opportunity for the curious."[10] The Commission also suggests that marijuana use "provides a shared group experience which offers the shy, lonely, socially awkward neophyte a means of entrance to the group, complete with its own ceremonial initiation."[11]

The Effects of Marijuana

In the minds of some people marijuana use leads to crime, abuse of other drugs, and loss of motivation. How accurate are these perceptions?

There are at least two erroneous beliefs behind the widely held idea that marijuana use leads to crime. First, it simply is not true that marijuana is a "killer weed" that triggers "crimes of violence and acts of sexual excess."[12] In reality, marijuana is nonaddictive and probably best classified as a mild intoxicant. The National Commission on Marijuana and Drug Abuse found that marijuana tends to relax and pacify the user, calming aggressive or violent tendencies.[13]

Second, marijuana is often thought to be extremely expensive, so that the marijuana user turns to crime to support his or her habit. Again, this simply is not true: most users in this country obtain marijuana from their friends at little or no cost. In sum, marijuana use does not seem to be linked with crime, unless the link is forged because society sometimes forces the marijuana user to associate with people whose behavior is deviant in other respects.

Similarly, little association appears to exist between the use of marijuana and the use of other drugs, although the Commission did find that people who use marijuana are more likely than nonusers to try other drugs such as hashish, LSD, methamphetamine, cocaine, and heroin.[14] But there are several explanations for this willingness to experiment. Since marijuana is both illegal and condemned by large segments of the public, the neophyte is often forced to associate with people who already use other drugs; these people may, in turn, supply the marijuana user with other drugs and encourage the user to try them.

The marijuana user may also be more willing to experiment with other drugs than the nonuser. In recent years, for example, the use of marijuana by the young has been associated with a complex of attitudes which favor experimentation. Unfortunately, in this atmosphere, some people come to use drugs as a way of escaping society. Some individuals, for psychological reasons, actually seek escape through drugs.[15] However, use of marijuana itself is not likely to cause the individual to progress to more dangerous drugs.

Finally, some people believe that the use of marijuana decreases motivation and, perhaps, causes young people to drop out. Although much more research is needed on the impact of marijuana on physical and mental health, little or no valid evidence has yet been found to support these claims. The moderate use of marijuana does not appear to represent a greater hazard to physical or mental health than the moderate use of tobacco or alcohol. But until more research is done, it would be unwise to speculate further.

Despite evidence to the contrary, some people continue to believe that marijuana is an extremely dangerous drug. As a result, laws against the sale or possession of marijuana are fairly stiff; in most jurisdictions, even today, a first offender convicted of possessing marijuana can potentially receive a prison sentence of up to one year. Such laws incur heavy law enforcement costs and may well do more harm than good.[16]

Given the extent of marijuana use in the United States today, our laws against the sale or possession of marijuana place an unnecessary and wasteful burden on our overtaxed court system. The time spent prosecuting marijuana cases could be much better spent alleviating the backlog of cases in our courts. Furthermore, a person convicted on a marijuana charge is criminalized and stamped with the label *deviant.* Neither the individual nor society benefits when a person begins to see himself or herself as a criminal, a deviant, or an outcast. In labeling a person *deviant,* society only encourages the very behavior that it seeks to discourage.

Our stiff marijuana laws may also engender a more generalized disrespect for the law among the young. Some young people may reason that "this law is stupid and unjust; probably a lot of other laws are stupid and unjust."[17] In other words, if society wants its young people to obey and respect the law, it must be sure that its laws deserve to be obeyed and respected.

In addition, the marijuana laws may seriously hamper efforts to educate young people about the dangers of drug abuse. The drug-abuse educator, for example, is in a difficult position. On the one hand, the educator who presents students with evidence that marijuana is not an extremely dangerous drug may well be accused of corrupting the young and encouraging disrespect for the law. On the other hand, the educator who attempts to convince students that marijuana is extremely dangerous simply won't be believed. The students probably also will not believe the educator's warnings about the dangers of cigarette smoking, excessive use of alcohol, and abuse of other drugs. Again, they might reason that if they weren't told the truth about marijuana, they are probably being lied to about the rest as well.

Our stiff laws against the possession of marijuana have other negative consequences, but it should already be clear that current marijuana laws do more harm than good. Most reasonable people would agree that if a law is counterproductive, it should be changed. But if one examines our current marijuana laws, it becomes clear that this is a point that many of our legislators, to say nothing of large segments of the general public, have not yet grasped.

LSD

During the middle and late '60s, a great deal was heard about LSD. By 1970 it was estimated that between one and two million

Americans had taken LSD.[18] LSD is usually classified as an hallucinogen, although some authorities object to this label.[19] In any event, LSD is supposed to make individuals more sensitive to sights and sounds, more insightful, and more in tune with themselves, nature, and other people. As with other drugs, the effects of LSD on the user depend upon a wide variety of factors, including the personality of the user, his or her emotional state when taking the drug, the expected effects of the drug, and the social context in which the use occurs. Obviously, an LSD trip will be experienced differently if a person is having a good time in the company of close friends than if he or she is lonely and depressed.

Today, relatively little is heard about LSD. While this may mean that LSD is no longer a popular drug, a 1970 Gallup Poll reported that 14 percent of a sample of college students had tried LSD. In 1969 a similar poll reported that only 4 percent had tried LSD.[20] On the other hand, the use of LSD may have decreased or stabilized because of highly publicized reports about bad trips; users who experience flashbacks long after discontinuing use of the drug; and the possibility of LSD-caused brain damage, deformed babies, and spontaneous abortions in pregnant women.

A number of studies, however, have tended to discredit the idea that LSD leads to brain damage, deformed babies, and spontaneous abortions.[21] But it is indisputable that during the '60s when LSD became an extremely controversial drug, there was a dramatic increase in the number of people who were hospitalized after taking LSD and in the number of accidents traceable to LSD. More and more people began complaining of bad trips and flashbacks.

The reasons for this increase in the number of reported negative effects resulting from the use of LSD are complex. After 1965, LSD was available only on the black market, and there was no control over its quality.[22] In addition, LSD became popular among young people who were not experienced in dealing with drugs and their effects. However, perhaps the most important reason why the number of LSD users reporting adverse effects from LSD increased dramatically in the '60s was because people were educated to expect negative effects:

> One effect of the nationwide warnings against LSD from 1962 on was to arouse "excessive initial apprehension" in the minds of countless LSD users. The result was what might have been anticipated. Bizarre behavior increased markedly from 1962 to 1969. Some users, warned that LSD might cause them to jump out of the window, did in fact jump out the window. Many who were warned that LSD would drive them crazy did in fact suffer severe panic reactions, fearing that LSD had driven them crazy. Thus the warnings proved self-fulfilling prophecies, and enhanced the hazards of the drug.[23]

In the public mind, probably the most significant aspect of drug abuse is narcotics addiction.

If this analysis is correct, the reason why LSD appears to be less of a problem today is probably because the mass media and government agencies no longer play up LSD use as a social problem with dire consequences for the individual and for society, and not because fewer people are taking LSD. Once more we encounter the fundamental principle that *people tend to act as other people expect them to act.*

Narcotics Addiction

In the public mind, probably the most significant aspect of drug abuse is narcotics addiction. Before we assess its real significance, however, we will look at its nature and causes.

The term *narcotics addiction* refers to a condition in which a person has an intense desire and craving for a particular drug.[24] The most commonly used illicit, addictive drug is heroin, but morphine, codeine, and methadone are others. Narcotics addicts display two essential traits—withdrawal and tolerance—that differentiate them from marijuana users and other individuals often mistakenly called addicts.

Withdrawal

Narcotics addicts display a withdrawal syndrome when they cease to take their drug. *Withdrawal syndrome* refers to an illness characterized by excessive tearing, a running nose, profuse sweating, and yawning. Other symptoms associated with withdrawal include nausea and vomiting, diarrhea, abdominal cramps, muscle spasms, and increased heart rate. The person may also make kicking movements (the origin of the expression "kicking the habit").[25]

Withdrawal symptoms reach their peak 48 to 72 hours after the last administration of the drug, and can range from very mild to extremely severe. Severity depends on many factors including the type of drug the person has been using, how long the drug has been used, and the health and personality of the user. Television and movies usually depict the withdrawal syndrome in its most severe form.

One expert suggests that it is the desire to avoid withdrawal and not the euphoric effects of narcotics that motivate an individual to continue using a drug: "The hook in addiction arises, not from the euphoria which the drug initially produces, but from the beginner's realization that the discomfort and misery of withdrawal is caused by the absence of the drug and can be dispelled almost magically by another dose of it."[26] Actually, the euphoric effects associated with narcotics use do not last very long and are not very dramatic. Narcotics do not produce extreme mood alterations nor do they produce spectacular changes in the person's perceptions of reality. Usually opiates give the user a "subtle feeling of being at home in the world and at peace with it."[27] This is especially true when the person is depressed, fatigued, or troubled.

Tolerance

Narcotics addicts tend to build up a *tolerance* for their drug. This means that users tend to take greater and greater quantities of drugs the longer they use them. There is some debate as to whether the body actually builds up a physiological tolerance for the drug so that it takes greater quantities to produce the desired effect or whether tolerance is psychological. There is more evidence to support the latter view. Often as an individual continues to take narcotics, he or she becomes increasingly aware of the beginning symptoms of withdrawal and thus increases dosage. In addition, the euphoric effects of the narcotic are most likely to be experienced when the person has not had the drug for some time. A user who recently had a fix must increase the dosage to experience the euphoric effects from the second shot. Finally, narcotics are both difficult and dangerous to secure, so the addicted person may be motivated to increase the dosage when the drug is available.

The hypothesis that tolerance is a psychological phenomenon gains further support by the finding that "an addict using large quantities daily may have the amount cut to a fraction of its former level and be none the wiser, providing he is unaware of the reduction."[28] In any event, because of tolerance, narcotics addiction soon ceases to be a cheap thrill and becomes instead an unbearably expensive habit.

Causes

Reasons for using narcotics are generally thought to be the same as reasons for abusing any other type of drug; probably a variety of psychological and social factors come together to produce the narcotics addict.

Thus, for many years, psychologists and psychiatrists have explained narcotics addiction in terms of its adjustive value for the individual in coping with emotional tension, anxiety, and frustration.[29] For example, "users . . . are seen as neurotic persons who have accepted an unpopular adjustment mechanism."[30] The causes of the anxiety and tension that the narcotics addict feels would presumably be many and varied, including deep-seated personality problems, an inability to play adult roles, and disturbed sexual adjustment.

Sociologists, however, have maintained that in order to understand narcotics addiction, we must understand our society and culture. For example, Merton's analysis of the causes of deviant behavior (see Chapter 2) leads to the theory that the narcotics addict is caught between the high value our society places on materialistic success and the difficulty he or she encounters in living up to this value. The addict, then, is a person who has seized upon narcotics as a way to make his or her "disadvantaged social position more tolerable."[31]

As early as the '50s, addiction was associated with weak social controls.[32] For example, rates of narcotics addiction are particularly high in urban slums and ghettos. This phenomenon suggests that narcotics addiction may be caused by the breakdown of mechanisms of social control which discourage drug abuse, coupled with the ready availability of drugs. Furthermore, in city areas with high rates of narcotics addiction, a drug subculture often flourishes which encourages the use of narcotics and which realizes financial gain from their sale.

Narcotics Addiction as a Social Problem

The lives of narcotics addicts, and often their families, are those of frustration and squalor. Although it is true that addicts contribute more than their fair share to the crime rates, experts have suggested that narcotics addiction may be a serious social problem chiefly because the public defines it as such. In this section, we'll look at two factors which offset the magnitude of narcotics addiction as a social problem.

Unknown terrors show in the eyes of this young woman who is "stoned" on drugs.

Social Problems and You

Student Drug Users and Abusers

For the Drug Abuse Council, we have just completed an ambitious program of field research to explore the behavior, values and attitudes of American students today regarding drugs. . . .

Drug experimentation and use is not limited to a small fringe of freaks, but is quite widespread. Two out of three college students (64 percent) and almost half of all high-school students (48 percent) have experimented at least once or twice with drugs, typically marijuana. About one third currently consider themselves regular users (26 percent in high school, 41 percent in college). Fewer smoke marijuana daily—six percent of the high-school students, eight percent of the college students.

College students do smoke marijuana more than their younger friends do, but they use other drugs less. High-school drug users are more likely to have regular highs from psychedelics (LSD), barbiturates, cocaine and even heroin, as well as marijuana, several times a month at least. Further, young people do not try drugs *instead* of alcohol, but in addition to it. Alcohol, in fact, continues to be used far more generally than drugs. We found twice as many drinkers as drug users —58 percent in high school and 79 percent in college. Most of the students, regardless of age, believe that alcohol is more dangerous than marijuana, but that doesn't keep them from drinking. . . .

Just as the alcoholic differs from the social drinker, the drug abuser differs from the occasional user. The alcoholic's whole life revolves around the search for booze, and the drug abuser's world is likewise defined by drugs. Abusers are far more likely than users to turn on by themselves, while users prefer social settings. Abusers confine their circle of friends to other heavy users. They are twice as likely as users to buy drugs to keep on hand (89 percent to 41 percent) and to sell drugs for profit (51 percent to 14 percent).

Most critically, users and abusers are separated by a clear psychological line. Whatever the reason, abusers are people who go through severe bouts of depression, anxiety, and frustration far more often than users and nonusers alike. . . .

Abusers also report feeling isolated, having little in common with their peers, and feeling like "black sheep" and second-class citizens. By a four-to-one margin, abusers report that "I never found a group where I belonged" (abusers 34 percent, users and nonusers eight percent). Abusers feel left out, alienated, lonely, and they have much more trouble at home and at school. By two to one, more abusers than users have run away from home (66 percent to 37 percent). Many more abusers than users report failing courses (36 percent to 16 percent), being expelled from school (70 percent to 41 percent), or damaging property on purpose (62 percent to 43 percent). Most student drug users, in short, show few of the characteristic symptoms of drug abuse: a preoccupation with drugs, exclusive association with other drug users, disturbances in psychological mood, a negative self-image, and inability to carry on the everyday life of the student.

College-student users, in particular, show few of the danger signs linked with drug abuse. However, a minority of high-school students may be at risk for drug abuse in the future. These students engage in various forms of "acting out": they damage property, run away from home, get expelled from school.

SOURCE: Daniel Yankelovich, "Drug Users Vs. Drug Abusers: How Students Control Their Drug Crisis," *Psychology Today*, 9 (October, 1975), pp. 39, 41.

First, relatively few people are addicted to narcotics. In 1970, the police and hospital authorities reported 68,864 civilian narcotics addicts in the United States.[33] Another estimate puts the number of addicts in the United States at between 200,000 and 350,000.[34] These numbers sound large but they pale beside the approximately 10 million alcoholic persons in the United States and the millions of people who suffer from debilitating mental illnesses. Alcoholism and mental illness are not normally associated with crime, but their disruptive effects on the individual, family, and society are as great as narcotics addiction. In addition, there is little direct evidence to suggest that the long-term use of narcotics has any noticeable impact on physical health, unlike tobacco and alcohol. The health hazards in using narcotics do not come from the narcotic itself but from contaminated drugs, unsterile needles, overdoses, and so forth.[35]

Few people question the need to have some regulations pertaining to the sale, transfer, or even possession of heroin, marijuana, and drugs like amphetamines and barbiturates.
▼

Second, the disruptive behavior patterns of narcotics addicts affect few regions and social classes. The general public has, in fact, probably overestimated the magnitude of narcotics addiction as a social problem. Narcotics addiction is, to a great extent, peculiar to disadvantaged minorities in run-down inner-city areas. Nevertheless, the problem is a serious one; and it may be that our programs for narcotics addicts are weak, punitive, and unsuccessful because narcotics addiction is, for the most part, confined to relatively small numbers of lower-class, minority people.

Social Control

Few people question the need to have some regulations pertaining to the sale, transfer, or even possession of heroin, marijuana, and drugs like the amphetamines and barbiturates. These drugs have dangers—dangers that would be compounded many times over if they were sold indiscriminately to anyone in pharmacies or grocery stores or college bookstores. But the debatable question is, Precisely what kind of regulations should we have?

In this section we shall examine the history of drug-control legislation in the United States. It will become clear that our past and present approaches to the control of narcotics addiction and drug abuse have, in many cases, been counterproductive. Instead of alleviating the problem, these approaches have sometimes aggravated it.

Social Control of Narcotics Addiction

Some people believe that social problems are created by laws which forbid some particular behavior. In other words, some patterns of behavior would not be thought of as social problems if there were no laws against them. This is, of course, an extreme position, but it seems to have some merit when we look at government responses to narcotics addiction.

Narcotics addiction is one social problem which has not been ameliorated by laws which make the sale, transfer, or possession of narcotics a criminal offense. Although these laws may have reduced the number of addicts, they have at the same time worsened their plight and have created other social problems.

Before 1914, no major laws prohibited the sale, transfer, or possession of narcotics. As a result, the use of narcotics was widespread, and there may have been more addicts in the United States before 1914 than there are today.[36] However, even though hundreds of thousands of people were addicted, they were not cut off from legitimate medical treatment and the link between narcotics addiction and crime did not exist.

In 1914 Congress passed the Harrison Act.[37] This act remained the basic antinarcotic statute until 1970 when it was replaced by the Comprehensive Drug Abuse Prevention and Control Act (see below). On the surface, the Harrison Act was fairly innocuous. Basically, it set up three controls. First, it placed a small excise tax on narcotics. Second, it required people who handled narcotics —physicians, dentists, veterinarians—to register with the Bureau of Internal Revenue and to keep records of their narcotics transactions. Third, it made it illegal for a person to obtain narcotics except from a registered physician.[38] In short, the Harrison Act sought to bring the flow of drugs into identifiable, controllable medical channels. But the Harrison Act did not completely deny the addict access to narcotics. In fact, the Act expressly stated that physicians could prescribe drugs if they did so "for legitimate medical purposes" and provided the drugs were "prescribed in good faith."[39]

Since the Harrison Act was essentially a tax act, responsibility for its enforcement was assigned to the U.S. Department of the Treasury and specifically to the Bureau of Internal Revenue. Shortly after the Act was passed, the staff of the Bureau's Narcotics Division began making the Division into much more than a tax collection unit. It soon emerged as a major law enforcement agency. To accomplish this transformation, the Narcotics Division staff first launched a well-organized publicity campaign to generate a "substantial public outcry against narcotics use."[40] This campaign mustered considerable public support for Division policies. Then, through a series of court cases, the Narcotics Division was able to increase its law enforcement powers. In the Webb case of 1919, the Supreme Court ruled that the Harrison Act did not allow the physician to prescribe narcotics simply to keep the addict comfortable by maintaining his customary dosage. In the Behrman case of 1922, the court made it clear that a physician could not prescribe narcotics even if the purpose was to rehabilitate the addict. These decisions, together with several others, effectively cut the addict off from any legal source of narcotics.[41]

The history of the Narcotics Division reads like a classic case of a government agency trying to legislate morality. As a result of its efforts, the Narcotics Division quickly changed the addict's image from a person who has a medical problem to a person who is a criminal and a moral outcast. The Division's motives are not entirely clear. It is true that in its early days the Division was a small, insignificant bureaucracy. With its campaigns, it ensured its own growth, development, and perpetuation.[42]

It has also been suggested that government bureaucracies, like the Narcotics Division, sometimes come to see themselves as moral entrepreneurs or moral reformers.[43] The Division staff probably did consider the use of narcotics an extreme threat to society and they very likely perceived themselves as protecting the public from a serious threat to health and welfare. In any event, efforts of the Narcotics Division quickly effected three important results:

1. The Division's efforts cut addicts off from legitimate medical treatment. As a result of the Supreme Court cases cited previously, physicians concluded that they dared not use narcotics to treat addicts even if their ultimate goal was to rehabilitate them.

2. The Division forged a link between narcotics addiction and crime. The Harrison Act did not make it illegal for the addict to obtain drugs through medical sources. But the Division soon cut off this source of supply as well. Narcotics distribution was thus driven underground where it became an attractive source of income for organized crime, and prices soared. Today, narcotics addicts are overrepresented among persons who commit crimes such as burglary and robbery.[44] It is not clear, though, why the relationship between narcotics addiction and crime exists. One argument is that narcotics addicts commit crimes to support their habit. Another is that addicts function in a social environment which is deviant in other respects and in which social controls against crime are weak or nonexistent.

3. The Division's rigid and repressive enforcement of the Harrison Act led to the growth of a narcotics subculture. Before the Webb, Behrman, and other Supreme Court decisions were handed down, addicts were likely to be members of stable family groups and to associate mainly with people who reinforced them in their efforts to kick the habit and solve their problems. However, when the addict was cut off from a legitimate supply of drugs, he or she was forced to go underground and to associate with other narcotics addicts. Deviant norms soon emerged, and narcotics addiction became not only a tragic medical problem but a furtive way of life. A social problem cannot be solved by creating a subculture that is devoted to its perpetuation.

Social Control of Marijuana

The sale, transfer, or possession of marijuana was not made illegal until 1937. By that time the responsibility for enforcing narcotic and drug laws had been assigned to the U.S. Bureau of Narcotics, a unit separate from the Bureau of Internal Revenue.

The reason why the Bureau of Narcotics and its chief, Henry J. Anslinger, pressed so vigorously for antimarijuana legislation seems pretty clearly to be another case of organizational survival: "Faced with a steadily declining budget, the Bureau responded as any other organization so threatened might react: it tried to appear more necessary, and it tried to increase its scope of operations. As a result of this response, the Marijuana Tax Act of 1937 was passed."[45] Possibly, too, Anslinger and those who worked under his direction saw themselves as moral entrepreneurs and righteous guardians of societal values.

Passing and enforcing the Marijuana Tax Act had many of the same effects as the Harrison Act. Perhaps its most important effect was to create a class of criminals out of a group of otherwise law-abiding citizens.

Social Control in the '70s

In 1970 Congress repealed the Harrison Act, the Marijuana Tax Act, and several other pieces of drug legislation and replaced them with the Comprehensive Drug Abuse Prevention and Control Act. This new act reduced the penalty for possession of dangerous drugs from a felony to a misdemeanor on the first offense and provided that the first offender can be committed to a treatment program in place of imprisonment.

However, the approach of the United States to the problem of narcotics addiction is still a punitive and repressive one. It is impossible to fully determine whether this approach has been a success or a failure. For example, we cannot tell how many people would be addicts today if the Bureau of Narcotics had not vigorously enforced the Harrison Act. A great deal of evidence suggests, however, that a legalistic, punitive approach to a problem as complex as narcotics addiction does more harm than good.

The Search for Solutions

Our first reaction, when confronted with problems like drug abuse or narcotics addiction, is to attempt to reform the abuser or addict. Few would argue against making treatment programs available to drug abusers and narcotics addicts, although many would vigorously debate how to implement them. Should the treatment program be therapeutically oriented or should it be punitive (lengthy imprisonment)? Should it be carried out on an individual doctor-patient basis or in a group setting (a therapeutic community)?

What we sometimes forget, though, is that often the best approach to solving a problem lies not so much in treating the individual as it does through changing the conditions that created the problem in the first place. This is particularly true of drug abuse and narcotics addiction.

In this section, then, we will first look at some of the approaches that have been developed to reform the individual drug abuser or narcotics addict. Second, we will explore changes in our current social policies on drug abuse and narcotics addiction that could help reduce the magnitude of these problems.

Individualized Treatment

A drug abuser or addict might seek treatment for at least two reasons. First, a person convicted on a drug charge might be ordered by a judge to undergo treatment in place of imprisonment. Second, a person may seek treatment voluntarily; in other words, the drug abuser or addict may really desire to be rehabilitated, although there may be other motives. In any case, we need to look at some of the available treatment facilities.

Drug treatment programs may be organized on either an outpatient or inpatient basis. In large cities, outpatient treatment programs may be made available through mental health clinics and similar facilities. Methadone maintenance programs for heroin addicts are often organized on an outpatient basis. Methadone is a synthetic opiate which can be administered in maintenance dosages to satisfy an addict's craving for heroin. Basically, it allows an addict to lead a relatively normal life, a factor conducive to rehabilitation. A good treatment program, however, views methadone merely as an adjunct to therapy, the goal being to get the addict off drugs completely. Indeed, methadone itself is addictive, and in a few large cities an active black market in methadone has developed.

Inpatient treatment for drug abusers is rendered by most mental hospitals and, on a short-term basis, by some general hospitals. But inpatient facilities have not had a good record in terms of permanent rehabilitation. For example, a follow-up study of ad-

Methadone maintenance programs for heroin addicts are often organized on an outpatient basis. ▶

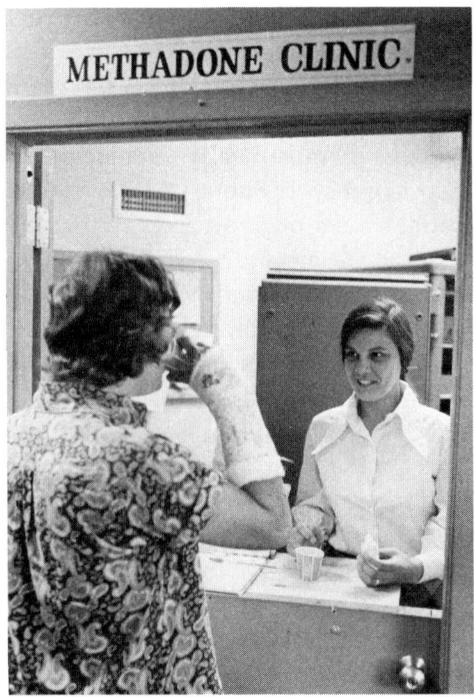

dicts released from the recently closed federal narcotics hospital in Lexington, Kentucky, found that "more than 90 percent of them became readdicted—generally within 6 months."[46] We can account for these relapses in two ways. First, when released from the hospital, the rehabilitated addict very often has no home and no legitimate contacts on the outside. He or she thus drifts back to the same environment that originally contributed to addiction. Second, the ex-addict is still labeled an addict by society. And, as we saw in Chapter 3, often the label alone is enough to trigger a return to deviant behavior.[47]

Another approach to treating narcotics addiction is the therapeutic community approach—for example, the Synanon program.[48] In 1958, a group of addicts and ex-addicts in Santa Monica, California, formed a residential treatment facility. Young addicts who enter Synanon live with older and more mature ex-addicts who understand them and their problems and who offer the opportunity to gain status within the system by staying away from narcotics. Most important, the environment of Synanon is antidrug and anticriminal. The residents of Synanon must avoid "street talk" and must never identify with the "code of the streets."[49] Similar therapeutic communities for rehabilitating addicts have appeared in a number of other communities.

During the '60s, Synanon and similar programs were widely hailed as a promising solution to the problem of reforming the narcotics addict. Recent findings, however, clearly show that these therapeutic communities have fallen far short of their goal. For one thing, they reach such a tiny portion of the addict population that, even if they were 100 percent successful, they still would not make a noticeable impact on the size of the addict population. Unfortunately, however, they are far from 100 percent successful. In 1971 the director of Synanon himself estimated that around 90 percent of the people who "graduated" from Synanon had returned to heroin within two years.[50] Synanon and similar programs appear to be reasonably successful only with addicts who are highly motivated to stay off drugs and who elect to stay on in the therapeutic community as staff members. This is an insignificant proportion of all addicts in the United States.

In recent years, several other, mostly community-based, facilities for helping addicts have been developed. These include switchboards and crisis lines, rap centers and crash pads, crisis intervention centers and free clinics.[51] Since no research data are available, we cannot even guess whether these facilities help addicts in a meaningful way. Many of them undoubtedly do help in an immediate sense in that they provide addicts with food and medical care, help them through withdrawal distress, and help them cope with bad trips. But these community-based facilities may not have much long-term impact in getting addicts off drugs.

Policy Changes

At this point, two facts appear clear. The reform approach to drug abuse and narcotics addiction simply does not seem to work—the vast majority of people who go through drug treatment programs eventually relapse. It also seems clear that many of the problems associated with drug abuse and narcotics addiction are rooted in our social policies concerning illicit drugs. As suggested earlier, drug abuse may be a serious social problem mainly because of the significance the public attaches to it. And the marijuana problem and drug problem may have been created largely because of the laws passed to control marijuana and drugs. Obviously, if a law or a social policy does more harm than good, the only prudent course of action is to change the law or the policy.

In recent years many students of the drug problem have suggested that we need a sweeping revision of our ways of dealing with drug abuse and narcotics addiction. Specific proposals, however, vary widely. For example, one expert argues that the responsibility for treating and rehabilitating the narcotics addict should be returned to the medical profession.[52] The National Commission on Marijuana and Drug Abuse recommends that the sale or distribution of marijuana for profit should still be criminalized but that the criminal penalties for possession of marijuana for private use should be dropped.[53] Another expert suggests that we should license marijuana distribution, much the same way as we license the distribution of alcohol.[54] We cannot review all of these proposals in detail, but we should note that they do have some common ground. First, they would decriminalize users. Nothing is gained by throwing them into jails and turning them into criminals simply because they use socially disapproved drugs. Second, all of these proposals would either wipe out or contain the black market in illicit drugs. This would strike a major blow to organized crime and destroy the link between drug abuse, narcotics addiction, and crime. If drugs were available to users at nominal cost, they would not be forced to commit crimes to support their habits nor would they have to deal with a criminal underground to obtain drugs.

The Consumers Union has developed a set of specific recommendations to reduce the scope of our drug problem and to deal more effectively with drug abuse.[55] Their recommendations have two advantages. First, they are general enough so that they apply to all types of problem-producing drugs, including marijuana and heroin. Second, they would also eliminate many of the undesirable consequences associated with our current approaches to the drug problem. The six major recommendations are:

1. We must "stop emphasizing measures designed to keep drugs away from people."[56] In other words, prohibition does not achieve positive results. Prohibition only serves to increase the price of drugs and attract black market operators to the drug scene. When a drug is difficult to secure, prices soar and drug abusers must sometimes resort to crime to support their habit. They thus become double criminals in the sense that they not only violate the drug laws but other criminal laws as well. And as long as drugs are in the hands of black market operators, there is no control over their quality; abusers may become victims of adulterated or contaminated drugs.

2. We must stop playing up the horrors of the "drug menace." Widespread antidrug publicity and propaganda only make people more aware of drugs and increase their interest in trying them. Before the massive anti-LSD campaigns of the '60s, for example, relatively few people had even heard of the drug. Once LSD became widely publicized as dangerous but exciting, many people were lured into trying it. Massive antidrug propaganda campaigns can also hamper calm and rational deliberations on drug abuse and how to cope with it.

3. We must stop increasing the damage done by drugs. Current drug laws criminalize the drug abuser and damage the individual's self-conception. The laws can also have the effect of forcing people to buy contaminated or adulterated drugs and, in the case of heroin, to use unsanitary and dangerous hypodermic needles. The risk of being caught and arrested keeps many drug abusers from seeking treatment, even if treatment is available.

4. We must stop misclassifying drugs. For example, the government puts marijuana and heroin in the same category, and says, in effect, that marijuana is as dangerous as heroin. As a result, the young marijuana user may be tempted to try heroin, assuming that since legal conceptions of marijuana are false perhaps official warnings about the dangers of heroin are equally false. Young people also realize that alcohol and nicotine are as hazardous as marijuana and may resent the hypocrisy of our drug laws. The accurate classification of drugs would greatly aid drug-abuse education programs because teachers would then be free to discuss tobacco, alcohol, marijuana, heroin, and other drugs openly and to compare their relative dangers.

5. We must stop viewing drug abuse as a national problem and instead develop programs to deal with it locally. A drug-abuse program that works well in New York City may have little relevance in a small southern community. Furthermore, it makes little sense to educate children in a rural community to the dangers of a drug of which they have never heard. At the same time, however, drug abuse *is* a national problem because the laws and policies have been formulated at the national level. Many of these laws and policies must be changed if the drug problem is to be dealt with realistically.

6. Finally, the Consumers Union suggests that we stop trying to stamp out illicit drug use completely. Some people will probably abuse drugs, whether it is legal or not; and little will be gained by getting tough with them. We should try instead to educate people not to want to use dangerous drugs and to seek help for the problems that drive them to drugs. By trying to stamp out the use of one drug (like marijuana), we may well only drive people to use others, such as alcohol, LSD, or heroin.

In summary, the thrust of the Consumers Union argument seems to be that since a certain percentage of the population will apparently abuse drugs, regardless of the law, we must minimize the dangerous and undesirable consequences of drug abuse. We must also stop creating the conditions which have the unintentional effect of encouraging drug abuse. Many students of drug abuse would concur with these recommendations.

Summary

Drug abuse and narcotics addiction are considered serious problems mostly because society defines them as such. In reality, relatively few people abuse drugs and narcotics except, of course, for the many people who abuse tobacco and alcohol. Narcotics addiction is mostly confined to minority groups in inner-city slums. The magnitude of the drug problem is probably overrated in the public eye.

Drug abuse is defined as the regular, excessive use of a drug so that it is damaging to the user's job, health, or social status, or to society in general. We live in a culture of pill poppers that encourages the abuse of both licit and illicit drugs. Our most widespread drug problem may be the legal use of substances like diet pills, sleeping pills, and tranquilizers. We have prohibited certain drugs and have outlawed them as dangerous. The use of nonapproved drugs is considered deviant behavior in our society.

Marijuana is a good example of a drug that seems to be meaninglessly defined as nonapproved. Marijuana is a nonaddictive, mild intoxicant, and we now have evidence which debunks the myth that marijuana leads to crime, the abuse of other drugs, and loss of motivation. However, our social policies on marijuana are very restrictive because some people *believe* it is a dangerous drug. This policy has had many ill effects, and the marijuana laws should perhaps be changed.

LSD is an hallucinogen which in the '60s was surrounded by a great deal of myth. It now appears, however, that many of the bizarre reactions, bad trips, flashbacks, and accidents which were blamed on LSD occurred because users were educated to expect these effects.

The general public considers narcotics addiction to be the most significant drug-abuse problem. It is characterized by two traits: withdrawal syndrome and tolerance buildup. Narcotics addiction is mostly confined to lower-class people in the inner city.

Social control of narcotics addiction began in 1914 with the Harrison Act. Charged with enforcing the Act, the Narcotics Division of the Bureau of Internal Revenue crusaded to turn public sentiment against narcotics use. Several Supreme Court decisions aided the Division's efforts. It is not clear whether the Division staff saw themselves as moral entrepreneurs or whether they were trying to ensure the survival of their agency. Nevertheless, they quickly cut addicts off from all legal drug sources, made possible the link between narcotics and crime, and contributed to the growth of a narcotics subculture.

The history of the social control of marijuana is similar: in 1937 the Bureau of Narcotics crusaded for antimarijuana laws, probably motivated by moral entrepreneurism and organizational survival. The resulting Marijuana Tax Act had the same effects as the Harrison Act.

Today, the 1970 Comprehensive Drug Abuse Prevention and Control Act has replaced previous laws and reduces penalties for possession on the first offense. However, the government still takes a legalistic, punitive approach to drug abuse.

Many other approaches have been tried in the search for solutions to drug abuse—especially drug treatment programs, including methadone maintenance for heroin addicts and the Synanon therapeutic community approach. However, ex-addicts leaving these programs have high rates of relapse. Many community-based facilities have been developed in recent years to help addicts, but no data are available on their effectiveness.

Since many of our drug-abuse and narcotics-addiction problems are rooted in our social policies regarding drugs, the best solution may be to change those policies. Rather than trying to make drugs unavailable, many proposals have been made which suggest decriminalizing the user and wiping out the black market to break the link between crime and drugs. We must minimize the dangerous consequences of drugs and we must change the conditions which encourage their use.

Discussion Questions

1. Experts in the area of drug research cannot agree on a completely acceptable definition of the term *drug abuse*. How would you define *drug abuse*? Would drinking one cup of coffee in the morning be considered a form of drug abuse? Smoking three packs of cigarettes a day? Getting drunk in the privacy of one's own home on Friday nights? Explain and justify your answers.
2. Why do you suppose that many Americans rely heavily on drugs, both licit and illicit, to get through life? Is it accurate to say that we live in a pill-popping culture? Given the present structure of our society, is it realistic to expect the average citizen to function without artificial crutches such as tranquilizers, barbiturates, amphetamines, alcohol, and so forth?
3. Watch two or three hours of prime time television. How many advertisements are presented which promote the sale of drugs? What do these advertisements promise the person who buys and uses the drugs?
4. Should the possession of marijuana for personal use be legalized? If not, how should we deal with people who desire to use marijuana? Support your argument with facts and data.
5. Discuss and evaluate the following statements: *(a)* Marijuana use leads to crime. *(b)* Marijuana use leads to the abuse of other drugs. *(c)* Marijuana use leads to the loss of motivation.
6. Discuss the following statement: If people are taught to believe that the use of certain types of drugs leads to extremely bizarre behavior, they will display extremely bizarre behavior. Is this an adequate explanation of the behavior of drug users?
7. Is narcotics addiction a serious social problem? Why or why not? What have been some of the negative consequences of passing and enforcing extremely stiff laws against the sale, transfer, or possession of narcotics? Did the government have any choice except to pass these laws?
8. What is meant by the term *narcotics subculture*? In what sense do narcotics subcultures help to perpetuate narcotics addiction?
9. Discuss the set of recommendations developed by the Consumers Union which supposedly would help us deal more effectively with drug abuse. Do you agree with all of the Consumers Union's recommendations? If not, which ones do you disagree with? Why do you disagree with them?

Glossary

Comprehensive Drug Abuse Prevention and Control Act This act, passed in 1970, reduced the federal penalties for possession of dangerous drugs from a felony to a misdemeanor on the first offense and provides that the first offender can be committed to a treatment program in place of imprisonment. It replaced the Harrison Act, the Marijuana Tax Act, and several other pieces of drug legislation.

drug abuse This term is defined as (1) the regular, excessive use of a drug so that it is damaging to the user's job, health, or social status, or to society in general; or (2) the use of drugs that society defines as dangerous or as lending themselves to abuse.

drug (or narcotic) subculture A group of people who share norms which encourage and perpetuate the use of socially disapproved drugs.

Harrison Act An act passed in 1914 which remained the basic antinarcotic statute in the United States until 1970. Its most important feature was that it made it illegal for a person to obtain narcotics from anyone except a registered physician.

Marijuana Tax Act An act passed in 1937 which made the sale, transfer, or possession of marijuana illegal. Many of its provisions were patterned after those of the Harrison Act.

methadone A synthetic opiate which relieves narcotics addicts of their craving for heroin. Ideally, a methadone treatment program is used as an adjunct to other types of therapy.

moral entrepreneurs People who see themselves as the guardians of society's values and who often attempt to impose their definitions of morality on other people.

narcotics addiction A condition in which a person has an intense craving for narcotics. Addicts build up a tolerance for narcotics and display a withdrawal syndrome when they are deprived of narcotics.

Synanon A residential treatment program for addicts staffed entirely by ex-addicts. The environment of Synanon is antidrug and anticriminal.

therapeutic community A residential treatment facility which makes use of the environment itself in an effort to rehabilitate the addict. Synanon, for example, is a therapeutic community in which a person can gain rewards by staying away from narcotics.

tolerance The tendency for addicts to take larger doses of narcotics the longer they use them.

withdrawal syndrome An illness experienced by addicts when they cease taking narcotics. Withdrawal syndrome is marked by a number of different symptoms ranging from very mild to extremely severe.

Suggestions for Further Reading

"The American Way of Drugging," *Society,* 10 (May/June, 1973), pp. 14–58. A series of articles which deals with various facets of the drug scene in the United States. Of particular interest is an article by Bruce Johnson which is critical of the work done by the National Commission on Marijuana and Drug Abuse.

Brecher, Edward M., and the Editors of Consumer Reports, *Licit and Illicit Drugs* (Boston: Little, Brown, 1972). An exceptionally comprehensive report on drugs and drug abuse in the United States. Must reading for any serious student of the drug problem.

Dickson, Donald T., "Bureaucracy and Morality: An Organizational Perspective on a Moral Crusade," *Social Problems,* 16 (Fall, 1968), pp. 143–56. In this insightful article, the author discusses the motives of the Narcotics Bureau in pressing for the passage of the Marijuana Tax Act. Dickson's basic thesis is that the Bureau pressed for the passage of the Marijuana Tax Act in order to assure its own growth and survival.

Geller, Allen, and Maxwell Boas, *The Drug Beat* (Chicago: Regnery, 1969). A look at marijuana, LSD, and amphetamines from a variety of different perspectives.

Goode, Erich, "Marijuana and the Politics of Reality," *Journal of Health and Social Behavior,* 10 (June, 1969), pp. 83–94. In this provocative article Goode suggests that the debate over marijuana is political rather than scientific. He also suggests that what we define as dangerous drugs is essentially arbitrary and that scientific evidence alone will not put the marijuana debate to rest.

Kaplan, John, *Marijuana: The New Prohibition* (New York: Pocket Books, 1971). A careful, well-balanced consideration of marijuana and its effects on the user and society. The author concludes by recommending a licensing system for distributing marijuana in a manner similar to our current methods of distributing alcoholic beverages.

Lindesmith, Alfred R., *The Addict and the Law* (Bloomington, Ind.: Indiana University, 1965). As the title of this volume implies, the author draws a picture of how the narcotic addict is treated by legal authorities in the United States and in other countries. The reader should not be deceived by the 1965 copyright date on this book. Most of the information contained in this classic work is still relevant and informative.

Lindesmith, Alfred R., *Addiction and Opiates* (Chicago: Aldine, 1968). Perhaps the best treatment available pertaining to the nature of addiction and to opiate addiction as a social problem.

McGrath, John H., and Frank R. Scarpitti, eds., *Youth and Drugs: Perspectives on a Social Problem* (Glenview, Ill.: Scott, Foresman, 1970). An excellent collection of articles on drug abuse and narcotics addiction in the United States. The introduction to this volume acquaints the reader with the psychological and sociological approaches to explaining drug abuse and narcotics addiction.

National Commission on Marijuana and Drug Abuse, *Marijuana: A Signal of Misunderstanding* (New York: New American Library, 1972). A comprehensive report on almost every facet of marijuana use as it occurs in the United States.

O'Donnell, John A., and John C. Ball, eds., *Narcotic Addiction* (New York: Harper & Row, 1966). Although somewhat dated, this volume contains many classic articles on narcotics addiction.

Notes

[1]Joel Fort, "A World View of Drugs," in Richard H. Blum et al., eds., *Society and Drugs: Social and Cultural Observations* (San Francisco: Jossey-Bass, 1969), p. 230.

[2]*Ibid.*, p. 229.

[3]Essentially the same argument is put forth by Erich Goode. See Erich Goode, "Marijuana and the Politics of Reality," *Journal of Health and Social Behavior*, 10 (June, 1969), pp. 83–93.

[4]Matthew P. Dumont, "Mainlining America: Why the Young Use Drugs," in John B. Williamson, Jerry J. Boren, and Linda Evans, eds., *Social Problems: The Contemporary Debates* (Boston: Little, Brown, 1974), p. 389.

[5]Joel Fort, "The Drug Explosion," in John W. Kinch, ed., *Social Problems in the World Today* (Reading, Mass.: Addison-Wesley, 1974), p. 50.

[6]For an interesting analysis see Arnold Bernstein and Henry L. Lennard, "Drugs, Doctors, and Junkies," *Society*, 10 (May/June, 1973), pp. 14–25.

[7]National Commission on Marijuana and Drug Abuse, *Marijuana: A Signal of Misunderstanding* (New York: New American Library, 1972), p. 38.

[8]*Ibid.*, p. 39.

[9]*Ibid.*, p. 41.

[10]*Ibid.*, pp. 51–52.

[11]*Ibid.*, p. 52.

[12]The phrases in quotations are cited in David Solomon, ed., *The Marijuana Papers* (New York: New American Library, 1966), p. xv.

[13]National Commission on Marijuana and Drug Abuse, *Marijuana*, esp. pp. 88–91.

[14]*Ibid.*, p. 54.

[15]Thus, in their classic study of heroin use, Isidor Chein and his associates maintain that "the evidence indicates that all addicts suffer from deep-rooted, major personality disorders." See Isidor Chein et al., *The Road to H: Narcotics, Delinquency, and Social Policy* (New York: Basic, 1964), p. 14.

[16]For a more extensive discussion of the costs of our marijuana laws, see John Kaplan, *Marijuana: The New Prohibition* (New York: Pocket Books, 1971), pp. 22–50. The following discussion leans heavily on that of Kaplan's.

[17]*Ibid.*, p. 35.

[18]Edward M. Brecher and the Editors of Consumer Reports, *Licit and Illicit Drugs* (Boston: Little, Brown, 1972), p. 367.

[19]*Ibid.*, p. 348.

[20]*Ibid.*, p. 384.

[21]Some of the more significant of these studies are summarized in *Ibid.*, Ch. 52.

[22]Thus, prior to 1962 LSD was manufactured by Sandoz Laboratories, a reputable drug firm, and distributed to physicians, psychologists, and psychiatrists who were qualified to use it for legitimate purposes. In 1965 Sandoz stopped distributing the drug completely, and it became available on a black market basis only.

[23]Brecher, *Licit and Illicit Drugs*, p. 375.

[24]Alfred R. Lindesmith, *Addiction and Opiates* (Chicago: Aldine, 1968), p. 49.

[25]Brecher, *Licit and Illicit Drugs*, p. 65.

[26]Lindesmith, *Addiction and Opiates*, pp. 73–74.

[27]*Ibid.*, p. 25.

[28]*Ibid.*, p. 90.

[29]For a brief review of psychological approaches to the explanation of narcotics addiction, see John H. McGrath and Frank R. Scarpitti, eds., *Youth and Drugs: Perspectives on a Social Problem* (Glenview, Ill.: Scott, Foresman, 1970), pp. 3–5.

[30]*Ibid.*, p. 3.

[31]*Ibid.*, p. 6.

[32]John A. Clausen, "Social and Psychological Factors in Narcotics Addiction," *Law and Contemporary Problems*, XXII (Winter, 1957), pp. 34–35.

[33]*Encyclopedia of Sociology* (Guilford, Conn.: Dushkin, 1974), p. 196.

[34]John A. Clausen, "Drug Use," in Robert K. Merton and Robert Nisbet, eds., *Contemporary Social Problems*, 4th Ed. (New York: Harcourt Brace Jovanovich, 1976), p. 157.

[35]Thus, in countries in which the use of heroin, for example, is legal and the addict is under medical supervision, there are numerous reports of addicts who lead essentially healthy, normal lives.

[36]Clausen, "Drug Use," p. 144.

[37]For a discussion of the Harrison Act and its enforcement see Alfred R. Lindesmith, *The Addict and the Law* (Bloomington, Ind.: Indiana University, 1965), esp. pp. 3–62.

[38]See Lindesmith, *Addiction and Opiates*, pp. 217–220.

[39]*Ibid.*, pp. 218–219.

[40]Donald T. Dickson, "Bureaucracy and Morality: An Organizational Perspective on a Moral Crusade," *Social Problems*, 16 (Fall, 1968), p. 149.

[41]For a more complete discussion of the Supreme Court's interpretations of the Harrison Act see Lindesmith, *The Addict and the Law*, esp. pp. 5–17.

[42]Dickson, "Bureaucracy and Morality," esp. pp. 149–51.

[43]Howard S. Becker, *Outsiders: Studies in the Sociology of Deviance* (New York: Free Press, 1963).

[44]See Harold Finestone, "Narcotics and Criminality," in John A. O'Donnell and John C. Ball, eds., *Narcotic Addiction* (New York: Harper & Row, 1966), pp. 141–64; and U. S. President's Commission on Law Enforcement and the Administration of Justice, *Task Force Report: Narcotics* (Washington, D.C.: U.S. Government Printing Office, 1967), pp. 10–11.

[45]Dickson, "Bureaucracy and Morality," p. 155.

[46]U.S. Department of Health, Education, and Welfare, *Narcotic Drug Addiction*, Public Health Service Publication No. 1021 (Washington, D.C.: U.S. Government Printing Office, 1965), p. 11.

[47]See Marsh B. Ray, "The Cycle of Abstinence and Relapse Among Heroin Addicts," in Howard S. Becker, ed., *The Other Side* (New York: Free Press, 1964), pp. 163–76.

[48]Among the more significant studies of Synanon are Daniel Cariel, *So Fair a House: The Story of Synanon* (Englewood Cliffs, N.J.: Prentice-Hall, 1963); Rita Volkman and Donald R. Cressey, "Differential Association and the Rehabilitation of Drug Addicts," *American Journal of Sociology*, 69 (September, 1963), pp. 129–42; Lewis Yablonsky, *The Tunnel Back: Synanon* (New York: Macmillan, 1965); and Guy Endore, *Synanon* (New York: Doubleday, 1968).

[49]Volkman and Cressey, "Differential Association and the Rehabilitation of Drug Addicts," pp. 133–34.

[50]Cited in Brecher, *Licit and Illicit Drugs*, p. 81.

[51]For further discussion of community-based facilities for drug abusers see *Ibid.*, pp. 499–506.

[52]Lindesmith, *The Addict and the Law*, pp. 269–302.

[53]National Commission on Marijuana and Drug Abuse, *Marijuana: A Signal of Misunderstanding*, pp. 188–95.

[54]Kaplan, *Marijuana*, pp. 346–60.

[55]The Consumers Union recommendations are to be found in Brecher, *Licit and Illicit Drugs*, pp. 521–527.

[56]*Ibid.*, p. 522.

Chapter 6

Deviant Sexual Behavior

In ancient Greece and Rome, homosexual relationships were approved of in certain social situations. More recently, in our own history, some Mormon men practiced polygamy, using Biblical precedents to justify their marital habits.

All societies have developed norms for human sexuality; and most, including Greek, Roman, and Mormon societies, have limited sex primarily to marriage or to relationships that lead to marriage. The reasons are simple. If most of us were homosexuals, rates of reproduction would be dangerously low. If we all engaged in frequent extramarital sex, the stability of the family and the socialization of children might be jeopardized.

In our country, deviancy from sexual norms often arouses severe social censure as not only immoral but evil, yet most sexual deviancy does not threaten society. Homosexuals, for example, do not affect birthrates in any significant way; and mate swapping involves only a very small percentage of married couples who, surprisingly, seem to sustain fairly stable marriages and family lives.

Is sexual deviancy, then, really a *social problem;* that is, a pattern of behavior which threatens society and/or the groups and institutions of which it is composed? Or is it, instead, a *social issue* that is important only because of widespread public attitudes and attention? Because the general public so strongly disapproves of the homosexual and the prostitute, for example, these people are lumped into the deviant category and thus are subject to all the negative effects of labeling.

In this chapter we will examine some of the patterns of sexual behavior that many people consider deviant—homosexuality, prostitution, the consumption of pornography, and mate swapping. Our examination will attempt to answer the question: If sexual deviance does not threaten society, should we stop labeling it *deviant* and recognize instead that human sexuality can be expressed and satisfied in alternative ways? More and more people are demanding that we answer this question in the affirmative. Yet much of society continues to define some forms of sexuality as immoral and evil. Thus, the issue of the individual's right to adopt alternative forms of sexual expression versus society's right to define certain forms of sexual expression as deviant or immoral promises to be a controversial one.

American Attitudes Toward Sex

In order to understand deviant sexual behavior, we must first understand American attitudes toward sex in general. Traditionally, our attitudes have been highly restrictive. For the most part, we have limited sex to the marital bed; any other expression of sexuality has been considered evil. Thus, all unmarried people, whether young or old, male or female, have been expected to be totally inactive sexually. But it is hardly likely that all unmarried people have adhered strictly to these norms.

In recent years we have heard a great deal about a sexual revolution. But *revolution,* meaning "a far-ranging, pervasive, radical change in part, or in many parts, of society,"[1] may be too strong a word. It would be extremely difficult to argue that our sexual behavior or attitudes have undergone far-ranging, pervasive, radical change. Most people today probably conduct their sex lives much like people did ten, twenty, or thirty years ago.[2]

However, some changes may be occurring. Specifically, the percentage of women who have premarital intercourse (coitus) has roughly doubled since the late '30s and '40s.[3] This trend is shown in Table 6.1, and two points should be made about these data.[4] First, between 1958 and 1968, the percentage of both intermountain (mostly Mormon) and midwestern females who experienced premarital coitus increased noticeably (22 percent for intermountain females and 13 percent for midwestern females). Second, and equally important, the percentage of both intermountain and midwestern boys who experienced premarital coitus changed little between 1958 and 1968 (although even in 1968 more males than females experienced premarital coitus).

Table 6.1

Percentage of Young People with Premarital Coital Experience

Year	Sample Culture					
	Intermountain[a]		Midwestern		Danish	
	Male	Female	Male	Female	Male	Female
1968	37	32	50	34	95	97
1958	39	10	51	21	64	60
Difference	−2	22	−1	13	31	37

[a]Comprises young people reared in the predominantly Mormon region of Utah and parts of surrounding states. Traditionally, Mormons have had the reputation of having very conservative attitudes toward sex.

Adapted from: Harold T. Christensen and Christina F. Gregg, "Changing Sex Norms in America and Scandinavia," *Journal of Marriage and the Family,* 32 (November, 1970), Table 3.

What the data in Table 6.1 seem to indicate is both that the double standard is gradually eroding and that it is no longer true that unmarried males have a great deal more sexual freedom than unmarried females. But the essential point is that the data do *not* show that we have become a highly permissive society. Compared to Danish males and females, American premarital coital experience is still quite limited.

Where then is the sexual revolution? Certainly Americans are more open today about sex than in the past; sex is more frequently and openly discussed on television, at social gatherings, and in the schools. But there is no solid evidence to suggest that our attitudes toward sex have become significantly more liberal in recent years. Most Americans continue to regard patterns of behavior like homosexuality, prostitution, the consumption of pornography, and swinging very unfavorably.

Male Homosexuality

In theory, homosexuality is easy to define. Under the entry *homosexuality* in *Webster's New Collegiate Dictionary,* for example, we find "the manifestation of sexual desire toward a member of one's own sex" or "erotic activity with a member of one's own sex." In practice, the question, What is homosexuality? is extremely difficult to answer.[5]

Homosexuality is a matter of degree. A great many men who are labeled heterosexual by society do have homosexual or pseudohomosexual experiences—for example, the adolescent boy who masturbates with his buddy; the frustrated middle-aged executive who occasionally visits public urinals to find young men to have oral-genital sex with; and the inmate of a penitentiary who, in frustration, turns to other prisoners for sexual gratification. Does their behavior mean that these people are homosexuals? Obviously, there is no ironclad answer to this question.

Human beings can be placed on a continuum ranging from those who are exclusively heterosexual to those who are exclusively homosexual.[6] Along the continuum male homosexuality can take various forms. One form is known as the tearoom trade.[7] Basically, tearoom (slang for *rest room*) participants seek fast, impersonal sexual gratification in men's rest rooms; they "want a form of orgasm-producing action that is less lonely than masturbation and less involving than a love relationship."[8] Most of them are married and most do not think of themselves as homosexual. Another form of homosexual is the man who is more or less committed to the gay life: he frequents gay bars, thinks of himself as a homosexual, and consistently chooses sexual relationships with various male partners. Still another form of homosexuality is the gay marriage in which two male partners live together and attempt to be sexually faithful to one another. At least one expert argues that these marriages are not likely to be successful for very long.[9] Jealousy is a continual threat to the gay marriage. Indeed, homosexuals who are married to one another seem to be a favorite sexual target for single homosexuals. But more importantly, the homosexual marriage exists in a society in which homosexuality is severely frowned upon. The couple must keep their marriage secret from their family, employers, and neighbors. This is extremely difficult, and the fear of being found out puts a severe strain on many homosexual marriages.

Extent of Male Homosexuality

In his research, first published in 1948, Alfred Kinsey found that about 37 percent of all American males have had at least one homosexual experience that resulted in orgasm and that about 4 percent of all males are exclusively homosexual.[10] However, Kinsey's figures, if anything, overestimate the extent of homosexuality. A more recent study found that about 1 percent of a nationwide sample of males considered themselves "mainly" homosexual; an additional 1 percent considered themselves bisexual.[11] Although it is extremely difficult to gather accurate data on the extent of male homosexuality, our statistics do make one point clear. Homosexuality is not especially common and therefore need not be considered a major threat to society.

Causes of Male Homosexuality

In the past, the human sex drive was widely thought to be almost totally determined by biological factors; thus, the normal person would naturally be attracted to a person of the opposite sex. Today, however, we realize that human beings can be sexually aroused by many different stimuli, including a person of his or her own sex, nude photographs, articles of clothing, etc. In short, the sex drive is innate, but the way in which it is expressed is learned. Most persons learn to be sexually aroused by persons of the opposite sex; the homosexual has learned to be aroused by persons of his or her own sex.

How a person learns a homosexual orientation is not fully understood. For the most part, efforts to explain homosexuality in psychiatric terms have failed. Perhaps homosexuals who seek psychiatric care are emotionally disturbed, but what about the vast majority of homosexuals who do not seek that care? A practicing psychologist states, "I have seen no homosexual man or woman in my practice who wasn't troubled, emotionally upset, or neurotic. On the other hand, if my concept of marriage in the United States were based on my practice, I would have to conclude that marriages are all fraught with strife and conflict, and that heterosexuality is an illness."[12] Some researchers have attempted to trace homosexuality to "undue attachment to the mother" or to "unsatisfactory relations with the father."[13] But these theories have not proven useful.

Labeling theory provides a more useful explanation of homosexuality. Basically, it suggests that in the course of their development some individuals gradually begin to define themselves as having homosexual tendencies. This initial self-definition may be the result of an exploratory homosexual contact during adolescence or of various other experiences. But the result is that:

People become entrapped in a false consciousness of identifying themselves as being homosexuals. They believe that they discover what they are. . . . Learning their "identity," they become involved in it, boxed into their own biographies. . . . There is no road back because they believe there is none. . . . Because they want to believe that they are not worthless (which they are not), and because they confuse the worth of a person with that of a characteristic, they go to the next step and say that gay is good.[14]

In the end, other people begin to identify the individual as a homosexual. Thus, the idea that people will be what other people consider them to be seems to apply to homosexuality.

Male Homosexual Subcultures

The labeling process is essentially complete when the individual begins to participate in a homosexual subculture (a group of homosexuals who to some degree interact with one another, who share common norms, and who often share a specialized argot). Most large cities contain one or more such subcultures. The following quote clearly points up their importance:

I knew there were homosexuals, queers and what not; I had read some books, and I was resigned to the fact that I was a foul, dirty person, but I actually wasn't calling myself a homosexual yet. . . . And the time I really caught myself coming out is the time I walked into this bar and saw a whole crowd of groovy, groovy guys. And I said to myself, there was the realization, that not all gay men are dirty old men or idiots, silly queens, but they are just normal looking and acting people. I saw gay society and I said, "Wow, I'm home."[15]

This is a perfect example of *coming out* in homosexual argot, when an individual firmly attaches the label of *homosexual* to himself and begins to identify with the homosexual subculture.

The homosexual subculture, particularly the gay bar, fulfills several very important functions for male homosexuals. First, the bar provides a setting in which the person can be himself and in which he can socialize with other homosexuals. This is important because in the outside world of work and family the individual usually must conceal his homosexuality and pretend he is straight. Such pretense can put a tremendous strain on him. However, at the end of the day the individual can, within the homosexual subculture, return to a more satisfying role. Second, the gay bar facilitates communication between and among homosexuals: "A characteristic of the homosexual subculture is that news travels very fast and information as to streets, public parks, and restrooms where homosexual contacts may be found is rapidly circulated among the members of the subculture."[16] Finally, and most importantly, the gay bar serves to bring the individual homosexual into contact with other persons who have similar sexual preferences.

The Homophile Movement

One of the most dramatic recent developments on the sexual scene has been the appearance of various **homophile organizations**. These voluntary associations of homosexuals seek to better the status of the homosexual. In 1969, about 150 such groups were known to exist in the United States.[17]

These associations have helped to improve the self-image of the homosexual. Through the homophile organization, the individual learns that thousands of other persons share his sexual orientation and that through collective action the status of the homosexual can perhaps be improved. Most importantly, the homophile movement holds out the hope that someday homosexuals can become a respected, integral part of society.

The homophile movement has also helped change psychiatric and legal views of the homosexual. A major breakthrough came in 1973 when the American Psychiatric Association decided to remove homosexuality from its list of mental disorders: "We will no longer insist on a label of sickness for individuals who insist that they are well and demonstrate no generalized impairment in social effectiveness."[18] Similarly, seven states—California, Connecticut, Colorado, Hawaii, Idaho, Illinois, and Oregon—have repealed their laws prohibiting homosexuality among consenting adults, and other states may do so in the near future. The liberalization of these state laws can be traced to the efforts of homophile organizations and to the generally greater visibility of homosexuality in our country.

Finally, the homophile movement has had some success in achieving its foremost goal—to change public attitudes toward the homosexual. There is much more openness today about homosexuality than in the past. However, the general public probably will not soon come around to the view that homosexuality is simply one of several alternative styles of sexual expression. Most people still view the homosexual with extreme disapproval.

Female Homosexuality

Less is known about female homosexuality, or lesbianism, than about male homosexuality.[19] For one thing, lesbians engender less public concern. Female homosexuality is less common than male homosexuality. Researchers fairly consistently find that about one-half as many women as men are "mainly" homosexuals.[20] Female homosexuality is also less visible than male homosexuality, occurring mostly in the privacy of the home and not involving the gay bar phenomenon which helps make male homosexuality so visible. Furthermore, in the United States, we approve of unmarried females living together and, to some extent, displaying affection for each other: most nonlesbian women on occasion display essentially the same behavior patterns as lesbians.

Since the '50s, several organizations have emerged to promote the rights of female homosexuals. ▶

We should emphasize that female homosexuality is a basically different phenomenon from male homosexuality.[21] Male homosexuals are oriented primarily toward simple sexual gratification. Although males do occasionally develop deep emotional commitments to one another, the customary emphasis in the male homosexual subculture is on a diversity of sexual experiences with a diversity of partners. Rates of promiscuity among male homosexuals are high. On the other hand, sexual encounters between women tend to grow out of an intense emotional relationship. Typically, the lesbian first develops a deep emotional and romantic commitment to another woman, and their sexual activities are an outgrowth of this emotional bond. It is interesting to note that the sexual orientations of male and female homosexuals closely parallel those of their heterosexual counterparts. In our society, males are socialized, at least subconsciously, to seek sexual gratification as an end in itself. The female, however, is much more likely to seek sexual gratification as a desirable outcome of deep romantic attachments.

Since the '50s, several organizations have emerged to promote the rights of female homosexuals. These include the Daughters of Bilitis, a California-based organization called the Society for Individual Rights, and the Lesbian Mothers' Union. The particular goals of these organizations are as diverse as their tactics. Essentially, however, they seek the same general ends as the homophile organizations. Their members want the right to live out their sexual life-styles without harassment or stigma, and they want to enjoy the same legal, political, and economic rights enjoyed by heterosexuals. Given contemporary public attitudes toward homosexuality, however, it is unlikely that these demands for liberation will soon be granted. In the sexual realm, our society continues to assign a higher priority to maintaining straitlaced definitions of morality than to allowing individuals to conduct their private lives as they choose.

Prostitution

Like homosexuality, prostitution is not easy to define.[22] Some have argued that any woman who exchanges sexual favors for tangible gain is a prostitute. But this definition could be construed to include the college girl who has sex once with her boyfriend after a date or even the faithful middle-class housewife whose husband provides her with the necessities of life. For our purposes, prostitution will be defined as selling sexual favors for monetary gain; that is, to the prostitute, prostitution is an occupation and source of income.

Extent of Prostitution

Estimates of the number of full-time prostitutes in the United States range between 250,000 and 550,000.[23] These estimates have changed little since World War II because there has been "a decline in the frequency with which men patronize prostitutes."[24] The chief reason why prostitution has not kept pace with our expanding population is because there is less need for commercialized sex; with the erosion of the double standard, more and more women are freely engaging in premarital sex.

Types of Prostitution

The types of prostitution are many and varied. The first type of prostitute is the *streetwalker*, who solicits her clients on the streets, in bars, in cheap hotels, and in other public places. The streetwalker's fee is usually less than $20 per customer, and of all prostitutes she is the most poorly paid and most frequently abused. The second type of prostitute is the *housegirl*. Formerly, the housegirl was most likely to work in a brothel but today she may work in a massage parlor or a "private club." In any case, she and her co-workers are supervised by a madam who takes a large percentage of their earnings. This type of prostitution may be less common today than it was in the past. The third type of prostitute is the *call girl*, who usually works out of a plush hotel or apartment building and may charge several hundred dollars per night for her services.[25] She is relatively selective in terms of whom she will accept as a client, and many of her clients are referred to her by regular customers. Finally, there is the more recent phenomenon of the *corporation prostitute*, who is retained by a large corporation to wine, dine, and otherwise entertain important customers.[26] How common corporation prostitution is cannot be determined.

Subculture of Prostitution

Some prostitutes work alone and do not interact with others who are involved in the business of commercial sex. Most prostitutes, though, are members of a complicated network of social relationships which includes other prostitutes, pimps, hotel operators, prostitution lawyers, prominent businessmen, and sometimes organized crime.[27]

The pimp is very important to the prostitute because he provides protection for her and serves as her business agent.

The most important persons in the life of the prostitute are other prostitutes and her pimp. Since the prostitute usually is not accepted by conventional society, she must seek companionship from other members of her profession. Furthermore, it is in her interaction with other prostitutes that she finds a rationale for her

behavior.[28] The subculture of prostitution is rife with stories about innocent girls tricked into a life of prostitution, of prostitutes who have married well-heeled businessmen or politicians, and of respectable women who have fallen into prostitution.[29] This body of folklore helps the prostitute define her place in society and relieves her from having to take personal responsibility for her behavior.

The pimp is very important to the prostitute because he provides protection for her and serves as her business agent. For this, he charges a large commission; for example, "The street pimp demands his girls bring in from $200 to $250 a night. The girls rarely see more than 5 percent. The pimp pockets all and doles out 'walk around money,' $5 at a time."[30] The pimp may also be the only person with whom the prostitute builds a close, affectionate relationship.

Several other individuals complete the subculture of prostitution. These include the skid-row hotel operator who rents the room that is used for only ten or fifteen minutes; on a good night the hotel operator can make about $200 an hour from prostitution.[31] Others include lawyers who charge high fees to represent prostitutes, policemen on the take, and the landlords who own the hotels, brothels, and massage parlors in which prostitution occurs. Indeed, prostitution seems to be lucrative for everyone but the prostitute herself.

Causes of Prostitution

In considering the causes of prostitution, we should ask two questions: (1) Why do some women become prostitutes? (2) Why is there a demand for prostitutes' services? Answering these questions will bring us close to understanding the causes of prostitution.

Psychologists and psychiatrists have provided various answers to our first question. In one study, for example, prostitutes had "early family experiences of parental conflict, neglect, and rejection. They also had rewarding sexual experiences with older men. These experiences led the girls to see sex as a commodity to barter for personal gain."[32] Prostitutes have also been described as having masochistic tendencies or as being incapable of forming mature interpersonal relationships with men. However, the variety of these psychological descriptions tend to indicate that there is no such thing as a "typical" prostitute. Prostitutes undoubtedly come from a variety of different backgrounds and display a wide variety of different personality traits.

Some women probably enter prostitution because of economic considerations. Compared to other jobs available to unskilled females, prostitution pays fairly well. In addition, the prostitute has a certain amount of freedom she would not have in a factory or clerical job, and she may see prostitution as a relatively glamorous, exciting profession. Many people cannot accept the fact that women enter prostitution because of economic considerations. But, "most women say they become prostitutes for very practical reasons. The occupation pays well, the work is reasonably pleasant, and they have a fair degree of independence and a chance of meeting a client they can marry."[33]

Why there is a demand for prostitutes is more difficult to explain, especially in a society where noncommercial sexual outlets are widely available. However, men seem to turn to prostitutes for three basic reasons.[34] First, in any society, some men are not able to compete for the available women: they may feel too shy, too old, or too unattractive, or they may be physically handicapped to the point that they cannot marry. Sometimes they may find themselves in settings, such as army bases, where there is a shortage of available women. Second, a man may turn to a prostitute to avoid entanglements. With a prostitute, a man need not worry about a possible pregnancy or make any emotional commitments. In short, prostitution is, for the man, a source of uncomplicated and impersonal sex. Finally, some men use prostitutes for sexual variety. For example, a man who derives gratification from fellatio (oral stimulation of the penis) may be reluctant or even afraid to ask his wife or girl friend to engage in it with him.

Liberalizing Attitudes and Laws

Unlike homosexuals and the homophile movement, prostitutes have not organized a strong proprostitution movement. They are, however, slowly moving in this direction. In 1974, a nationwide organization of prostitutes called COYOTE (Call Off Your Old Tired Ethics) held its first convention in San Francisco and articulated three main goals. Their first and overriding goal is to secure both the legalization of prostitution and full civil rights for prostitutes. Second, until prostitution is legalized, COYOTE advocates passing laws against the customers who use prostitutes so that they too face potential arrest. In this regard, the prostitutes seem motivated not so much by a desire for equality before the law as by a desire to pressure men to change the laws.[35] Finally, COYOTE seeks to improve the public image of prostitutes and to destroy the myths that surround prostitution. One such myth, for example, is that prostitutes are the main source of venereal disease.[36] Other groups interested in achieving more equitable treatment for prostitutes include NOW (National Organization for Women) and the ACLU (American Civil Liberties Union).

So far, however, little public response has been stirred by these groups. Certainly prostitutes have not experienced the kind of backlash that the gay liberation movement has. This is probably because the proprostitution movement is so weak and relatively unorganized. However, if this movement becomes a viable challenge to traditional sexual norms and values, considerable public controversy will most likely develop.

Pornography

Pornography consists of written or visual materials read or viewed primarily for the purpose of sexual arousal, including "dirty" books, "stag" films, "nudie" pictures. Whether a statue from ancient Greece that has long been considered a work of art or a contemporary men's magazine such as *Playboy* are pornographic is impossible to determine. As two researchers point out, "Almost anything may be sexually exciting—to some people. And many people can be completely bored by, sexually uninterested in, and unresponsive to materials that others become wildly excited by."[37]

It is important, in discussing pornography, to bear in mind the distinction between a social issue and a social problem. The manufacture, sale, and consumption of pornographic materials is one of the most controversial social issues. Citizens in one western Kentucky city, for example, disputed the local showing of the X-rated movie *Deep Throat;* and, once or twice a year, their outcries force local bookstores and magazine stands to remove certain materials from their shelves. These materials reappear within a month or two. This pattern is not unique to western Kentucky but is observable throughout the country. To the public mind, pornography represents an extreme threat both to the individual and to society. Yet, from a sociological perspective, pornography has relatively few harmful effects and thus cannot be called a social problem.

Probably the chief reason for the controversy over pornography is that the public so poorly understands the consequences of its use. The U.S. Commission on Obscenity and Pornography found that between 40 and 60 percent of the public believes that pornography leads to moral breakdown and to rape.[38] In general, many people believe that pornography causes all kinds of sex crimes. However, the evidence does not bear this belief out. After carefully examining the entire issue of pornography, the Commission on Obscenity and Pornography concluded that there is "no evidence to date that exposure to explicit sexual materials plays a significant role in the causation of delinquent or criminal behavior among youth or adults."[39] Indeed, the primary use of pornography seems to be to facilitate masturbation.[40]

Nevertheless, in 1973, the Supreme Court responded to public attitudes by tightening its definitions of obscenity and ruling that "different states and communities may set their own standards as to what constitutes obscenity."[41] Since that time, however, the production and consumption of pornographic materials has actually increased—and with little interference from the law. The simple reason pornography is produced and distributed in such prodigious quantities is because it is profitable and in demand: "By any definition, porn has mushroomed in the past decade, from a marginal underground cottage industry into an open, aggressive $2 billion-a-year, crime-ridden growth enterprise."[42] Among the people who profit from pornography are writers, publishers, actors, filmmakers, and newstand and theater owners.

Future years, however, may see an eventual decline in the demand for pornographic materials. In Denmark, for example, where very liberal pornography laws were adopted in the late '60s, a sharp initial increase in demand just after the laws were passed was followed by a decline about three years later.[43] Similarly, experimental data reported by the Commission on Obscenity and Pornography point to a saturation effect; repeated exposure to pornographic materials seems to reduce its ability to arouse

The simple reason pornography is produced and distributed in prodigious quantities is because it is profitable and in demand.
▼

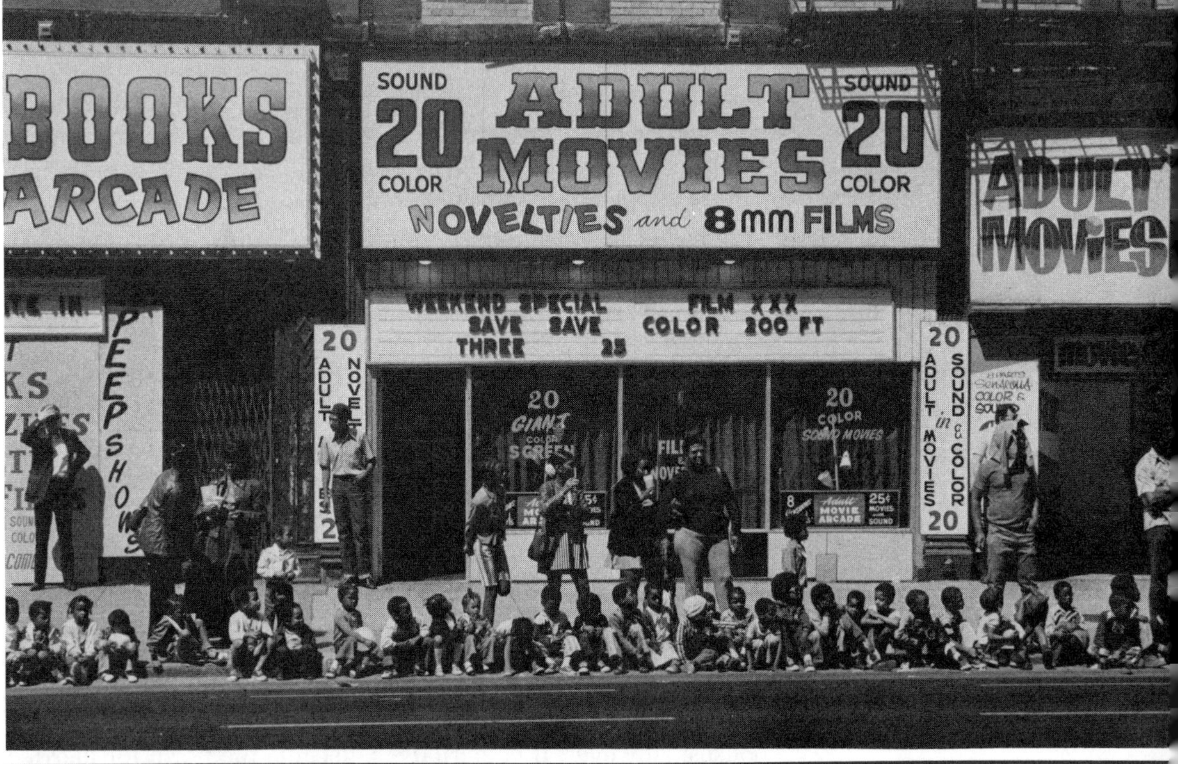

people sexually.[44] Findings such as these suggest that pornography could become much less of an issue in this country in the next few years.

Swinging

In recent years swinging, or mate swapping, has received considerable attention in popular magazines and from commentators and filmmakers. It has also been investigated intensively by sociologists and anthropologists. The phenomenon deserves the attention of social scientists: if swinging, or comarital sex, becomes a popular mode of sexual expression among married people, there will be some justification in talking about a sexual revolution.

Comarital sex is essentially different from adultery or an old-fashioned extramarital affair in two ways.[45] First, both husband and wife are aware that their spouses are engaging in comarital sex. They have comarital sex with each other's consent, and no lying or cheating is involved. Second, the couple engages in comarital sex as a couple, at a specific time and place with other couples. Sometimes the sexual interaction may be a "closet" gathering in which the parties involved pair off in separate rooms. On other occasions, the sexual interaction may be open with all participants in the same room. "[I]n open swinging, a 'pretzel,' 'flesh pile,' or 'scene' may take place, all terms which signify groups of more than two people having sex with each other."[46] Most swingers apparently see themselves not as deviants but as people who have been able to escape the confining, constricting boundaries of middle-class morality.[47]

Comarital sex, as presently practiced, is hardly a social problem or a major contributor to other social problems. Despite its publicity, it is rare: "Those who practice mate swapping with frequency or regularity are too few in number to justify precise percentaging, and amount to tiny fractions of 1 percent of our married males and females."[48] And, contrary to what might be expected, comarital sex does not seem to contribute to marital unhappiness or instability. Indeed, "one of the most common themes pervading the discussions of swinging leaders is that comarital sex embellishes and enriches marriages in all areas, and especially in the erotic sector."[49]

But only a tiny percentage of the married people in the United States engages in comarital sex. Possibly these are essentially avant-garde, "liberated" people who have been able to overcome their sexual tensions and to outgrow any jealousies of their spouses. However, if comarital sex became the norm for married

Social Problems and You

Pornography: Its Impact on Users

To many, porn is innocent escapism, a healthy device for fantasizing, a safety valve for dangerous impulses, a useful antidote to Puritan attitudes. Alan Dundes, professor of folklore at Berkeley, argues that it is an informal part of the nation's sex-education program, "the way American culture prepares people for sexuality." To Social Psychologist Douglas Wallace of the University of California Medical Center, porn is needed to bring sexual pleasure to the losers in the sexual game—the shy, the unattractive, the crippled. "Are you," he asks, "to deny these victims of our socialization process the satisfaction they might enjoy from looking at these kinds of stimuli?"

Sex researchers and therapists routinely use porn films to prod troubled couples into overcoming their sexual inhibitions. Says Dr. Zev Wanderer of the Center for Behavior Therapy in Beverly Hills: "Watching explicit sex makes the patient willing to try in his own life what he has seen on film."

To opponents of porn, that is one of the problems. Will porn's power to lessen inhibitions, which has perhaps already won some acceptance for practices long regarded as aberrant, do the same for rape and sadomasochism, both now part of the usual repertoire of film and printed porn? Writer Irving Kristol complains porn is considered harmless "by the very same people who seem convinced that advertisements in magazines or displays of violence on television do indeed have the power to corrupt."

Manhattan Psychoanalyst Natalie Shainess fears the new acceptability of pornography has convinced many of her young male patients that their perverse compulsions are not really problems at all. Result: they do nothing to deal with their compulsions. Claims Shainess: "That is happening everywhere today." Anthropologist Edgar Gregersen makes a similar point about sadomasochists: "A great many people with S-M tendencies now conceptualize themselves as S-M people. This has a very great consequence. They are not so willing to change."

U.C.L.A. Psychiatrist Robert J. Stoller, author of *Perversion: The Erotic Form of Hatred*, argues that hostility is the essential dynamic of all pornography. In his eyes, even the mildest porn is tinged with aggressive voyeurism and the sadomasochistic search for a sexual victim. Says he: "Societies fear pornography as they fear sexuality, but perhaps there is a less sick reason: they respond intuitively to the hostile fantasies disguised but still active in pornography." In Stoller's view, porn is two-edged; it "disperses rage" that might tear society apart, but it also threatens society by serving as propaganda for the unleashing of sexual hostility.

Such allegations of harm were laboriously investigated by the Commission on Obscenity and Pornography. After two years of study and ten volumes of research, in 1970 it reported "no substantial basis" for the belief that exposure to erotica causes sex crimes or bad moral character. Yet the Commission's ten volumes hardly settled the matter. Says Herbert Abelson, president of the Response Analysis Corporation in Princeton: "You can use studies to demonstrate whatever you want." Harvard Political Scientist James Q. Wilson argues that the National Commission on the Causes and Prevention of Violence decided television violence was dangerous, with as little real proof at hand as the obscenity commission had when it decided pornography was harmless. Says Wilson: "In the cases of violence and obscenity, it is unlikely that social science can either show harmful effects or prove there are no harmful effects."

SOURCE: "The Porno Plague," *Time*, 107 (April 5, 1976), pp. 62–63.

people, the picture could change considerably. In a sexually "up-tight" society such as our own, a norm that subtly forced couples into comarital sex could produce tremendous guilt and anxiety in at least some people. And the average American might not be able to control his or her jealousies as well as more liberated people can. If these jealousies were not controlled, the stability of the family and the socialization of children could be jeopardized—and comarital sex would be a true social problem.

Experts have speculated on the future of comarital sex. Some argue it is largely associated with the economic prosperity that until recently has characterized our country. Comarital sex may thus decline in popularity or disappear as our country faces more and more economic woes. Periods of economic recession and depression have typically been followed by periods of sexual repression.[50] Other experts estimate that, under optimal conditions, 15 to 25 percent of married couples may become involved in comarital sex.[51] If such an estimate proves correct, the changing American sexual scene could accurately be called revolutionary.

On Legislating Morality

Having developed social norms which limit sexual relations to the marriage bed, we have attempted to deal legalistically with deviancy from these norms.[52] As mentioned, all but seven states have laws which forbid homosexuality between consenting adults, and very few jurisdictions have legalized prostitution. The Supreme Court has devoted a great deal of time to the issue of pornography, attempting to formulate definitions of obscenity and searching for a valid legal basis for restricting the availability of pornography. What this means is that through our legal system we attempt to impose a narrow view of morality on everyone. Manifestations of human sexuality—other than the approved ways—are considered deviant and are repressed.

Most people would agree that there are times when we should control homosexuality, prostitution, and pornography. Laws regarding sexual behavior should protect the immature from sexual exploitation. In this context, the word *immature* includes not only young people but mentally ill, mentally retarded, alcoholic, and other persons who are incapable of making sound decisions about their sexual behavior. Perhaps an individual should have the right to have sexual relations with persons of his or her own sex or to enter into prostitution as an occupation—but only if he or she fully understands the nature and consequences of the decision to do so. Laws should also protect the innocent bystander from affronts to public decency. One of the paradoxes of our society is that we are willing to spend billions of dollars each year to see sexual behavior, deviant or straight, on the movie screen but most of us are not yet prepared to see the same thing free of charge in the city park.

Beyond these two instances, our laws against homosexuality, prostitution, and pornography may do more harm than good, and their rigid enforcement seems to have these drawbacks:

1. Our laws against homosexuality and prostitution lead to questionable law-enforcement practices. Plain-clothed police officers sometimes loiter around public rest rooms for hours in order to apprehend a tearoom queen. Similarly, homosexuals in some cities are subjected to constant police harrassment and they may in some areas be particularly likely targets for police brutality.[53] The same is essentially true for prostitutes. Do we really want a society in which the police enforce the law using dishonest tactics? Do we really need laws which cannot be enforced or are not enforced equally? (Only a small percentage of homosexuals or prostitutes are ever actually arrested.)

In March of 1977, the codirectors of the National Gay Task Force, Bruce Voeller and Jean O'Leary, met with an assistant to President Carter in the White House. At a later press conference, the two declared that their meeting demonstrated that the President's commitment to human rights extends to gay people.
◀

2. Our laws against homosexuality and prostitution help create deviant subcultures by forcing the homosexual or the prostitute to go underground. Here they have no social or legal protection and they are vulnerable to people who take advantage of them, including pimps, corrupt police officers, small-time robbers, and sadistic customers. Is this really better than allowing homosexuals to live their sex lives the way that we allow heterosexuals to live theirs? Is this really fairer than allowing the prostitute to conduct her business legally?

3. Finally, our laws constitute an attempt to legislate morality. Most of us probably do not personally approve of homosexuality or prostitution, but how do we know that they are inherently any worse than many of the things we do? We do not define smoking cigarettes, drinking liquor, or working ourselves to death as immoral or illegal, but each of these activities can harm the individual and sometimes society.

So perhaps, in an open, free, and democratic society, we should allow each person to choose his or her own sexual life-style as long as no harm or injury is done to other individuals.

Summary

American social norms traditionally confine sexual relations to husbands and wives, although in recent years the so-called sexual revolution has received widespread public attention. However, studies comparing past and present sexual practices in America reveal that most people conduct their sex lives today much as people did in the past. Two changes have occurred: premarital coitus rates among women have increased significantly in the last generation; and people are much more open and frank about sex than in the past.

Otherwise, our attitudes have changed little, and we continue to regard deviancy from the traditional norm very unfavorably. Nonetheless, an examination of some of the most visible forms of sexual deviancy fails to reveal a true social problem. Homosexuality involves too few men and women to be regarded as a threat to society; nor do prostitutes comprise a large enough group to jeopardize the family unit. Studies show no link between pornography and sex crimes; and comarital sex involves only a very small number of people, most of whom claim their marriages are enhanced—not endangered—by swinging.

Yet we continue to condemn certain sexual life-styles and even pass laws against them in an attempt to deal legalistically with deviancy. These laws have three drawbacks: they encourage questionable law-enforcement tactics; they help create deviant subcultures; and they constitute an attempt to legislate morality.

Perhaps our attitudes and laws do more harm than good, and we should recognize instead the individual's right to choose alternative expressions of sexuality.

Discussion Questions

1. Is sexual deviancy a *social problem* or a *social issue*? What is the difference between a social problem and a social issue?
2. Discuss and analyze American attitudes toward sex. Has there been a sexual revolution in the United States during recent years? Explain your answer fully.
3. Why do you think that Americans have traditionally had such negative attitudes toward homosexuality? Are these negative attitudes gradually changing? Will they change dramatically in the foreseeable future?
4. What is meant when we refer to *the subculture of prostitution*? What are some of the functions of the subculture of prostitution? How would you account for the existence of these subcultures?
5. Is the consumption of pornographic materials a threat to the individual and/or to society? What might be some of the consequences of making pornographic materials more readily available to the public?
6. During recent years swinging, or mate swapping, has been extensively investigated by sociologists and anthropologists. Yet, it is relatively rare. Why do you suppose that social scientists are so interested in doing extensive research on a phenomenon that involves only a fraction of 1 percent of married males and females?
7. What should our laws pertaining to sexual behavior be designed to do? What are some of the negative consequences of our laws against homosexuality, prostitution, and pornography?

Glossary

coming out Homosexual argot which refers to the point at which an individual attaches the label *homosexual* to himself or herself and begins to identify with a homosexual subculture.

homophile organizations Voluntary associations of homosexuals (and sometimes their heterosexual supporters) which seek to better the social and legal status of homosexuals.

homosexuality Erotic activity with a member of one's own sex. Human beings can be regarded as being on a continuum ranging from those who are exclusively heterosexual to those who are exclusively homosexual.

homosexual subculture A group of homosexuals who to some degree interact with one another, who share common norms, and who often share a specialized argot.

pornography Written or visual materials read or viewed primarily for the purpose of sexual arousal.

prostitution The selling of sexual favors for monetary gain. To the prostitute, prostitution is an occupation and source of income.

subculture of prostitution A network of social relationships which includes prostitutes, pimps, hotel operators, and so forth. The subculture of prostitution is often characterized by specialized norms and a specialized argot.

tearoom trade Fast, impersonal homosexual encounters in men's rest rooms.

Suggestions for Further Reading

Bell, Robert R., *Social Deviance: A Substantive Analysis,* rev. ed. (Homewood, Ill.: Dorsey, 1976). This basic textbook contains excellent chapters on premarital and extramarital sex, pornography, prostitution, and male and female homosexuality.

Bowers, Faubion, "Homosex: Living the Life," *Saturday Review* (February 12, 1972), pp. 23–28. An engrossing article which discusses the current status of homosexuality in America.

Edwards, John N., ed., *Sex and Society* (Chicago: Markham, 1972). An anthology of some of the most significant recent articles on social and cultural dimensions of human sexuality.

Gagnon, John H., and Bruce Henderson, *Human Sexuality: An Age of Ambiguity,* Social Issue Series No. 1 (Boston: Little, Brown, 1975). This book was produced by a noted authority on human sexuality and by a professional writer on the staff of *Time* magazine. As such, it "offers a view of human sexuality as a changing attribute in a culture that is itself undergoing widespread change."

Gagnon, John H., and William Simon, eds., *The Sexual Scene,* rev. 2nd ed. (New Brunswick, N.J.: Transaction, 1973). A collection of essays on various facets of the current sexual scene in America. All of the articles originally appeared in *Transaction.*

Goode, Erich, and Richard Troiden, eds., *Sexual Deviance and Sexual Deviants* (New York: Morrow, 1974). Probably the most complete and interesting collection of readings on sexual deviancy that is available today.

Hunt, Morton, *Sexual Behavior in the 1970s* (Chicago: Playboy, 1974). A highly praised and widely quoted book that contains a wealth of data on the contemporary sexual behavior of Americans.

Libby, Roger W., and Robert N. Whitehurst, *Marriage and Alternatives: Exploring Intimate Relationships* (Glenview, Ill.: Scott, Foresman, 1977). A fascinating collection of articles pertaining, for the most part, to sexuality within marriage. Most of these articles are of a decidedly liberal bent.

"The Porno Plague," *Time*, 107 (April 5, 1976), pp. 58–63. Although this article engages in some moralizing, it nonetheless provides a fairly good overview of pornography in America as of 1976.

Notes

[1]*Encyclopedia of Sociology* (Guilford, Conn.: Dushkin, 1974), p. 224.

[2]Some support is lent to this thesis by Ira L. Reiss. See Ira L. Reiss, "Consistency and Sexual Ethics," in Edwin M. Schur, ed., *The Family and the Sexual Revolution* (Bloomington, Ind.: Indiana, 1964), esp. pp. 90–91; and Ira L. Reiss, "How and Why America's Sex Standards Are Changing," *Transaction*, 5 (March, 1968), pp. 26–32.

[3]Morton Hunt, *Sexual Behavior in the 1970s* (Chicago: Playboy, 1974), p. 149.

[4]See Harold T. Christensen and Christina F. Gregg, "Changing Sex Norms in America and Scandinavia," *Journal of Marriage and the Family*, 32 (November, 1970), p. 621.

[5]For an interesting discussion of the problems involved in defining homosexuality see Erich Goode and Richard Troiden, eds., *Sexual Deviance and Sexual Deviants* (New York: Morrow, 1974), pp. 149–60.

[6]Apparently this idea was first suggested by Alfred C. Kinsey and his associates. See Alfred C. Kinsey et al., *Sexual Behavior in the Human Male* (Philadelphia: Saunders, 1948), pp. 636–55.

[7]The definitive study of tearoom trade was performed by Laud Humphreys. See Laud Humphreys, "Tearoom Trade: Impersonal Sex in Public Places," *Transaction*, 7 (January, 1970), pp. 10–25.

[8]*Ibid.*, p. 18.

[9]See Barry M. Dank, "The Homosexual," in Goode and Troiden, eds., *Sexual Deviance and Sexual Deviants*, pp. 187–88.

[10]Kinsey, *Sexual Behavior in the Human Male*, pp. 650–51.

[11]Hunt, *Sexual Behavior in the 1970s*, p. 310.

[12]Wardell B. Pomeroy, "Homosexuality," in Ralph A. Weltge, ed., *The Same Sex: An Appraisal of Homosexuality* (Philadelphia: United Church, 1969), p. 13.

[13]See Eva Bene, "On the Genesis of Male Homosexuality," in William A. Rushing, ed., *Deviant Behavior and Social Process* (Chicago: Rand McNally, 1969), p. 164.

[14]Edward Sagarin, "The Good Guys, the Bad Guys, and the Gay Guys," *Contemporary Sociology*, 2 (January, 1973), p. 10.

[15]Dank, "The Homosexual," p. 181.

[16]Robert R. Bell, *Social Deviance: A Substantive Analysis*, rev. ed. (Homewood, Ill.: Dorsey, 1976), p. 295.

[17]Edward Sagarin, *Odd Man In: Societies of Deviants in America* (New York: Watts, 1969), p. 87.

[18]Cited in John H. Gagnon and Bruce Henderson, *Human Sexuality: An Age of Ambiguity*, Social Issue Series No. 1 (Boston: Little, Brown, 1975), p. 55.

[19]Some significant discussions of lesbianism are contained in Denise M. Cronin, "Coming Out Among Lesbians," in Goode and Troiden, *Sexual Deviance and Sexual Deviants*, pp. 268–77; Charles H. McCagny and James K. Skipper, Jr., "Lesbian Behavior as an Adaptation to the Occupation of Stripping," *Social Problems*, 17 (Fall, 1969), pp. 262–70; and William Simon and John H. Gagnon, "Femininity in the Lesbian Community," *Social Problems*, 15 (Fall, 1967), pp. 212–21.

[20]Hunt, *Sexual Behavior in the 1970s*, p. 310.

[21]Bell, *Social Deviance*, pp. 308–33; Simon and Gagnon, "Femininity in the Lesbian Community," pp. 212–21.

[22]For a discussion of the problems involved in defining prostitution, see Goode and Troiden, eds., *Sexual Deviance and Sexual Deviants*, pp. 101–102.

[23]Charles Winick and Paul M. Kinsie, *The Lively Commerce: Prostitution in the United States* (Chicago: Quadrangle, 1971), p. 5.

[24]T. C. Esselyn, "Prostitution in the United States," *The Annals*, 376 (March, 1968), p. 127.

[25]The call girl has been extensively studied by Harold Greenwald. See Harold Greenwald, *The Elegant Prostitute: A Social and Psychoanalytic Study* (New York: Walker, 1970).

[26]At least one former corporation prostitute has told her story. See "The Corporation Prostitute," in Judson R. Landis, ed., *Current Perspectives on Social Problems*, 3rd Ed. (Belmont, Calif.: Wadsworth, 1973), pp. 27–32.

[27]See Gail Sheehy, "The Economics of Prostitution: Who Profits? Who Pays?" in Goode and Troiden, eds., *Sexual Deviance and Sexual Deviants*, pp. 110–23.

[28]See James H. Bryan, "Occupational Ideologies and Individual Attitudes of Call Girls," *Social Problems*, 13 (Spring, 1966), pp. 441–50.

[29]Bell, *Social Deviance*, p. 240.

[30]Sheehy, "The Economics of Prostitution," pp. 112–13.

[31]*Ibid.*, p. 114.

[32]Cited in Bell, *Social Deviance*, p. 237.

[33]*Ibid.*, p. 238.

[34]The discussion in this paragraph is based on ideas generated by Kingsley Davis. See Kingsley Davis, "The Sociology of Prostitution," *American Sociological Review*, 2 (October, 1937), pp. 746–55.

[35]Armand L. Mauss, *Social Problems as Social Movements* (Philadelphia: Lippincott, 1975), p. 368.

[36]*Ibid.*, p. 368.

[37]Goode and Troiden, eds., *Sexual Deviance and Sexual Deviants*, p. 60.

[38]*The Report of the Commission on Obscenity and Pornography* (Washington, D.C.: U.S. Government Printing Office, 1970), p. 24.

[39]*Ibid.*, p. 27.

[40]Ned Polsky, "On the Sociology of Pornography," in Alfred M. Mirande, ed., *The Age of Crisis: Deviance, Disorganization, and Societal Problems* (New York: Harper & Row, 1975), p. 350.

[41]Goode and Troiden, eds., *Sexual Deviance and Sexual Deviants*, p. 61.

[42]"The Porno Plague," *Time*, 107 (April 5, 1976), p. 58.

[43]See "When Pornography Curbs Are Lifted," *U.S. News & World Report*, LXIX (Oct. 19, 1970), p. 68.

[44]*The Report of the Commission on Obscenity and Pornography*, pp. 25, 178–82.

[45]See Charles A. Varni, "Contexts of Conversion: The Case of Swinging," in Roger W. Libby and Robert N. Whitehurst, eds., *Renovating Marriage: Toward New Sexual Life-Styles* (Danville, Calif.: Consensus, 1973), pp. 168–69.

[46]Charles Palson and Rebecca Palson,"Swinging in Wedlock," in Frank R. Scarpitti and Paul T. McFarlane, eds., *Deviance: Action, Reaction, Interaction* (Reading, Mass.: Addison-Wesley, 1975), p. 50.

[47]Varni, "Contexts of Conversion," p. 169.

[48]Hunt, *Sexual Behavior in the 1970s*, p. 272.

[49]Brian G. Gilmartin and Dave V. Kusisto, "Some Personal and Social Characteristics of Mate-Sharing Swingers," in Libby and Whitehurst, eds., *Renovating Marriage*, p. 156.

[50]Palson and Palson, "Swinging in Wedlock," p. 57.

[51]Cited in Gilmartin and Kusisto, "Some Personal and Social Characteristics of Mate-Sharing Swingers," p. 150.

[52]For a many-sided discussion of the legislation of sexual morality see Stephen D. Ford, *The American Legal System: Its Dynamics and Limits* (St. Paul, Minn.: West, 1970), pp. 638–82. Many of the ideas contained in this section are drawn from Edwin M. Schur, *Crimes Without Victims: Deviant Behavior and Public Policy* (Englewood Cliffs, N.J.: Prentice-Hall, 1965).

[53]Goode and Troiden, eds., *Sexual Deviance and Sexual Deviants*, p. 196.

Chapter 7

Juvenile Delinquency

What Is Juvenile Delinquency?
Extent of Juvenile Delinquency
Correlates of Juvenile Delinquency
Age
Sex
Race
Social Class
Social Institutions and Juvenile Delinquency
The Family
The School
Theories of Juvenile Delinquency
Nonsociological Theories
Sociological Theories
Culture
Social Disorganization
Middle-Class Delinquency
Labeling
Social Control
Traditional Approaches
Probation
Incarceration
Other Alternatives
Diversion
Society and Juvenile Delinquency: A Broader View
Summary

It probably wasn't too long ago that you hung out with your friends at the drugstore, pizza parlor, local school yard, shopping mall, or wherever was *the* place. And if parents and other adults thought of you as young hoodlums, that was cool. But you probably didn't really think of yourself as a hoodlum.

Yet juvenile delinquency is on the increase in middle-class suburban neighborhoods as well as inner-city slums. And it is increasing even though Americans are of the opinion that young people constitute our greatest resource. Not surprisingly, many communities and parents everywhere are badly shaken by the increase in delinquency and regard it as a major social problem.

Much juvenile delinquency is simply a reflection of adult values and norms; many adults abuse alcohol and drugs, wink at sexual promiscuity, and indulge in verbal and physical aggression. We shouldn't be surprised then when juveniles mimic these so-called adult patterns of behavior and get in trouble with the law. But we should remember that, for the most part, juvenile delinquency is a self-containing social problem, that is, for many young people it is simply a passing phase in their growth and development. Happily, most juvenile delinquents eventually mature into law-abiding adults.[1]

One of the most serious—perhaps tragic—aspects of juvenile delinquency in this country is that, despite national pride in our children, we very often fail to treat them with social and legal justice when they are in trouble. We shall consider these injustices and the other aspects of juvenile delinquency in this chapter.

What Is Juvenile Delinquency?

One definition states that "legally a juvenile delinquent is a youth who has been so adjudged by a juvenile court."[2] This definition, though hard to quibble with, leaves some questions: What behaviors could cause a court to judge a youth delinquent? What age must an offender be to be accorded juvenile status? While it is clearly up to state legislatures to define what behaviors are delinquent, no two do so in exactly the same way. An examination of various state juvenile codes, however, suggests that there are essentially three categories of delinquents.[3]

1. A child can be declared delinquent for committing an offense which would be a misdemeanor or a felony if committed by an adult. The child can also be declared delinquent for violating a penal ordinance of any subdivision of the state, such as a city or county. This category includes all offenses, from petty theft and shoplifting to armed robbery, rape, and murder.

2. A child can be declared delinquent for violating any state law which pertains specifically to juveniles. Every state has laws that require children to attend school until a certain age and that forbid young people from being truant from school, running away from home, smoking or drinking, patronizing bars, taking certain types of employment, and so forth.

3. Most state juvenile codes have a clause which says, in effect, that a child can be declared delinquent for engaging in any other pattern of behavior which could constitute a threat to his or her own health, welfare, or morals, or those of other people. This category includes such diverse behaviors as association with vicious and immoral people, incorrigibility, growing up in idleness and crime, engaging in immoral conduct or displaying sexual irregularities, loitering, or being beyond the control of parent or guardian.

The third category is obviously a catchall which allows police and juvenile authorities wide latitude in deciding who is delinquent and who is not. The purpose of such catchall clauses is to allow the juvenile court to reach children who have not violated a specific law but who nevertheless need court supervision and guidance. Unfortunately, however, this category is often so broadly and vaguely defined that the child cannot tell what is forbidden and what is not. A child can actually be taken into

Probably all children at some time commit acts forbidden by the juvenile codes of the states in which they live, but only a small percentage of these children ever come to the attention of the police.
▼

custody for appearing to have a bad attitude. In direct contrast, an adult can only be arrested for behavior specifically forbidden by law. Because only children can be arrested for committing them, the catchall offenses are often called *juvenile status offenses.*

The upper age limit used to distinguish the juvenile delinquent from the adult criminal varies from state to state. In most states, the juvenile court has jurisdiction over the child up to age 18, but in some states the age limit is set at 16, 17, or 21 years. In many states, a child can be bound over to the adult court for criminal prosecution if it is in the interest of the child or society to do so. In some states, the criminal court has exclusive jurisdiction over the child when the offense is extremely serious, such as murder.[4]

Extent of Juvenile Delinquency

It is impossible to determine the extent of juvenile delinquency. As already noted, the police and juvenile authorities have tremendous latitude in deciding who is labeled delinquent and who is not. Even within the same community, one officer may completely ignore a child loitering for no apparent reason around a bus depot; another officer might promptly take that child into custody. Thus, our statistics on juvenile delinquency are really a record of decisions made by law enforcement officials rather than a real record of youthful misbehavior.

Over 65 percent of all arrests for vandalism in 1975 involved juveniles —about 114,000 cases.
▼

Furthermore, our statistics on juvenile delinquency refer either to the number of children arrested or to the number of cases actually adjusted by the juvenile court.[5] However, only a small percentage of young people who come to the attention of the police are actually arrested, and in many cases the arrested child is not brought to the attention of the juvenile court. For example, a classic study of the juvenile bureau of a metropolitan police department found that of sixty-six cases dealt with by the bureau, only sixteen youths were actually arrested. The remainder were admonished and released, informally reprimanded, or cited and given an official reprimand.[6] Of the sixty-six youths involved, only the sixteen who were arrested would show up as statistics in the F.B.I. *Uniform Crime Reports.*

Probably the most serious problem with our statistics on juvenile delinquency is that not all children who engage in delinquent behavior are brought to the attention of official correctional agencies; in fact, probably all children at some time commit acts forbidden by the juvenile codes of the states in which they live. But only a small percentage of these children ever come to the attention of the police and other correctional agencies. Most delinquency is hidden delinquency.

Thus, our official statistics on juvenile delinquency are far from perfect. They can only hint at how serious a problem juvenile delinquency really is. In 1973, a total of 1,717,366 persons under

Runaway boards like the one below can be found in police stations throughout the country. In 1975 alone, parents reported 189,000 runaway children.
▼

age 18 were arrested in the United States, or about 26.4 percent of all the arrests that year.[7] The importance of this statistic is that, because of hidden delinquency, these arrests represent only a fraction of offenses actually committed.

The leading juvenile offenses according to police records include larceny, running away, burglary, breaking and entering, the violation of narcotics and drug laws, and disorderly conduct. Again, however, we must point out that this information can be misleading; because these are serious offenses, the youth who commits them is especially likely to be arrested. Thus, they are probably not typical of the kinds of offenses that most juveniles commit.

Correlates of Juvenile Delinquency

One of the goals of this chapter is to try to explain why some children become delinquent. Before we can attempt this kind of explanation, however, we need to know what kinds of children are most likely to run afoul of the law. Once we know the characteristics of those children most likely and least likely to be declared delinquent, we will be in a better position to offer sound explanations for juvenile delinquency.

Age

According to F.B.I. statistics, rates of arrest peak at age 16 and then taper off in both directions.[8] Other statistics show that the overall rate of arrests for persons of all ages in 1971 was 3,365.0 per 100,000 total population; for persons 15 to 17, the comparable rate was 9,410.4; and for persons 18 to 20, it was 8,549.6.[9] It seems likely that more crimes may be committed by persons age 16 than by persons of any other age.

Some sociologists have suggested that "the relationship between age and juvenile delinquency is more than a statistical association."[10] We all know that the role of the adolescent, and particularly the 16- and 17-year-old, is a difficult one in our society. For example, this is the age that most states allow young people to drop out of school. After dropping out, they often cannot find jobs. As a result, these young people have no money and nothing to do with their time. These conditions seem to be conducive to delinquent behavior.[11] In addition, young people age 15 to 18 are struggling to discover and establish their identities as adults; they have reached maturity in terms of material, social, and sexual wants. Yet, without money they cannot begin to fulfill these wants.

Social Problems and You

Juvenile Crime: Some Statistics and Case Histories

Between 1960 and 1973, according to the Federal Bureau of Investigation's Uniform Crime Reports, the number of "juveniles" arrested, for all types of offenses, increased by 144 percent. For "serious crimes," the increase was 116 percent.

Last year, 45 percent of all the serious crimes committed in this country were done by "juveniles"—youngsters under 18 years of age.

By "serious crimes," the FBI does not mean petty thievery or vandalism or "pot" smoking or other such offenses commonly associated with youth. It means such crimes as these: killing, forcible rape, robbery, aggravated assault, burglary by breaking and entering, auto theft or larceny of money or valuable property. . . .

Many of those arrested are not even yet into their teens. Last year, more than 30,000 "kids" aged 10 or younger were arrested and charged with "serious" crimes.

The total number of juveniles arrested in 1973 for all offenses reported by the FBI was 1,717,366—more than one fourth of the total for all age groups.

Youngsters under 18 accounted for 11 percent of all arrests for killings, 34 percent of those for armed or strong-armed robberies, 20 percent of those for rapes, 17 percent of those for aggravated assaults, 54 percent of those for burglaries, 56 percent of those for auto thefts and 48 percent of those for larceny thefts.

While the statistics themselves are disturbing, the case histories recorded on police blotters are even more alarming to officials as illustrating the kinds of crimes being committed by the youngsters of today.

In Falls Church, Va., a 17-year-old high-school student was charged with killing a 16-year-old schoolmate and neighbor by shooting him three times as they stood on their tree-lined street in a middle-class neighborhood of well-groomed lawns and tidy white frame houses. They had resumed an argument which had begun earlier at school. . . .

Three boys—13, 15, and 16 years old—were arrested in November in El Paso, Tex., for stealing more than $6,000 from suburban-area banks.

In Miami, two 13-year-olds and a 12-year-old were charged with first-degree murder after the death of one of three sleeping vagrants the boys allegedly doused with lighter fluid and set afire.

A 14-year-old boy in Chicago, expelled from school for disciplinary problems and transferred to a correctional school, allegedly returned to his old school "with two guns blazing," shot the principal to death and wounded the assistant principal and a teacher. . . .

In New York City's Bronx area, at least four elderly persons have died this fall from wounds suffered in brutal assaults by small groups of children and teen-agers. Police said that hundreds of elderly persons have been pummeled and knifed in similar robberies in New York.

In Los Angeles high schools, there is a gang called "The Crips"—short for Cripples—so named because its objective is to permanently cripple its victims. It has a female auxiliary called the "Crippettes" and the "Junior Crips" for elementary students. . . .

While the statistics are high, law-enforcement officers agree that they do not reflect in any way the total picture of youthful crime. There are many instances in which young people are handled informally by police or by social workers instead of being arrested or referred to court.

In addition to that, many juveniles who participate in crimes are not caught.

SOURCE: "All Kinds of Crime—Growing, Growing, Growing," *U.S. News & World Report*, (December 16, 1974), pp. 33–34.

Sex

The juvenile delinquent is more likely to be a boy than a girl. In 1973, 2,378 police departments reported arrests by sex to the F.B.I. Of the persons under age 18 who were arrested, 889,333 were males and 248,713 were females—a ratio of approximately 4 to 1.[12] However, between 1960 and 1973 the number of males arrested under age 18 increased 123.5 percent while the number of females arrested under age 18 increased 264.1 percent.[13] The crime rate among young females is increasing more than twice as rapidly as the crime rate among young males.

One reason for the narrowing gap between the number of male and female delinquents may be tied up with the feminist movement. More and more women, regardless of age, are beginning to assume more active and aggressive social roles. Law enforcement officials may also be less reluctant to arrest females now than in the past. At least two researchers have found that "the centuries-old tendency to protect the young female from arrest, confinement, and trial has apparently been modified: young women are no longer immune to arrest."[14]

Race

In 1973, blacks constituted 11.3 percent of the U.S. population.[15] Yet, of all persons under age 18 arrested that year, 23.3 percent were black; blacks under age 18 were involved in over one-half of all arrests for murder, forcible rape, and robbery which involved juveniles.[16] Likewise, black delinquents are heavily involved in gambling, prostitution, and commercialized vice.[17]

The reasons why young blacks are especially likely to engage in delinquent behavior are many and varied. Dropping out of school is quite common among young blacks, and it is even more difficult for them to find employment than for young whites. The young black is also more likely to be raised in an atmosphere of poverty and family instability. As we will see, these background conditions seem to be associated with high rates of juvenile delinquency.

Several other minority groups, for example, Mexican Americans, are also characterized by high rates of juvenile delinquency; although others, like Jews and Orientals, have extremely low rates.[18] However, since the number of young people who belong to these other racial and ethnic groups is relatively small, their impact on the overall rate of juvenile delinquency is not significant.

Social Class

Several studies suggest that rates of juvenile delinquency are increasing among middle-class youth.[19] Despite this more or less recent finding, there generally seems to be an inverse correlation between social class and rates of delinquency: lower-class youths are more likely to have trouble with the law than are middle- or upper-class youths. There are several reasons for this phenomenon. First, the correlation between social class and rates of delinquency may reflect a bias on the part of law enforcement officers. Some officers are more likely to arrest a lower-class youth for committing a relatively minor offense than a middle-class youth. Second, lower-class life-styles may be more conducive to juvenile delinquency; lower-class culture, for example, often puts emphasis on attributes such as fearlessness, bravery, daring, the ability to outsmart or con other people, freedom from authority, and independence.[20] Finally, lower-class youths tend to live in areas where rates of delinquency are high: "The low status boy has the greatest chance of becoming delinquent, although to be sure, his chances are only one in a hundred in [a] low delinquency area, while they are one in five in . . . high delinquency areas."[21]

Social Institutions and Juvenile Delinquency

We have seen that the youth most likely to be labeled delinquent is the 16- or 17-year-old nonwhite, lower-class male. Not surprisingly, there are two other important factors which can help determine the likelihood of a child's becoming delinquent—family life and school experience.

The Family

The question as to whether broken homes contribute to juvenile delinquency is difficult to answer. Although a disproportionate share of juvenile delinquents do come from homes broken by divorce, desertion, or death, the majority do not.[22] Most likely it is the *quality* of the child's family experiences that determines whether the child will become delinquent. A severely disorganized family life may well be conducive to juvenile delinquency. In families where the adults fight constantly, drink excessively, and are inconsistent in disciplining and in displaying affection, the child certainly has every reason to leave home and "hit the streets." With nothing to do, the child may meet others with the same problems, and the outcome may be delinquent behavior. Parents also have a profound impact upon whether children will succeed in school. If parents provide too little intellectual stimulation—either because they are ill-equipped themselves and do not know how or because their own difficulties in coping with life leave them too drained and exhausted to attend to their children's

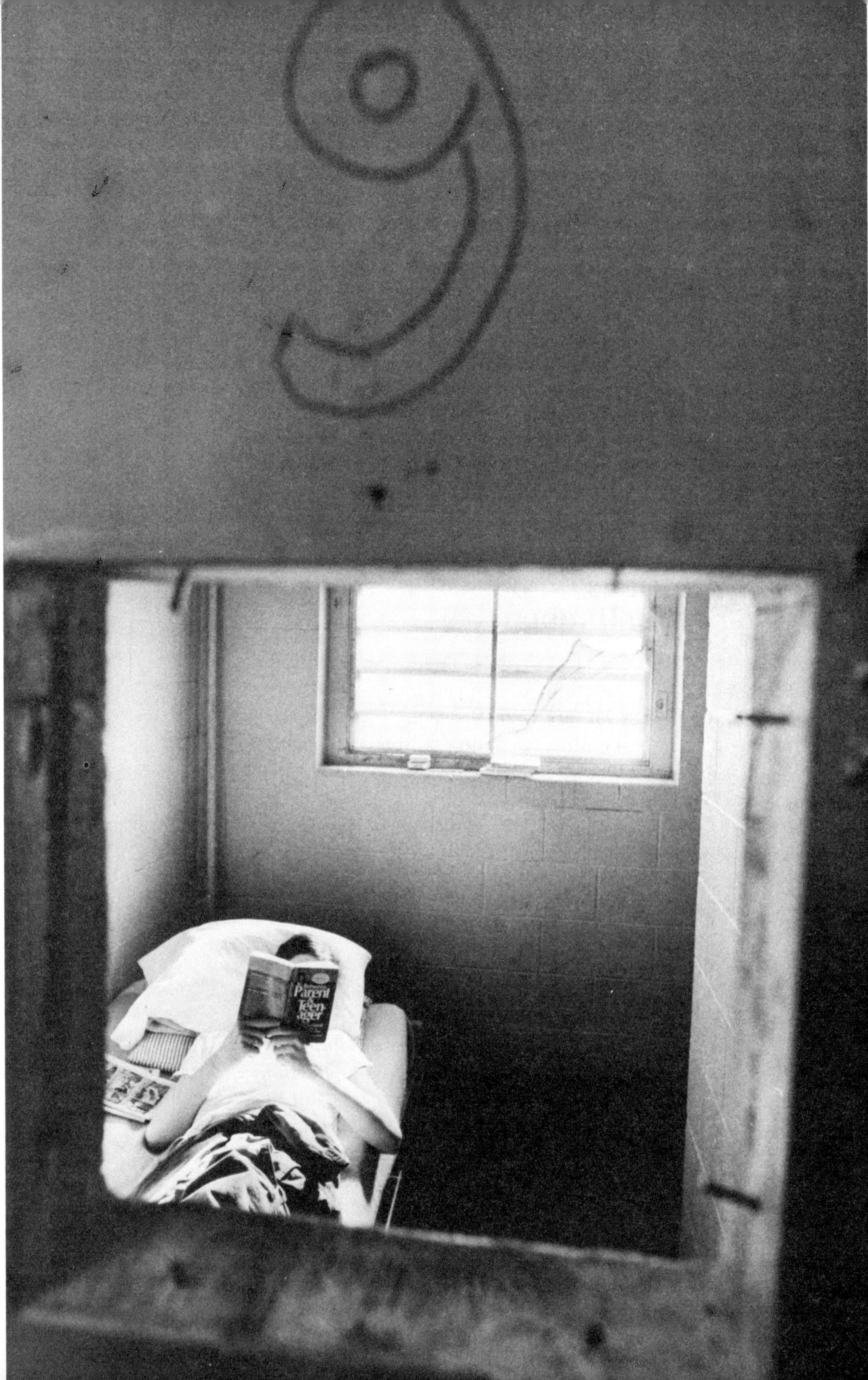
9
Parent
Teen-
ager

needs, problems, and aspirations—their children are more likely to fail in school.

The School

Failure in school seems to contribute to juvenile delinquency. One study revealed that approximately 61 percent of delinquents age 8 to 17 are not in school.[23] A comparison of a group of A and B students with a group of C and D students found that the latter are seven times more likely to be delinquent than the former.[24] Still another study found that the delinquency rate for dropouts is ten times higher than that for high-school graduates.[25]

The relationship between failure in school and juvenile delinquency is complex. First, it is not clear whether failure in school leads to juvenile delinquency or whether juvenile delinquency leads to failure in school. What is clear is that difficulties in school do seem likely to contribute to delinquent behavior. Social class is also a factor here because, as already mentioned, lower-class children are more likely to be declared delinquent than middle-class children, and lower-class children are more likely to have difficulties in school than their middle- or upper-class peers.

The lower-class child's difficulties in school may stem from lack of intellectual stimulation at home. Furthermore, the school he or she attends may well be inadequate. Schools in lower-class areas tend to be poorly staffed and overcrowded. Often, instruction at these schools is not geared to students' needs—the folktales, norms, and values of middle-class America have little relevance to the ghetto-raised child.

Failure in school seems to contribute to juvenile delinquency in three ways. First, children who continually experience failure in their school work begin to define themselves as inadequate, different, or deviant. These negative self-images are, of course, reenforced if teachers define them as "goof-offs" and if school officials assign them to special classes for slow learners, exclude them from meaningful extracurricular activities, and deny them access to coveted school tasks and responsibilities.[26] Second, an ever growing sense of failure makes it particularly important for these children to prove their self-worth in some other way. One way is to engage in illegal or forbidden activities—such as fighting, drag racing, sexual exploits, breaking and entering—which require a certain amount of bravery, toughness, and smartness. Third, if school experiences become frustrating enough, these children will simply drop out; as we have already seen, if they cannot find jobs, they are likely to drift into delinquent activities.

It is most likely the *quality* of the child's family experiences that determines whether the child will become delinquent. Perhaps this young inmate is trying to discover what was wrong with his family experiences as he reads the popular *Between Parent and Teenager* by Haim Ginott.

Theories of Juvenile Delinquency

We have just looked at several factors which may contribute to juvenile delinquency. Now we will turn our attention to explanations of juvenile delinquency developed by scholars in the field of delinquency theory and research.

Nonsociological Theories

Since it is always tempting to look for simple explanations of complex phenomena, some theorists have looked to biological factors for the causes of delinquency. For example, Cesare Lombroso, a nineteenth-century Italian medical doctor, concluded that criminals are by birth a distinct biological type characterized by physiological features such as a long lower jaw, scanty beard, and low sensitivity to pain.[27] According to Lombroso, these traits indicated that the criminal was a throwback to an earlier stage of human development and evolution.

In the '40s, American criminologist William H. Sheldon studied the relationship between body build and juvenile delinquency.[28] He concluded that people with mesomorphic body builds (muscular, athletic, and agile) would be especially likely, because of their energy and restlessness, to become great athletes, generals, or politicians. They would also be particularly likely to drift into delinquent activities. Several other studies conducted earlier in this century suggested that, on the whole, delinquents tend to be of lower intelligence than nondelinquents.[29]

Lombroso's and Sheldon's theories of juvenile delinquency have been thoroughly discredited. Many of the criminals observed by Lombroso were Sicilians who perhaps have some distinct physical features. But, more importantly, they grew up in a criminally oriented culture. In 1950 a careful replication of Sheldon's study found that the association between body build and juvenile delinquency is so slight as to be of little or no predictive value.[30] And as early as the '20s studies showed that any difference in the intelligence of delinquent and nondelinquent youths can be traced to the fact that the delinquent child is more likely than the nondelinquent child to have had inferior schooling.[31] In addition, intelligence tests have a built-in middle-class bias. We can reasonably conclude, then, that no meaningful relationship exists between intelligence and juvenile delinquency.

Juvenile delinquency has also been explained in Freudian terms. The Freudian psychologist would argue that a delinquent child has failed to develop an adequate ego (the individual's picture of physical and social reality, of which things are possible in the world as actually perceived), superego (the repository of an individual's values, including moral attitudes implanted by society), or both, and is thus unable to control impulses from the id (the primitive, unconscious part of the personality containing inherited urges and impulses; the id includes our aggressive and destructive tendencies, our sexual urges, and our desires for self-preservation). According to Freudian theory, the juvenile delinquent would not be able to control impulses from the id because of some fault in the socialization process, such as the failure to learn the difference between right and wrong.

Freudian theories of juvenile delinquency have many of the same limitations as biological theories of juvenile delinquency. In general terms, they suggest that all of us are, in effect, born criminals and that we only learn *not to be* criminals through socialization. Freudian theories do not take into account the real possibility that a person learns to be a delinquent. Furthermore, the theories tend to be circular, saying "in effect, we behave thus-and-so because of an instinct, and we know there is such an instinct because we behave thus-and-so."[32]

Modern psychodynamic theories of juvenile delinquency are considerably different from Freudian theories. Basically, they suggest that juvenile delinquency represents the child's attempt to cope with a problem—a problem he or she is not even aware of. These theories assume that "the delinquent act . . . does not mean what it seems to mean."[33] For example, juvenile delinquency might represent the child's subconscious desire to be caught and punished because he or she does not feel deserving of others' respect and esteem. The child, of course, does not recognize this subconscious desire as the motivating force in his or her behavior.

One study offers a succinct and pointed critique of modern psychodynamic theories of juvenile delinquency.[34] First, they are extremely difficult to prove or disprove. Trying to find hidden motives for behavior can become complicated because the person cannot tell us what the motives truly were. Do boys really steal cars because they are motivated by subconscious drives, or do they steal cars for thousands of other possible reasons? Second, modern psychodynamic theories of juvenile delinquency can also make the explanation of delinquent behavior too easy. All too often, the analyst simply finds some hidden or unresolved conflict and concludes that the cause of the child's behavior has been found. In reality, the purported cause-and-effect relationship is extremely difficult to demonstrate. Finally, psychodynamic theories of juvenile delinquency raise the old question of what causes what. While it is possible that a hidden and unresolved conflict could cause a youth to engage in delinquent activities, it is equally possible that the mere fact of being labeled a delinquent could bring years of hatred, hostility, and resentment to the surface. When we are under pressure, most of us say and do things we would not normally say or do.

Sociological Theories

Sociologists have developed many theories of juvenile delinquency, far more than we can explore in this chapter. Some have already been mentioned, and others will be explored in Chapter 8. But nearly all sociological theories of juvenile delinquency have one point in common—they view delinquency as a group phenomenon which must be examined against the background of American culture. The sociologist maintains that, to properly understand delinquent behavior, we must look at the groups and the cultural settings in which the individual delinquent functions. The causes of delinquent behavior are not to be found in the child's personal characteristics.

Culture

One group of sociological theorists emphasizes the role of culture in explaining juvenile delinquency. For example, Robert Merton has applied his anomie theory to juvenile delinquency.[35] According to this theory we set extremely high standards of material success for all our youth, but we deny the lower-class youth the opportunity to attain this success. Juvenile delinquency thus becomes an illegitimate means to a legitimate end. To oversimplify the case, the lower-class child who lacks the money to buy cars, tape decks, and other consumer goods simply steals them. Although Merton's theory seems to make sense at first glance, it does not explain all delinquent acts. Merton assumes that most delinquent acts are utilitarian, yet much, if not most, juvenile delinquency involves running away, fighting, sexual misconduct, and destruction of property. In practice, most juvenile delinquency is nonutilitarian—it does not represent a means for obtaining something wanted or needed.[36]

Albert K. Cohen also recognizes that we set extremely high standards for all our young people without regard to social class. We expect teenagers to be ambitious, to act responsibly, to develop skills and show signs of tangible achievement, and to control physical aggression and violence.[37] However, the lower-class child is less able to live up to these standards than the middle- or upper-class child. This creates tension and frustration in the lower-class child that must be alleviated in some way.

Cohen suggests that middle-class values and standards can be frustrating to the lower-class child only as long as the child accepts them. Once the child rejects them, they are no longer a source of tension and frustration. The lower-class youth who destroys our property and scorns our values is telling the world that middle-class values aren't worth pursuing. This way of coping with middle-class standards can best be understood in terms of a delinquent subculture because the youth still needs support and status. He or she gets them by becoming a loyal member of a delinquent subculture.[38]

Of all the analyses of delinquent subcultures, one of the most perceptive is that by Richard A. Cloward and Lloyd E. Ohlin.[39] They identify three types of delinquent subculture—the *criminal*, the *conflict*, and the *retreatist*. Which of these three the child drifts into depends on the social setting. "The criminal subculture is likely to arise in a neighborhood milieu characterized by close bonds between different age-levels of offender, and between criminal and conventional elements."[40] Conflict subcultures tend to appear in highly disorganized neighborhoods where young people have little opportunity to participate in either legitimate or illegitimate opportunity structures.[41] Retreatist subcultures, devoted to alcohol and drug abuse, appear in yet another type of social setting. Cloward and Ohlin share Merton's view that delinquent subcultures have their origin "in marked discrepancies between culturally induced aspirations among lower-class youth and the possibilities of achieving them by legitimate means."[42]

Social Disorganization

A second group of sociological theorists emphasizes social disorganization in explaining juvenile delinquency. Social disorganization theories are fundamentally different from cultural theories. The latter emphasize the conflict the child experiences between middle-class values and lower-class reality; they almost seem to say that the delinquent child takes middle-class values too seriously. In contrast, social disorganization theories suggest that, rather than taking middle-class norms and values too seriously, the delinquent child learns *no* consistent set of norms and values at all.

Social disorganization theories are based on the observation, documented in many cities, that rates of delinquency tend to be highest in areas that also have high rates of crime, mental illness, narcotics addiction, alcoholism, family instability, and so forth.[43] In such highly disorganized areas the child has little chance to identify with any consistent set of positive norms and values. While some parents may attempt to teach their children values such as honesty and sobriety, their children readily observe that few people live up to these values so why should they.

Middle-Class Delinquency

Most sociological theories of juvenile delinquency, including those discussed above, are principally concerned with delinquency among lower-class youth. However, many middle-class children become involved in delinquent activities, and sometimes their offenses are rather serious. For example, one study found that "it was middle-status boys, as contrasted with lower- and upper-status boys, who committed the most serious offenses, including forgery, breaking and entering, destroying property, and arson."[44]

Since theories of lower-class delinquency do not adequately account for middle-class delinquency, a different set of theories is needed to explain why some middle-class children became involved in juvenile delinquency. Sociologist Fred J. Shanley has succinctly summarized the many theories of middle-class delinquency.[45] According to Shanley, there are eight different dimensions of middle-class delinquency.

1. Several theorists think that middle-class delinquency stems from anxiety over sex-role identification. According to these theories, middle-class male delinquency is a form of " 'masculine protest' against the dominance of a mother who is the principal exemplar of morality, source of discipline and object of identification in the middle-class home."[46]

2. Middle-class delinquency has been explained in terms of the ambiguity of the adolescent's role in our society. The adolescent reaches physical maturity long before he or she is allowed to enter into sexual relationships, acquire adult possessions, and so forth. The failure of society to grant the adolescent adult prerogatives may thus induce frustration that can lead to delinquent behavior.

3. Middle-class delinquency has been attributed to feelings of status deprivation which may arise when adolescents are unable to achieve status because they lack skills or are defined by themselves and others as failures at conventional activities such as schoolwork or dating.

4. A number of theories attribute middle-class delinquency to our society's decreasing emphasis on deferred gratification ("work before play") and our increasing emphasis on hedonism, that is, the idea that pleasure and happiness should be the main goals of life.

5. Middle-class delinquency has been attributed to inadequate parent-child relationships. Because of inadequate childhood training, for example, the child may not learn to control his antisocial drives and impulses.

6. Some theorists link middle-class delinquency to ineffective performance in school coupled with compulsory school attendance laws. These laws lock children who perform poorly in school into frustrating roles and activities and, in effect, punish them for their inadequacies.

7. Middle-class delinquency has been tied to the influence of peer groups which, while providing acceptance and status, often embrace delinquent norms and values. For example, stealing, fighting, or sexual promiscuity might become the means by which the child gains status among his or her peers.

8. Middle-class delinquency has also been seen as "a type of irresponsible, temporary experimentation with deviant behavior which will terminate without serious consequence upon entry into adult status."[47]

Much of the debate about juvenile delinquency, particularly middle-class delinquency, has centered on whether it is a form of rebellion or whether it simply represents an extension of the values held widely throughout American society. Most of the theories that Shanley outlines reflect this debate and can be classified as either a rebellion against or an extension of American values.

Others have suggested that there is a subterranean value system in our society which stresses and approves such behavior as avoiding hard work, pursuing kicks and thrills, sexual promiscuity, heavy drinking, and playing it cool.[48] Very often, middle-class delinquents seem, in an exaggerated way, to be adopting these values.

Labeling

We have already used the labeling perspective to shed light on different problem behaviors, including mental illness, alcoholism, and narcotics addiction. Happily, the theory also sheds some light on juvenile delinquency.

Although labeling does not explain the underlying causes of delinquency, it does help explain why some children continue to engage in delinquent activities after society has tagged them delinquent.[49] Once a child realizes that he or she is labeled delinquent, the chances are greater that he or she will adopt delinquency as a social role, motivated perhaps to "live up to" the reputation. Having been labeled delinquent, the child is also more likely to begin to associate more and more with other delinquent children and less and less with nondelinquent children. This association, in turn, increases the likelihood that the child, partly because of peer group pressure, will engage in further delinquent acts. Finally, a child who is labeled delinquent is much more likely to come under surveillance by parents, school authorities, and the police. The child is thus likely to be apprehended again and again for delinquent activities. Each apprehension will reinforce the child's self-image as a "bad egg" who is different from and perhaps inferior to "good" kids.

Social Control

Since juvenile delinquency is such a widespread and persistent problem, we will now take a look at what we are doing about it. What happens to the juvenile who comes in contact with official correctional agencies? Do these agencies help the juvenile avoid further delinquencies? Do we punish or rehabilitate delinquents?

Traditional Approaches

Few young people are referred to the juvenile authorities by their parents or school officials. By and large, the delinquent child's first contact with official correctional agencies is with the police. The path of treatment and corrections leading from this first contact may lead no farther than the officer's car or as far as the state reformatory.[50]

In most jurisdictions the police are authorized to dispose of a juvenile delinquency case themselves if they see fit. An individual police officer or the juvenile division of the police department can counsel the child, reprimand the child, or place the child under police supervision without making a referral to the juvenile authorities.

Whether informal handling by the police helps deter children from further delinquencies is impossible to determine because no studies have been done along this line. It is possible that the police may have some correctional impact if the child's misbehavior is minor. If nothing else, informal handling by the police saves the child from the negative effects of being officially labeled delinquent. One point is certain—whether the police dispose of the case informally depends a great deal on the character of the child. The police are more likely to refer the older, nonwhite, lower-class youth to the juvenile authorities than the young, white, middle-class child. The youth who is polite and respectful in his interaction with the officer is more likely to get no farther than the officer's car, regardless of the seriousness of the offense.[51]

The officer who decides to take formal action against a child has two options. First, the child can be released to the custody of the parents pending action by the juvenile authorities. Second, the child can be taken before a judge or a magistrate who, in turn, can either release the child to parental custody or hold the child in detention pending further action.

Normally a child is placed in detention when there is reason to think that (1) the child will not voluntarily report to the juvenile authorities or appear at a court hearing; (2) the child, if released, would constitute a threat to himself or others; or (3) the child's parents are unavailable or are unable to provide supervision. Ideally, every juvenile court should have a detention facility completely separate from the adult jail; however, this is often not the case:

> Although model juvenile sentencing law states that no child shall be confined in an adult jail, a survey found that 93 percent of all juvenile court jurisdictions (in places comprising 44 percent of the nation's population) had no facilities except the county jail to confine children. Only Connecticut and Vermont and the government of Puerto Rico report never using jails. Nine states prohibit jailing of children but do not always observe the law, and in 19 other states the law does allow adult jails to be used if there is some separation of children from adults. In a 1970 census of the 3,919 jails in the USA, 95 percent were reported to have no educational facilities and 86 percent to have no exercise facilities. This practice is on the face of it a serious problem. . . . When juveniles are segregated from adults in a jail, they may be segregated from attention as well. Physical and sexual aggression from other minors and suicides have been reported.[52]

Detention is not jail; it is merely a step between the time the child is taken into custody and when he or she appears in juvenile court. It should be a short step. However, it is not unusual for a child to languish in detention for days or even weeks.

After detention, the next step is the juvenile court hearing. The purpose of the hearing is to determine whether the child is delinquent and, if so, to prescribe a program of treatment and rehabilitation. If the juvenile court judge finds the child delinquent, there are several alternatives.

Probation

Probation is not simply a form of leniency. The goal of probation is to help and rehabilitate juveniles while allowing them to remain at home and continue attending school. The probation officer can assist the child in making use of community resources and can advise, guide, and counsel the child.

Although one study reported that success rates for rehabilitating children placed on probation ranged between 60 and 90 percent, it is very possible that probation itself does not prevent further delinquencies.[53] The high success rates reported in the study may *not* be the direct result of probation officers' efforts. We should point out that probation officers carry very heavy case loads and frequently have little contact with each child. One major factor in the success rate of probation may be that the youth

placed on probation is likely to be less disturbed and less hardened than the youth sent to a reformatory. Another factor may be the simple fact that most juvenile delinquency is self-correcting—the child usually grows out of it whether or not official correctional agencies intervene.[54]

The juvenile court judge can order that the child be placed in a state correctional institution. These institutions vary tremendously from minimum security "forestry camps" to maximum security reformatories.

Incarceration

If probation is not feasible, the juvenile court judge can order that the child be placed in a state correctional institution. These institutions vary tremendously from minimum security "forestry camps" to maximum security reformatories. Whatever their nature, however, correctional institutions generally have very low success rates. It is difficult for a child to learn the norms and values of the law-abiding community when he or she is isolated from that community and incarcerated with other children who re-enforce his or her self-image as a delinquent. Not only will a child's nondelinquent norms and values deteriorate during incarceration, but his or her knowledge of delinquent behavior will very probably increase.

Compounding the problem is the fact that many correctional facilities—like lower-class schools—are poorly staffed, ill equipped, and overcrowded. In fairness, we must point out that these facilities carry a heavy burden; for the most part they receive hard-core delinquents who have not responded to other rehabilitative approaches such as reprimands and probation. But this argues for exceptionally good correctional facilities, not exceptionally bad ones.

Other Alternatives

A judge also has the option of reprimanding a child and sending him or her home, placing a child in a foster home, or making a child a ward of the court. Just how many cases fall into these categories is unclear, although the numbers are probably fairly low.

In summary, our traditional approaches to juvenile delinquency appear to have little impact on the problem. Most juvenile delinquents do not become adult criminals. Yet even where high success rates for rehabilitation occur, such as probation, we cannot attribute them directly to the work of the police and juvenile authorities.

Diversion

For the most part, local officials continue to take the traditional approaches to juvenile delinquency outlined above. However, there is a growing recognition that in many cases our methods of dealing with the young offender do more harm than good. As we have seen, the juvenile justice system re-enforces the child's self-image as delinquent and forces the predelinquent or delinquent child to associate with other delinquents. One critic puts it this way, "Not surprisingly, children whose delinquency has been minimal (or even nonexistent) prior to such an encounter with juvenile justice (and other delinquents), may learn behavior that proves of far more concern to police than the original problem."[55]

Some communities are now trying to divert juvenile offenders, particularly less hardened ones, into other, nontraditional treatment programs.[56] Children involved in such offenses as incorrigibility, truancy, running away from home, and sexual misconduct often do not benefit at all from the traditional juvenile justice system which puts heavy emphasis on punishment. For these children some communities now have youth service bureaus (staffed by police, probation, social-work, and mental-health personnel) which provide a variety of services for these children *and*

It is difficult for a child to learn the norms and values of the law-abiding community when he or she is isolated from that community and incarcerated with other children who re-enforce his or her self-image as a delinquent.
▼

their families, including counseling and job placement. The bureau also often serves as a referral service to put problem children into contact with other agencies equipped to deal with them and their needs.

This movement to divert children away from the traditional juvenile justice system is new, and few communities have fully developed their resources for dealing with youthful offenders. Despite its newness, however, diversion looks promising; it is an approach to rehabilitating juvenile delinquents without forcing them to associate with other delinquents and without burdening them with the label delinquent.

Society and Juvenile Delinquency: A Broader View

At the start of this chapter we stated that Americans regard children as our nation's greatest resource. We appear to take pride in our children and in how we treat them. However, the evidence we have just considered regarding our treatment of juvenile delinquents forces us to wonder just how well we really treat our children.

We have failed to create conditions that would give *all* children the chance to enjoy a healthy family life. While it is against the principles of a democratic society to regulate marriage so that only people with the potential to be truly fit parents are allowed to reproduce, we could take steps to eliminate many of the conditions conducive to juvenile delinquency, such as poverty, unemployment, and slum neighborhoods. We have also failed to create an educational system to meet the need of *all* young people. To many lower-class urban youths, going to school is a painful, humiliating experience; participation in a delinquent gang is much more meaningful. Surely we can revamp and revitalize our school system to meet these children's needs. And finally, we have failed to create a truly just system of juvenile justice. Not until 1967, for example, did the Supreme Court give children threatened with incarceration the right to a written notice of the charges against them, the right to counsel, the right to call and cross-examine witnesses, and other basic rights—rights that have always been extended to adults involved in criminal proceedings.[57] In addition, our juvenile probation offices are understaffed, our juvenile court judges are poorly trained, and our correctional institutions for young offenders are among the most inadequate treatment institutions in our country.

There is very little to be proud of in this record. Surely our nation's greatest resource deserves more.

Summary

Juvenile delinquency has traditionally been defined by the courts, although no two courts do so in the same way. It is impossible to accurately determine the extent of juvenile delinquency because (1) police and juvenile authorities have so much latitude in deciding who is to be labeled delinquent, (2) so few of the delinquents who come to the authorities' attention are actually arrested, and (3) so much delinquency is hidden.

The juvenile delinquent is most likely to be a 16- or 17-year-old nonwhite, lower-class male, although middle-class delinquency is a growing problem. The delinquent is also likely to come from a disorganized family and to have experienced failure in school.

Many theories of juvenile delinquency have been advanced, including simplistic, and now discredited, biological theories. Among some of the others, Freudian theories explain juvenile delinquency in terms of uncontrolled impulses from the id. Modern psychodynamic theories look for unresolved conflicts hidden in the child's subconscious.

Of the sociological explanations of delinquency, one group of theorists suggests that it is rooted in the conflict between high middle-class standards and the lower-class child's inability to live up to these standards. A second group of sociological theorists suggests that social disorganization can help explain juvenile delinquency; this group claims that the delinquent child never learns a consistent set of norms and values.

Most theories of middle-class delinquency characterize it as either an extension of or a rebellion against American values. Other theories suggest that middle-class delinquents incorporate a subterranean value system that accounts for their behavior.

Labeling theory is valuable in explaining not the underlying causes of delinquency but why some children continue to engage in delinquent activities.

Traditional approaches to the social control of juvenile delinquency—for example, probation and incarceration—seem largely ineffective. A new approach to dealing with young offenders is *diversion*. This approach looks promising in that delinquent children are neither forced to associate with other delinquent children nor are they labeled delinquent.

Discussion Questions

1. Most Americans believe that children are our nation's greatest resource. Given this fact, how can you account for the sometimes less than just and desirable ways that we treat many children when they get into trouble?

2. Go to your college library and examine your state's juvenile code. Have you ever engaged in behaviors that could have caused you to be declared delinquent? Do your state's definitions of juvenile delinquency seem to be too broad, too narrow, or about right?
3. Do the police and juvenile authorities have too much latitude in deciding who is delinquent and who is not? Explain and justify your answer.
4. What is meant by the statement that "our statistics on juvenile delinquency are really a record of decisions made by law enforcement officials rather than a record of youthful misbehavior"? To what extent do you think juvenile crime statistics *are* reliable?
5. How would you account for the fact that more crimes seem to be committed by persons aged 15 to 17 than by persons in any other age group? How would you account for the fact that the crime rate among young females is increasing more rapidly than the crime rate among young males?
6. Discuss the following statements: (*a*) Failure in school contributes to juvenile delinquency. (*b*) Juvenile delinquency contributes to failure in school. Do you agree with either, neither, or both of these statements? Why?
7. There has been much debate as to whether juvenile delinquency, and particularly middle-class delinquency, is a form of rebellion or whether it simply represents an extension of values held widely throughout society. Where do you stand in regard to this debate? Explain your answer fully.
8. What are some of the consequences of labeling a child *delinquent*? Common sense would seem to dictate that a child who is called *delinquent* or *bad* would be motivated to improve his or her behavior. Is this necessarily the case? Why or why not?
9. What is meant by *diversion* as a means of dealing with a juvenile offender? What are some of the advantages of diverting young people away from the traditional juvenile justice system? Are there any disadvantages to diversion?
10. Some people have claimed that our system of juvenile justice is not really a system of juvenile justice at all. Rather, they argue that it is a system of juvenile *in*justice. Is there any truth to this claim? Explain.

Glossary

anomie theory A theory of deviant behavior, including juvenile delinquency, which holds that deviant behavior results when there is a lack of socially approved means to achieve a socially approved goal. Anomie theory views juvenile delinquency as an illegitimate means to a legitimate end.

delinquent subculture A group of young people whose shared values and norms favor delinquent over nondelinquent patterns of behavior.

detention The holding of delinquent children in custody between the time that they are apprehended and the time that they appear in court or the case is disposed of in some other way.

diversion (of juvenile offenders) A treatment approach in which the young offender is placed in programs such as those offered by youth service bureaus, child guidance clinics, and so forth.

Freudian theory (of juvenile delinquency) A theory which holds that a delinquent child has failed to develop an adequate ego, superego, or both, and is thus unable to control inborn impulses and urges.

hidden delinquency Delinquent acts which are not brought to the attention of official correctional agencies. The term *hidden delinquency* reminds us that our statistics tell us only how many children get caught committing delinquent acts and not how many actually commit such acts.

juvenile delinquency Behavior on the part of persons under a certain age, usually 18, which is in violation of local, state, or federal law, or which could constitute a threat to the child's own health, welfare, or morals, or those of other people.

juvenile status offenses Offenses for which a child, but not an adult, can be taken into custody, for example, failure to attend school is a juvenile status offense.

probation Supervision of the delinquent child in the community in place of incarcerating the child in a state correctional facility.

psychodynamic theories (of juvenile delinquency) Theories that assume that delinquency represents a child's attempt to cope with a problem, a problem of which the child is not even aware. Psychodynamic theories assume that the delinquent act does not mean what it seems to mean.

subterranean value system A partially hidden value system in our society which stresses and approves behavior such as avoiding hard work, pursuing kicks and thrills, sexual promiscuity, heavy drinking, and playing it cool.

Suggestions for Further Reading

Haskell, Martin R., and Lewis Yablonsky, *Crime and Delinquency,* 2nd Ed. (Skokie, Ill.: Rand McNally, 1975). A good basic textbook on crime and delinquency. Of particular interest are Parts III, IV, and V which deal respectively with the concept of juvenile delinquency, the causes of crime and delinquency, and the treatment and control of crime and delinquency.

James, Howard, *Children in Trouble: A National Scandal* (New York: Pocket Books, 1971). A perceptive and readable indictment of our methods of dealing with children in trouble.

Lemert, Edwin M., "The Juvenile Court: Quest and Realities," in Carl A. Bersani, ed., *Crime and Delinquency: A Reader in Selected Areas* (New York: Macmillan, 1970), pp. 424–35. Lemert discusses the functions and philosophy of the juvenile court, and argues that, as a court of law, the juvenile court should deal only with those children who have committed serious offenses.

Lerman, Paul, ed., *Delinquency and Social Policy* (New York: Praeger, 1970). A wide-ranging and comprehensive anthology of readings on virtually every facet of juvenile delinquency.

Reed, John P., and Fuad Baali, eds., *Faces of Delinquency* (Englewood Cliffs, N.J.: Prentice-Hall, 1972). Probably the best collection of readings on juvenile delinquency that is available today. Contains forty-four articles, some of which are cited in this chapter.

Sheridan, William H., "Juveniles Who Commit Noncriminal Acts: Why Treat in a Correctional System?" in Simon Dinitz, Russell R. Dynes, and Alfred C. Clarke, eds., *Deviance: Studies in the Process of Stigmatization and Societal Reaction* (New York: Oxford, 1969), pp. 204–11. Sheridan argues that children who have committed noncriminal acts (for example, truancy, incorrigibility, and running away) should not be treated in correctional settings. He suggests some alternative strategies for dealing with these children.

Trojanowicz, Robert C., *Juvenile Delinquency: Concepts and Control* (Englewood Cliffs, N.J.: Prentice-Hall, 1973). A thorough treatment of the causes, prevention, treatment, and control of juvenile delinquency. The author draws on the perspectives of several different academic disciplines to analyze delinquency.

Notes

[1]See Sheldon Glueck and Eleanor Glueck, *Delinquents and Nondelinquents in Perspective* (Cambridge, Mass.: Harvard, 1968), esp. Ch. 14.

[2]Martin R. Haskell and Lewis Yablonsky, *Crime and Delinquency* (Skokie, Ill.: Rand McNally, 1970), p. 252.

[3]See John P. Reed and Fuad Baali, eds., *Faces of Delinquency* (Englewood Cliffs, N.J.: Prentice-Hall, 1972), pp. 5–11.

[4]See *Ibid.*, p. 8.

[5]Data on the number of children who are arrested are contained in the *F.B.I. Uniform Crime Reports.* The U. S. Children's Bureau, a branch of the Department of Health, Education, and Welfare, publishes data on the number of cases that are processed by the courts. For a discussion of the latter statistics, see *Ibid.*, pp. 40–41.

[6]Irving Piliavin and Scott Briar, "Police Encounters with Juveniles," *American Journal of Sociology*, 70 (September, 1964), p. 210.

[7]See F.B.I., *Crime in the United States: 1973* (Washington, D.C.: U.S. Government Printing Office, 1974), Table 31.

[8]*Ibid.*, Table 30.

[9]Edwin H. Sutherland and Donald R. Cressey, *Criminology*, 9th Ed. (Philadelphia: J. B. Lippincott Company, 1974), p. 123.

[10]Haskell and Yablonsky, *Crime and Delinquency*, p. 275.

[11]See Belton M. Fleisher, *The Economics of Delinquency* (New York: Quadrangle, 1966), pp. 83–84.

[12]F.B.I., *Crime in the United States*, Table 28.

[13]*Ibid.*

[14]Haskell and Yablonsky, *Crime and Delinquency*, p. 279.

[15]U.S. Bureau of the Census, *Statistical Abstract of the United States: 1975*, 96th Ed. (Washington, D.C.: U.S. Government Printing Office, 1975), Table 26.

[16]F.B.I., *Crime in the United States*, Table 34.

[17]*Ibid.*

[18]See Gwynn Nettler, *Explaining Crime* (New York: McGraw-Hill, 1974), pp. 122–23.

[19]For a review of these studies, see Fred J. Shanley, "Middle-Class Delinquency as a Social Problem," in Reed and Baali, eds., *Faces of Delinquency*, pp. 260–70.

[20]See Walter B. Miller, "Lower-Class Culture as a Generating Milieu of Gang Delinquency," in Reed and Baali, eds., *Faces of Delinquency*, pp. 228–36.

[21]Albert J. Reiss, Jr., and Albert Lewis Rhodes, "The Distribution of Juvenile Delinquency in the Social Class Structure," *American Sociological Review*, 26 (October, 1961), p. 727.

[22]See Thomas P. Monahan, "Family Status and the Delinquent Child: A Reappraisal and Some New Findings," *Social Forces*, 35 (January, 1957), pp. 250–58.

[23]Bernice Milburn Moore, "The Schools and the Problems of Juvenile Delinquency: Research Studies and Findings," *Crime and Delinquency*, 7 (July, 1961), p. 202.

[24]President's Commission on Law Enforcement and Administration of Justice, *The Challenge of Crime in a Free Society* (Washington, D.C.: U.S. Government Printing Office, 1967), p. 71.

[25]W. E. Schafer and Kenneth Polk, "Delinquency and the Schools," in *Task Force Report: Juvenile Delinquency and Youth Crime* (Washington, D.C.: U.S. Government Printing Office, 1967), p. 256.

[26]See President's Commission on Law Enforcement and Administration of Justice, *The Challenge of Crime in a Free Society*, p. 71.

[27]For a survey of the biological theories of juvenile delinquency, including that of Cesare Lombroso, see William McCord, "The Biological Basis of Juvenile Delinquency," in Joseph S. Roucek, ed., *Juvenile Delinquency* (New York: Philosophical Library, 1958), pp. 59–78.

[28]See William H. Sheldon, *The Varieties of Delinquent Youth* (New York: Harper & Row, 1949).

[29]See especially Henry H. Goddard, *Human Efficiency and Levels of Intelligence* (Princeton, N.J.: Princeton, 1920), pp. 73–74; and Henry H. Goddard, *Feeblemindedness: Its Causes and Consequences* (New York: Macmillan, 1912).

[30]See Sheldon Glueck and Eleanor Glueck, *Unraveling Juvenile Delinquency* (New York: Commonwealth Fund, 1950).

[31]See Carl Murchison, *Criminal Intelligence* (Worcester, Mass: Clark University Press, 1926).

[32]Albert K. Cohen and James F. Short, Jr., "A Survey of Delinquency Theories," in Reed and Baali, eds., *Faces of Delinquency*, p. 219.

[33]*Ibid.*

[34]*Ibid.*, pp. 220–21.

[35]Robert K. Merton, *Social Theory and Social Structure*, Rev. and Enlarged Ed. (New York: Free Press, 1957), esp. pp. 176–81.

[36]Cohen and Short, "A Survey of Delinquency Theories," p. 223.

[37]For a complete list of the values to which Cohen believes that we expect young people to aspire, see Albert K. Cohen, *Delinquent Boys: The Culture of the Gang* (New York: Free Press, 1955), pp. 88–93.

[38]*Ibid.*, esp. pp. 129–37.

[39]See Richard A. Cloward and Lloyd E. Ohlin, *Delinquency and Opportunity* (New York: Free Press, 1960).

[40]*Ibid.*, p. 171.

[41]*Ibid.*, p. 178.

[42]Haskell and Yablonsky, *Crime and Delinquency*, p. 379.

[43]For example, see Clifford R. Shaw and Henry McKay, *Juvenile Delinquency and Urban Areas* (Chicago: University of Chicago, 1942).

[44]Shanley, "Middle-Class Delinquency as a Social Problem," p. 261.

[45]*Ibid.*, esp. pp. 266–67.

[46]*Ibid.*, p. 266.

[47]*Ibid.*, p. 267.

[48]See David Matza and Gresham M. Sykes, "Juvenile Delinquency and Subterranean Values," *American Sociological Review*, 26 (October, 1961), pp. 712–19.

[49]See Robert W. Winslow and Virginia Winslow, *Deviant Reality: Alternative World Views* (Boston: Allyn & Bacon, 1974), pp. 28–29.

[50]For an account of the procedures involved in processing the juvenile offender, see Robert C. Trojanowicz, *Juvenile Delinquency: Concepts and Control* (Englewood Cliffs, N.J.: Prentice-Hall, 1973), pp. 158–85.

[51]Piliavin and Briar, "Police Encounters with Juveniles," pp. 206–14.

[52]Gene Kassebaum, *Delinquency and Social Policy* (Englewood Cliffs, N.J.: Prentice-Hall, 1973), p. 102.

[53]Cited in LaMar T. Empey, "Alternatives to Incarceration," in Paul Lerman, ed., *Delinquency and Social Policy* (New York: Praeger, 1970).

[54]Glueck and Glueck, *Delinquents and Nondelinquents in Perspective*, pp. 151–52.

[55]Alan R. Coffey, *Juvenile Justice as a System: Law Enforcement to Rehabilitation* (Englewood Cliffs, N.J.: Prentice-Hall, 1974), p. 52.

[56]There have been several good analyses of diversion as a correctional tool. For example, see Robert M. Carter, "The Diversion of Offenders," *Federal Probation*, 36 (December, 1972), pp. 31–36; and U.S. Department of Justice, *New Approaches to Diversion and Treatment of Juvenile Offenders* (Washington, D.C.: U.S. Government Printing Office, 1973).

[57]For an excellent discussion of the Gault decision see Alan Neigher, "The Gault Decision: Due Process and the Juvenile Courts," *Federal Probation*, 31 (December, 1967), pp. 8–18.

Chapter 8
Crime

What Is Crime?
How Much Crime?
Cost of Crime
Correlates of Crime
- Age
- Sex
- Race
- Social Class

Types of Crime
- Common Crime
- White-Collar Crime
- Terrorism
- Organized Crime

Causes of Crime
- Differential Association
- Containment Theory
- Social Reality of Crime

Crime and Punishment
- The Present
- The Future

Summary

In mid-1975 Seattle police apprehended a 31-year-old parking meter thief. Statistically, the man was a one-man crime wave, responsible for 15 percent of the city's 14,000 serious crimes reported from January through April 1975. And he may have single-handedly ripped off over 90 percent of the 2,300 Seattle parking meters stolen in that period.

While even crime has a lighter side, most of us agree that crime, or lawlessness, is among the most serious problems we face as a nation[1]—each year costing billions of dollars and thousands of lives.

But what is crime? Who commits it? Why? How big a problem is it? How are we coping with it? Crime is a big subject—there are many views of it and theories about it. Since we do not have the space here to say all that can be said, we will try, instead, to present a broad picture of crime as a social problem in the United States.

What Is Crime?

Crime has been defined as "any pattern of behavior for which the state may lawfully punish the individual."[2] In all societies individuals are expected to obey many rules. Some of these rules, or norms, are cast into law; and certain people in the society are given the right to judge and direct punishment of those who break the rules. In a primitive society, these judges may be the tribal chieftain or the council of elders. In modern, democratic societies, the courts alone usually have the right to judge the criminal and decide punishment. Among the punishments are exile, fine, imprisonment, death.

In the United States, there are two major types of crime—misdemeanors and felonies. Generally, a misdemeanor is any crime punishable by a fine or by imprisonment in a local jail. But we should point out that a criminal act classified as a felony in one state may be classified as a misdemeanor in another state, and vice versa. In most states, a person is sent to the state penitentiary only if his or her sentence exceeds one year. For all practical purposes, a misdemeanor is any crime which calls for confinement of one year or less; a felony carries a penalty of more than one year.

In all societies individuals are expected to obey many rules. Some of these rules, or norms, are cast into law; and certain people in the society are given the right to judge and direct punishment of those who break the rules.

How Much Crime?

We don't know how much crime really occurs in the United States since many crimes go unreported. The *Uniform Crime Reports*, published yearly by the F.B.I. and covering 90 to 95 percent of the

population, are the most comprehensive data source available.[3] But these data are only the tip of the iceberg.

The *Uniform Crime Reports* tabulate statistics on major crimes known by or reported to the police and the numbers of arrests made. The major crimes are murder, forcible rape, robbery, aggravated assault, burglary, larceny, and auto theft. For example, as shown in Table 8.1, over seven million crimes against property were reported in 1973. At a later point in this chapter, we shall see that many of these crimes were *not* cleared by the arrest of a suspect (see Figure 8.1 below). However, some major crimes are never discovered or reported, either because there are no witnesses or because the witnesses or victims fear reprisals, hesitate to become involved, or consider the crime unimportant. Thus we can safely assume that more major crimes occur than are reported to the police.

Less than 5 percent of the known crime in this country, however, involves the major, violent crimes of murder, forcible rape, robbery, and aggravated assault. Over 50 percent involves larceny, the violation of narcotic and drug laws, drunken driving, and disorderly conduct. Many of these crimes are listed, as in Table 8.1, under "Other Offenses," for which category the F.B.I. does not publish data on the numbers reported to police. One reason these data are not published is that the "Other Offenses" are frequently not reported or discovered.

Finally, we cannot always assume that a constant relationship exists between the true incidence of crime, which is unknown, and the number of arrests made. Clearly, given a new police chief, new methods of fighting crime, community pressure, and so forth, the number of arrests could increase while the true incidence of crime remained the same.

What, then, does Table 8.1 tell us about crime? First, it reveals the enormity of the crime problem in our country. Second, it shows the relative distribution of crime; the most publicized crimes are only a very small portion of all crimes committed. Most crimes today either involve some form of theft or are "victimless crimes" (see Chapter 6).

In sum, the *Uniform Crime Reports* constitute a very crude measure. They give us only the minimum statistics on the number of crimes that occur in the United States. We can only speculate on what lies below the tip of the crime iceberg.

Cost of Crime

The costs of even the known amount of crime are very difficult to estimate. For example, Table 8.2 presents estimates of the mone-

Table 8.1
Major Crimes Reported to the Police and Arrests for All Crimes, 1973 [a]

	Major Crimes Reported to Police	Number of Arrests for All Crimes	Percent of Total Arrests
TOTAL	**8,638,375**	**6,499,864**	**100.0**
Major Crimes:			
Murder and nonnegligent manslaughter	19,509	14,399	.2
Forcible rape	51,002	19,198	.3
Robbery	382,683	101,894	1.6
Aggravated assault	416,271	154,891	2.4
Violent crime[b]	**869,465**	**290,382**	**4.5**
Burglary—breaking and/or entering	2,540,907	316,272	4.9
Larceny—theft	4,304,363	644,190	9.9
Auto theft	923,640	118,380	1.8
Property crime[c]	**7,768,910**	**1,078,842**	**16.6**
Other Offenses:			
Manslaughter by negligence		2,996	(d)
Other assaults		275,105	4.2
Arson		11,096	.2
Forgery and counterfeiting		41,975	.6
Fraud		85,467	1.3
Embezzlement		5,612	.1
Stolen property; buying, receiving, possessing		70,238	1.1
Vandalism		121,011	1.9
Weapons; carrying, possessing, etc.		115,918	1.8
Prostitution and commercialized vice		45,308	.7
Sex offenses (except forcible rape and prostitution)		48,673	.7
Narcotic drug laws		484,242	7.5
Gambling		54,938	.8
Offenses against family and children		42,784	.7
Driving under the influence of alcohol		653,914	10.1
Liquor laws		183,813	2.8
Drunkenness		1,189,489	18.3
Disorderly conduct		461,553	7.1
Vagrancy		50,310	.8
All other offenses (except traffic)		848,835	13.1
Suspicion		40,927	.6
Curfew and loitering law violations		118,003	1.8
Runaways		178,433	2.7

[a]Data on major crimes reported to the police were collected from police agencies which, as of 1973, served 209,851,000 people. The data on number of arrests were collected from 6,004 police agencies serving an estimated population of 154,995,000. Thus the number of arrests made in 1973 would actually be higher than the number indicated on the table.

[b]Violent crimes include murder, forcible rape, robbery, and aggravated assault.

[c]Property crimes include burglary, larceny, and auto theft.

[d]Less than one-tenth of 1 percent.

SOURCE: Compiled from F.B.I., *Crime in the United States: 1973* (Washington, D.C.: U.S. Government Printing Office, 1974), Tables 1 and 32.

tary costs of the seven major crimes. Some of these figures are arbitrary. For example, how can we put a dollar value on human life? The F.B.I. sets the cost of a murder at $50,000, which, among other things, supposedly takes into account the income the victim could have earned during his or her lifetime.

The estimated cost of the crimes listed in Table 8.2 was over $4 billion. A 1967 estimate put the cost of all crime, including gambling, loansharking, and tax fraud, at about $15 billion.[4] If we add to these figures such indirect costs as law enforcement and the loss of productivity, crime becomes enormously expensive.

Table 8.2
Costs of Crimes, 1971

Crime	Total Offenses	Value per Offense in Dollars	Total Value in Dollars
Murder	17,630	50,000	881,500,000
Assault	364,600	3,000	1,093,800,000
Rape	41,890	3,000	125,670,000
Robbery	385,910	226	87,000,000
Burglary	2,368,400	312	739,000,000
Larceny, $50 and up	1,875,200	110	485,000,000
Auto theft	941,600	933	878,512,000
Total			**4,290,482,000**

SOURCE: Keith D. Harries, *The Geography of Crime and Justice* (New York: McGraw-Hill, 1974), p. 10.

Correlates of Crime

The tendency to commit crime is not spread evenly throughout our society. Some parts of the population have high crime rates; others do not. We must look closely, then, at the correlates of crime. What groups are most likely and what groups are least likely to commit crimes? Once we identify the groups most likely to commit crime (and what crimes they are likely to commit) we will be better able to examine theories about crime.

Age

Table 8.3 shows the striking relationship between youth and crime. The rates of arrest peak in the 15- to 20-year-old age group; both younger and older age groups have far fewer arrests. Persons age 50 and over are infrequently involved in major crimes of any type. Apparently young people are not only America's greatest resource, they are also its most active criminal element.

People under age 18 tend to commit certain types of crime. In

Table 8.3
Arrest Rates by Age Group, 1971

Rates per 100,000 population			
Age Groups	Arrest Rates for All Offenses (Excluding Traffic)	Arrest Rates for Willful Homicide, Forcible Rape, Robbery, Aggravated Assault	Arrest Rates for Larceny, Burglary, Motor Vehicle Theft
11 to 14	3,455.7	107.1	1,312.5
15 to 17	9,410.4	354.7	2,636.9
18 to 20	8,549.6	417.4	1,697.5
21 to 24	6,723.5	364.3	954.2
25 to 29	4,974.7	266.8	557.5
30 to 34	4,305.8	197.7	370.7
35 to 39	4,078.0	149.7	265.9
40 to 44	3,790.8	105.8	194.5
45 to 49	3,299.2	71.7	138.0
50 and over	1,457.9	24.5	59.7
Overall rate	3,365.0	131.9	541.6

SOURCE: Edwin H. Sutherland and Donald R. Cressey, *Criminology*, 9th Ed. (Philadelphia: Lippincott, 1974), p. 123.

Rates of arrest peak in the 15- to 20-year old age group.
▼

1973, for example, this group accounted for 57 percent of all arrests for auto theft, 54 percent of all arrests for burglary, and 48 percent of all arrests for larceny. On the other hand, the under-18 age group accounted for only 4 percent of all arrests for prostitution and commercialized vice, 3 percent of all arrests for drunkenness, and 4 percent of all arrests for fraud.[5]

Persons age 18 to 24 commit a large proportion of all narcotic and sex offenses. In 1973, this group accounted for about 41 percent of all arrests for forcible rape, 59 percent of all arrests for prostitution and commercialized vice, and 54 percent of all arrests for violation of narcotics laws.[6]

Sex

Men are much more likely to break the law than women. In 1973, approximately 5.5 million males were arrested compared with slightly under 1 million females.[7] Indeed, "if an investigator were asked to use a single trait to predict which persons in a town of 10,000 population would become criminals, he would make the fewest mistakes if he simply chose sex status and predicted criminality for the males and noncriminality for the females."[8]

Perhaps this difference can, in part, be traced to the different ways we expect males and females to behave in our society. Traditionally, females are taught not to be violent, not to take their anger out on other people, not to own and use guns. On the other hand, aggressiveness and violence have been traditionally defined as desirable traits for males.

But there is some recent evidence that sex differences in arrest rates may narrow as role expectations and the socialization of women change.[9] As Table 8.4 shows, between 1960 and 1973 the arrest rates for women increased more rapidly than those for men in most categories of crime. Overall, during this thirteen-year period the total number of arrests involving males increased 28 percent while the total number of arrests involving females rose 95 percent.[10] Even so, the number of men arrested still far exceeds the number of women arrested in all crime categories except prostitution and commercialized vice.

It would probably be naive to conclude that the dramatic increase in the number of females arrested is due entirely to the women's changing role expectations. The number of crimes committed by women may have increased dramatically for other—perhaps economic—reasons. It is always possible that the police may simply have become more diligent in tracking down and arresting women suspected of crime. There are many possible reasons for the dramatic increase.

Race

As Table 8.5 shows, blacks are far more likely to be arrested than whites. While they total only about 11 percent of the U.S. popula-

Table 8.4

Arrests by Sex for Selected Crimes, 1973, and Percent Change in Number Arrested, 1960–1973[a]

	Males		Females	
	Number Arrested 1973	Percent Change 1960–73	Number Arrested 1973	Percent Change 1960–73
Major Crimes:				
Murder and nonnegligent manslaughter	12,223	+140.6	2,176	+102.7
Forcible rape	19,198	+101.6	—	—
Robbery	94,998	+160.1	6,896	+286.6
Aggravated assault	134,381	+115.8	20,510	+106.3
Burglary—breaking and/or entering	299,286	+76.4	16,986	+193.3
Larceny-theft	441,075	+83.7	203,115	+341.1
Auto theft	111,324	+58.6	7,056	+155.4
Other Offenses:				
Forgery and counterfeiting	30,769	+15.3	11,206	+116.8
Fraud and embezzlement	91,079	+49.6	62,999	+281.3
Stolen property; buying, receiving, possessing	63,171	+416.8	7,067	+526.0
Weapons; carrying, possessing, etc.	106,651	+170.2	9,267	+304.0
Prostitution and commercialized vice	11,082	+49.9	34,226	+72.0
Sex offenses (except forcible rape and prostitution)	44,873	−1.8	3,800	−55.2
Narcotic drug laws	414,174	+995.1	70,068	+1,026.6
Gambling	50,153	−58.3	4,785	−59.3
Offenses against family and children	38,855	−34.2	3,929	−18.8
Driving under the influence	606,560	+185.8	47,354	+254.3
Liquor laws	156,223	+32.0	27,590	+45.3
Drunkenness	1,103,181	−30.3	86,308	−39.9
Disorderly conduct	379,407	−18.5	82,146	+22.7
Vagrancy	33,113	−78.3	17,197	+43.7

[a]Data on the number of persons arrested in 1973 are based on statistics collected from 6,004 police agencies throughout the country. The percent change in the arrest rate is based on data reported to the FBI by 2,378 police agencies.

SOURCE: Adapted from F.B.I., *Crime in the United States: 1973* (Washington, D.C.: U.S. Government Printing Office, 1974), Tables 28, 32.

Between 1960 and 1973 ▶ the arrest rates for women increased more rapidly than those for men in most categories of crime.

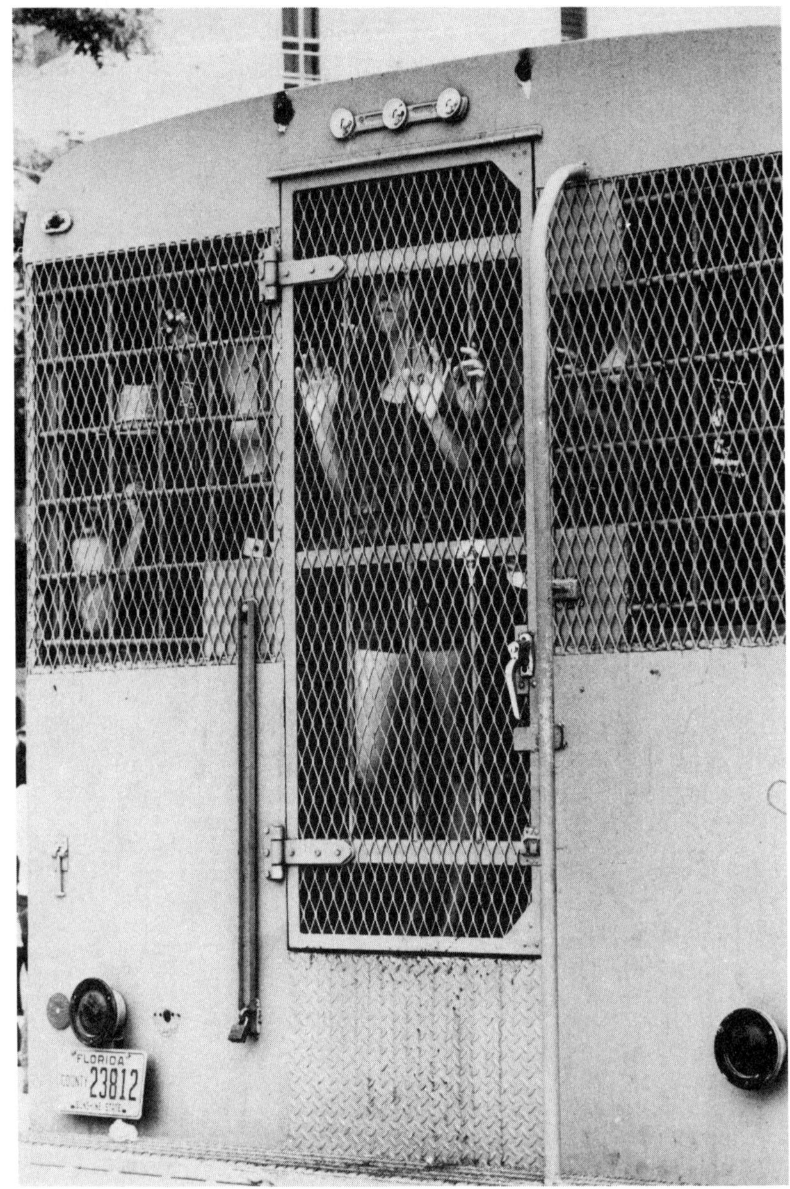

tion, blacks account for over 60 percent of all arrests for robbery and about 70 percent of all arrests for gambling. Table 8.5 shows that they are also overrepresented for aggravated assault, carrying and possessing weapons, and prostitution and commercialized vice.

On the other hand, blacks are only slightly overrepresented, if at all, in arrests involving the violation of liquor laws, drunkenness, and drunken driving. Other nonwhite Americans make a negligi-

Table 8.5
Total Arrests by Race, 1973

Offense	Total Arrests							Percent Distribution[a]						
	Total	White	Black	Indian	Chinese	Japanese	All others	Total	White	Black	Indian	Chinese	Japanese	All others
TOTAL	6,248,286	4,458,567	1,636,237	110,433	3,049	2,134	37,866	100.0	71.4	26.2	1.8	(b)	(b)	0.6
Criminal homicide:														
(a) Murder and nonnegligent manslaughter	12,913	5,236	7,478	118	18	3	60	100.0	40.5	57.9	.9	.1		.5
(b) Manslaughter by negligence	2,852	2,095	658	21		2	76	100.0	73.5	23.1	.7		.1	2.7
Forcible rape	17,178	8,832	8,022	189	5	2	128	100.0	51.4	46.7	1.1			.7
Robbery	83,953	29,688	53,206	607	57	21	374	100.0	35.4	63.4	.7	.1		.4
Aggravated assault	137,427	74,785	60,294	1,298	109	24	917	100.0	54.4	43.9	.9	.1		.7
Burglary—breaking or entering	297,286	203,086	90,221	2,264	118	82	1,515	100.0	68.3	30.3	.8			.5
Larceny—theft	625,719	425,920	190,495	4,912	701	398	3,293	100.0	68.1	30.4	.8	.1	.1	.5
Auto theft	106,829	70,114	34,504	1,381	53	33	744	100.0	65.6	32.3	1.3			.7
Violent crime[c]	251,471	118,541	129,000	2,212	189	50	1,479	100.0	47.1	51.3	.9	.1		.6
Property crime[d]	1,029,834	699,120	315,220	8,557	872	513	5,552	100.0	67.9	30.6	.8	.1		.5
Subtotal for above offenses	1,284,157	819,756	444,878	10,790	1,061	565	7,107	100.0	63.8	34.6	.8	.1		.6
Other assaults	260,748	162,863	93,846	2,621	103	59	1,256	100.0	62.5	36.0	1.0			.5
Arson	10,423	7,961	2,366	48	4	5	39	100.0	76.4	22.7	.5			.4
Forgery and counterfeiting	39,053	25,998	12,637	252	17	13	136	100.0	66.6	32.4	.6			.3
Fraud	82,499	59,267	22,605	400	32	7	188	100.0	71.8	27.4	.5			.2
Embezzlement	5,087	3,946	1,106	18	4	3	10	100.0	77.6	21.7	.4	.1	.1	.2
Stolen property; buying, receiving, possessing	64,393	40,334	23,376	286	29	18	350	100.0	62.6	36.3	.4			.5
Vandalism	116,165	95,492	19,208	857	38	35	535	100.0	82.2	16.5	.7			.5
Weapons; carrying, possessing, etc	106,135	52,914	51,867	612	55	29	658	100.0	49.9	48.9	.6	.1		.6
Prostitution and commercialized vice	41,928	16,894	24,651	149	33	24	177	100.0	40.3	58.8	.4	.1	.1	.4
Sex offenses (except forcible rape and prostitution)	45,951	34,963	10,367	310	59	20	232	100.0	76.1	22.6	.7	.1		.5
Narcotic drug laws	463,443	373,861	85,826	1,610	211	266	1,669	100.0	80.7	18.5	.3		.1	.4
Gambling	52,880	15,516	36,856	39	112	65	292	100.0	29.3	69.7	.1	.2	.1	.6
Offenses against family and children	42,045	29,956	11,625	271	6	11	176	100.0	71.2	27.6	.6			.4
Driving under the influence	641,038	521,495	101,212	8,444	220	367	9,300	100.0	81.4	15.8	1.3		.1	1.5
Liquor laws	181,405	156,232	19,977	4,114	42	45	995	100.0	86.1	11.0	2.3			.5
Drunkenness	1,178,605	866,739	245,737	59,934	434	159	5,602	100.0	73.5	20.8	5.1			.5
Disorderly conduct	432,418	299,413	124,684	6,397	121	54	1,749	100.0	69.2	28.8	1.5			.4
Vagrancy	35,654	23,098	11,210	907	96	11	332	100.0	64.8	31.4	2.5	.3		.9
All other offenses (except traffic)	829,056	588,548	225,415	8,888	272	227	5,706	100.0	71.0	27.2	1.1			.7
Suspicion	40,242	26,177	13,626	286	4	12	137	100.0	65.0	33.9	.7			.3
Curfew and loitering law violations	117,640	80,794	35,239	1,118	34	47	408	100.0	68.7	30.0	1.0			.3
Runaways	177,321	156,350	17,923	2,082	62	92	812	100.0	88.2	10.1	1.2		.1	.5

[a]Because of rounding, the percentages may not add to total.
[b]Less than one-tenth of 1 percent.
[c]Violent crimes include murder, forcible rape, robbery, and aggravated assault.
[d]Property crimes include burglary, larceny, and auto theft.
SOURCE: F.B.I., *Crime in the United States: 1973* (Washington, D.C.: U.S. Government Printing Office, 1974), p. 133.

ble statistical contribution to our overall crime rate, perhaps because they are a small percentage of the total population.

Two factors may help explain the association between race and criminality. The first may be prejudicial treatment in the administration of the law. There is fairly convincing evidence that black Americans fare less well with law enforcement agencies and the entire legal system than white Americans.[11] Second, the resident of an urban slum, regardless of race, is more likely to be exposed to a subculture that teaches, rewards, and encourages criminality than the person who lives in a middle-class environment. In any case, race by itself is no cause of crime.

Social Class

Statistically, lower-class persons appear more likely to commit crimes than middle- or upper-class persons. Several studies over the past thirty-five years report a relation between socioeconomic status and rates of arrest. For example, a now classic 1940 study showed that members of the lower-lower class made up only 25 percent of the population of an eastern city (Newburyport, Massachusetts) but accounted for 65 percent of the arrests there.[12] However, research findings relating social class and rates of crime must be interpreted with caution.

The types of crime that lower-class persons tend to commit—burglary, larceny, robbery, and assault—are more likely to be reported to the police than the types of crimes committed by middle- and upper-class persons. The lower-class person is also more likely to be apprehended and convicted. Upper-class criminals are rarely caught; and when they are, they are rarely punished with severity. If an association exists between poverty and crime, it is probably because the poor live in neighborhoods where there is a greater chance of learning about crime, of committing crime, and of getting caught.

Types of Crime

There is great diversity in types of crime and criminal behavior. The term *crime* is a broad one which includes, among other things, the common burglary, the major income-tax swindle, and an international narcotics operation. There is also great diversity in the people who commit different types of crime. We must work, then, to develop a sociologically meaningful classification of types of criminal behavior.

Common Crime

Common crimes range from petty theft and shoplifting to armed robbery and rape. These offenses are committed by widely different types of people—the occasional criminal, the habitual or professional criminal, and the violent criminal. Some behavior which offends the public's sense of propriety or morals is also classified as criminal.

The *occasional criminal* does not make a life of crime but is not above stealing or committing other offenses from time to time. Apparently, many Americans engage in occasional shoplifting or stealing from their employers. In a study of 1,020 adult males and 678 adult females conducted in the 1940s, 91 percent had committed one or more offenses for which they could have been jailed *had they been caught and convicted.* Overall, the men averaged eighteen offenses and the women eleven.[13] It should be remembered that these findings were obtained from a cross section of people considered law-abiding.

In 1973, shoplifters hauled off $5.6 billion in merchandise.[14] A large part of this merchandise was probably taken by people who were otherwise noncriminal. Similarly, in the same year, approximately 121,000 arrests were made for vandalism. Since hardened criminals do not waste their time breaking windows in school buildings, shooting holes in stop signs, and carving their initials on park tables, most of these crimes were probably committed by people who do not even think of themselves as criminals.

The *habitual criminal* more or less makes a career of burglary, robbery, or other offenses for monetary gain. Many are paroled from prison, only to be returned again later on the same or a similar offense. Others manage to pursue their criminal careers for years without interference from the law. In fact, a suspect is arrested in only about 21 percent of all serious crimes, and only about 5 percent of all serious crimes result in conviction.[15]

Violent criminals commit crimes such as murder or rape—but not the kinds that television melodramas, so often set in dark alleys, have stereotyped for us. In reality, most murders occur in the home; and, in about half the cases, the murderer and his or her victim are close friends or relatives.[16] Furthermore, most murders seem to be accidents—a quarrel starts and before the perpetrator knows it, a friend, relative, or spouse is fatally injured. In over half the murder cases, both murderer and victim have been drinking.[17]

Rape cases are somewhat more complex, but most do not involve extreme violence beyond the rape itself. In almost half of all rape cases, the victim and perpetrator are acquainted, in some instances intimately acquainted. Furthermore, most rapes are planned.[18] The traditional stereotype of the crazed man beating, raping, and perhaps even killing a totally unsuspecting woman does not, in most cases, correspond with reality.

Criminals without victims engage in a pattern of behavior

which is repugnant to the general public but which, in reality, does not irreversibly harm either themselves or other people. In short, the criminal without a victim is defined by society's notions of how the average person should behave. Criminals without victims include the prostitute, the homosexual, the public drunk, the exhibitionist, and those who from time to time engage in sexual or other types of behavior which violate the letter of the law.

White-Collar Crime

Crimes committed by members of the middle and upper classes in the course of their business and professional activities are termed *white-collar crime.* For example, violating antitrust laws, receiving kickbacks, embezzling, false advertising, selling fraudulent securities, accepting bribes, violating clean air laws, and evading income taxes are all white-collar crimes.

Particularly disturbing is the white-collar crime that some politicians and government officials commit in the course of their careers—like the crimes connected with the Watergate scandal.[19] But despite the political crimes that occur at national, state, and local levels, the average level of honesty among government officials is probably as high as or higher than that of the average citizen. One must remember that government officials often find themselves in positions that afford them great opportunity to grab money or power illegally.

Except for the political variety, white-collar crime is not usually highly publicized. Yet its social and economic costs are high. For example, over a forty-five-year period, seventy of this country's largest corporations were found guilty of approximately one thousand violations involving restraint of trade; infringements of patents, trademarks, and copyrights; unfair labor practices; misrepresentation in advertising; and others.[20] Similarly, "one chain of stores has about five hundred burglaries and robberies a year, with a total loss of about $100,000 a year. The same chain had one embezzlement which caused a loss of more than $600,000."[21] In 1974 the costs of white-collar crime to its victims were estimated to be over $40 billion a year, and this figure does not reflect price-fixing and industrial spying.[22]

Despite the high incidence and cost of white-collar crime, the criminals are rarely caught. If they are caught, they are rarely punished severely. There are several reasons for this. First, in much business, professional, and political activity, white-collar crime tends to become prevailing practice. Kickbacks, bribes, and extortion may be a regular part of the routine workday. As a result, neither the specific people involved nor the general public

Social Problems and You

A Case Study of Consumer Fraud

The phrase "white-collar crime" suggests paneled boardrooms, manicured nails, and expensively dressed executives making millions through canny stock manipulations or embezzlement.

The fact is that most economic crime is much grubbier and closer to everyday life. Repair fraud, shortweighting in food stores, product misrepresentation, and similar incidents are so common that people often don't realize they've been taken. Or if they do, they figure the money lost isn't worth the hassle to get it back.

Sociologists Diane Vaughan and Giovanna Carlo studied one case of repair fraud in detail to learn what they could about the white-collar criminal and his victims. Ohio appliance repairman Bill Jones (a pseudonym) was indicted by the county prosecutor's office on four counts of larceny by trick, a felony under an Ohio statute that covers consumer fraud. . . .

Jones would ask for money before making any repairs, saying it was needed to buy parts. According to the complaints, he overcharged for parts, sometimes charged for new parts when he installed used ones, and occasionally took a deposit or removed a part and was never heard from again. Many complaints said the used appliances he sold didn't work, and that he didn't honor his guarantees. . . .

By [interviewing Jones's] victims, as well as a similar number of other people living in the same neighborhoods, the researchers hunted for social, economic or personality differences between victims and nonvictims. . . .

When Vaughan and Carlo analyzed their interviews, they uncovered no real social, economic or personality differences between the victims and nonvictims. . . .

There were good reasons for these similarities, as the researchers found when they compared what victims and nonvictims reported about their experience with consumer fraud and street crimes. Forty-three percent of Jones's victims said they had suffered consumer fraud earlier—but so did 42 percent of the nonvictims. Similarly, 32 percent of the victims and 31 percent of the nonvictims had had experience with street crime. It appears that we are all vulnerable to a rip-off. The difference between Jones's victims and the rest was a matter of chance rather than personality, character, social class or some other clear difference. In view of this, Vaughan and Carlo combined the two groups to see what they could learn about victims who reported consumer fraud and those who didn't. . . .

When individuals were asked why they didn't report frauds, their answers generally fell into four categories. The most common (39 percent) was the belief that complaining wouldn't do any good. Individuals felt that they'd have trouble proving their case, that they didn't have money to hire a lawyer, or that nothing would be done anyway. Twenty-eight percent didn't report the fraud for personal reasons. . . .

Twenty-two percent said they didn't know why they failed to take action—a nonanswer that the researchers believe reflects a general public apathy about consumer fraud.

Consumer fraud affects nearly everyone. One reason for this mass vulnerability is a general lack of technological knowledge. In a time of specialization and technological advance, we are forced to trust strangers to meet our needs, a trust that is easily abused.

Another factor which makes us easy marks is the difficulty of knowing where to complain if we feel we've been victimized, and of getting satisfaction if we do complain. In the community Vaughan and Carlo studied, complaints were scattered among four agencies, only some of which could take legal action.

SOURCE: Jack Horn, "Economic Crime: Portrait of an Arrogant Crook," *Psychology Today*, 9 (April, 1976), pp. 76, 79.

consider what is regarded as "common practice" to really be criminal activity.

Second, the effects of white-collar crime are difficult to trace. Oftentimes, no individual suffers unduly, and no one is injured in a physical sense. The public is not aware of what price-fixing costs them; and the stockholders in a corporation may receive excellent dividends even though a company official systematically embezzles company funds.

Finally, the public and law enforcement agencies seem reluctant to label businesspeople, doctors, or politicians as criminals. This may be because we have traditionally considered these people the backbone of our society and find it hard to believe that someone who is sophisticated, well educated, and successful could also break the law. Thus, the white-collar criminal is often punished by a warning, license revocation, or small fine—a far cry from the way we punish a mugger or a thief.

As a social problem, white-collar crime is of interest for two reasons. First, because it tends to discredit the idea that crime is associated with or caused by poverty. Second, white-collar crime points up some of society's flaws and inconsistencies. Something is very wrong with our norms and values when the most successful and respected people in our society—physicians, lawyers, executives, and politicians—routinely engage in criminal practices to gain money or power.

Terrorism

In recent years we have witnessed an increase in violent or potentially violent crimes for the purpose of either disrupting social (particularly government) institutions or forcing a third party to give in to the (usually political) demands of the perpetrators. Such acts are termed *terrorism*. The most obvious examples of the first type of terrorism are assassinations and placing bombs in public buildings. Although this form of crime has not met with particular success in the United States, it has been quite successful in certain other countries.

The second type of terrorism is, perhaps, best exemplified by acts such as the bizarre political kidnapping of Patricia Hearst by the Symbionese Liberation Army.[23] Among the demands made for her release was a multimillion-dollar food giveaway program for the poor financed by her wealthy father.

Some acts of terrorism are meant to benefit only the perpetrator but still constitute a threat to the safety of large numbers of people. An aircraft hijacking, in which the perpetrator demands a large ransom in return for allowing the plane to land safely, is a good example. Hijackings and in-flight bomb threats have dropped off dramatically, however, with the installation of fairly rigid airport security checks.

Organized Crime

The term *organized crime* refers to crime syndicates which often operate much like reputable businesses but which deal in gambling, narcotics, prostitution, loansharking, and other illegal activities that are relatively safe and profitable. While organized crime today bears little resemblance to the stereotypes of mobs and gangsters in the '30s, gangland murders occasionally occur today.

The full extent of organized crime in America is unknown. Federal officials estimate that about 5,000 individuals constitute the inner core of organized crime. These individuals, in turn, command about 150,000 "helpers" or "soldiers."[24] The most powerful syndicate is controlled by persons of Sicilian origin or descent, commonly called the Mafia. Reliable estimates list the most lucrative sources of profit for organized crime as illegal gambling; loansharking; and the importation, sale, and distribution of

In a rare public appearance, some leaders of organized crime can be spotted in the crowd attending funeral services for underworld "Godfather" Carlo Gambino in October of 1976. Gambino, 74, died of a heart ailment at his home.
▼

narcotics—in that order.[25] Organized crime took in an estimated $37 billion during 1973.[26]

In addition, organized crime invests heavily in reputable businesses. As might be expected, however, such businesses do not long remain very reputable. For example, a chain of restaurants controlled by organized crime may be forced to buy all supplies from other syndicate-owned businesses. This constitutes price fixing and stifles competition among reputable restaurant supply firms. Another form of racketeering consists of payments for syndicate protection.

Like white-collar crime, organized crime could not exist if the public did not condone it; that is, the public wants the goods and services organized crime offers. The billions upon billions of dollars organized crime takes in each year come mostly from people who like to bet on the horses, who cannot qualify for a loan from a reputable bank, who are addicted to drugs, and so forth. Organized crime also could not exist without the cooperation and connivance of some law enforcement officials and politicians.

Organized crime is clever at creating bonds of obligation between it and the legitimate world. For example, organized crime is suspected of contributing heavily to the campaign coffers of certain elected officials. Obviously, the crime syndicates, like other organizations contributing to election campaigns, expect something in return. Such returns may include protection from raids or arrests, the right to operate an illegal business without police interference, and so on. But bribes, fixes, and illegal campaign contributions, although they do occur, are not the primary reason the United States has organized crime. The primary reason is that the public wants and enjoys the goods and services of organized crime.

Causes of Crime

Crime has been explained in much the same way as juvenile delinquency—the biological, psychological, and sociological theories of juvenile delinquency explored in Chapter 7 also apply to crime. To these previously discussed theories, we will add several other theories of the genesis of crime.

Differential Association

One of the most widely respected explanations of criminal behavior is the *learning theory* of crime developed by the late Edwin H. Sutherland.[27] Called the principle of *differential association,* this theory essentially states that "in some societies an individual is surrounded by persons who invariably define the legal codes as rules to be observed, while in others he is surrounded by persons whose definitions are favorable to the violation of the legal codes. In our American society these definitions are almost always mixed, with the consequence that we have culture conflict in relation to legal codes."[28] A person therefore "*becomes delinquent because of an excess of definitions favorable to violation of law over definitions unfavorable to the violation of law.*"[29] In other words, if a person's environment encourages law-abiding behavior, he or she will probably be law-abiding; but in an environment that encourages and rewards criminality, he or she may well engage in criminal behavior.

From one perspective, the principle of differential association appears limited to explaining why some individuals become criminals and others do not. However, Sutherland and his colleague, Donald Cressey, maintain that the theory also sheds light on crime-rate variations from group to group. Specifically, they suggest that "most communities are organized for both criminal and anticriminal behavior, and, in that sense, the crime rate is an expression of differential group organization."[30] For example, in many slums and ghettos, people's perceptions of the law favor criminality over law-abiding behavior. As a result, the crime rate tends to be high. In contrast, perceptions of the law in some middle-class suburban communities and rural areas favor law-abiding behavior, and the crime rate tends to be lower.

Containment Theory

If two boys are raised in the same environment, why does one eventually engage in criminal behavior while the other does not? This is the question Walter C. Reckless addresses in his *containment theory;* he postulates that two forces determine whether or not a person will engage in criminal acts. The first is *outer containment,* or social pressure. Like Sutherland, Reckless recognizes that some people grow up in environments where family, friends, and the community exert strong social pressures to obey social norms and the law. Other persons grow up in environments where such pressures are less intense.

At the same time, no society counts exclusively on social pressure to make people obey the law. One of the aims of socialization is the development of self-control, or what Reckless calls *inner containment.* The inner ability to control or contain behavior is a key factor in distinguishing the law-abiding from the law-breaking citizen.[31]

Social Reality of Crime

Richard Quinney argues that crime is created by the law: "Crime is not inherent in behavior, but is a judgment made by some about the actions and characteristics of others."[32] Those who have the power to influence public policy define certain acts as criminal and the persons who engage in those acts as criminals. In this sense, crime is created by the legal institutions of society—the police, courts, and legislative bodies.

An interesting implication of Quinney's theory is that legislative bodies, in defining crime and judging criminals, actually *regulate* the crime rate. For example, if a law was passed forbidding the sale, transfer, or possession of tobacco, the crime rate would soar because large numbers of people would persist in smoking. On the other hand, if all laws forbidding the sale or possession of marijuana were repealed, the crime rate would drop because those who sell or possess marijuana would no longer be defined as criminals.

To explain why certain people engage in behavior defined as illegal, Quinney subscribes to Sutherland's theory of differential association.[33] He thus states that a person's tendency to engage in acts defined as criminal depends upon several factors—opportunity to commit crime, learning experiences, associations, persons identified with, and conception of self as law-abiding.[34]

Crime and Punishment

Since crime is so widespread and costly, we must examine how we deal with criminals. What happens to them when they are convicted? Does their treatment achieve positive and worthwhile goals?

The United States has always taken an essentially punitive approach toward criminals; that is, we believe in punishing them and making them pay for their offense. Usually they are fined or imprisoned, sometimes for many years. Society has many motives for imposing punishment. One is simple revenge. Another is to remove the criminal from society so he or she can do no further harm. A third is to reform through fear. We reason that if the price for committing a crime is high enough, the person will not commit a crime again and others will be deterred from committing crime. A final and more noble motive for imprisonment is rehabilitation. If a criminal can be resocialized and retrained for a useful life in society, imprisonment has served a positive social purpose.

▲ The United States has always taken an essentially punitive approach toward criminals; that is, we believe in punishing them and making them pay for their offense. Usually they are fined or imprisoned, sometimes for many years.

The Present

There is little evidence to suggest that severely punishing criminals deters them from committing further crimes. In fact, much evidence supports the contrary: "About 85 percent of the offenders admitted to the prisons and reformatories of Massachusetts in 1971, and about 85 percent of the male felons admitted to California prisons in 1969, had been in correctional institutions previously."[35] Similarly high rates of *recidivism* (repetition of criminal behavior) have been reported by the F.B.I.[36]

Clearly, we cannot reform criminals by simply locking them up with other criminals and isolating them from the law-abiding community. As they serve their time, they are likely to become even more bitter and hostile toward the society that placed them in prison; association with other criminals may only strengthen their criminal values and skills. Conversely, any noncriminal skills and values they may have possessed will deterioriate.

The argument that punishing criminals deters other people from committing crime is difficult to prove or disprove.[37] There is no way to know whether law-abiding citizens refrain from committing crimes because they fear punishment or because of other factors. Perhaps most of us are law-abiding either because we have been taught that it is wrong to violate the law or because we fear the disapproval of our family, friends, and associates. In any event, there is no evidence which proves that harsh punishments reduce crime or that light punishments encourage crime.

The crime rate might possibly be reduced if potential criminals were *certain* they would be punished. As Figure 8.1 shows, however, most crimes, particularly crimes against property, are not cleared by the arrest of a suspect. Furthermore, only a relatively small percentage of the persons arrested are convicted and sentenced to prison.

Figure 8.1 **Crimes Cleared by Arrest, 1973**

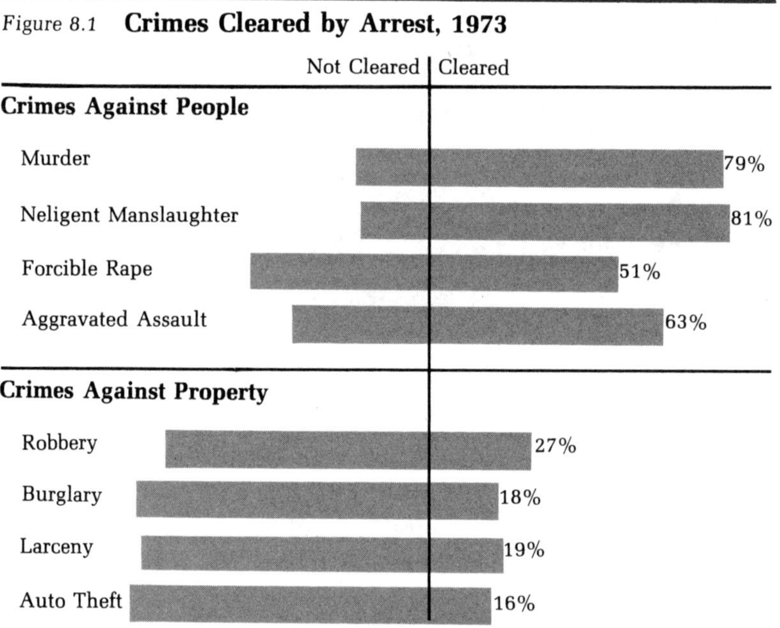

SOURCE: F.B.I., *Crime in the United States: 1973* (Washington, D.C.: U.S. Government Printing Office, 1974), Chart 16.

The Future

Because punishment does not effectively reform criminals, we must improve our methods of dealing with crime and the criminal. A suggestion has been made to decriminalize certain patterns of behavior currently defined as illegal, including such offenses as public drunkenness, the possession of drugs and narcotics, gambling, and homosexuality among consenting adults. Those who argue that these activities should be legalized point out that the alcoholic individual, the narcotic addict, the gambler, and the homosexual are not rehabilitated through imprisonment. Rather, while they are in prison, they simply learn more about crime and make contacts that will be useful or gratifying to them after their release. Supporters of this argument also feel that if certain patterns of behavior were decriminalized, the persons involved in them might be more likely to seek professional, therapeutic help.

But these activities are only one aspect of crime. More importantly, we must develop effective ways of bringing criminals back into society upon their release from prison. Many ex-convicts have difficulty finding employment, and "about 90 percent of reported felonies are crimes against property, so most of the recidivism of releasees may be regarded as a substitute for legitimate employment."[38] If so, the number of repeaters might be decreased significantly by helping the ex-convict find employment that is both economically and personally rewarding.

We must also develop programs which place the ex-convict in groups and institutions that reward and encourage law-abiding behavior. If ex-convicts can be helped to define themselves as constructive, law-abiding members of their community, the threat of losing their new status might well motivate them to obey the law. The task of bringing the ex-convict into law-abiding groups might be achieved if parole officers could help parolees form positive group affiliations. Unfortunately, many parole officers now seem to define their task negatively—as surveillance or checking up on the parolee to make sure he or she is not violating the law.

Summary

Crime is one of our most pressing social problems—one that costs too many lives and too many dollars.

We don't even know how much crime there is. The F.B.I. *Uniform Crime Reports* tell us only how much crime is known by and reported to police authorities, not how much actually occurs. The reports, however, can give us some idea of the magnitude of the problem. In 1973, over 8.6 million major crimes were reported in the United States. Of the arrests made, over 50 percent involved larceny and victimless crimes such as drug and alcohol abuse. Less than 5 percent involved the violent crimes of murder, rape, robbery, and aggravated assault. As long ago as 1967, crime was estimated to cost $15 billion per year.

Some population groups have higher crime rates than others. Youths aged 15 to 20 have the highest rates of arrest, and men are arrested much more often than women. As a percent of total population, more blacks are arrested than whites for many types of crime. This may be due to prejudicial treatment by the law or to the fact that people in urban slums, regardless of race, are exposed to a criminal subculture. But race is not a cause of crime. Finally, although the case is far from closed, it appears that lower-class persons are more likely to commit crimes than middle- or upper-class persons.

Common crimes range from petty theft and shoplifting to armed robbery and murder and are committed by three different types of people—by essentially law-abiding people who commit crimes on an occasional basis, by those who commit crime habitually, and by those who commit violent crimes. In addition, some behavior classified as *criminal* really only offends the public sense of propriety.

White-collar crime is committed by members of the middle and upper classes, usually in their business and professional activities. The costs of white-collar crime are much higher than those of common crime, but the white-collar criminal is rarely caught and even more rarely punished.

Terrorism involves violent or potentially violent criminal acts to disrupt social institutions (particularly government) or to force a third party to give in to specific demands (usually political). The first type of terrorism is exemplified by placing bombs in public buildings. Political kidnappings and airline hijackings are examples of the second type.

In organized crime, syndicates operate like legitimate businesses but deal in gambling, narcotics, loansharking, and other illegal but relatively safe and profitable activities. Organized crime pervades our society largely because the public wants the goods and services it offers.

One of the most popular explanations of criminal behavior, Sutherland's learning theory of crime, or differential association, says that a person becomes delinquent because his or her associations favor violating the law more than they favor keeping the law. Also widely accepted is Walter C. Reckless's theory of outer and inner containment, or outward social pressure plus inward socialized self-control directing the individual. Richard Quinney, on the other hand, argues that the source of crime lies in the law and that those who influence public policy and legislation define certain acts as crimes and persons who engage in those acts as criminals.

In the United States we have always believed in punishing the criminal through fines or imprisonment. Among our motives are revenge, the protection of society, deterrence, and rehabilitation. However, there is little evidence that severely punishing criminals deters them from committing further crime.

Because punishment does little to reduce crime, it has been suggested that certain patterns of behavior should be decriminalized. In addition, it has been suggested that the ex-convict should be helped to find employment, to make associations in the law-abiding community, and to become a part of groups which encourage respect for law.

Discussion Questions

1. Carefully examine the data presented in Table 8.1. What sort of picture of crime in the United States does this Table give you? What are the most common crimes? Are most of the crimes extremely serious?
2. It has often been maintained that crime doesn't pay. After recalling the data presented in this chapter, do you believe this to be a true statement? Why or why not?
3. How would you account for the fact that so few crimes against property, such as burglary, larceny, and auto theft, are solved by the arrest of a suspect?
4. How would you account for the fact that men are much more likely to break the law than women? Why do you suppose that the arrest rate for women is now increasing much more rapidly than for men? Is this due entirely to women's changing role expectations? Explain your answer.
5. Reread the section on the occasional criminal in this chapter. How would you account for the fact that the vast majority of Americans apparently commit crimes for which they could be jailed if they were caught and convicted?
6. What are some of the reasons why white-collar criminals are rarely caught and, if they are caught, rarely punished severely? Why is white-collar crime of particular interest to the sociologist?
7. Compare the theories of crime that have been developed by Edwin H. Sutherland and Walter C. Reckless. How would each of these theorists account for our high crime rate? What, if any, are the similarities between the two theories?
8. What does Richard Quinney mean when he says that "crime is not inherent in behavior, but is a judgment made by some about the actions and characteristics of others"? Does Quinney's theory seem reasonable to you? What are some of the possible criticisms that might be aimed at Quinney's theory?
9. How do you account for the fact that rates of recidivism among ex-convicts are so high? What suggestions do you have for helping the ex-convict avoid further scrapes with the law?
10. It has been suggested that some behaviors, such as public drunkenness, the possession of narcotics, and homosexuality among consenting adults, should be decriminalized. Do you agree? What would be some of the advantages of removing these, and similar behaviors, from regulation by criminal law? Are there any disadvantages to decriminalizing these behaviors?

Glossary

common crimes Crimes ranging from petty theft and shoplifting to armed robbery, rape, and murder.

containment theory (of crime) A theory which postulates that two forces determine whether or not a person will engage in criminal acts—social pressure (outer containment) and a person's inner ability to control his or her behavior (inner containment).

crime Any pattern of behavior for which the state, and specifically the courts, may lawfully punish the individual.

criminals without victims Persons who engage in patterns of behavior which are repugnant to the general public but which, in reality, do not irreversibly harm either themselves or other people. Prostitutes, homosexuals, and exhibitionists are among those considered criminals without victims.

differential association (principle of) A theory of crime which postulates that a person will engage in criminal activities if he or she is exposed to an excess of definitions favorable to the violation of law over definitions unfavorable to the violation of law.

felony A crime which carries a minimum penalty of one year or more in prison.

habitual criminal A person who more or less makes a career of burglary, robbery, or other offenses for monetary gain.

misdemeanor Any crime that carries a maximum penalty of one year or less in jail.

occasional criminal A person, such as a shoplifter, who does not make a life of crime but is not above stealing or committing other offenses from time to time.

organized crime Crime syndicates which often operate much like reputable businesses but which deal in gambling, loansharking, narcotics, and other illegal activities that are relatively safe and profitable.

recidivism The tendency of ex-convicts to relapse into criminal behavior.

terrorism Violent or potentially violent crimes which have the purpose of either disrupting social (particularly government) institutions or forcing a third party to give into the demands of the perpetrators. Examples include assassinations and political kidnappings.

white-collar crime Crimes committed by members of the middle and upper classes in the course of their business and professional endeavors. Examples include embezzlement, receiving kickbacks, income tax evasion, and so forth.

Suggestions for Further Reading

Adler, R., *Sisters in Crime: The Rise of the New Female Criminal* (New York: McGraw-Hill, 1975). According to the *New York Times Book Review,* Adler "gives us a copiously footnoted look at the 'liberation of the female criminal.' Her main point is that women aren't any more honest or less willing to engage in criminal activities than men; they simply have lacked the opportunities."

Bersani, Carl, ed., *Crime and Delinquency: A Reader* (New York: Macmillan, 1970). Probably the best collection of readings on crime and delinquency that is available today. This volume contains fifty-one readings, many of which are classics in criminology and related fields.

Dinitz, Simon, Russell R. Dynes, and Alfred C. Clarke, eds., *Deviance: Studies in the Process of Stigmatization and Societal Reaction* (New York: Oxford, 1969), esp. Part II. Part II of this diverse collection of readings contains some interesting and informative materials on the crime problem. Of particular interest are the readings taken from The President's Commission on Law Enforcement and the Administration of Justice.

Glaser, Daniel, *Adult Crime and Social Policy* (Englewood Cliffs, N.J.: Prentice-Hall, 1972). This slim volume sheds more light on the problem of adult crime in the United States than many longer and, on the surface, more thorough treatments of the crime problem.

Griffin, Susan, "Rape: The All-American Crime," *Ramparts,* 10 (September, 1971), pp. 26–35. An interesting discussion of rape, written from the standpoint of a leading feminist. Griffin maintains that "the existence of rape in any form is beneficial to the ruling class of white males."

Hacker, Andrew, "Getting Used to Mugging," in Henry Etzkowitz, ed., *Is America Possible?* (St. Paul, Minn.: West, 1974), pp. 79–86. After examining some of the alternative strategies for dealing with "street crime," and particularly robbery, Hacker infers that our best recourse may be to simply learn to live with the problem.

Nettler, Gwynn, *Explaining Crime* (New York: McGraw-Hill, 1973). A thorough review of currently popular explanations of crime. This volume also contains excellent chapters on the meaning of crime, the counting of crime, and the correlates of crime.

Quinney, Richard, *Criminology: Analysis and Critique of Crime in America* (Boston: Little, Brown, 1975). This new textbook covers essentially the same topics as other criminology texts, but with a different slant. Quinney's basic thesis is that crime is created by political authorities who define certain patterns of behavior as criminal.

Reckless, Walter C., *The Crime Problem,* 5th Ed. (Englewood Cliffs, N.J.: Prentice-Hall, 1973). A basic introductory text in criminology. Contains chapters on the major forms of crime, on the punishment and control of crime, and much more.

"Revolt Against Rape," *Time*, 106 (October 13, 1975), pp. 48–54. In what is ostensibly a review of a book by Susan Brownmiller *(Against our Will: Men, Women and Rape)*, this article provides some interesting information about rape and the growing anger of its female victims.

Sutherland, Edwin H., and Donald R. Cressey, *Criminology*, 9th Ed. (Philadelphia: Lippincott, 1974). One of the most widely used introductory texts in criminology. This book sets forth the classic theory of differential association and a wealth of other information.

Wilson, James Q., *Thinking About Crime* (New York: Basic, 1975). In this provocative book, an eminent authority concludes that we must make some basic changes in how we think about criminal behavior.

Notes

[1]See Gwynn Nettler, *Explaining Crime* (New York: McGraw-Hill, 1973), p. 3; and "The Thin Blue Line," *Time*, 92 (July 19, 1968), p. 39.

[2]Daniel Glaser, *Adult Crime and Social Policy* (Englewood Cliffs, N.J.: Prentice-Hall, 1972), p. 1.

[3]For a discussion and critique of the F.B.I. *Uniform Crime Reports*, see Marvin E. Wolfgang, "Limitations in the Use of Official Statistics," in Anthony L. Guenther, ed., *Criminal Behavior and Social Systems* (Skokie, Ill.: Rand McNally, 1970), pp. 60–76.

[4]President's Commission on Law Enforcement and the Administration of Justice, *The Challenge of Crime in a Free Society* (Washington, D.C.: U.S. Government Printing Office, 1967), p. 33.

[5]Computed from F.B.I., *Crime in the United States: 1973* (Washington, D.C.: U.S. Government Printing Office, 1974), Table 30.

[6]Computed from *Ibid.*, Table 30.

[7]*Ibid.*, Table 32.

[8]Edwin H. Sutherland and Donald R. Cressey, *Criminology*, 9th Ed. (Philadelphia: Lippincott, 1974), p. 126.

[9]For a new and interesting look at the female criminal in America, see R. Adler, *Sisters in Crime: The Rise of the New Female Criminal* (New York: McGraw-Hill, 1975).

[10]F.B.I., *Crime in the United States: 1973*, Table 28.

[11]See Haywood Burns, "Can a Black Man Get a Fair Trial in this Country?" in Joel B. Grossman and Mary H. Grossman, eds., *Law and Change in Modern America* (Pacific Palisades, Calif.: Goodyear, 1971), pp. 330 –39. A somewhat more mixed picture of how black Americans fare before the law is presented by Michael J. Hindelang, "Equality Under the Law," *Journal of Criminal Law, Criminology, and Police Science*, 60 (September, 1969), pp. 306–13.

[12]W. L. Warner and P. S. Lunt, *The Social Life of a Modern Community* (New Haven: Yale, 1941), p. 376.

[13]James S. Wallerstein and Clement J. Wyle, "Our Law-Abiding Law-Breakers," *Probation*, 25 (April, 1947), pp. 107–12.

[14]"The Losing Battle Against Crime in America," *U.S. News and World Report* (December 16, 1974), p. 36.

[15]*Ibid.*, p. 31.

[16]Harwin W. Voss and John R. Hepburn, "Patterns of Criminal Homicide in Chicago," *Journal of Criminal Law, Criminology, and Police Science,* 59 (December, 1968), p. 506.

[17]Glaser, *Adult Crime and Social Policy,* p. 34.

[18]Monachem Amir, "Forcible Rape," in Simon Dinitz, Russell R. Dynes, and Alfred C. Clarke, eds., *Deviance: Studies in the Process of Stigmatization and Societal Reaction* (New York: Oxford, 1969), pp. 67–74.

[19]For an account of the Watergate affair, for example, see Carl Bernstein and Bob Woodward, *All the President's Men* (New York: Simon & Schuster, 1974).

[20]Edwin H. Sutherland, *White Collar Crime* (New York: Dryden, 1949).

[21]Sutherland and Cressey, *Criminology,* p. 21.

[22]U.S. News and World Report, "The Losing Battle Against Crime in America," p. 40.

[23]For a summary of this bizarre case, see "The Hearst Nightmare," *Time,* 103 (April 29, 1974). pp. 11–18. For a more in-depth account of the Hearst case by a reporter who seemingly "scooped the F.B.I., the police, and the media," see Marilyn Baker with Sally Brompton, *Exclusive!: The Inside Story of Patricia Hearst and the SLA* (New York: Macmillan, 1974).

[24]U.S. News and World Report, "The Losing Battle Against Crime in America," p. 39.

[25]President's Commission on Law Enforcement and the Administration of Justice, *Task Force Report: Organized Crime* (Washington, D.C.: U.S. Government Printing Office, 1967), pp. 2–3.

[26]U.S. News and World Report, "The Losing Battle Against Crime in America," p. 39.

[27]The latest statement of the principle of differential association is to be found in Sutherland and Cressey, *Criminology,* pp. 75–77.

[28]*Ibid.*, p. 75.

[29]*Ibid.*, p. 75. Italics in original.

[30]*Ibid.*, p. 77.

[31]See Walter C. Reckless, *The Crime Problem,* 5th Ed. (Englewood Cliffs, N.J.: Prentice-Hall, 1973), esp. pp. 50–51, 55–57.

[32]Richard Quinney, *The Social Reality of Crime* (Boston: Little, Brown, 1970), p. 16.

[33]*Ibid.*, p. 21.

[34]*Ibid.*

[35]Sutherland and Cressey, *Criminology,* p. 608.

[36]See F.B.I., *Uniform Crime Reports: 1970* (Washington, D.C.: U.S. Government Printing Office, 1971), pp. 39–40.

[37]For an interesting discussion of the deterrent effects of punishment, see Johannes Andenaes, "The General Preventive Effects of Punishment," in Grossman and Grossman, eds., *Law and Change in Modern America,* pp. 77–91.

[38]Glaser, *Adult Crime and Social Policy,* p. 104.

PART III

PROBLEMS OF STRUCTURE

Poverty

Growing Old

Racial and Ethnic Prejudice and Discrimination

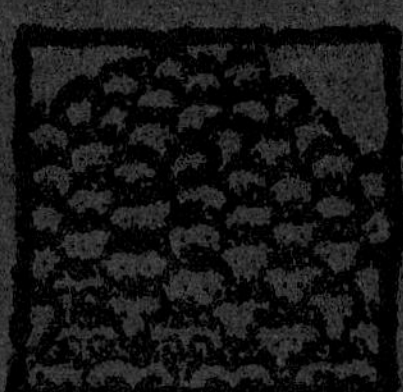
Overpopulation

Sex Roles and Sexism

Chapter 9
Poverty

Poverty, Social Stratification, and Social Problems
What Is Poverty?
Who Are the Poor?
Being Poor in an Affluent Society
- Education and the Poor
- The Poor Pay More
- The Law and the Poor
- Poverty and Health

Causes of Poverty
- Effects of Schooling
- Unemployability
- Racism
- Sexism
- Recession

Perpetuating Poverty
- Cycle of Poverty
- Culture of Poverty

A Search for Solutions
- The War on Poverty
- The Welfare System Today
- Redistribution of Income

Summary

Try to imagine anyone today seriously arguing that children are just no-good bums who should be made to go to work and earn their own keep. Or that old people and severely handicapped persons could improve their lots if they wanted to by "pulling themselves up by their bootstraps."

These notions sound absurd—and inhumane. Yet many, many Americans believe that poor people are poor because they are lazy and shiftless and simply do not want to work. What many of us fail to realize is that the majority of poor people are too young, too old, or too infirm to work. For the most part, poverty is not the fault of the poor; it is not entirely their problem.

Poverty is, in fact, both an individual and a social problem. Clearly, it is a big problem for the individuals who are poor—they can get little or no medical care; they often suffer from malnutrition; they usually must live in overcrowded, unsafe housing; and they are hassled constantly by landlords and creditors. In addition, their lives are often filled with frustration, hopelessness, and despair.

But why is poverty also a social problem? Does it really matter if a few people, more or less, are in a financial bind compared with the rest of us? Does poverty really threaten society and the groups and institutions of which it is composed? And if it does, are we doing anything to solve this social problem? These are difficult questions. In this chapter we will examine them and try to put the problems of poverty into perspective.

Poverty, Social Stratification, and Social Problems

Every society has a system of stratification.[1] This means that some people are more highly rewarded than others. For example, in our society, middle- and upper-class people have the money to buy nourishing food, good medical care, adequate housing, and a good education for their children. Their money also gives them power because money opens up choices. People with money and the power it brings can choose where to live, what schools to send their children to, and what doctors to see. This wide range of choices is not open to poor people. Indeed, "poverty is an important area in the study of social stratification and can be adequately understood only in this larger context."[2]

Position in the stratification system is determined by social forces. Lower-class people are not poor because they are lazy and unmotivated. They are poor because they are victims of structured inequality; that is, society is structured in such a way that they are not given the opportunity to acquire the means (money) to obtain adequate food, housing, education, and medical care. This, in turn, means that they are not equipped to make meaningful contributions to society. For example, it is not unusual to find many job opportunities for skilled laborers going unfilled at the very time millions of poor people are unemployed. Poor people simply do not have the requisite skills.

In addition, because they have no money, poor people are often forced to live in run-down, dilapidated neighborhoods surrounded on all sides by drug and alcohol abuse, crime, and other patterns of deviant behavior.

The United States has what is called an *open class system* of stratification. In theory, this means that there are channels of upward mobility and that the individual rises or falls through these channels in the class structure according to the amount of effort he or she exerts. Thus, people who take advantage of educational opportunities and work diligently can hypothetically improve their positions in the class structure.

However, it has become increasingly difficult to keep the channels of upward mobility open so that lower-class people can acquire the tools that would help them climb out of poverty. "The opportunity to achieve tends to be ascribed. Rich parents' children, even if they are stupid, are much more likely to go to college than the children of the poor, even if they are quite intelligent and have good grades."[3] As a result, poverty often becomes self-perpetuating. Society is structured to deny them opportunities, so the children of poor people are likely to be poor themselves when they reach adulthood. This waste of talent is tragic. Because their parents are poor, millions of bright lower-class youngsters will never have the opportunity to develop the skills and abilities that benefit society.

Poverty, then, is a social problem in the same sense that racism and sexism are social problems—some people are channeled into unrewarding and unproductive roles simply because of a status that they acquired at birth. In sum, society creates the conditions that lock people into poverty and then it pays the price in urban blight, high crime rates, and excessive unemployment.

What Is Poverty?

Against the backdrop of social stratification,poverty itself can be examined. In general, we all know what constitutes poverty. The poor are disadvantaged and deprived compared with other members of society. "They are easily distinguished from other classes by their housing, diet, education, economic goods, occupation, and employment. . . . [T]he poor stand out by their lack of the goods and the access to services that we take for granted in an affluent society."[4]

As we have seen, the poor also have little power and influence. For example, affluent Americans who wish to influence public policy can contribute to election campaigns, join volunteer and professional associations, or even run for election themselves. The poor normally are not able to do any of these. Thus, poverty implies (1) lack of sufficient income, and (2) lack of control over one's fate.

The federal government defines poverty in terms of the amount of income an individual or family receives. As Table 9.1 indicates, in 1974 the poverty line for a nonfarm family of four was set at $5,038. Persons whose incomes were below this line were considered poor while those whose incomes were above it were not.

Table 9.1
Poverty-Line Income, 1974

Number of Family Members	Nonfarm Family Income in Dollars	Farm Family Income in Dollars
1	2,495	2,092
2	3,211	2,707
3	3,936	3,331
4	5,038	4,302
5	5,950	5,057
6	6,699	5,700
7 or More	8,253	7,018

SOURCE: *The World Almanac and Book of Facts: 1976* (New York: Newspaper Enterprise Association, 1975), p. 206.

The government calculates the figures shown in Table 9.1 by determining the weekly cost of maintaining an adequate diet and multiplying by three to take into account other basic expenses such as rent and clothing. The weekly costs are then multiplied by fifty-two to determine annual poverty-line incomes. By this standard, 24.3 million Americans, or about 12 percent of the population, live at or below the poverty line.[5] However, a nonfarm family of four with an income of $5,038 per year must live very frugally. If they spent exactly one-third of their income on food, each family member would receive approximately $1.15 per day for breakfast, lunch, and dinner combined. People have tried eating on this amount and pretty much found that they could not eat nutritionally. How many of us, for example, could eat satisfactorily on this meager amount?

Some experts question the value of an absolute standard, such as income, to distinguish between poor and nonpoor.[6] They prefer to define poverty in terms of the person's inability to maintain a decent standard of living as defined by the larger society. In any society, certain things are considered "necessary" to lead a comfortable life. In the United States today, "necessities" include much more than adequate food, clothing, and shelter. Many Americans consider at least one nice car, color television, any number of appliances, a nice house, and money for restaurants and shows to be "necessities." And every year this list of "necessities" increases. The poor then are defined as people who, by virtue of their low incomes, cannot acquire many of the things the average American takes for granted. In short, they are deprived relative to other people and they "have fallen behind the grades and standards of the society as a whole."[7]

Scholars who define poverty in relative terms usually consider persons who are in the lowest income brackets (the bottom 10 or 20 percent) to be poor. The important implication of this definition of poverty is that if poverty is a matter of relative deprivation, it will not be eliminated from American society in the foreseeable future. Without a drastic redistribution of income, there will always be people who lack many or most of the things that, by the standards of our society, are necessary to a decent life.

But no matter how we define it, poverty is a way of life for many Americans. Although compared to people in many developing countries America's poor are well-off, poverty is nonetheless a serious problem. Being poor in a country of affluence is a humiliating, degrading experience. And the situation begs the question: If most of us have so much, why do some of us have so little?

Who Are the Poor?

There is no simple statistical picture of the poor in America. Some poor people are young and some are old, some are black and some are white, some are men and some are women. And they live in both rural and urban areas throughout the north, south, east, and west. However, sufficient data exist to allow us to draw a rough picture of the poor in America.[8]

While about 78 percent of all poor families and individuals in this country are white, poverty is closely related to racism and sexism. Black Americans and other minority groups are grossly overrepresented among the poor, and "about one-fourth of the poor families in America are headed by a female."[9] Approximately one-fourth of all poor families are headed by an old person whose retirement income is not sufficient to meet family needs;

nonetheless, a high percentage of poor people are young. The impoverished young fall into two categories: dependent children and unemployed young adults. Since most poor families have children, dependent youngsters constitute the largest single group within the poverty population. The young adults among the poor are usually those who have dropped out of school, are unskilled, and are unable to find jobs.

Although the poor live in every section of the country, the South has a higher percentage of poor than other sections. About 50 percent of the nation's poor live in rural areas, even though only about 27 percent of the total population live in rural areas. Although every state has its poor, the rural poor tend to be concentrated in Appalachia, California, the Ozarks, Wisconsin, and Minnesota.[10] In at least one-quarter of America's poor families, someone, usually the family head, works full time. This suggests, first, that, contrary to popular opinion, the poor are not lazy; and, second, that even today small wages are a leading cause of poverty. In recent years, another group of people has joined the poor—millions of competent, skilled men and women who have lost their jobs because of economic recession.

On the basis of these statistics, then, we can conclude that there is no such thing as a typical poor person. The poor person in America may be young or old, white or nonwhite, employed or unemployed. Many poor people live in the South, but all regions of the country have people who live in poverty. About the only thing that all poor people have in common is their lack of an adequate income.

Being Poor in an Affluent Society

Up to this point, we have examined poverty in conceptual and statistical terms. In the United States, however, being poor means much more than simply not having enough money. Rather, it means being assigned to a social class whose members are denied the basic rights to lead a dignified, healthy life and to enjoy the respect of their fellow citizens. In this section, we will examine some of the many actual costs and consequences of being poor in an affluent society.

Education and the Poor

Position in the American class structure is often measured by an index that combines the variables of education, income, and occupation. Not surprisingly, children from poor families complete fewer years of education than children from affluent families, and

Some poor people are young and some are old, some are black and some are white, some are men and some are women. And they live in both rural and urban areas throughout the north, south, east, and west.

▲
In at least one-quarter of America's poor families, someone, usually the family head, works full time. Inadequate wages are a leading cause of poverty.

the education poor children receive is often inferior to that of affluent children. This, in turn, means that children from poor families are disadvantaged when it comes to getting good jobs and earning adequate incomes. In our country, educational credentials seem to count more than innate abilities in the competition for jobs.[11]

Children from poor families are educationally disadvantaged for several reasons.[12] Lower-class children may not be as motivated as their middle- and upper-class peers to achieve in school. In lower-class families, children often are neither socialized to place a high value on educational achievement nor instilled with the kind of self-discipline required for success in high school and college. The elementary and secondary schools which serve children from poor families often have inferior teachers and facilities, inadequate supplies, overcrowded classrooms, and so forth. For these reasons, children from poor families often lack the academic preparation required for admission to college; and, if they are admitted, they lack the necessary skills for success. Moreover, poor children who are able to get into college may be unable to afford tuition and other expenses.

Social Problems and You

Some Notes on Measuring Poverty

The "war on poverty" that Lyndon Johnson launched in the mid-1960s began winding down when Richard Nixon and the Republicans moved into the White House in 1969, but many signs of L.B.J.'s battle are still around. One of them is the U.S. Census Bureau's annual reckoning of how many Americans are "poor." The latest report . . . was a shocker: it counted 12.3% of the total population—precisely 25.9 million Americans—as living at or below the poverty line, the highest percentage of poor since 1970. Worse still, there were 2.5 million more poor than in 1974, a record increase suggesting that a long period of decline in their number since the Eisenhower recession days of the late 1950s and early '60s had come to an end.

Measuring poverty is a peculiarly American compulsion. With the exception of Israel, no other country regularly assembles—and publishes—official statistics on its poor. Government interest in measuring poverty goes back to the 19th century, but today's system of annual reports began in 1965, when Congress decided that the flood of Great Society legislation demanded some useful yardsticks of prosperity. The result has been a system that is necessarily arbitrary and, some critics say, paints an unnecessarily lurid picture of U.S. poverty.

Basically, the statisticians define the poor by establishing a series of poverty-threshold incomes that are adjusted every year according to the inflation rate. For 1975, the poverty cutoffs ranged from $2,717 for a single person to $5,500 for a nonfarm family of four. But how are the numbers determined? Deep down underneath a maze of statistical formulas designed to compensate for assorted variables such as sex, age, race, geographic location and family status, the definition of poverty rests on one bedrock invariable: people must eat.

In the mid-'60s, the statisticians decided to establish the poverty line for individuals and families simply by multiplying what it cost them to eat for a year by three. Why three? Because a 1955 survey of food spending habits showed that the average U.S. family spent about $1 of every $3 of income on food. Over the years, various refinements have been made in the system, most notably a linking of the poverty figures to all of the components in the Consumer Price Index, including fuel and clothing as well as food. Distinctions are also made for price differences in various parts of the country, and the fact that it generally costs less to live on a farm than it does in an urban area.

Still, Government statisticians themselves warn that poverty figures serve only as relative measures and not hard and fast pictures of reality. The '75 figures, for example, include only money income. They do not include such "in kind" payments as food stamps or the value of subsidized public housing.

The poverty figures are more than just an interesting—and imprecise—measure of the nation's well-being. They are used to determine, among other billion-dollar matters, which citizens are exempted from paying federal income taxes (almost all of those below the poverty line) and what communities receive federal school aid. A small rise in the poverty line, for example, could cause a shift of millions in federal education aid from the South to Northern states, as more low-income citizens in and around Northern cities officially joined the "poor." Thus, the poverty yardstick has become a policy tool as well as a measure, making further refinement in it all the more imperative.

SOURCE: "Those 26 Million 'Poor,'" *Time*, 108 (October 18, 1976), p. 78.

The Poor Pay More

Obviously, people are poor because they lack the money to adequately meet their needs for food, clothing, and shelter. Yet, for what they do buy, the poor actually pay more.[13] Unlike more affluent consumers, the poor "tend to lack the information and training needed to be effective consumers in a bureaucratic society."[14] They cannot always take advantage of sales, they often do not engage in comparative shopping, and they are frequently ill-equipped to evaluate the quality of merchandise in relation to its price. So the goods and services that the poor do purchase are sometimes sold to them at inflated prices.

Credit transactions are a source of economic discrimination for the poor. Poor people usually do not qualify for loans from reputable banks and other lending institutions; as a result, they must get loans from pawnbrokers, unaccredited loan companies, or loan sharks.
▼

Credit transactions are another source of economic discrimination for the poor. Poor people usually do not qualify for loans from reputable banks and other lending institutions; as a result, they must get loans from pawnbrokers, unaccredited loan companies, or loan sharks. This means that they pay much higher interest rates than more affluent people who are good credit risks. Furthermore, the poor often do not understand the terms and conditions of the credit transactions that they do make. They do not realize that they are responsible for collection fees and court costs if they fall behind on their payments. Likewise, some credit contracts allow the merchant to repossess all of the goods that the

person has bought from the store if that person fails to keep up the payments on one item. This is sometimes true even if the other items have been paid for in full.[15]

Taxes also work to the particular disadvantage of the poor. Sales taxes, which are fixed percentages of the cost of items, eat up a larger proportion of a poor person's income than an affluent person's income. In addition, affluent people can use tax loopholes and shelters to reduce their federal and state income taxes: some rich people pay no income taxes. The poor, on the other hand, get very few tax breaks.

The Law and the Poor

Poor people also encounter gross discrimination within the legal system.[16] The poor are more likely to be arrested for relatively minor offenses such as public drunkenness, disorderly conduct, and vagrancy. Once arrested, they have less chance of "beating the rap" than affluent people. Since most poor people cannot afford bail, they must sit in a jail for weeks or even months awaiting trial. During this time, they are separated from their families, they lose their jobs, and, most important, they lose their liberty.

Furthermore, the cards are often stacked against poor people when they go to trial. "Recent studies have statistically determined that defendants remaining in jail are handicapped in preparing their defense, are much more likely to be found guilty, and much less likely to be granted probation."[17] The Supreme Court *requires* an attorney in criminal cases, but the poor person will very likely be represented by inferior counsel. Often, the poor person's attorney will advise that the case cannot be won and that he or she should plead guilty to a lesser charge to get a lighter sentence. This is called *plea bargaining* or *bargain basement justice.* Plea bargaining saves the prosecuting attorney, the defense attorney, and the court time and money at the poor person's expense. This practice is certainly not what most of us think of as "equal justice for all."

The poor are equally handicapped in civil lawsuits. For example, when the poor are victimized by unethical and unreasonable credit schemes, they normally cannot afford attorneys to take action against the credit companies. The same is true when they are ripped off by slum landlords. Very often, the poor are barred from using the court system simply because they cannot afford to pay court costs. The problem is particularly vexing regarding divorce. Because a divorce means court costs and attorneys' fees, it is a luxury most poor people cannot afford.[18] As a result, the poor often end their marriages by desertion, not by divorce, so that neither partner is free to remarry (see also Chapter 14).

Poverty and Health

Few data are available on the health status of the poor. However, poor people are probably much less likely to lead long, healthy lives than affluent people. For example, the average white person born in 1973 could expect to live approximately 72.2 years; the average nonwhite person, however, could expect to live only about 65.9 years.[19] This differential cannot be attributed to the fact of race itself. Since nonwhites represent a disproportionately high percentage of the poor (they make up 22 percent of the poor but only about 12.9 percent of the whole population), this life expectancy differential is in large part traceable to differentials in income and in the ability to obtain and pay for good health care.

A recent study found that infant mortality rates were 75 percent higher in the poverty areas than in nonpoverty areas of Chicago.[20] This is a particularly depressing statistic since the overall infant mortality rate in the United States is high compared with many other countries.[21] In addition, poor people get sick more often than affluent people: "Those in families with income of under $2,000 a year have 29 restricted activity days a year, while those with family income over $4,000 a year have less than half that, 13 restricted activity days a year."[22]

But lack of money is only one reason why poor people do not live as long and are not as healthy as affluent people. Very often medical services are not available to the poor even if they can afford them; and overwork, malnutrition, inadequate housing, and poor sanitary facilities adversely affect poor people's health. Some experts have suggested that there is a culture of poverty that affects health levels among the poor.[23] For example, definitions of what constitutes sickness seem to differ among the poor and among the affluent: "Only about one-half [of the poor] recognizes excessive vaginal bleeding as a reason for concern. Loss of appetite will be ignored by 80 percent of the lower class, fainting spells by 67 percent, and continued coughing by 77 percent."[24] Each of these, however, can denote a serious health problem. Poor people also do not always go to a physician when they are sick. They are much more likely to rely instead on home remedies and folk medicines which can adversely affect their general health and life expectancy.

Finally, "with few exceptions, . . . poverty status groups have startingly higher rates of mental illness than do other segments of the population."[25] The causes of mental illness are complex, and the association between poverty and high rates of mental illness could be explained in many ways. For example, lower-class people certainly face a great deal of stress and frustration in their lives: they are poor in the midst of affluence and they have few of the things society considers necessary and by which society defines success (see also Chapter 2). There is also the very real possibility that poor people are more likely to be labeled mentally ill than affluent people: "Many more persons from low income backgrounds may be 'diagnosed' mentally ill because their patterns of behavior and life-styles do not fit the standards of the basically middle-class 'judges.' "[26]

Causes of Poverty

The causes of poverty are many and varied. As we examine them, one underlying principle will emerge—the vast majority of poor people are poor through no fault of their own.

Effects of Schooling

As we have already pointed out, our society is structured so that poor people are less well educated than the middle and upper classes. Table 9.2 shows the high correlation between the number of school years completed and the amount an individual earns. To a certain extent, our educational system helps propagate poverty and inequality.

Table 9.2
Median Family Income, by Race and Years of Schooling Completed, 1974

	White Family Income in Dollars	Black Family Income in Dollars
Elementary School		
Less than 8 Years	7,501	5,736
8 Years	10,011	7,184
High School		
1–3 Years	12,080	7,238
4 Years	14,226	10,283
College		
1–3 Years	16,139	13,220
4 Years or More	20,267	16,434

SOURCE: U.S. Bureau of the Census, *Statistical Abstract of the United States: 1975*, 96th Ed. (Washington, D.C.: U.S. Government Printing Office, 1975), p. 396.

Equal educational opportunity for all young people, however, would by no means be a cure-all for poverty in the United States. A large percentage of the poor, as we have pointed out, are people who are elderly or disabled and would be unable to work even if they had college diplomas. And, even with equal education, members of minority groups, including women, are often paid less than white men for doing the same jobs. Furthermore, our

PUBL C SCHOOL 37
BONE
Son
of
ceasar

occupational system is structured in such a way that some people will always be forced into low-paying jobs regardless of their education. In sum, making good educational opportunities available to everyone would help to lessen the effects of poverty but would not eliminate them.

Unemployability

In a survey conducted in 1972, the U.S. Bureau of the Census found that 36 percent of all whites who are poor and about 52 percent of all blacks who are poor are children under age 18. About 15 percent of the poor are people age 65 and over.[27] People who are chronically sick or disabled make up still another significant component of the poverty population. Thus, a large percentage (perhaps over 50 percent) of the poor people in this country could not work even if jobs were available for them. In addition, about 43 percent of our poor families are headed by women; many of them do not work because they must stay at home to care for their children.[28] Clearly, then, employment opportunities alone will not solve the problem of poverty.

Racism

Another important cause of poverty is the racism that characterizes our society:

> The average yearly income for blacks, Chicanos, and Indians is, at best, only around 65 percent of that for whites; Chicanos earn somewhat more than blacks, and Indians earn only a very small percentage of the white income. This income gap has been closing at a very slow rate and has changed little since 1960; and in fact, it has dropped for blacks over the last years.[29]

Blacks, Chicanos, and American Indians are from three to five times more likely to be poor than whites.[30] About 33 percent of the nonwhite population are poor, as opposed to 9 percent of the white population.[31]

One reason for the high rates of nonwhite poverty is job discrimination. Until relatively recently, blacks were denied all but the most menial jobs, were not allowed to join most labor unions, and in parts of the country worked for lower pay scales than white workers in the same job. Even in federal government jobs, blacks are underrepresented in high-paying jobs and overrepresented in low-paying jobs.[32] Much of this discrimination can be traced directly to the traditional practice of treating white job applicants and workers more favorably than black job applicants and workers.

To a certain extent, our educational system helps propagate poverty and inequality.

Another reason for the higher poverty levels of minorities is educational discrimination. Most better-paying jobs today demand not only many years of education but also that the education be of high quality. Blacks, Chicanos, and American Indians have been denied access to this education and, as a result, are either unemployed or forced to take menial jobs which are neither economically nor personally rewarding.

Sexism

Sexism also contributes to poverty. As we have pointed out, 43 percent of all poor families are headed by women—many of whom might work if they could. But the costs of work for these women may be more than its rewards. A baby-sitter or day-care service may cost a mother as much or more than she can earn. Leaving her children unattended is hardly a desirable alternative. Furthermore, even if the female head of household does take a job, her wages are likely to be low. In all occupational categories, women earn considerably less than men.[33] Thus, encouraging female heads of household to work will not significantly reduce the number of poor families until the problems of day care and sexism are solved.

Recession

The inability of able-bodied men and women to find jobs has always been a cause of poverty. Automation, for example, has taken jobs from many coal miners in Appalachia and from blacks in the South. These two groups alone account for a large percentage of the people who have migrated into northern and western states seeking jobs. In every section of the country, there are numbers of able-bodied adults who are technically able to work but, because they lack skills or training, are unemployable.

The recent economic recession which began in 1969 has helped create another group of able-bodied adults who are unemployable. In 1969, the nation's unemployment rate stood at 3.9 percent, but by May, 1972, it had steadily risen to 5.9 percent.[34] That year, members of President Nixon's administration told us that joblessness would be reduced to 5 percent by year end and that it would be even lower in 1973.[35] Unfortunately, the rate continued to increase and in June, 1975, reached a high of 9.2 percent. Among the hardest hit have been automobile, aerospace, and construction workers. In June, 1975, for example, one out of every five automobile workers was unemployed. Neither the causes of nor the solutions to this serious national problem are very clear.

Some economists feel that the dramatic price rise of raw materials used in the manufacturing and construction industries—oil, electricity, steel, and building materials—during the early '70s contributed to the national recession. Rapid inflation in the costs of raw materials affects unemployment rates in several ways. Manufacturers and builders compensate for their increased costs by trimming their labor costs and raising the prices on the goods they produce. Higher price tags reduce the demand for the goods so still fewer employees are needed to supply sufficient goods. And the more people are thrown out of work, the more the demand for goods drops.

In addition, as the costs of electricity, building materials, supplies, and other goods rise, public-sector jobs in government and education are affected. These jobs too are cut back to compensate for the increased materials costs and to keep budgets balanced. (As one college professor observed, universities can get by with fewer professors but not with fewer rolls of toilet paper.) As a result, millions of men and women are without jobs and facing potential poverty.

There may be no way to return to unemployment rates of 3 and 4 percent. Reducing the unemployment rate to an acceptable level may increase the inflation rate to a totally unacceptable level. Employed people buy things, and, if they are competing for scarce commodities, prices are driven up. Thus, we face the economic paradox—full employment creates inflation, but inflation, in turn, creates unemployment.

More importantly, we may be quickly approaching the point in the historic development of our national economy at which it is not feasible to provide every able-bodied head of household with a job. With the development of completely automated assembly lines, highly mechanized farm equipment, and thousands of other labor-saving devices, we no longer need a huge force of unskilled, semiskilled, or even skilled laborers. This means that, in the future, millions of people, regardless of skill, talent, or education, may be thrown into poverty simply because there are no jobs for them.

> Another potential multiplier of dependency is automation. This is becoming an old, documented story. In the last decade, the population of the United States increased by 20 percent, production increased 43 percent, but the number of factory workers decreased 10 percent. We will need twelve million jobs in the next decade—at present rates, which may decline, we supply six.[36]

Perpetuating Poverty

Many people agree that the causes of poverty are rooted in the structure of our society, that poor people are poor through no fault of their own. Some have also suggested that poverty may be self-perpetuating, that is, passed on from generation to generation. In this section we will examine two of the most important of such theories—the cycle-of-poverty theory and the culture-of-poverty theory. Both theories suggest that there are built-in barriers which discourage the poor from attempting to improve their economic and social position.

Cycle of Poverty

Developed by social scientist and political leader Daniel P. Moynihan, the cycle-of-poverty theory asserts that poverty is a vicious cycle that makes it difficult if not impossible for the children of poor parents to break out of poverty.[37] According to the theory, people who live in poverty often face severe cultural and environmental obstacles that keep them from improving their own economic status and that of their children. For example, poor parents are often unable to motivate their children to do well in school, and the schools in the poor neighborhoods where they live are inferior. As a result, their children either receive a second-rate education or become school dropouts at an early age. Isolated from the middle- and upper-classes, poor children often do not learn the norms of the larger society relating to employment, punctuality, and good workmanship. Lower-class children grow up poorly educated, poorly equipped to find and keep jobs, and in poor health. They are thus severely hampered in terms of improving their economic status. So they remain in the lower class. When they marry and have children, the cycle of poverty begins again.

Perhaps the greatest limitation of the cycle-of-poverty theory is that it oversimplifies the causes of poverty. One influential critic states, "This vision of poverty is not wrong, merely incomplete."[38] People are not poor simply because their parents were poor. As we have seen, people are poor because our educational system does not provide adequate opportunities, because their job skills are no longer needed, or because they are too young, too old, or too infirm to work. But the theory does make one point clear—if you are poor, you are very likely to stay poor.

Culture of Poverty

In 1959, eminent anthropologist Oscar Lewis suggested that there may be a culture of poverty; that is, a set of shared ways of thinking, doing, and having that characterize poor people regardless of whether they live in the United States or in another country, in a city or on a farm.

As an anthropologist I have tried to understand poverty and its associated traits as a culture or, more accurately, as a subculture with its own structure and rationale, *as a way of life which is passed down from generation to generation along family lines.*[39]

Lewis argues that poor people live in a culture of poverty which instills in each generation a distinctive set of values, attitudes, and behavioral norms. These values, attitudes, and behavioral norms make it difficult for the poor to take advantage of any opportunities they may have to climb out of poverty.

Lewis gives a quite detailed description of the culture of poverty.[40] He maintains that people who share in this culture participate little in the major institutions of the larger society and that they develop distinctive patterns of family life. Children are introduced to sex at an early age, rates of illegitimacy are high, and marriages tend to be very unstable. People who are socialized into the culture of poverty usually have a strong sense of marginality, helplessness, dependence, and inferiority. In addition, the culture of poverty is marked by "a lack of impulse control, a strong present-time orientation with relatively little ability to defer gratification and to plan for the future, a sense of resignation and fatalism, a widespread belief in male superiority, and a high tolerance for psychological pathology of all sorts."[41]

This may be a reasonably accurate picture of the lives of *some* poor people. But for the most part, Lewis's formulations have undergone devastating criticism.[42] First, the culture-of-poverty theory inadequately explains the persistence of poverty. According to the theory, young people are instilled with values which hamper their success—if they do not defer gratification, it is because of the way they have been socialized. But a better explanation of why the poor adopt the life-styles they do is because society is not structured to give the poor the opportunity to participate in a rewarding way in our occupational and educational institutions. To a person who has no chance of getting ahead in life, the idea of deferring gratification today so that life will be better tomorrow is meaningless. The life-styles of the poor, then, are better seen as a reaction to, not a cause of, their poverty.

The culture-of-poverty theory has also been criticized because it leads to the conclusion that poor people are poor because of their own failings. But if poor people socialize their children to believe that they cannot succeed, the only way to eradicate poverty would be to launch a massive effort to change the values and attitudes of the poor. Yet simply instilling in the poor a middle-class emphasis on hard work and material success would have a negligible effect on poverty unless actual opportunities for the poor were opened up as well. Much poverty can be traced to lack of employment opportunities, low wages, racism, and sexism.

Changing the values of the poor will not change these things. So the culture-of-poverty theory, as one critic concludes, "is little more than a middle-class rationale for blaming poverty on the poor and thus avoiding recognition of the need for radical change in our society."[43]

A Search for Solutions

Since poverty is not the fault of the poor, since it is rooted in our social structure, it will not be eliminated by merely urging the poor to lift themselves up by their bootstraps. In this section, we will look at what we have done in the recent past, what we are doing presently, and what we can do in the near future to eliminate poverty.

The War on Poverty

In 1962, Michael Harrington published his influential book, *The Other America,* which drew attention to the poverty amidst affluence in our society.[44] He suggested that up to 25 percent of all Americans may be poor and that hunger and malnutrition marred the lives of millions. About two years later, President Lyndon B. Johnson declared a War on Poverty and created the Office of Economic Opportunity (OEO) to coordinate our antipoverty efforts. When the late President announced his program to "strike at poverty at its source," it was widely hoped that the United States would be the first country in the world to conquer the persistent problem of poverty.[45] If poverty could be conquered, our creaky, inefficient welfare system could be dismantled.

A vast array of antipoverty programs were launched under the OEO, including the Job Corps to train unskilled workers, the Head Start Program to help disadvantaged youngsters, the Neighborhood Youth Corps to provide summer employment, the Upward Bound Program to get blacks into college, and the Volunteers in Service to America (VISTA) program which sought general public involvement in the War on Poverty.[46] In addition, local communities "were encouraged to create their own community action boards. These boards, in turn, would enlist the cooperation of schools, welfare agencies, and other community resources in waging a grass roots war on poverty."[47] In sum, the War on Poverty sought to eliminate poverty by giving the poor skills which would allow them to successfully compete in a capitalistic society.

Despite all these programs, we lost the War on Poverty; our efforts drew attention to the existence of poverty but they did little to eliminate it. There are several reasons why this experiment in social engineering failed so badly. From an administrative point

▲ This OEO photo from the mid-1960s shows a volunteer advising poor youths in a Job Corps program. At that time, it was hoped that the United States would be the first country in the world to conquer the persistent problem of poverty.

of view, the War on Poverty was poorly conceived. From the beginning, it was plagued by inadequate funding, lack of coordination between the various participating agencies, and constant squabbling at the local level over who would control local OEO programs. But most importantly, the War on Poverty failed to provide the poor with the two things that they needed most—jobs and money.

The Welfare System Today

Two major programs constitute the core of the federal government's present efforts to combat poverty: the Supplemental Security Income (SSI) program and the Aid to Families with Dependent Children (AFDC) program. Administered by the Social Security Administration, the SSI program was launched in 1974 to replace the Old Age Assistance, Aid to the Blind, and Aid to the Permanently and Totally Disabled programs. The latter programs were jointly financed by the federal and state governments and, by the early '70s, had become completely unwieldy. Eligibility requirements, for example, varied greatly from state to state as did the average monthly payment per recipient. Under SSI, an eligible individual recipient in 1974 could receive up to $146 per month in aid and an eligible couple could receive up to $219 per month. In December 1974, nearly four million persons received assistance under this program.[48] Most SSI recipients are old people (see also Chapter 12).

The AFDC program provides aid to children whose parents are poor. Under this program, a monthly payment is also made to the mother of the children so she can stay home and care for them (occasionally the payments are made to the father). In 1974, almost eleven million persons received AFDC assistance. Average monthly AFDC payments per family ran from a high of $362 in Massachusetts to a low of $46 in Puerto Rico.[49]

Other federal programs designed to help poor people are Medicaid and the Food Stamp program (see Chapter 12). Some state and local governments also have their own public assistance programs which make limited financial aid available to poor people who do not qualify for SSI or AFDC aid.

As attempts to aid poor people, SSI and AFDC have been feeble. In most states, for example, average AFDC payments fall short of lifting a family above the federally defined poverty line. As a result, our welfare system has been subjected to devastating criticism.[50] The three most important criticisms of our welfare programs are the following: (1) they do not pay enough to provide a decent standard of living; (2) they do not aid all the poor; and (3) they are inefficient.

Few of our public assistance programs pay enough to ensure a decent standard of living. For example, in 1968, only New Jersey and Connecticut made AFDC payments high enough to lift a family of four above the officially defined poverty line. In five states (Alabama, Arkansas, Florida, Mississippi, and South Carolina) poor families of four received less than $100 a month each.[51] Clearly, the AFDC and other public assistance programs are not eliminating poverty.

Another shortcoming of our welfare system is that it is not even intended to aid all poor people. The programs extend aid only to poverty-stricken families with children, to the needy blind, to the permanently and totally disabled, and to old people who are poor. There are no national welfare programs for single adults or for married couples without children, nor is assistance usually available for people who work but who do not earn enough to meet their basic needs. Yet a large percentage of the poor fall into these categories. These people deserve assistance.

Finally, a number of inefficiencies and absurdities are built into our public assistance programs. For one thing, the rules and regulations pertaining to who is and who is not eligible for assistance (particularly under the AFDC program) are so complex that even highly qualified caseworkers sometimes have difficulty in explaining them. Furthermore, our current welfare system is designed in such a way that some welfare recipients are kept permanently dependent.

In Berkeley, Calif., a young husband and father, unemployed but trying to improve his future by attending college at night, is receiving aid. His caseworker informs him that by going to school he is violating the rules: he must be available for employment at all times. He quits school and is still on welfare.

In Oakland, Calif., a middle-aged man, after receiving aid for 13 months, gets a post at last as a security guard. There is one problem: he needs $40 for a deposit on the uniform he will have to wear. Sorry, no money in the rule book. A caseworker deliberately breaks the law to advance the money. The man repays it within a month.[52]

What do we gain by preventing welfare recipients from attending college? Or, what would have happened if the caseworker had not advanced the $40? Very likely, that man would still be receiving assistance today, at a cost to taxpayers far above $40. Unfortunately, these are not exceptional incidents; our welfare system has become a maze of rules and regulations that defies explanation. The tragic result of these rules and regulations seem to be to discourage the poor from attempting to improve their situation.

What is the way out of our current welfare mess? If we are serious about eliminating poverty, we must take two steps. First, we must ensure that every head of household who is able to work can find a job which pays adequately. But we should point out that we are quickly approaching the time when it may not be possible to provide jobs for every able head of household. The second step, then, is to design some means by which all Americans are *guaranteed* the right to share in the nation's wealth.

Redistribution of Income

One method of distributing wealth more equitably is through a negative income tax.[53] Properly designed and implemented, a negative income tax could guarantee that no American would have to live in poverty. At the same time, it could be regulated so that it would not unduly penalize the middle and upper classes.

Figure 9.1 indicates how one proposed negative income tax scheme would work. Under this particular plan, a family of four with no income would receive $2,600 a year from the Internal Revenue Service (negative tax payment). This money would be paid to the family even if one of its members was employable. In short, every family would be guaranteed an annual income of a certain amount with no strings attached.

Figure 9.1 **How the Negative Income Tax Would Work**

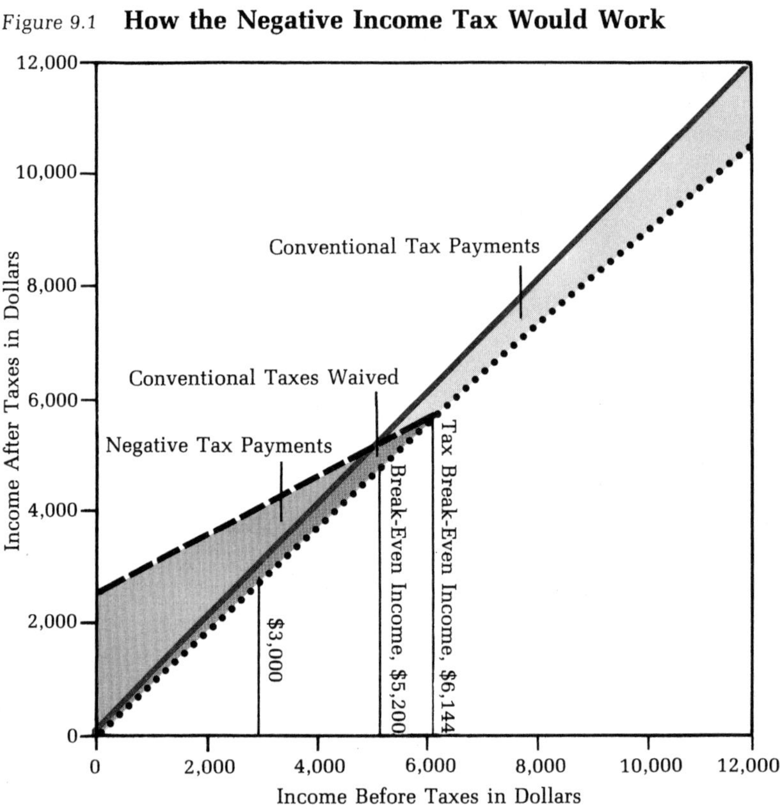

SOURCE: Edmund K. Faltermeyer, "A Way Out of the Welfare Mess," *Fortune*, LXXVII (July, 1968), p. 134.

However, it would still be in the interest of family members to seek work because their negative tax payment from the Internal Revenue Service would be reduced by only $0.50 for every $1.00 earned. For example, if a family of four earned $1,000 during a year, their $2,600 from the government would be reduced $500, leaving them a payment of $2,100. Their total income then would be $3,100. The family would no longer be entitled to a negative tax payment when its earned income reached $5,200 per year; at this point the reduction in their negative tax payment ($.50 on every dollar earned) would equal $2,600 and cancel out their payment.

Under the proposed tax scheme, a family would not begin paying conventional income taxes until its annual income reached $6,144. If they had to begin paying taxes immediately and were liable for, say $300 in taxes on $5,201 in earnings, they would have less money than before they reached the breakeven point of $5,200. Not taxing them until they earn $6,144 gives the family the incentive to keep working after their earnings pass the breakeven point.

Since the negative income tax would provide every person with an income regardless of employability, it is a means of redistributing income. Such a program, however, would be quite a bit more expensive than our present welfare system: "The total cost to the federal government would be $26 billion a year, or about $20 billion more than federal and state agencies currently pay out in cash benefits under the welfare system."[54] The cost of a fully adequate negative income tax system would be even more since the proposed annual income of $2,600 a year is not sufficient for a family of four. But a good negative income tax program could easily pay for itself in time if it helped millions of Americans escape from poverty.

Shortly after taking office, President Richard M. Nixon proposed a Family Assistance Plan (FAP) that had many of the features of a negative income tax. Under his plan, every family would have been guaranteed an annual income of $1,600 plus $800 in food stamps.[55] However, Nixon's proposal was killed by the Senate Finance Committee and never revived.

In conclusion, then, we are not yet ready to launch a meaningful attack on poverty. And until we are ready, we will continue to pay the high price that poverty exacts from its victims and from society in general.

Summary

Poverty is a problem both for those individuals who do not have enough money for food, housing, education, or health care and for society in general. Poverty is a social problem for the simple reason that it is built into our system of social stratification. Poor people, through lack of training and opportunities, are locked into poverty.

Poverty means being disadvantaged in terms of material goods, power, and influence. The government defines poverty in absolute terms—people whose incomes are below a certain amount are considered to be poor. Others define it in relative terms—people are poor who lack many or most things our society considers necessary for a decent life.

Poverty knows few boundaries. The poor are young, old, black, white, male, female, unemployed, and full-time wage earners; they live in both urban and rural areas in the North, South, East, and West.

Being poor in an affluent society means getting an inferior education, being discriminated against by lending institutions and the law, and getting poor health care. Poor people, in short, are denied the right to live a dignified, healthy life and to enjoy the respect of their fellow citizens.

The vast majority of poor people are poor through no fault of their own. They are poor because they are less well educated than the affluent; because they are too young, too old, or too infirm to work; because their race or sex is a handicap to them in getting good jobs; or because our economic system cannot provide enough jobs.

Several theories have been advanced suggesting that poverty may be self-perpetuating. According to the cycle-of-poverty theory, poverty is a vicious circle that makes it difficult for the children of poor parents to break out of poverty. The culture-of-poverty theory suggests that shared ways of thinking, doing, and having characterize the poor. These shared ways of thinking handicap them in improving their economic situation. However, this latter theory leads to the conclusion that the poor are to blame for their poverty. Both theories fail to take into account certain facts—that our social system denies people opportunities, that our economic system denies them jobs, and that many are unable to work.

To date our solutions for poverty have failed dismally. The federal government makes aid available to the poor through Aid to Families with Dependent Children (AFDC) and Supplemental Security Income (SSI). However, these programs do not pay enough to provide a decent standard of living; they are inefficient; and they do not aid all poor people.

The War on Poverty launched in the '60s ended in defeat; it drew attention to the existence of poverty but did little to eliminate it.

Eliminating poverty will most likely require a redistribution of the nation's wealth. Plans such as a negative income tax or guaranteed annual income look promising. Although they would be very expensive, they would pay for themselves in time if they helped eliminate poverty. But at the present time we are apparently unwilling to launch such programs and begin a meaningful attack on poverty.

Discussion Questions

1. Why is poverty a social problem? Does poverty really constitute a threat to society and the groups and institutions of which it is composed? Explain your answer fully.

2. Discuss the relationship between poverty and social stratification. What is meant by the statement that "poverty is an important area in the study of social stratification and can be adequately understood only in this larger context"?
3. Review the section in this chapter entitled "Who Are the Poor?" Describe the characteristics of poor people in America. Is there any such thing as a "typical" poor person?
4. Does the lack of equal educational opportunities for poor children help to perpetuate poverty? Would equal education opportunities for all young people solve the problem of poverty in the United States? Why or why not?
5. Does unemployment contribute to poverty? What is meant by the statement that "full employment creates inflation, but inflation, in turn, creates unemployment"?
6. Discuss the cycle-of-poverty and the culture-of-poverty theories. What are their respective merits? What, if any, are their limitations as explanations for the persistence of poverty?
7. What were some of the specific programs developed as part of the War on Poverty? What were some of the reasons for the failure of the War on Poverty?
8. Our efforts to eliminate poverty have been feeble and halfhearted. How would you account for this? Could our reluctance to launch meaningful programs to eradicate poverty be traced to some core American values (see Chapter 2)? If so, which ones?
9. Indicate that you understand how a negative income tax would work. Do you favor such a program? Why or why not?

Glossary

Aid to Families with Dependent Children (AFDC) A joint federal-state program which makes financial assistance available to children whose parents are poor. A monthly payment is also made to the mother so she can stay home and care for her children.

culture-of-poverty theory A theory which asserts that poor people share a subculture which makes it difficult for them to take advantage of any opportunities they may have to climb out of poverty.

cycle-of-poverty theory A theory which asserts that it is difficult if not impossible for the children of poor parents to break out of poverty.

negative income tax A method of redistributing wealth in which people would receive a cash payment from the government until their earnings reach a specified amount.

open class system (of stratification) A system of stratification in which the individual theoretically can rise or fall in the class structure according to the amount of effort he or she exerts.

poverty A lack of sufficient income and a lack of control over one's fate.

stratification The ranking of individuals into levels that share unequally in the distribution of wealth, status, and power.

structured inequality Inequalities in income, educational opportunities, and so on that are a product of the way in which society itself is organized.

Supplemental Security Income (SSI) Program A federally financed program which makes financial assistance available to certain categories of poor people; SSI replaced Old Age Assistance, Aid to the Blind and Aid to the Permanently and Totally Disabled programs in 1974.

Suggestions for Further Reading

Caplovitz, David, *The Poor Pay More: Consumer Practices of Low Income Families* (New York: Free Press, 1967). An important book which shows how the poor are victimized by unethical sales practices and business schemes. Even though this book was originally published in 1963, most of its findings are still applicable.

Gans, Herbert J., "The Uses of Poverty: The Poor Pay All," in John B. Williamson et al., eds., *Social Problems: The Contemporary Debates* (Boston: Little, Brown, 1974), pp. 140–46. With a great deal of insight, Gans shows how affluent Americans benefit by having the poverty-stricken in their midst. However, he also argues that poverty has many more dysfunctions than functions.

Harrington, Michael, *The Other America: Poverty in the United States* (Baltimore: Penguin, 1962). An extremely important book which helped inspire the ill-fated War on Poverty. Harrington convincingly argues that there are two groups of people in the United States—affluent people much like most of us, and the poor who are isolated and invisible and powerless.

Huber, Joan, and H. Paul Chalfant, eds., *The Sociology of American Poverty* (Morristown, N.J.: General Learning Press, 1974). An excellent collection of articles and essays on various aspects of poverty, many of which were prepared especially for this volume.

Meissner, Hanna H., ed., *Poverty in the Affluent Society* (New York: Harper & Row, 1966). A somewhat dated but nonetheless useful collection of articles on poverty in the United States. Most of the good literature on poverty was published in the '60s as a spin-off from President Johnson's ill-fated War on Poverty.

Moynihan, Daniel P., ed., *On Understanding Poverty: Perspectives from the Social Sciences* (New York: Basic, 1969). A series of important readings on poverty, compiled by one of the leading authorities on this persistent national problem. Of particular interest is Moynihan's own article, "The Professors and the Poor."

Moynihan, Daniel P., *The Politics of a Guaranteed Income* (New York: Random House, 1973). An account of the rise—and fall—of the controversial Family Assistance Plan proposed by President Nixon shortly after he took office.

Reissman, Leonard, *Inequality in American Society: Social Stratification* (Glenview, Ill.: Scott, Foresman, 1973), esp. Ch. 3. A highly sophisticated discussion of poverty as it manifests itself in the United States. Recommended for the more advanced reader.

Turner, Jonathan H., *American Society: Problems of Structure*, 2nd Ed. (New York: Harper & Row, 1976), esp. Ch. 7. A lucid discussion of poverty, what has been done about it, and what could be done about it.

Notes

[1]See Kingsley Davis and W. E. Moore, "Some Principles of Stratification," *American Sociological Review*, 10 (April, 1945), pp. 242–49.

[2]Joan Huber, "Poverty, Stratification, and Ideology," in Joan Huber and H. Paul Chalfant, eds., *The Sociology of American Poverty* (Morristown, N.J.: General Learning Press, 1974), p. 1.

[3]Huber, "Poverty, Stratification, and Ideology," p. 5.

[4]Leonard Reissman, *Inequality in American Society* (Glenview, Ill.: Scott, Foresman, 1973), p. 53.

[5]U.S. Bureau of the Census, *Statistical Abstract of the United States: 1975*, 96th Ed. (Washington, D.C.: U.S. Government Printing Office, 1975), p. 379.

[6]For example, see Herman Miller, "Changes in the Number and Composition of the Poor," in Edward C. Budd, ed., *Inequality and Poverty* (New York: Norton, 1967), esp. p. 165.

[7]S. M. Miller and Pamela A. Roby, *The Future of Inequality* (New York: Basic, 1970), p. 34.

[8]See Jonathan H. Turner, *American Society: Problems of Structure*, 2nd Ed. (New York: Harper & Row, 1976), p. 153.

[9]*Ibid.*

[10]*Ibid.*

[11]For further discussion of the so-called credentials trap, see S. M. Miller and Frank Riessman, *Social Class and Social Policy* (New York: Basic, 1968), Ch. 5.

[12]See David Popenoe, *Sociology*, 2nd Ed. (Englewood Cliffs, N.J.: Prentice-Hall, 1974), pp. 376–79.

[13]See David Caplovitz, *The Poor Pay More* (New York: Free Press, 1963), esp. pp. 13–20.

[14]*Ibid.*, p. 14.

[15]*Ibid.*, esp. pp. 155–69.

[16]For a discussion of the problems which the poor face when they come into contact with the legal system, see Zona Fairbanks Hostetler, "Poverty and the Law," in Ben B. Seligman, ed., *Poverty as a Public Issue* (New York: Free Press, 1965), pp. 177–216.

[17]*Ibid.*, pp. 194–95.

[18]*Ibid.*, p. 190.

[19]U.S. Bureau of the Census, *Statistical Abstract of the United States: 1975,* p. 59.

[20]Nathan Glazer, "Paradoxes of Health Care," in Henry Etzkowitz, ed., *Is America Possible?* (St. Paul, Minn.: West, 1974), p. 134.

[21]See Abraham Ribicoff, "The 'Healthiest Nation' Myth," *Saturday Review,* 53 (August 22, 1970), p. 20.

[22]Glazer, "Paradoxes of Health Care," p. 134.

[23]See Robert L. Eichhorn and Edward G. Ludwig, "Poverty and Health," in Hanna H. Meissner, ed., *Poverty in the Affluent Society* (New York: Harper & Row, 1966), pp. 178–80.

[24]*Ibid.,* pp. 178–79.

[25]H. Paul Chalfant, "Poverty and Mental Illness," in Huber and Chalfant, eds., *The Sociology of American Poverty,* p. 232.

[26]*Ibid.,* p. 233.

[27]U.S. Bureau of the Census, "Characteristics of the Low Income Population: 1972," *Current Population Reports,* Series p-60, No. 88 (Washington, D.C.: U.S. Government Printing Office, 1973), pp. 1–2.

[28]*Ibid.,* p. 1.

[29]Turner, *American Society: Problems of Structure,* p. 176.

[30]*Ibid.*

[31]U.S. Bureau of the Census, "Characteristics of the Low Income Population," p. 1.

[32]Alphonso Pinkney, *Black Americans* (Englewood Cliffs, N.J.: Prentice-Hall, 1969), p. 80.

[33]U.S. Bureau of the Census, *Statistical Abstract of the United States: 1975,* pp. 361–64.

[34]"Unemployment: Any Quick Remedy in Sight?" *U.S. News and World Report,* LXXII (June 19, 1972), p. 43.

[35]*Ibid.,* p. 45.

[36]Martin Rein, *Social Policy: Issues of Choice and Change* (New York: Random House, 1970), p. 90.

[37]See Daniel P. Moynihan, ed., *On Understanding Poverty: Perspectives from the Social Sciences* (New York: Basic, 1969), p. 9.

[38]Jonathan H. Turner, *American Society: Problems of Structure* (New York: Harper & Row, 1972), p. 81.

[39]Oscar Lewis, *Anthropological Essays* (New York: Random House, 1970), p. 68. Italics added.

[40]See *Ibid.*, pp. 70–73.

[41]*Ibid.*, p. 73.

[42]For example, see Eleanor Burke Leacock, ed., *The Culture of Poverty: A Critique* (New York: Simon & Schuster, 1971); Charles A. Valentine, *Culture and Poverty: Critique and Counter-Proposals* (Chicago: University of Chicago, 1968); and William Ryan, *Blaming the Victim* (New York: Pantheon, 1971), pp. 112–35.

[43]Valentine, *Culture and Poverty: Critique and Counter-Proposals*, p. 144.

[44]See Michael Harrington, *The Other America* (Baltimore: Penguin, 1962).

[45]For a more extensive discussion of the War on Poverty, see Moynihan, ed., *On Understanding Poverty: Perspectives from the Social Sciences*, pp. 3–35; Louis A. Ferman, ed., "Evaluating the War on Poverty," *The Annals of the American Academy of Political and Social Science*, 385 (September, 1969), pp. 1–156; and Ben B. Seligman, *Permanent Poverty: An American Syndrome* (New York: Watts, 1968), pp. 161–218.

[46]Turner, *American Society: Problems of Structure*, p. 160.

[47]Dennis E. Poplin, *Communities: A Survey of Theories and Methods of Research* (New York: Macmillan, 1972), p. 236.

[48]U.S. Bureau of the Census, *Statistical Abstract of the United States: 1975*, p. 305.

[49]*Ibid.*, pp. 304, 306.

[50]For example, see Edmund K. Faltermeyer, "A Way Out of the Welfare Mess," *Fortune*, LXXVIII (July, 1968), pp. 62ff. For a more comprehensive evaluation of federal welfare programs, see John Williamson et al., *Strategies Against Poverty in America* (New York: Halsted, 1974).

[51]Committee for Economic Development, *Improving the Public Welfare System* (New York: Committee for Economic Development, 1970), p. 34.

[52]From "Welfare: Trying to End the Nightmare," *Time* (February 8, 1971), p. 15.

[53]For an insightful series of essays on guaranteed annual incomes and negative income taxes, see Robert Theobold, ed., *The Guaranteed Income: Next Step in Economic Evolution?* (Garden City, N.Y.: Doubleday, 1966).

[54]Faltermeyer, "A Way Out of the Welfare Mess," p. 134.

[55]See Daniel P. Moynihan, *The Politics of a Guaranteed Income* (New York: Random House, 1973).

Chapter 10

Racial and Ethnic Prejudice and Discrimination

Our democratic ideal of equality is over two hundred years old. Yet even today millions of Americans are denied employment, education, housing, and political privileges just because of the color of their skin, their national origin, their religion, or their sex. Because some of us are defined as belonging to some *minority*, some of us are the victims of *discrimination*.

Minority group status may have little to do with actual numbers; for example, women constitute about 51 percent of our population, but they are still considered a minority group. In general, a minority group is one that is treated as though it is different from and subordinate to the groups that dominate society.[1] In our country and in our culture, most social, economic, and political power lies with the white male. Among the groups that are accorded minority group status are women, blacks, Chicanos, Puerto Ricans, and American Indians.

This chapter will focus on racial and ethnic discrimination, that is, the systematic denial of equal opportunities to people because they belong to a minority racial or ethnic group. (Chapter 11 will examine the special disadvantaged status of women in our society.) We will deal here chiefly with blacks because they constitute our largest racial minority and because a wealth of data exists on them. We will also touch on the plight of some of America's other minority groups.[2]

Racial and Ethnic Minorities in the United States

Blacks constitute the largest nonwhite minority group in our country.[3] The 1970 census counted 22.5 million blacks, or about 12 percent of the total population. American Indians total about 764,000; most live on reservations in the southwestern and western states and have "the sad distinction of being the most depressed of America's racial and ethnic groups."[4] There are about 4.5 million Mexican-Americans (or Chicanos) in the United States, most of whom live in cities in the southwestern and western states. Mexican-Americans are plagued by low levels of education and income to say nothing of high rates of unemployment. Puerto Ricans number about 1.4 million. They are heavily concentrated in New York City where they are "in more straitened circumstances than blacks."[5] Among other groups who are sometimes discriminated against are Jews, Chinese, and Japanese.

Institutionalized Discrimination

Discrimination means denying to certain individuals and groups equal access to the goods and services we value; it is a part of the very foundation of our society. Our educational, economic, legal, and political institutions are structured to deny blacks and other minorities opportunities to achieve at the same levels as whites. Furthermore, we must add segregation to this interconnecting web of institutional discrimination. Segregation entails the spatial and social separation of minority groups from the dominant sector of our society.

Educational

If society denies a person a good education, it also denies him or her many other benefits. Among many other disadvantages, the poorly educated person is less able to use the ballot box intelligently and less likely to live a long and healthy life.

The existence of educational discrimination is well documented. The Bureau of the Census, for example, reports that in 1970 the average white adult completed 12.1 years of education, the average black 9.8 years, the average Chicano 8.1 years, and the average Puerto Rican 8.7 years.[6] Table 10.1 bears this report out. Blacks do tend to leave school much earlier than whites. In 1972 slightly over 50 percent of all blacks age 25 or older had completed only one year of high school or less. The comparable figure for whites was 27 percent. Conversely, nearly twice as many whites as blacks completed four or more years of college.

Table 10.1

Years of Education Completed by Persons 25 Years of Age and Over, 1972

Years of Education	Blacks	Whites
Less than 5 years	12.8%	3.7%
Less than 1 year of high school	38.2%	23.3%
4 years of high school or more	39.1%	60.4%
4 years of college or more	6.9%	12.6%

SOURCE: Adapted from Sar A. Levitan, William B. Johnston, and Robert Taggart, *Still a Dream: The Changing Status of Blacks Since 1960* (Cambridge, Mass.: Harvard, 1975), Table 4-1.

Not only do our educational institutions provide less education for minority children, they provide inferior education. For each year that they are in school, ghetto children fall further behind white children in reading ability and other skills.[7] Many factors account for this, including a lack of teachers who can work effectively with minority children, overcrowded schools, home environments that do not encourage success in school, and segregation.

In a landmark decision in 1954, the Supreme Court declared that the practice of segregating schools denies black Americans the equal protection of the laws (*Brown v. The Board of Education of Topeka*). One year later, school systems across the country were ordered to desegregate "with all deliberate speed." Yet school desegregation is yet to be achieved because of *de facto* (actual) urban segregation—in many cities black students live in one part of the city and white students live in another. *De facto* school segregation exists because segregated housing exists.

Economic and Occupational

In our economic world, whites fare best. The median family income for white families in 1969 was $9,590, for black families $6,067, and for Spanish-surname families $7,534.[8] It is tempting to attribute these income differentials to the lower overall education levels of racial and ethnic minorities and the lower likelihood that minority members will attain high-status occupations. However, the data indicate that even with education and occupation held constant, nonwhites earn less than whites. For example, in 1969 black professional and technical workers made only 77 percent as much as all professional and technical workers in the United States.[9] Black males with seventeen years or more of education earned only 73 percent as much as white workers with equivalent education.[10] Blacks on the whole, then, are simply paid less than whites regardless of their educational and occupational achievements.

High unemployment rates are also a chronic problem for nonwhite Americans. As Figure 10.1 indicates, unemployment rates for whites have hovered around 5 percent since 1954 while unemployment rates for nonwhites have been near 10 percent. Nonwhite teenagers have particularly high unemployment rates.

Poor pay and frequent unemployment means that racial and ethnic minorities have trouble improving their economic status. Nonwhite families are less likely to be able to afford to send their children to college. As a result, these children fall into the same pattern of economic deprivation that characterized their parents and grandparents. Economic discrimination also means that nonwhite Americans obtain less adequate diets, housing, and health care than whites. In 1971, for example, white females could expect to live an average of 75.8 years; nonwhite females could expect to live 69.7 years. The comparable figures for males were 68.3 years and 61.6 years.[11]

Legal and Political

Throughout our history our legal system has been intentionally used to keep blacks in a subservient position. In 1896, for example, the Supreme Court upheld the constitutionality of a Louisiana

Social Problems and You

The Role of the School in a Democratic Society

What should be the role of the school within a democratic society which has a dominant culture and many other cultures? The school in this type of society has a difficult task, especially when those who make most of the major public decisions do not value, and often disdain, the minority cultures. . . .

The school must help Anglo-Americans to break out of their ethnic encapsulations and to learn that there are other viable cultures in the United States, aspects of which can help to redeem and to revivify the dominant culture. The school should also help all students to develop *ethnic literacy,* since most Americans are very ignorant about cultures other than their own. To attain social and economic mobility, minorities are required to function in the dominant culture and are thus forced out of their ethnic encapsulations. Most minorities, nevertheless, are very ignorant about other minorities.

Broadly conceptualized ethnic heritage programs should be devised and implemented in all schools. Such programs should teach about the experiences of *all* American ethnic groups. Most ethnic studies programs now in the schools deal only with the history and culture of the ethnic minority group which is present or dominant within the local school population. . . .

The school within a pluralistic society should maximize the cultural and economic options of students from all income and ethnic groups. Minority students should be helped to attain the skills needed to function effectively both within their ethnic cultures and within the dominant culture.

By arguing that the school must help minority youths to attain the skills needed to function effectively within the dominant culture, I do not mean to suggest that the school should continue to demean the languages and cultures of minority students. Rather, educators should respect the cultural and linguistic characteristics of minority youths, and change the curriculum so that it will reflect their learning and cultural styles and greatly enhance their achievement. . . .

Anglo-American students should also be taught that they have cultural options. They should realize that using Black English is one effective way to communicate, that Native Americans have values, beliefs, and life styles which may be functional for them, and that there are alternative ways of behaving and of viewing the universe which are practiced within the United States that they can freely embrace. . . .

It is necessary but not sufficient for the school to help minority children to acquire the skills which they need to attain economic and social mobility. It must also help equip them with the skills, attitudes, and abilities needed to attain *power* so that they can effectively participate in the reformation of the social system.

While the school should reflect and perpetuate cultural diversity, it has a responsibility to teach a commitment to and respect for the core values expressed in our major historical documents. If carried to the extreme, cultural pluralism can be used to justify racism, cultural genocide, and related practices. Thus, this concept must be rigorously examined for all of its social and philosophical ramifications.

We should not exaggerate the extent of cultural pluralism in the United States, and should realize that widespread cultural assimilation has taken place in America. To try to perceive cultural differences where none exist may be as detrimental as ignoring those which are real. The school should foster those cultural differences which maximize opportunities for democratic living but vigorously oppose those which do not. Emerging concepts and unexamined ideas must not be used to divert attention from the humanistic goals that we have too long deferred, or from the major cause of our social ills—*institutional racism.*

SOURCE: James A. Banks, "Cultural Pluralism and the Schools," condensed from *Educational Leadership,* XXXII (December, 1974), pp. 163–66, in *The Education Digest,* 40 (April, 1975), pp. 21–23.

Figure 10.1 **Annual Unemployment Rates for Whites and Nonwhites, 1954–1973**

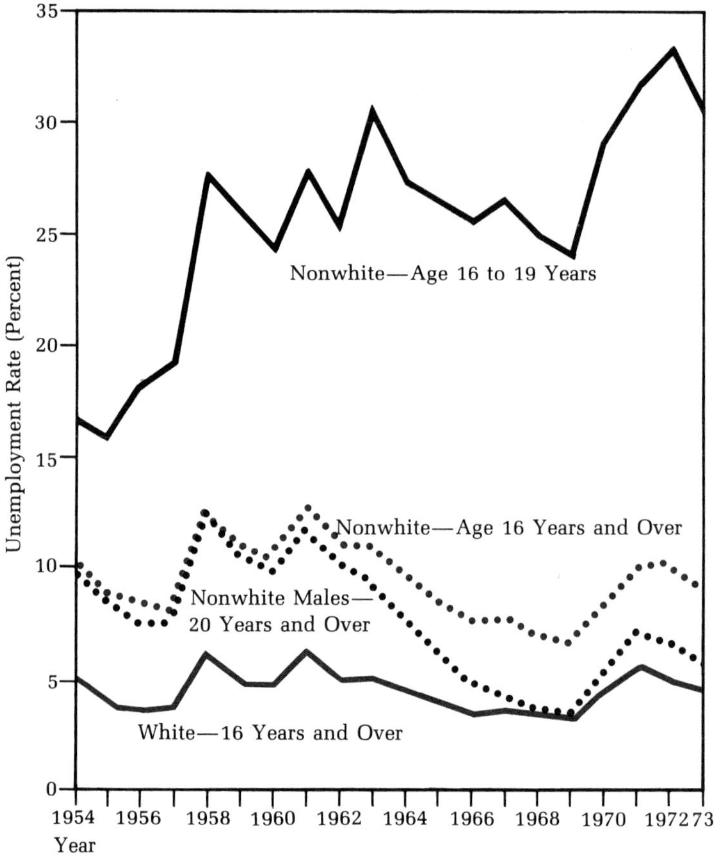

35
30
25
20
15
10
5
0
Unemployment Rate (Percent)
Nonwhite—Age 16 to 19 Years
Nonwhite—Age 16 Years and Over
Nonwhite Males—
20 Years and Over
White—16 Years and Over
1954 1956 1958 1960 1962 1964 1966 1968 1970 197273
Year

SOURCE: Sar A. Levitan, William B. Johnston, and Robert Taggart, *Still a Dream: The Changing Status of Blacks Since 1960* (Cambridge, Mass.: Harvard, 1975), p. 66.

statute which required passenger trains to provide "separate but equal" accommodations for the two races. Although this ruling pertained specifically to passenger trains, it was used until the middle of the present century to justify segregated schools, parks, and other public facilities.[12]

Black Americans have also frequently been denied the right to vote. The Fifteenth Amendment to the Constitution, ratified in 1870, clearly specified that no state could deny a person the right to vote on the basis of skin color or condition of previous servitude. However, it was not until 1965 that Congress passed the Voting Rights Act which put teeth into this amendment. The practice of denying minority group members the right to vote makes it clear to them that they are not respected members of society:

"democracy in the United States is for the white man." It also deprives the group of its right to have people in government who will represent their interests effectively. Even today, blacks are grossly underrepresented in local, state, and national political offices. There is only one black senator (Senator Edward Brooke of Massachusetts), and a handful of black congressmen and mayors. No black has ever been elected president, vice-president, or governor.

Blacks and other minorities also experience severe discrimination in the administration of justice. Black defendants in criminal cases are less likely to be released on bail, less likely to have their own attorneys, more likely to be found guilty, and more likely to be sent to prison for relatively minor offenses than whites (see Chapter 16). In many ways our system of justice treats ethnic and racial minorities differently than it treats the white majority.

Segregation

The practice of physically separating blacks and other minorities from the dominant white population has taken many forms in our history. Until laws were passed in the early '60s to forbid such practices, blacks were often barred from using public accommodations such as hotels, theaters, and restaurants. Despite laws which forbid discrimination in the sale or rental of housing, segregation in housing is still widespread. Every year blacks become increasingly concentrated in the run-down, dilapidated cores of our large metropolitan areas.[13] Here they pay inflated rent for inferior housing. Table 10.2 indicates that blacks are most likely to occupy housing that is overcrowded, old, and lacking in such amenities as washing machines, freezers, air conditioners, and television sets. Inferior housing in run-down neighborhoods can often contribute to health problems and feelings of demoralization and

The practice of physically separating blacks and other minorities from the dominant white population has taken many forms in our history. Until laws were passed in the early '60s to forbid such practices, blacks were often barred from using public accommodations—as this laundry advertisement indicates.
◄

alienation among residents. Segregated housing is also a major cause of *de facto* school segregation. Integrated housing is a major key to integrated schools.

Table 10.2
Housing Characteristics, Black Americans as Compared to Total Population, 1970

Characteristic	Black Americans	Total Population
Median Number of Rooms	4.6	5.0
More than One Person per Room	19.4%	8.0%
Single Family House	57.7%	69.4%
Owner Occupied	41.6%	62.8%
Median Value	$10,800	$17,100
Renter Occupied	58.4%	37.2%
Monthly Rent	$72	$89
Structure Built During Last 10 Years	15.8%	24.8%
Percent Lacking		
Clothes Washer	49.3%	28.9%
Clothes Dryer	88.2%	58.3%
Freezer	79.0%	71.8%
Air Conditioner	82.0%	69.0%
Television	8.0%	4.5%

SOURCE: Adapted from Sar A. Levitan, William B. Johnston, and Robert Taggart, *Still a Dream: The Changing Status of Blacks Since 1960* (Cambridge, Mass.: Harvard, 1975), Table 7-3.

Prejudice

It is important to bear in mind the difference between *discrimination* and *prejudice*—the first refers to behavior, the second to attitudes. So far in this chapter the word *prejudice* has not been used. We have not used the word because sociologists are primarily interested in how societies are structured and organized. As we have seen, virtually every institution in our society is structured to discriminate against blacks and other racial and ethnic minorities. Thus, discrimination is the sociologist's first interest. However, an intelligent understanding of discrimination requires an examination of prejudice.

The Nature of Prejudice

The term *prejudice* means a value-loaded attitude toward another person because that person belongs to a different group.[14] Technically, prejudice can be positive or negative; that is, a person can be prejudiced in favor of a group as well as against it. Usually, however, when we say that someone is prejudiced we mean that he or she looks down on or is hostile to all members of another group, such as blacks, Jews, Chicanos, Puerto Ricans. There are four basic traits associated with prejudice—ethnocentricity, stereotyping, scapegoating, and rationalization.

Ethnocentricity

An ethnocentric person tends to put his or her own group or culture on an unrealistically high pedestal and to see virtue only in that group or culture. So the person who believes that blacks are exceptionally crude, rude, and ignorant may also believe that whites are exceptionally polished, polite, and knowledgeable. Why highly prejudiced persons tend to be ethnocentric is not clear. Perhaps such persons can only feel self-esteem if they believe they belong to the best group or the "in" crowd. In any event, "it is . . . ethnocentrism which lays the foundation for prejudice. If there were no strong feelings for one's own group, there would not be strong consciousness of other groups."[15]

Stereotyping

When a person forms an image of a "typical" member of a minority group in his or her mind and then assumes that this image applies to all members of the minority group, that person is stereotyping. For example, in our society highly prejudiced people may see the black American as a happy-go-lucky, foot-shuffling child; the Jewish American as a greedy, cunning merchant; and the Mexican-American as a dirty, lazy con artist.

Stereotyping is, needless to say, a big liability for the particular group in question. Some black Americans, for instance, intentionally do act in accordance with the stereotype that sees them as intellectually inferior; they feel that if they act any other way they will "be put in their place." Furthermore, stereotyping can become a self-fulfilling prophecy—the prejudiced person assumes that all members of a minority group are inferior and then denies them the right to act in any way that disproves their inferiority.

Scapegoating

The tendency to blame another group for all sorts of social ills and evils is called scapegoating. Blacks, for example, take much of the blame for our high rates of crime, narcotics addiction, and illegitimacy. Similarly, as more blacks and other minority group members assume positions of equality and responsibility, many whites who have not succeeded in their occupations are likely to use blacks and others as convenient scapegoats. Admitting failure is very painful; psychologically, it is much easier to blame "smart" blacks or "cunning" Jews.

Rationalization

Prejudice flies in the face of some basic American values. In principle, we believe that all people are created equal and that all people have the right to be treated with dignity and respect. It is not surprising, therefore, that prejudiced people often develop elaborate rationalizations to justify their prejudice.[16] In short, prejudiced people manage to find some excuse for being prejudiced. Often they rely on racism.

Racism

Racism is the belief that some groups are inherently—biologically—inferior to other groups. True racists may literally believe that blacks have not evolved as far as whites. The racist maintains that this alleged inferiority manifests itself in differences in intelligence, temperament, health and average length of life, morality, and the capacity to create superior cultures.[17] Obviously, if racist dogma were true, the disadvantaged positions of blacks and other racial and ethnic minorities would be both justified and understandable.

However, very few people today take racist theories seriously. Nobody has been able to successfully identify any meaningful differences between racial groups that can be traced to the fact of race itself. Nonetheless, racism continues to have a few champions, including some intellectuals. One spokesman for "scientific racism" is scientist Arthur Jensen. He maintains that "since genetically conditioned physical characteristics differ markedly between racial groups, there is strong *a priori* likelihood that genetically conditioned behavioral or mental characteristics will also differ."[18] Jensen points out that black children tend to score about fifteen points lower on intelligence tests than white children. However, he discounts cultural and environmental variables and ignores pervasive social inequalities that make meaningful research on the heredity-environment question virtually impossible. The chances are very great that if all social inequalities could be eliminated, the I.Q.s of black children would no longer be lower. Jensen's research has also been criticized on other grounds, including inaccurate and misleading data.[19]

Although very few people today take racist theories seriously, racism continues to have a few champions as evidenced by these demonstrators in Chicago.

Origins of Prejudice and Discrimination

We know that prejudice exists because some people define certain groups as superior to others. However, we do not know why prejudice is so deeply rooted in our society nor do we know why virtually all our social institutions are structured to systematically discriminate against blacks and other minorities.

59th ST
WHITE POWER
THE SYMBOL OF WHITE POWER
THE SYMBOL WHITE POWER
WHITE POWER
WHITE POWER NOW!
59th STREET
UP WITH

At least two approaches can be taken to explaining the disadvantaged positions of racial and ethnic minorities in our society. The first attributes systems of discrimination to prejudice; the second attributes prejudice to the need to justify discrimination. Some important psychological and economic theories take the first approach, that is, they argue that prejudicial attitudes lead to or cause discriminatory behavior. On the other hand, some major sociohistorical theories maintain that discrimination comes first: prejudicial attitudes arise to justify and perpetuate discriminatory institutional arrangements.

Psychological Factors

Two major theories trace prejudice to the personality needs of the prejudiced individual. One of these theories links prejudice to a particular personality syndrome called the *authoritarian personality.*[20] This theory grew out of the finding that highly prejudiced, ethnocentric people tend to have an undue respect for authority, they see people as all good or all bad, they view the world in terms of black and white, and they are extremely aware of differences in status. According to this theory, the authoritarian personality is a product of an individual's interaction with a very stern, punitive father whom the individual eventually grows to hate. In our society, however, an individual cannot hate his or her father without experiencing at least some guilt and anxiety. So, the authoritarian personality deflects this hatred onto groups that are different from his or her own and which rank lower in terms of status. The authoritarian personality not only reveres strong and powerful groups but hates those that are powerless and weak. Obviously, an individual with an authoritarian personality would support discriminatory institutional arrangements and would discriminate against members of disadvantaged minority groups.

The second theory, advanced by psychologist John Dollard, is the *frustration-aggression hypothesis.*[21] This hypothesis rests on two premises: the first is that as we go through life we constantly meet with frustrating situations (that is, situations in which we cannot achieve our goals); and the second is that typical reactions to frustration are aggression and hostility. Normally, a person would vent his or her aggression on the individual or group which causes the frustration. For example, if denied a pay raise, a person should logically tell the boss off, not beat the children or kick the dog. However, advocates of the frustration-aggression hypothesis point out that very often the sources of a person's frustration are unknown or are individuals or groups which the person dares not attack. The person thus seeks a convenient substitute target on which to vent pent up hostility. This substitute could be any group that is weak and unable to fight back. It is possible then, for example, that white southerners after the Civil War turned their wrath on blacks because blacks were convenient scapegoats and because they dared not attack the real source of their frustration—white northerners.

Economic Factors

Some researchers have tried to trace prejudice to economic factors:

> Race prejudice . . . is a social attitude propagated among the public by an exploiting class for the purpose of stigmatizing some group as inferior so that the exploitation of either the group itself or its resources may both be justified.[22]

Recently, colonialism has been used to explain prejudice and discrimination.[23] Colonialism is a process by which a conquering group obtains political, economic, and social power over a previously independent people. According to this theory, the dominant white group in the United States has acquired colonial power over blacks and other minority groups by forcing them into ghettos (internal colonies) where they can be economically exploited.

Economic forces clearly play a role in creating prejudice. Researchers, for example, "have found anti-semitism and anti-Negro sentiments to be most common among people dissatisfied with their own economic position or among those whose status has declined."[24] Even prosperous whites may, to some extent, resent blacks who are economically successful because the blacks represent a threat to their jobs and economic security.

However, economic theories of prejudice do not provide a complete explanation of institutionalized discrimination. For example, white manual laborers are discriminated against in an economic sense because they are frequently not paid enough to afford adequate food, housing, clothing, and medical care. Yet this is not because the middle and upper classes are prejudiced against them. Rather, our society is structured so that people born into a disadvantaged economic position, regardless of race, find it extremely difficult to climb out of that position.

Sociohistorical Factors

The psychological and economic theories examined so far assume that people acquire negative attitudes toward racial and ethnic minorities and then translate these attitudes into discriminatory institutional structures. However, the causal relationship between prejudiced attitudes and discriminatory behavior can be just the opposite—discrimination may lead to prejudice.

Several writers maintain that racist ideologies develop to justify discriminatory practices and institutions. For example, a study of plantations concluded that racist ideologies developed as a way to keep slaves subservient; the notion that blacks are inherently inferior to whites was, to some extent, accepted by blacks as well as whites and therefore helped ensure that blacks would accept their own subjugation and exploitation.[25] Racist ideologies, it is interesting to note, did not develop until the late eighteenth century.[26] "[R]acist ideas and practices emerged from a need to justify and perpetuate slavery. Once ideas are mobilized, they linger on for a time after the disappearance of the conditions that produced them."[27]

Moreover, "although there is a correlation between the two, racism [or prejudice] can be completely independent of discrimination."[28] A person can behave discriminatorily toward other people without harboring any personal prejudice toward them.[29] For example, a white contractor who has close friends who are black and who employs black carpenters and electricians at above average wages may nonetheless refuse to sell one of his homes to a black family because he fears that his white customers will look elsewhere. Very often racial and ethnic minorities are discriminated against because it is the norm to do so. If we deviate too far from the norm, we may be subject to gossip and ridicule, economic losses, or other forms of punishment.

A Concluding Note

Like the chicken and the egg, it probably does not matter in the end which came first—prejudice or discrimination. On the one hand, prejudiced attitudes are reinforced when people constantly see members of racial and ethnic minorities holding unskilled, poorly paid jobs, living in run-down neighborhoods, getting into trouble with the law. On the other hand, people's attitudes have a very profound impact on their behavior. If some whites did not believe that blacks are inferior, they would be less able to rationalize educational, economic, and legal discrimination and segregation.

We learn our prejudiced attitudes and discriminatory behavior just as we learn any other pattern of culture, that is, through the process of socialization. A white American child has every opportunity to become prejudiced. He or she is not only taught that some groups are inferior to others, but also observes filthy urban ghettos populated by blacks, Chicanos, Puerto Ricans, and other racial and ethnic minorities who most likely work in menial jobs. Unfortunately, a child's attitudes can crystallize at an early age. And if a child needs further lessons in discrimination and prejudice, he or she need only observe and listen to adults.

We learn our prejudiced attitudes and discriminatory behavior just as we learn any other pattern of culture, that is, through the process of socialization. Unfortunately, a child's attitudes can crystallize at an early age.

Liberation Movements and the Demand for Change

So far we have established two major ideas in this chapter. First, we have shown that prejudicial attitudes and discriminatory practices are thoroughly institutionalized in the United States. A thoroughgoing system of social and economic relationships keeps racial and ethnic minorities subservient, and a complex set of prejudicial attitudes and rationalizations support our discriminatory practices. Second, we have pointed out that the costs of discrimination—tallied in wasted human potential and talent—are prohibitive for both the individual and society.

It is natural to conclude this chapter by looking at what steps we have taken to end the prejudice and discrimination we have talked about. In recent years there have been a number of social movements that have sought to liberate racial and ethnic minorities. Again, we will primarily focus on black liberation efforts because they are the largest and best documented.

Most improvements in the status of American racial and ethnic minorities have come at the absolute insistence of the minority groups, not of the white majority. Black individuals and black organizations have long worked to improve the status of black Americans. The National Association for the Advancement of

Colored People (NAACP) was formed in 1909 to fight discrimination and segregation. Between its founding and 1954, it won several court cases for blacks and their rights. However, major progress was first made in 1954 when the Supreme Court declared school segregation unconstitutional. The years between 1954 and 1970 can be divided into two phases in the black struggle for equality—the civil rights phase (1954 to 1965) and the militant phase (1965 to 1970).

The Civil Rights Phase

The civil rights phase of the struggle for black equality was initiated in 1954 when the Supreme Court handed down its decision in the case of *Brown* v. *the Board of Education of Topeka.* As mentioned earlier, this decision struck down the doctrine of "separate but equal." A year later school districts across the country were ordered to desegregate with all deliberate speed.

At about this time black leaders were emerging who could spearhead the drive for equality. A key figure was the Reverend Martin Luther King, Jr.[30] King inspired several successful nonviolent protests against discrimination and segregation, such as the Montgomery city bus boycott (1955), the battle for voting rights in

The Reverend Martin Luther King, Jr., (seventh from right) inspired several successful nonviolent protests against discrimination and segregation, such as this 1963 March on Washington.
▼

Selma, Alabama (1963), and the March on Washington (1963). But perhaps most importantly, he imbued millions of Americans, both black and white, with his dream that "we shall overcome." During these years, lower federal courts applied the *Brown* case and ruled against segregation in other public facilities besides schools. The Supreme Court also handed down decisions pertaining to voting, employment, and due process, and in 1968 declared state laws forbidding interracial marriage unconstitutional.[31]

The Supreme Court was not the only branch of government supporting equal rights in the '50s and '60s. Presidents Kennedy and Johnson were both sensitive to the discrimination, poverty, and suffering in the midst of American prosperity.

In 1964 Congress overcame southern opposition and passed the Civil Rights Act banning discrimination in the use of public facilities such as hotels, restaurants, parks, and hospitals. One year later, Congress passed a strong Voting Rights Act banning literacy tests that had frequently been used to disenfranchise black voters. The Voting Rights Act also empowered federal examiners to oversee voter registration procedures in states that seemed intent on denying blacks the right to vote. Other needed legislation was passed during the '50s and '60s pertaining to discrimination in employment and in the sale or rental of housing. School lunch programs, Headstart, the Job Corps, and Upward Bound, all part of President Johnson's War on Poverty (see Chapter 9), also benefited blacks and other racial and ethnic minorities.

The goal of the civil rights phase of the black struggle for equality was the total integration of blacks into American society. If total integration could be achieved, problems of inequality would disappear.

> The ideology of the movement was based on an orderly and pluralistic conception of society committed to nonviolence and passive resistance. The movement was biracial: liberal whites and, to some extent, the Federal government were allies in the struggle against bigotry and discrimination.[32]

Unfortunately, not all whites embraced the idea of finding peaceful solutions to the problems that beset American society. In Birmingham and Selma, in Greensboro, in Little Rock, and in many other places, civil rights leaders and their followers met with violence in their peaceful struggle for racial equality.

Since the mid-1960s there has been little legislative and judicial action on civil rights. No significant new civil rights laws have been passed and no major Supreme Court decisions have been handed down.

The Militant Phase

The mid-1960s brought a period of violence to the black struggle for equality, beginning with the bloody Watts riot in Los Angeles in 1965. During the summer of 1965, massive riots broke out in Detroit, Newark, New Brunswick, and many other cities. This was not, of course, the first time that violence had marked race relations—blacks have often been the victims of beatings, lynchings, and other acts of terrorism.[33] But the summer of 1965 was the first time that blacks collectively reacted with violence to the injustices they suffered.

Why, at this point in American history, did many blacks resort to violence as a tactic for overcoming suppression? After all, the years between 1945 and 1965 had been marked by judicial and legislative victories in the civil rights movement. Yet, these victories seemed hollow; in 1965, most blacks still lived in enforced poverty, most blacks were still treated as second-class citizens, and in many ways the situation appeared to be getting worse. At that time the National Advisory Commission on Civil Disorders stated that "our nation is moving toward two societies, one black, one white—separate and unequal."[34] Black Americans still had many very serious grievances, including the following:

1. unfair police practices
2. unemployment and underemployment
3. inadequate housing
4. inadequate education
5. poor recreation facilities and programs
6. ineffectiveness of the political structure and grievance mechanisms
7. disrespectful white attitudes
8. discriminatory administration of justice
9. inadequacy of federal programs
10. inadequacy of municipal services
11. discriminatory consumer and credit practices
12. inadequate welfare programs[35]

Given all these grievances, it is surprising that blacks did not turn to violence much sooner.

The militant phase of the black liberation movement ended as abruptly as it began. The summer of 1967 was the last of the "long hot summers."

The Black Movement in the '70s

Today, two issues that grew out of the civil rights phase are very much alive—busing and equal employment opportunities. It was one thing for the Supreme Court to order the desegregation of schools. Actually finding ways to overcome school segregation, especially that of a *de facto* variety, has proven to be extremely difficult. The task of assuring that all Americans enjoy equal employment opportunities has also been problematic.

Busing

More than two decades after the Supreme Court's decision in *Brown v. The Board of Education of Topeka,* our schools are still not integrated. As we have seen, *de facto* housing segregation is a major stumbling block to school desegregation—in many cities black students live in neighborhoods quite some distance from neighborhoods where white students live. Nonetheless, the courts have consistently ruled that schools must be integrated. One way to achieve a balanced racial mix of students is to transport them to different schools—white children to black schools, black children to white schools.

Not only has busing not helped black-white relations, in many instances it has actually hurt them. In Boston in 1976, for example, busing led to violence and increased racial antagonisms.
◀

Busing sounds like a simple and obvious solution but it has become one of the most controversial issues of the '70s. A 1971 Gallup Poll found that 77 percent of the public is against busing.[36] Clearly, opposition to busing reflects racism to some degree. Although busing foes publicly state that they oppose busing because it inconveniences their children and because they want to maintain neighborhood schools, a more likely reason is that they do not want their children sent to black schools nor do they want black students to attend their schools.

Not only has busing not helped black-white relations, in many instances it has actually hurt them. In several cities, notably Boston and Louisville, busing has led to violence and increased racial antagonisms. It has also helped speed up the white flight to the suburbs as white parents move farther from central cities to escape school integration. Many white parents in cities and suburbs in all parts of the country have been motivated to place their children in all-white private schools. Busing, then, although intended to help integrate schools, has in some cases led to increased segregation in both education and housing. As a result, even a leading proponent of school integration has concluded that "busing does not work."[37]

There is a possibility that the courts will partially abandon busing, at least in northern cities. Nonetheless, the Supreme Court's ruling that schools must be integrated with all deliberate speed still stands both as a legal principle and as an essential goal of civil rights.

Equal Employment Opportunities

The federal government has forged several tools to help ensure equal employment opportunities. For example, the Equal Opportunities Employment Commission has fairly broad powers to enforce Title VII of the Civil Rights Act of 1964. This act forbids discrimination in hiring, compensation, and promotion on the basis of race, color, religion, sex, or national origin. Similarly, the Office of Federal Contract Compliance, a branch of the Department of Labor, is empowered to withhold federal funds from companies which discriminate in their employment practices. In all, about 250,000 companies, employing about a third of the U.S. labor force, depend enough on federal contracts and grants that they must comply with guidelines established by the Office of Federal Contract Compliance.[38]

There is some confusion as to what an employer must do to comply with federal policies on nondiscriminatory employment practices. Is it sufficient for the employer to hire, pay, and promote people without considering their race, ethnicity, or sex; or must the employer have an affirmative action program? The latter would entail preferential treatment for women and minorities in order to eliminate past inequities in hiring, pay, and promotions. In some cases, employers have been required to develop specific plans to increase the percentage of women and racial and ethnic minorities in their total labor force.[39]

Affirmative action programs have aroused considerable controversy. Opponents argue that such programs run counter to the idea that people should be hired, paid, and promoted on the basis of merit. Conceivably, under a rigorously enforced affirmative action program an employer would have to hire a minority group member who is less qualified than a white male applicant for the same job. This is closely related to a second charge that affirmative action programs promote reverse discrimination. This means that employers might discriminate against white males simply because they are under pressure to hire and promote blacks and other minorities. But reverse discrimination is also illegal. Able white male workers do not appear to be adversely affected by government programs designed to assure equal employment opportunities.[40]

The Black Movement in Retrospect

It is difficult to assess the accomplishments of the postwar black liberation movement. The civil rights phase appears to have achieved minor progress through the passage of legislation banning discrimination in employment, voting, housing, education, and so forth. But today blacks still earn less than whites, complete fewer years of education, and have higher rates of unemployment. American cities continue to become increasingly segregated.[41] The one area of undisputed progress has been in ensuring blacks the right to vote.

Why the militant phase of the liberation movement ended so abruptly is unclear. Possibly the rioting that marked the mid-1960s subsided because it proved to be an ineffective tactic. However, a more likely reason is that it was impossible to sustain the emotional fervor that riots feed on. Emotion-charged feelings died down and those who led the protest movements moved on to other things. For example, groups like the Black Panthers have either disbanded or have turned to service projects in urban ghettos as a means of restoring black American pride.

It is extremely difficult to determine where we stand now and where we shall go in the future in terms of race and ethnic relations. Since 1968, the government has done little or nothing to substantially further the cause of civil rights. In the early '70s, President Nixon appeared to advocate a policy of benign neglect toward blacks; he openly opposed busing. Furthermore, little activism has emerged from the urban slums and ghettos. Just because little seems to be happening, however, does not mean that the problems of racial and ethnic minorities have been solved. They still exist and they can surface any time.

Summary

Despite our verbal and legal commitments to the ideal of equality, many Americans today are denied equal opportunities because of the color of their skin, their national origin, their religion, or their sex. They are given minority status and treated as subservient to the dominant society. This chapter focuses on the black minority.

Discrimination means denying to certain individuals and groups equal access to the goods and services we value. Discrimination is part of the structure of our society and is in evidence in our educational, economic, legal, and political institutions. Segregation means the spatial and social separation of minority groups from the dominant sector of our society. Although now illegal, segregated housing is still widespread and is the primary cause of *de facto* school segregation.

Prejudice means a value-loaded attitude toward a person who belongs to a minority group. There are four basic traits associated with prejudice—ethnocentricity, stereotyping, scapegoating, and rationalization.

To rationalize their stand, prejudiced people often turn to racism—the belief that some are inherently (biologically) inferior. Racist dogmas have never been proven but are taken seriously by some people.

There are two approaches to the origins of prejudice and discrimination. Psychological and economic theories (authoritarian personality syndrome, frustration-aggression hypothesis, and colonialism) hold that discrimination grows out of prejudice. On the other hand, sociohistorical theories maintain that prejudiced attitudes emerged to justify discriminatory practices (slavery). It is also possible to behave discriminatorily without being prejudiced.

Discrimination and prejudice are learned, like any other pattern of culture, through socialization.

The black liberation movement can be roughly divided into two phases—the civil rights phase and the militant phase. The civil rights phase (1954–1965) saw many court decisions in favor of equality and many government programs to improve the status of minority groups. The militant phase (1965–1970) was marked by violence and massive summer riots. Today, we face two highly controversial issues that grew out of the civil rights phase—busing and equal employment opportunities.

It is difficult to assess the accomplishments of the postwar black liberation movements. Minor progress has certainly been made, but significant inequalities still exist in education, housing, and employment. The passage of the Voting Rights Act in 1965 represented a major victory for the civil rights movement. Although there is little evidence of activism at the present time, many problems of racial and ethnic minorities remain to be solved.

Discussion Questions

1. What do we mean by the term *minority group*? Are women a minority group? What about old people? Explain and justify your answer.

2. Discuss the difference between *prejudice* and *discrimination*. Is it possible for a person to be prejudiced but not to discriminate? Is this likely to happen very often? Are people who are non-prejudiced likely to engage in discriminatory behavior from time to time? Why or why not?

3. Define and discuss the four traits that are associated with prejudice. Do you think that it is possible to grow up in the United States without acquiring any prejudices?

4. Discuss the following statements: (*a*) prejudicial attitudes cause discriminatory behavior, (*b*) prejudicial attitudes arise from a need to justify discrimination. With which of these statements do you agree? Why?

5. Discuss those theories that trace prejudice to the personality needs of the prejudiced individual. How do these theories differ from the theories that trace prejudice to sociohistorial factors?

6. Discuss the civil rights phase of the black liberation movement. What were some of its significant accomplishments? Why do you suppose that laws and Supreme Court decisions have not been entirely successful in bringing about full equality of opportunity?

7. Why do you suppose that some blacks in the mid-1960s resorted to violence in an effort to improve their disadvantaged position? Why did the militant phase of the black liberation movement end so abruptly?

8. Busing does not seem to be a fully satisfactory method of integrating schools. Could busing be made to work? Can you think of some alternative ways by which school integration can be achieved?

9. How would you assess the accomplishments of the postwar black liberation movement? Has major progress been made in solving the problems of racial and ethnic minorities? Explain and justify your answer.

Glossary

affirmative action programs Hiring programs designed to increase the percentage of women and racial and ethnic minorities in an employer's labor force.

de facto segregation Segregation brought about by the fact that racial and ethnic minorities live in one part of the city whereas the dominant majority lives in another, and sometimes far removed, part of the city.

discrimination The practice of denying certain individuals and groups equal access to the goods and services we value.

ethnocentricity The tendency to put one's own group or culture on an unrealistically high pedestal and to look down on the cultures of other groups.

minority group A racial, ethnic, or other group assigned to a low level in the system of social ranking.

prejudice A value-loaded attitude toward another person because that person belongs to a different group. The prejudiced person looks down on or is hostile to all members of another group.

racism The belief that some groups are biologically inferior to other groups.

scapegoating The tendency to blame minority groups for all sorts of social ills and evils.

segregation The spatial and social separation of minority groups from the groups that dominate society.

stereotyping The common tendency to characterize a whole category or group of people without regard for individual differences.

Suggestions for Further Reading

Griessman, B. Eugene, ed. *Minorities: A Text with Readings in Intergroup Relations* (Hinsdale, Ill.: Dryden, 1975). A general discussion of various facets of minority group relations. This book serves as a good introduction to the field of racial and ethnic minorities.

Grimshaw, Allen D., *Racial Violence in the United States* (Chicago: Aldine, 1969). Probably the most comprehensive collection of articles on racial violence in the United States that has ever been assembled. The time span covered by these articles runs from 1640 to the present.

Jordan, Winthrop D., *White Over Black: American Attitudes Toward the Negro, 1550–1812* (Chapel Hill, N.C.: University of North Carolina, 1968). A monumental exploration of white attitudes toward blacks in America from 1550 to 1812. This book provides the reader with an excellent background for understanding American race relations today.

Levitan, Sar A., William B. Johnston, and Robert Taggart, *Still a Dream: The Changing Status of Blacks Since 1960* (Cambridge, Mass.: Harvard, 1975). An outstanding review of the changing status of black Americans since 1960 and of how these changes were brought about. This volume is a virtual gold mine of data on the black American.

Mack, Raymond W., *Race, Class, and Power*, 2nd Ed. (New York: Van Nostrand Reinhold, 1968). Although somewhat dated, this volume contains a comprehensive and well-selected collection of articles on race and ethnic relations. Many of these articles have become classics and are still widely cited in the professional literature.

"Racism in Sports," *Social Science Quarterly,* 55 (March, 1975), pp. 919–66. This collection of five articles advances some hypotheses that are important both to the sociology of race relations and the sociology of sports. Especially recommended for students who are themselves involved in intercollegiate athletics.

Rose, Peter I., *They and We: Racial and Ethnic Relations in the United States,* 2nd Ed. (New York: Random House, 1974). A simple but intelligent introduction to race and ethnic relations in the United States, written by one of the leading students of minority group relations.

Simpson, George Eaton, and J. Milton Yinger, *Racial and Cultural Minorities: An Analysis of Prejudice and Discrimination,* 3rd Ed. (New York: Harper & Row, 1965). Even though this volume was published in 1965, this is still the most complete treatment of prejudice and discrimination available.

Staples, Robert, *Introduction to Black Sociology* (New York: McGraw-Hill, 1976). An exciting, easily read volume which sheds much new light on the black experience in America.

Notes

[1]The term *minority group* is more complicated than this definition suggests. For further discussion see George Eaton Simpson and J. Milton Yinger, *Racial and Cultural Minorities: An Analysis of Prejudice and Discrimination,* 3rd ed. (New York: Harper & Row, 1965), pp. 16–19.

[2]There are several books that the reader can consult for in-depth information on America's other minority groups. For example, see Judith Kramer, *The American Minority Community* (New York: Crowell, 1970); S. J. Makielski, Jr., *Beleagured Minorities: Cultural Politics in America* (San Francisco: Freeman, 1973); and Rudolph Gomez, Clement Cottingham, Jr., Russell Endo, and Kathleen Jackson, eds., *The Social Reality of Ethnic America* (Lexington, Mass.: Heath, 1974).

[3]All data in the following paragraph are taken from U.S. Bureau of the Census, *Census of Population: 1970, Subject Reports* PC(2)-1B, 1C, and 1F (Washington, D.C.: U.S. Government Printing Office, 1973).

[4]John R. Howard, *The Cutting Edge: Social Movements and Social Change in America* (Philadelphia: Lippincott, 1974), p. 109.

[5]*Ibid.,* p. 103.

[6]U.S. Bureau of the Census, *Census of Population: 1970,* Vol. I, *Characteristics of the Population,* Part I, *U.S. Summary* (Washington, D.C.: U.S. Government Printing Office, 1973), Table 70; and U.S. Bureau of the Census, *Census of Population: 1970, Subject Reports,* PC(2)-1C, Table 4.

[7]For example, see Kenneth B. Clark, *Dark Ghetto: Dilemmas of Social Power* (New York: Harper & Row, 1965), pp. 120–24.

[8]U.S. Bureau of the Census, *Census of Population: 1970,* Vol. I, *Characteristics of the Population,* Table 94.

[9]Sar A. Levitan, William B. Johnston, and Robert Taggart, *Still a Dream: The Changing Status of Blacks Since 1960* (Cambridge, Mass.: Harvard, 1975), Table 3-6.

[10]*Ibid.*, Table 3–8.

[11]National Center for Health Statistics, *Vital Statistics of the United States: 1971*, Vol. II, *Mortality* (Washington, D.C.: U.S. Government Printing Office, 1975), Table 5–1.

[12]Laws that require the operation of segregated facilities are often referred to as "Jim Crow" laws. See C. Vann Woodward, *The Strange Career of Jim Crow*, 2nd. Rev. Ed. (New York: Oxford, 1966).

[13]See Jonathan H. Turner, *American Society: Problems of Structure*, 2nd Ed. (New York: Harper & Row, 1976), esp. pp. 233–34.

[14]For further discussion, see Peter I. Rose, *They and We: Racial and Ethnic Relations in the United States*, 2nd Ed. (New York: Random House, 1974), pp. 100–102.

[15]Cited in *Ibid.*, p. 100.

[16]See Simpson and Yinger, *Racial and Cultural Minorities*, p. 53.

[17]For further discussion, see *Ibid.*, pp. 41–48.

[18]Arthur Jensen, "The Differences Are Real," *Psychology Today*, 7 (December, 1973), p. 81.

[19]For a thorough and rigorous critique of Jensen's research, see Martin Deutsch, "Happenings on the Way Back to the Forum: Social Science, IQ, and Race Differences Revisited," *Harvard Educational Review*, 39 (Summer, 1969), pp. 523–51.

[20]See T. W. Adorno, Else Frenkel-Brunswik, D. J. Levinson, and R. N. Sanford, *The Authoritarian Personality* (New York: Harper & Row, 1950).

[21]See John Dollard et al., *Frustration and Aggression* (New Haven: Yale, 1939).

[22]Oliver C. Cox, *Caste, Class, and Race* (New York: Doubleday, 1948), p. 393.

[23]For example, see Graham C. Kinloch, *The Dynamics of Race Relations: A Sociological Analysis* (New York: McGraw-Hill, 1974); and Robert Blauner, "Internal Colonialism and Ghetto Revolt," *Social Problems*, 16 (Spring, 1969), pp. 393–408.

[24]Rose, *They and We*, p. 114.

[25]See Edgar T. Thompson, "The Plantation as a Race-Making Situation," in B. Eugene Griessman, ed., *Minorities: A Text with Readings in Inter-group Relations* (Hinsdale, Ill.: Dryden, 1975), pp. 102–103.

[26]See Ashley Montague, *Man's Most Dangerous Myth: The Fallacy of Race*, 5th Ed. (New York: Oxford, 1974), esp. p. 15.

[27]Robert Staples, *Introduction to Black Sociology* (New York: McGraw-Hill, 1976), p. 46.

[28]*Ibid.*,

[29]Indeed, Merton points out that one can be an unprejudiced nondiscriminator, an unprejudiced discriminator, a prejudiced nondiscriminator, or a prejudiced discriminator. See Robert K. Merton, "Discrimination and the American Creed," in R. M. Maclver, ed., *Discrimination and National Welfare* (New York: Harper & Row, 1949), pp. 99–126.

[30]There have been several biographies of Martin Luther King, Jr., one of the best of which is David L. Lewis, *King: A Critical Biography* (New York: Praeger, 1970).

[31]One of the most important decisions pertaining to due process was handed down in the case of *Gideon* v. *Wainwright.* This decision gave indigent defendants the right to counsel in a criminal trial. See Anthony Lewis, *Gideon's Trumpet* (New York: Random House, 1964).

[32]Alfred M. Mirandi, *The Age of Crisis: Deviance, Disorganization, and Societal Problems* (New York: Harper & Row, 1975), p. 113.

[33]For an extensive collection of articles on racial violence in the United States, see Allen D. Grimshaw, ed., *Racial Violence in the United States* (Chicago: Aldine, 1969).

[34]National Advisory Commission on Civil Disorders, *Report of the National Advisory Commission on Civil Disorders* (Washington, D.C.: U.S. Government Printing Office, 1968), p. 1.

[35]*Ibid.*, p. 81.

[36]Levitan, Johnston, and Taggart, *Still a Dream*, p. 283.

[37]"New Coleman Report," *Time*, 105 (June 23, 1975), p. 60.

[38]Daniel Seligman, "How 'Equal Opportunity' Turned into Employment Quotas," *Fortune*, 57 (March, 1973), p. 162.

[39]Thus, in 1969 the U.S. Department of Labor required federal construction contractors in Philadelphia to increase the number of minority craftsmen that they employed from 2 percent to 4 to 9 percent during the first year and to 19 to 26 percent by the fourth year. The federal courts have upheld the right of the federal government to require that federal contractors develop affirmative action plans. See Levitan, Johnston, and Taggart, *Still a Dream*, pp. 271–72.

[40]It should be noted that reverse discrimination is clearly illegal. Thus, section 703(a) of Title VII of the Civil Rights Act of 1964 makes it illegal for an employer "to . . . classify his employees in any way which would deprive or tend to deprive any individual of employment opportunities . . . because of such individual's race, color, religion, sex, or national origin." Seligman, "How 'Equal Opportunity' Turned into Employment Quotas," pp. 166–67.

[41]Reynolds Farley and Karl E. Taeuber, "Population Trends and Residential Segregation Since 1960," *Science* 159 (March 1, 1968), pp. 953–56.

Chapter 11

Sex Roles and Sexism

Almost every day our newspapers carry stories on women who are competently performing jobs once considered "men's work." For example, we read of women carpenters, coal miners, Episcopalian priests, truck drivers, and linepersons for the telephone company. In addition, in a few families, the men are "househusbands" while their wives are "breadwinners." We also read about more and more men becoming nurses, secretaries, and telephone operators. And former football star Rosey Grier has published a book on needlepoint for men. Sex-role stereotypes in this country are unquestionably being challenged.

In most societies the division of labor is based on sex—certain tasks are assigned to men, certain others are assigned to women. Men are also expected to behave differently from women. For example, in our society, men are traditionally expected to be independent, aggressive, and tough-minded; women are traditionally expected to be dependent, passive, and emotional.

Today, however, millions of American women are beginning to question the traditional division of labor. Why can't they have the same career opportunities and rewards as men? Many American men are also beginning to question the roles assigned to them. Frequently male sex roles force men into jobs which are tedious and unrewarding and virtually cut them off from full participation in family life. Many men and women have come to the realization that they live in a sexist society.

Almost every day newspapers carry stories about women who are competently performing jobs once considered "men's work."
▼

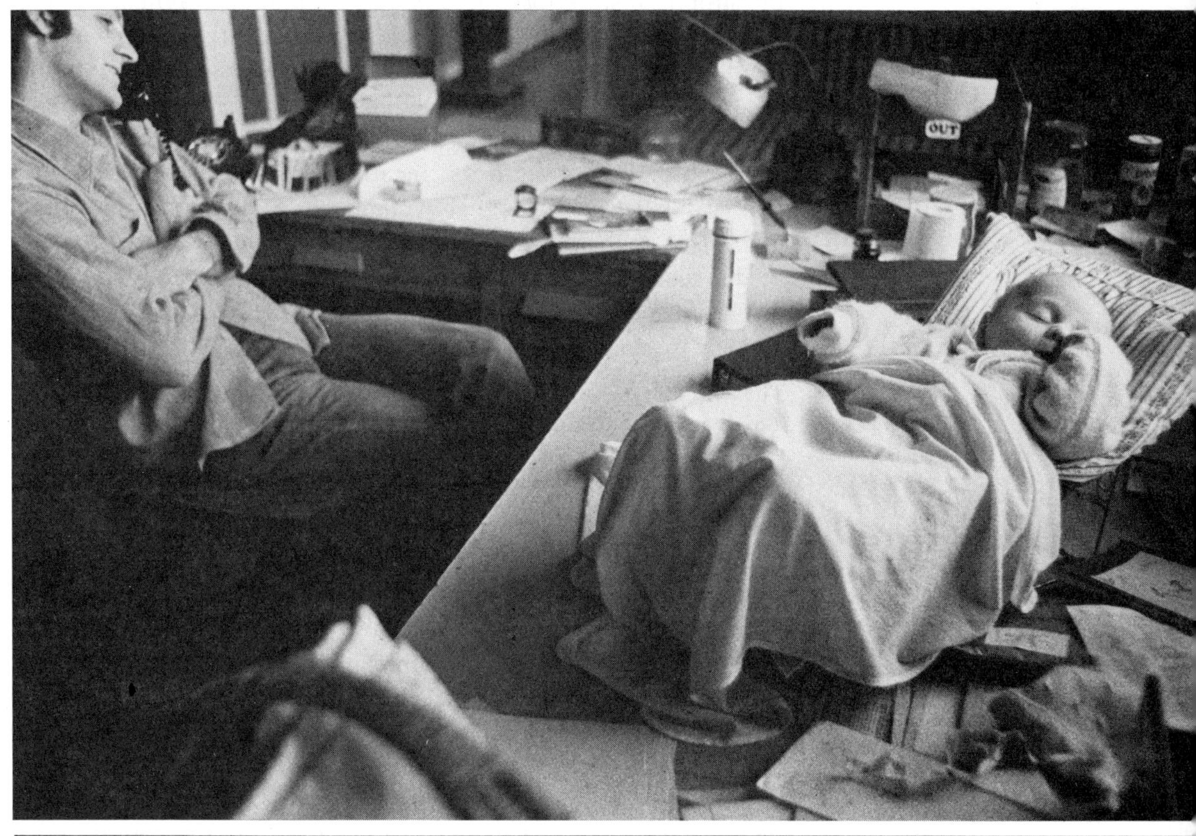

▲
In a few families, the men are becoming "househusbands."

Sexism

The words *sexist* and *sexism* crop up almost daily in the press, and many of us have probably asked ourselves the question, Am I a sexist? But most of us are probably not even sure what sexism is, nor could we explain why it is a social problem. This is not surprising. Even the literature on sexism lacks a rigorous definition of sexism; and, although sexism is widely considered a social problem, there are few coherent statements as to why it is.

What Is Sexism?

Sexism means different things to different people; but, generally speaking, we can distinguish two separate, but interrelated, meanings.

First, sexism means "the belief in the superiority of the male principle."[1] Some people consider men stronger than and superior to women in a number of different respects—for example, men are supposed to be more intelligent than women. Often, the supposed superiority of men is attributed to the innate biological differences between men and women. Here, the remarkable similarity between sexism and racism is clear. Racists, as we discussed in Chapter 10, believe that black persons have not evolved as far as white persons and that blacks are, because of their presumed biological inferiority, incapable of achieving as much as whites. Sexists believe that women are biologically inferior to men and are therefore incapable of achieving as much as men.

The second meaning of sexism is more direct and is the one usually used by feminists—sexism means the subjugation of women by men.

> The truth of woman's life and of her actual experience is engulfed again and again by those institutions of our society, owned and operated by men, that act as a kind of policing force to keep her in line, to keep her believing that she is what men say she is, that she wants what men say she wants, that she knows only what men say she knows.[2]

In other words, men have structured society so that they benefit at women's expense. Sexism, in effect, is a set of social relations which keeps women in subservient positions.

According to either definition, sexism is clearly rooted in the structure of our society. Sexist thinking and behavior is taught by virtually every social institution. We are socialized by our culture to be sexists. Sexism is also self-perpetuating—if men are socialized to believe that women are inferior, they will structure institutions so that women are treated as inferior; similarly, if women believe that they are inferior, they will act inferior.

Consequences of Sexism

Sexism is a social problem for the same reason racism is a social problem—it produces discrimination in education, employment, law, and politics. This, in turn, means that women are effectively cut off from power since most power in this country comes from a high position in the occupational hierarchy and the money that accompanies this high position. Sexism locks *both* men and women into restricted social roles and hampers them in developing their full potentials as human beings. Sexism is at odds with the democratic ideology of our society.

Educational

In theory, our schools are thoroughly democratic institutions. With the exception of a few all-male or all-female schools and colleges, our educational system is available to all students regardless of sex. Women seem to be encouraged to excel in school just as much as men. However, statistics and research studies show that our educational system in many ways discourages females.

At first glance, females appear to complete about as much schooling as males. In 1974, for example, white females 25 years of age or over had completed an average of 12.3 years of education and white males had completed an average of 12.4 years of education.[3] However, these figures must be interpreted with extreme caution. They do not mean that women are almost as likely as men to go to college. In fact, in 1967, about 71 percent of male high-school graduates went on to colleges compared to 54 percent of female high-school graduates.[4] The difference between the percentages of males and females going on to graduate school is even greater. The reason females *appear* to complete about as many years of school as males is that fewer females drop out of school before high-school graduation. The average number of years of schooling completed by males is reduced by the fairly high number who drop out of high school.

The failure of girls to pursue higher education as frequently as boys do is largely due to sexism. We have traditionally defined competitiveness, aggressiveness, and other personality traits which go along with academic achievement as unfeminine: "While boys are often afraid of failing, girls are additionally afraid of succeeding. The adolescent girl, her parents, her girl friends, and her boy friends perceive success, as measured by objective, visible achievement as antithetical to femininity."[5] Several other studies support this view, suggesting that academically successful college girls often try to hide their success and/or intelligence from their male peers.[6]

Occupational

Women tend to fare less well than men in their earnings. In 1973, for example, the median income of women was only 56.6 percent that of men. Men employed full-time had median 1973 earnings of $11,186 per year, while women employed full-time had median earnings of $6,335 per year.[7] We might be tempted to explain this discrepancy by pointing out that women are less likely than men to have earned college degrees. However, Table 11.1 suggests that this is not the case. With education held constant, women still make far less than men. One reason for their lower earnings is that women are concentrated in clerical and sales jobs and in professions such as teaching and social work. None of these occupations offer high pay.

Women's lower incomes are particularly important for society when women are the sole providers for their families. About one-

Table 11.1
Comparison of Median Income of Year-Round, Full-Time Workers by Sex and Educational Attainment, 1974

Years of School Completed	Median Income Women	Median Income Men	Women's Income as a Percent of Men's[a]
Elementary School			
Less Than 8 Years	$ 5,022	$ 7,912	63.5
8 Years	5,606	9,891	56.7
High School			
1 to 3 Years	5,919	11,225	52.7
4 Years	7,150	12,642	56.6
College			
1 to 3 Years	8,072	13,718	58.8
4 Years	9,523	16,240	58.6
5 Years or More	11,790	18,214	64.7

[a]Column 1 divided by column 2.

SOURCE: U.S. Bureau of the Census, *Current Population Reports*, P-60, No. 101 (Washington, D.C.: U.S. Government Printing Office, 1976).

quarter of all poor families in America are headed by women.[8] Some of these women are unable to work, some cannot find work, and some are employed in jobs that pay poorly. The children of these women pay a heavy price for the economic and occupational discrimination against their mothers. Eventually, society also pays—children in poor families are less likely to get an adequate education and more likely to have health problems, to run afoul of the law, and to end up as welfare dependents (see also Chapter 9).

Legal

Until 1920, women did not have the right to vote. Even today, the laws in most states still reflect the belief that women are not quite the equals of men. In Alabama, Florida, Indiana, and Texas, for example, a woman cannot sell her own property without the consent of her husband; in Kentucky and Georgia a woman cannot borrow money without her husband's signature.[9]

Women are treated particularly unfairly by the law in regard to rape and abortion. In many states the law treats women who have been raped as second-class citizens. The woman must sometimes prove that she resisted the rape until overcome by force or violence before the accused rapist can be convicted. Furthermore, in many states a woman's testimony is not enough to convict the rapist; the woman's testimony must be corroborated by independent witnesses. Similarly, many states place severe restrictions on a woman's right to have an abortion—even though most of these restrictions are unconstitutional. These laws say, in effect, that a woman must give birth to a child even if she strongly desires not to do so.

The Supreme Court has not been as diligent in trying to eliminate sex discrimination as it has been in trying to eliminate racial discrimination.[10] In fact, in several instances the Supreme Court has upheld the constitutionality of laws which obviously favor one sex over the other.

Political

Women have, to a great extent, been excluded from political office. No woman has ever been seriously considered as a potential president or vice-president of our country, no woman has ever served on the Supreme Court, and only three women have served as governors. Between 1917 and 1971, there were only ten women in the Senate and only sixty-nine in the House.[11]

President Carter has expressed his intention to try to rectify political inequalities based on sex and has appointed a few women to top-level governmental positions. Nonetheless, a massive effort will be required before women come anywhere near being equally represented in government.

Other

Any kind of discrimination, including sexism, can make the victim feel useless and locked into unrewarding roles:

> The problem lay buried, unspoken, for many years in the minds of American women. It was a strange stirring, a sense of dissatisfaction, a yearning that women suffered in the middle of the twentieth century in the United States. Each suburban wife struggled with it alone. As she made the beds, shopped for groceries, matched slipcover material, ate peanut butter sandwiches with her children, chauffeured Cub Scouts and Brownies, lay beside her husband at night—she was afraid to even ask herself the silent question—"Is this all?"[12]

Today, a great many American women are asking themselves the question, Is this all? Perhaps one reason why many women no longer find the traditional wife-mother role fully satisfying is that they are socialized, like men, to value achievement and success. Yet, as we have seen, women are to a great extent denied the opportunities men have. Thus, in a society which stresses the importance of achievement and success, over half the population is to a great extent discouraged from pursuing these goals.

Sexism also takes its toll on men. For example, in our society men are socialized to be unexpressive and unaffectionate; yet many people identify the key to a good marriage as the ability to express feelings and emotions. "The possibility of an affectionate and companionable conjugal relationship carries with it the assumption that both the husband and wife are bringing into marriage the expressive capabilities to make such a relationship work. This being the case, American society is ironically shortchanging males in terms of their ability to fulfill this role expectation."[13] In addition, because a father is away at work during most of his day, the ties between him and his children tend to be very weak.[14]

There are many other ways in which sexism and sex-role stereotyping affect us. For example, many more women than men suffer from mental depression, and this suffering has been attributed to the sexist character of our society.[15] Similarly, rates of juvenile delinquency, crime, alcoholism, and narcotics addiction are higher among men than among women, possibly because of the way appropriate male behavior is defined in our society.

Origins of Sexism

Sexism hurts both individuals and society. It hurts individuals because it prevents them from using their full potentials by locking them into unrewarding roles. It hurts society because it wastes needed talent and ability. For example, even in the '50s and early '60s when we suffered from a shortage of scientifically trained personnel, women were not encouraged to become scientists and engineers. In this section we will examine why our society is sexist and why sexism remains so embedded in our society. We will begin by determining what we mean by the terms *sex* and *sex roles*.

Sex

The term *sex* refers to certain features of a person's anatomy and physiology. The person who marks *female* on a questionnaire indicates that she is potentially capable, during part of her life, of bearing and suckling young. The person who marks *male* indicates that he is potentially capable of producing and ejaculating sperm. In short, the term *sex* refers to what our bodies can or cannot do in the reproduction process.

After determining a person's sex, we can hazard some guesses about that person. For example, if we know that *X* is a male and *Y* is a female, we can predict that *X* may be stronger than *Y*. But we can't be certain. Except for the ability to bear children, the differences within sex groups are greater than the differences between sex groups. Some men are weak and nonmuscular, and some women are strong and muscular.

Sex Role

The term *sex role* refers to how a person is expected to behave by virtue of his or her sex. Men and women differ not only in their anatomies but in their attitudes and behavior. The traits we ascribe to the male sex role include "independence, aggression, competitiveness, leadership, task orientation, outward orientation, assertiveness, innovation, self-discipline, stoicism, activity, objectivity, analytic-mindedness, courage, unsentimentality, rationality, confidence, and emotional control." The traits we ascribe to the female sex role include "dependence, passivity, fragility, low pain tolerance, nonaggression, noncompetitiveness, inner orientation, interpersonal orientation, empathy, sensitivity, nurturance, subjectivity, intuitiveness, yieldingness, receptivity, inability to risk, emotional liability, supportiveness."[16]

But there is much overlap between males and females in terms of the degree to which they display these traits. As Figure 11.1 suggests, the differences between men and women, in terms of both their anatomical characteristics and their sex-role traits, are best thought of as two overlapping, bell-shaped curves.

Figure 11.1 **Overlapping Sex and Sex-Role Differences Between Men and Women**

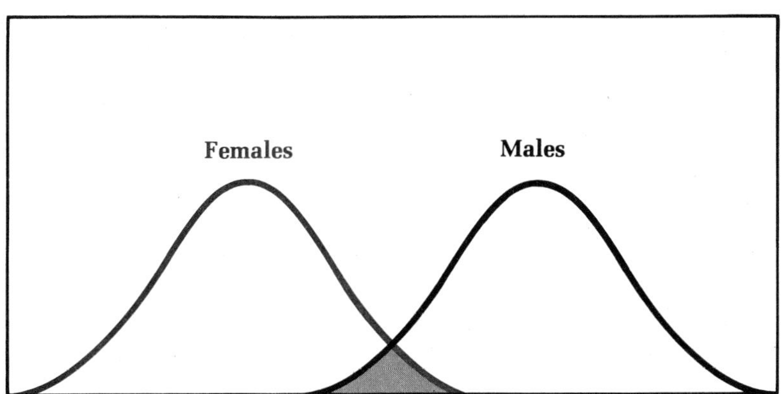

As the shaded area indicates, the social and anatomical differences between males and females are best thought of in terms of two overlapping, bell-shaped curves. Thus, men are generally stronger than women, but some women are stronger than some men. Men may generally be more aggressive than women, but some women are more aggressive than many men.

The reason that the "typical" male comports himself differently than the "typical" female is most likely that society expects males to act differently than females. Every role we play is surrounded by a set of norms, that is, rules and regulations which tell us what we should and should not do, must and must not do. For example, in our society, men "should" be aggressive and independent, women "should" be passive and nonaggressive; men "must not" wear dresses and makeup, women "must not" get into fist fights and barroom brawls.

The sex roles assigned to us affect us in at least two ways. First, our roles influence the goals we pursue and the aspirations we hold. In our society, men are more likely, on the whole, than women to aspire to be doctors, lawyers, engineers, and scientists because we define these roles as roles which are appropriately filled by men. On the other hand, women are more likely, on the whole, than men to aspire to be housewives, secretaries, teachers, and nurses because these roles are socially defined as women's roles. Role distinctions are even reflected in our vocabulary—according to most dictionaries, there are no such words as *househusband* or *salesboy*.

Second, the roles assigned to us affect how other people expect us to behave. In our society women are expected to be passive and noncompetitive, and men are expected to be aggressive and competitive, especially in dealing with the larger society. Furthermore, the price for deviating too far from the behavior expected of us may be high—we may be criticized, ridiculed, gossiped about, and even ostracized.

Thus, the origins of sexism lie in sex roles—women play subsidiary roles because they are expected to and men assume domineering attitudes toward women because they are expected to. If we wish to eliminate sexism, we must change our stereotypes of how men and women should behave. Before we can change these stereotypes, however, we need to understand where sex roles come from.

Biological Origins

Throughout most of history, it has been assumed that sex-role differences originate in the biological differences between men and women; that is, sex-role differences were thought to be inborn. Even as recently as 1969, Dr. Benjamin Spock, a widely read and respected pediatrician and scholar, stated, "Biologically and temperamentally, I believe women were made to be concerned first and foremost with child care, husband care, and home care."[17] Obviously, the key words in Spock's statement are *biologically* and *made*. What evidence is there to suggest that women are biologically made to play different roles than men?

As we have pointed out, there are certain anatomical differences between men and women. In addition, normal women usually produce a preponderance of female sex hormones, and normal men produce a preponderance of male sex hormones. However, there is no evidence to suggest that these hormones have any significant impact on the individual's personality or behavior.[18]

It has also been traditionally assumed that, on the whole, men are larger and stronger than women. This seems to be generally true, at least in Western societies. However, even here some question arises as to whether size and strength are inborn, immutable differences. For example, in Bali men do little heavy work; as a result, Balinese men and women resemble each other in body size and shape: "The greater strength of the male is at least partly a result of the fact that he exerts himself more, and in cultures where this is not the tradition there may hence be much less difference between men and women."[19] As depicted in Figure 11.1, there is considerable overlap between the sexes in terms of strength.

Further differences between men and women that may be linked to biological factors are hard to pin down. Based on a review of the pertinent literature, one study reports that, in infancy and very early childhood, males in general tend to differ from females in general in terms of the following characteristics:

1. Males tend to display a higher activity level than females. Males cry more and have a slightly higher metabolic rate than females.

2. Female infants tend to be more sensual than male infants and are sensitive to a wider range of stimuli than males.

3. Girls speak earlier, read earlier, and count earlier than boys.

4. Female infants tend to respond more readily than males to social stimuli and are more likely to seek satisfaction from other human beings.

5. Even during early childhood, males tend to be more aggressive than females and seem to have a lower tolerance for frustration.

6. During early childhood, girls tend to score higher than boys on intelligence and aptitude tests. By the time the child reaches high school, these differences have evaporated or reversed themselves.[20]

But again, we must stress that boys and girls overlap in terms of these characteristics. Furthermore, the differences are not great: "That these developmental differences are not sizeable is evidenced by the fact that the girl and the boy will be very much alike for the most part. Girls may speak earlier, but not so much so that it is noticeable to parents, pediatricians, or teachers."[21]

In summary, a survey of the biological differences between males and females merely demonstrates how insignificant those differences really are. About the only striking difference is that, between the ages of about 14 and 45, women are potentially capable of bearing children; men are not. Beyond this, biological differences between the sexes do not appear to influence behavior patterns nor do they determine sex roles—biology is not destiny.

Sociocultural Origins

The field of anthropology has provided much insight into the origins of sex-role differences. In her famous study, *Sex and Temperament in Three Primitive Societies*, anthropologist Margaret Mead found that personality differences between the sexes are "cultural creations to which each generation, male or female, is trained to conform."[22] In one of the societies she studied, both men and women were expected to be mild, sympathetic, and cooperative—traits we associate with femininity and motherliness. In the second society, Mead found that both men and women were expected to be fierce and aggressive, or masculine by our standards. In the third society, she found that the sex roles were the exact opposites of our own. The women shaved their heads, were prone to hearty laughter, and displayed a good deal of comradely solidarity and aggressiveness. The men of the tribe, on the other hand, were "preoccupied with art, spent a great deal of time on their hairdos, and [were] always gossiping about the opposite sex."[23] According to our definitions, the women acted like men, and the men acted like women.

Mead's evidence strongly suggests that sex-role differences grow out of the socialization process. In other words, society has expectations as to how females should behave and it carefully teaches the female what these expectations are. If she deviates from these expectations or fails to incorporate them into her personality and behavior, she may face gossip, ridicule, and ostracism. The same is true for the male.

In our society, every major social institution participates in the process of socializing males to act "like men" and females to act "like women." Three institutions are essential in the socialization process—the family, the school, and the mass media.

The Family

The family is crucially significant in socializing children to play all the various roles assigned to them, especially their sex roles. Several good studies have been conducted on how families contribute to the origin of sex-role differences. One of the best suggests that there are three processes by which families socialize children into their sex roles.[24]

The first of these processes is *molding and canalization.* As an example of molding, "young mothers of female runarounds report they 'fuss with' the baby's hair, dress them 'feminine,' and tell them how pretty they are."[25] As a result, young females incorporate these aspects of female comportment and behavior into their personalities.

Canalization refers to the practice of giving the female infant objects and playthings specifically defined as feminine, such as dolls, carriages, and nurse's kits. This is a form of anticipatory socialization—the child is subtly told that when she grows up, these are the objects that she will be expected to manipulate. The same process applies to boys. Boys are dressed up as soldiers or cowboys and given doctor's kits, toy trucks, and toy guns.

The second process is *symbol manipulation.* This usually begins on a simple level—the female child is told that she is "a good girl" or "daddy's girl," while the male child is told that he is "a good boy" or "all boy." These expressions impress on the child that he or she belongs to one group which is different from another group. As the child grows older, the process of symbol manipulation becomes more complex. For example, the little girl is told that someday she will grow up to be "a lady just like mommy"; and when she engages in masculine behavior such as attempting to urinate standing up, she is told that only daddies and boys do that, but mommies and little girls sit down to go to the bathroom. Again, the child is told that she belongs to a group (females) which is different from another group (males).

The third process by which families teach their children their sex roles is by *exposing them to different activities.* Little girls help their mothers around the house by doing dishes, making beds, and setting the table. Little boys, on the other hand, emulate their fathers by working in the yard, washing the car, going hunting, and taking out the garbage.

Through the processes of molding and canalization, symbol manipulation, and being exposed to different activities, the child learns to identify with his or her sex role. These three processes also constitute forms of anticipatory socialization in that children learn the behavior patterns that will be expected of them when they reach adulthood. Parents participate in the processes of sex-role socialization with little or no awareness of what they are doing. One study found that "many mothers did not recognize any efforts they might be making to produce appropriate sex-role behavior. . . . They thought a mother had to adjust her behavior to the sex-determined temperament of her child, but did not consider that her own actions might be responsible for any such characteristics."[26]

The School

Like the family, schools encourage sex-role identification through the processes of molding and canalization, symbol manipulation, and exposure to different activities. For example, a study of sex-role socialization at the nursery-school level reveals a prime example of molding and symbol manipulation: "M. walks in

Like the family, schools encourage sex-role identification through the processes of molding and canalization, symbol manipulation, and exposure to different activities. ▶

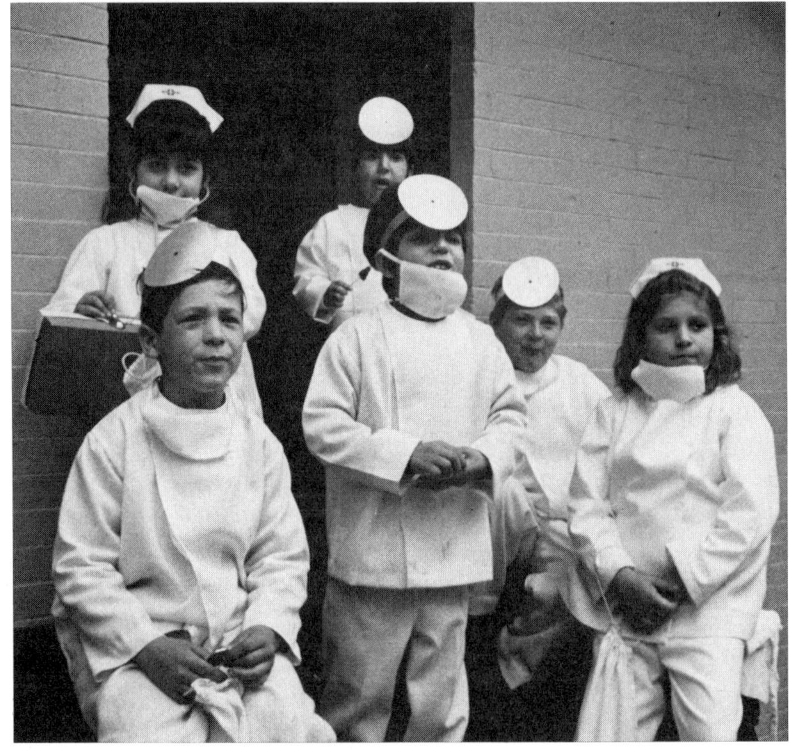

wearing a dress she has not worn before. One of the mothers says to her, 'M., what a pretty little lady you are today.' "[27]

Schools also contribute to the origin and perpetuation of sex-role differences in many other ways. For example, a survey of textbooks adopted by or recommended for use in the second through sixth grades in California found that "at least 75 percent of the stories' main characters are male" and that "the average book devotes less than 20 percent of its story space to the female sex."[28] Furthermore, the stories that do center on females tend to show women in traditional or subservient roles: "Textbook writers seem to have reduced all women to a common denominator of cook, cleaner, and seamstress."[29] Clearly, many school textbooks perpetuate and reinforce sexist ideology.

Another interesting study shows how the educational system in effect "teams up" with society to mold the female into her sex role and to discourage her from being academically successful.[30] Before puberty, girls as well as boys are encouraged to excel in school and allowed to display the traits, such as aggressiveness and competitiveness, that are conducive to academic success. However, with the onset of puberty, pressure is put on girls to adopt the traits we associate with femininity and to develop good interpersonal relationships with boys. With this socially induced change in priorities, "personal qualities, such as independence, aggression, and competitive achievement, qualities that might threaten success in heterosexual relationships, are largely given up."[31] This change in female priorities occurs near the end of high school and again near the end of college.

The Mass Media

The mass media play a major role in creating and perpetuating sexism and sex-role differences, particularly through advertising.

> Advertising did not create these images about women, but it is a powerful force for their reinforcement. It legitimizes the idealized, stereotyped roles of woman as temptress, wife, mother, and sex object, and portrays women as less intelligent and more dependent than men. It makes women believe that their chief role is to please men and that their fulfillment will be as wives, mothers, and homemakers. It makes women feel unfeminine if they are not pretty enough and guilty if they do not spend most of their time in desperate attempts to imitate gourmet cooks and eighteenth-century scullery maids. It makes women believe that their own lives, talents, and interests ought to be secondary to the needs of their husbands and families and that they are almost totally defined by these relationships.[32]

> Advertising also reinforces men's concepts about women's place and women's role—and about their own roles. It makes masculine dominance legitimate—and conversely questions the manhood of men who do not want to go along with the stereotypes. . . . Advertising prolongs the myths of male supremacy, painting pictures of men who are superior to women and etching these images in the eyes of men who use these "eternal verities" as the excuse for forcing women's continued subjugation.[33]

In one example of sexist advertising, the Dictaphone Corporation once carried an advertisement for calculators in which an attractive blonde woman sat behind a desk polishing her nails. The punch line for the advertisement read, "Our new line of calculators goes through its final ordeal. The dumb blonde test."[34] In other advertisements women are shown as essentially simple-minded creatures whose primary goal in life is to produce a dazzling white wash, a dining room table made sparkling with lemon-fresh Pledge, or a smile made sexy with Ultra-Brite.

The mass media also help propagate sexism and sex-role differences in their programming. For example, almost every intelligent and perceptive analyst of the national and world scene is a man; Walter Cronkite, David Brinkley, Harry Reasoner, Eric Sevareid, and Howard K. Smith have few female counterparts besides Bar-

▲
Advertising did not create sexist images about women, but it is a powerful force for their reinforcement. Advertising legitimizes the idealized, stereotyped roles of woman as temptress, wife, mother, and sex object.

bara Walters. News broadcasts are filled with reports of successful men. When women are shown as successful, it is often in conjunction with their husband's success. For example, Pat Nixon was once shown visiting schoolchildren in China while her husband worked for détente between two of the world's great powers. This, of course, is not the fault of the networks themselves. Their task is to report on those who make the news, and in a sexist society women generally lack the opportunity to make news. If a woman were running for the presidency of the United States, she would receive wide news coverage.

More research is needed before we can determine to what actual extent the mass media influence the role behavior of men and women and propagate sexist stereotypes. We do know, however, that millions of people watch television for hours every day: to many people, it is their primary source of knowledge, information, and truth. Even if the mass media eventually were shown not to have a great impact in propagating sex-role stereotyping, much of its content is degrading to both men and women.

Social Problems and You

Girls, Boys, and Books

We've done some research recently . . . to study an activity nearly everyone has shared—book-carrying. Books are a common burden, but boys and girls handle them differently almost from the start, on their way to developing two distinct styles.

By high-school age, nearly all men carry books at their sides, with their arms relatively straight. Eight out of 10 women, in contrast, rest the lower edge of the book or books on their hip or pelvic bones, holding them against their bodies with one or both arms bent.

The obvious explanation for this difference in style is that there are sex differences in size, strength, and body shape. But other forces must be at work, too, because the book-carrying differences develop earlier in life than the physical ones.

We directed a team of researchers who observed the behavior of 3,100 Knoxville students. The students ranged in age from kindergarten through college. We studied a nearly equal number of working-class blacks, working-class whites and middle-class whites, enabling us to examine racial and socioeconomic differences among the three groups.

Researchers recorded how students carried books on a checklist that described eight different carrying positions. In position A, the person holds the book at his side, gripping the top of the book with his fingers pointing down toward the ground. In position H, the carrier clutches the book directly in front of her body with both hands or arms. In the six in-between positions, the book is raised gradually until it is held against the body about waist-high, usually cradled in the arms.

Kindergarten boys and girls lug their books in similar ways, with both favoring "masculine" position B. By second grade, boys and girls in all three groups use significantly different carrying methods. Boys employ position B increasingly in succeeding grades, until by high school other positions are rare.

Except for working-class whites, girls' book-carrying techniques shift much more abruptly. Position B remains the favorite through the sixth grade, although G and similar "feminine" positions gradually become more popular. A dramatic shift takes place in junior high. Position B almost disappears from the girls' repertoire, to be replaced by G and similar positions.

In contrast, working-class white girls adopt female positions much earlier. This difference could develop because white working-class mothers put more emphasis than do middle-class mothers on their daughters' femininity. There were no obvious racial or socioeconomic differences in the development of male book-carrying methods.

Physical factors may account for most of the book-carrying differences in college and in the late high-school years, but the differences exist earlier. Height, weight, and body shape are quite similar in boys and girls until about age 12. These sexually similar growth patterns contrast sharply with the sexually different book-carrying methods. . . .

We believe that the desire to imitate older children and adults, along with other social factors, helps explain the different carrying styles. In addition, position B appears to be more comfortable for men and position G for women because of their physical differences. It also seems true that boys are under greater pressure from their friends to "carry their books like a man" than girls are to use feminine methods. This would also account for the greater variety of methods used by females.

SOURCE: Thomas P. Hanaway and Gordon M. Burghardt, "Girls, Boys and Books," *Psychology Today,* 10 (August, 1976), p. 67.

The Contemporary Women's Rights Movement

Sociologists frequently classify social problems as *manifest* or *latent.*[35] A latent social problem is one which presents a very real threat to social order or personal well-being but is not recognized as a social problem. A manifest social problem, on the other hand, is one which a significant number of people recognize as a threat to social order or personal well-being and for which they seek some remedy.

Sexism as a social problem has recently made the transition from latent to manifest. It has always been with us, but only during recent years has it been defined by a significant segment of the public as a social problem.

As a latent social problem, of course, sexism—with its tremendous costs and consequences—has been with us for a long time. The subjugation of women has always been a waste of talent and ability. Through the ages, millions of men and women have been locked into roles which they have found unrewarding and unfulfilling. Although there have been feminist movements in the past, they have usually been confined to pursuing very specific, limited, short-term objectives, such as the right to vote.[36] A full-scale, long-range women's rights movement has developed in the United States only recently. For the first time, women are now demanding that the sexist structure of society be changed.

Several factors have contributed to the emergence of the contemporary women's rights movement; two are of particular importance. The first was the publication, in 1963, of Betty Friedan's best-selling book, *The Feminine Mystique.* In this book, Friedan gave form and substance to an idea that had been growing in the minds of many women for years—that they were not being allowed to realize their full potentials as human beings. Friedan's book was widely read and convinced many people of the crucial need to redefine and reassess the role of women in our society. As Friedan said, "It is my thesis that as the Victorian culture did not permit women to accept or gratify their basic sexual needs, our own culture does not permit women to accept or gratify their basic needs to grow and fulfill their potentialities as human beings, a need which is not solely defined by their sexual roles."[37]

The second important contributing factor to the emergence of the women's rights movement was the civil rights movement of the '60s.[38] This latter movement demonstrated that suppressed groups can improve their condition through collective action. The civil rights movement also made a lot of women angry because, although supposedly dedicated to the betterment of all humankind, it was sexist. It was the men who did the planning and took the action; the women participants were expected to cook and otherwise meet the men's needs. One black leader even declared that "the position of women in [the] movement should be prone."[39]

Goals

The women's rights movement is more difficult to analyze than the postwar civil rights movement. One reason for this is that the goals of the women's rights movement are sometimes difficult to identify. The unmistakable goal of the civil rights movement in its early phases was the total integration of black Americans into American society; in its later phases, the movement clearly sought to liberate blacks from suppression and tyranny. In contrast, the goals of the women's rights movement are much more diverse.

Most women's rights organizations share at least two goals: (1) to eliminate discrimination against women in education, jobs, law, and politics; and (2) to change the ways we socialize boys and girls. As we have illustrated, women are less likely to go to college and graduate school than men, they earn less than men, and they are grossly underrepresented in government.

That we need to change the ways we socialize children is beyond dispute. In our society, little girls are socialized to believe that it is better to be attractive than bright. We tend "to produce women who are rather timid, unventuresome, unoriginal, conformist types."[40] Sex-role socialization also concerns men. In our society, "The boy is constantly open to a challenge to prove his masculinity. He must perform, adequately and publicly, a variety of physical feats that will have very little utility in most cases in adulthood. . . . The boy is not adequately socialized for adulthood."[41] Clearly, we are wasting many people's talents and abilities.

Beyond these two goals, the aims of the women's rights movement are many and varied. Some women's groups seek to liberalize abortion laws and establish a nationwide system of day-care centers that would be available to everyone. One radical women's group maintains that "it is now technically possible . . . to produce only females. We must begin immediately to do so."[42] Yet another radical group, the Female Liberation Front, counsels women to leave their husbands and children and abstain from sexual relations.[43] Some women's groups seek only the passage of the Equal Rights Amendment, while others pursue much wider goals. Perhaps the most comprehensive and the most widely known women's group is the National Organization for Women

(NOW). This group seeks a variety of different goals, including the passage of the Equal Rights Amendment, the establishment of day-care centers, and equal opportunities for women in all spheres of life.[44]

▲ Some women's groups seek only the passage of the Equal Rights Amendment, while others pursue much wider goals.

Methods

In their efforts to eliminate discrimination and sex-role stereotyping, women have used several tactics. Like blacks, they have relied heavily on the legal system as a tool to bring about change. Right now, for example, women are working for the passage of the Equal Rights Amendment (ERA). The key section of this amendment simply states that "equality of rights under the law shall not be denied or abridged by the United States or by any State on account of sex." If ratified, ERA will effectively strike down hundreds of state laws which discriminate against women. It will also make unconstitutional several laws which operate in favor of women; for example, women will no longer be treated preferentially in divorce courts and they may no longer have a legal claim on their husband's earnings. For ERA to become law, thirty-eight states must ratify it by 1979.

Ironically, the strongest opposition to ERA has come not from men but from women. "While 'male chauvinism' has often been blamed by today's feminists as largely responsible for women's subordination, the most vocal opposition to emerge in response to the feminist movement has come from women."[45] Why do many women appear to be "antiwomen"? "Probably the most hostile reaction to the women's liberation movement has come from women who have spent a good part of their adult years doing the things that the liberation women say are demeaning and valueless. . . . The middle-aged woman who has spent her adult years as a wife, mother, and housekeeper feels very threatened by the young woman who tells her that her life has been empty and that she has been a victim of male viciousness."[46] A study in Texas found that the most active ERA opponents are well-educated, conservative women who hold fundamentalistic religious beliefs. These ERA opponents not only have a strong commitment to traditional values, but their money and status give them considerable influence over state legislative bodies.[47]

Women also worked for the passage of other laws, such as the Civil Rights Act of 1964. Title VII of this act states that employers cannot discriminate on the basis of race, color, religion, sex, or national origin. This means that employers cannot bar women from being airline pilots, truck drivers, or mechanics; likewise, they cannot refuse to hire men as nurses, telephone operators, or secretaries.

The goal of breaking down traditional patterns of sex-role socialization may be even more difficult to achieve than eliminating sex discrimination: "This kind of goal does not lend itself to legislative focus. One cannot legislate the manner in which people raise their children."[48] Likewise, the task of eliminating age-old sex-role stereotypes will be difficult since they are instilled in us almost from the day that we are born.

In order to break down traditional patterns of sex-role socialization and to eliminate sexist stereotypes, feminists have relied heavily on what might be called a public education approach. Thus, a number of books have been published during recent years which deal with the problems of women in a sexist society. These books have undoubtedly had a major impact on the thinking of the millions of women—and men—who have read them. The same is true of *Ms.* magazine which was first published in 1972 and which now has a wide readership. Furthermore, more and more women are receiving coverage on television—coverage which tends to bring sexist stereotypes into question.

A modification of this public education approach has been consciousness-raising groups. A consciousness-raising group usually consists of five to ten women who meet periodically in a joint effort to change their self-conceptions and to increase their understanding of the problems women face in a sexist society.

Just how successful these efforts at modifying traditional patterns of sex-role socialization and sex-role stereotypes have been is unclear. It is likely that many parents are fearful of breaking away from the traditional patterns of sex-role socialization which have been with us, in one form or another, since our country was founded.

Is the Women's Movement Succeeding?

The U.S. Census represents the most complete information that we have on the economic, occupational, and educational status of the population. Our next census will be conducted in 1980. At that time, we can put together a reasonably accurate statistical picture of the impact that the current women's movement has had.

In the meantime, we can get some idea of how women are faring vis-à-vis men by consulting the *Statistical Abstract of the United States*, published annually by the U.S. Bureau of the Census. In 1965 there was a gap of $3,502 in the median annual incomes of males as compared to females. By 1974, this gap had widened to $5,286.[49] Likewise, in 1969, 5.5 percent more males than females 25 years of age and over had completed four or more years of college. By 1974, the figure had risen to 6.9 percent.[50] About the only place in which women seemed to hold their own vis-à-vis men was in terms of the unemployment rate. Between 1968 and 1974 the unemployment rate for females increased 4 percent whereas the unemployment rate for males increased 5 percent.[51] Nonetheless, in both years a larger percentage of females than males were unemployed.[52]

These figures would seem to indicate that the women's movement has achieved little in terms of eliminating inequalities between men and women in regard to earnings, educational attainment, and unemployment. The differences are greater today than they were when the current women's movement began. On the basis of these data alone, however, we cannot say that the women's movement has been totally unsuccessful. There is no way to assess what impact the women's movement has had on the self-images of women and on the attitudes that men have toward women. One thing is clear—sexist ideologies continue to pervade our society, handicapping both men and women. Americans must work to overcome them.

Summary

Many men and women today have come to realize that we live in a sexist society, and they are challenging our sex-role stereotypes.

Sexism has two separate but interrelated meanings: (1) male superiority and (2) the subjugation of women by men. Feminists most frequently use the latter meaning; but according to either definition, sexism is rooted in the structure of society.

Sexism is a social problem because it produces educational, occupational, legal, and political discrimination. Fewer women than men go on to college; and even with equal education, women earn less than men. In many states, laws discriminate against women, and women are grossly underrepresented in both elected and appointed political offices. Sexism locks both women and men into unrewarding roles and may affect rates of mental illness, crime, alcoholism, and drug addiction.

A determination of the origins of sexism must begin by defining what we mean by *sex* and *sex roles*. *Sex* refers to what our bodies can and cannot do in terms of reproducing. *Sex role* refers to behavior—we consider certain traits "male" and certain others "female."

Except for the female ability to bear children, the differences within sex groups are greater than the differences between sex groups. In fact, the anatomical and behavioral differences between men and women are probably best thought of as two overlapping, bell-shaped curves.

Sex roles are socially determined and are the basis for sexism. Women play subsidiary roles because they are expected to and men assume domineering attitudes toward women for the same reason.

The origins of sex-role differences are sociocultural. Although many people believe that sex-role differences are biologically determined, the evidence does not indicate that sex differences produce behavior differences or determine the roles that people play.

Anthropological studies indicate that sex-role differences grow out of the socialization process. The most important institutions in this process are the family, the school, and the media. Families and schools socialize males to act "like men" and females to act "like women" in three ways: *molding and canalization*, *symbol manipulation*, and *differing activity exposure*. Many school textbooks reinforce sexist ideology, and, after puberty, girls are discouraged from pursuing academic success. The mass media create and reinforce sex-role stereotyping by constantly showing subservient women and successful men.

Until recently, sexism was a latent social problem; the women's rights movement has made it a manifest social problem. For the first time, women are demanding that the sexist structure of society be changed. The publication of *The Feminine Mystique* by Betty Friedan and the civil rights movement were particularly important to the emergence of the women's rights movement.

Although the goals of women's groups are sometimes difficult to identify, most groups share at least two goals—to eliminate discrimination on the basis of sex and to change the ways we socialize boys and girls. Working to achieve these goals, women have relied heavily on the legal system as a tool for social change and on the media to educate the public. If we are to overcome the sexist inequities that pervade our society and that create a tremendous waste of people's talents and abilities, men and women must work together.

Discussion Questions

1. What is meant by the term *sexism*? What is meant by the statement that "sexism is clearly rooted in the structure of our society"? Are all of us, including women, in a sense sexists?
2. Why is sexism a social problem? What are some of the costs and consequences of sexism for males, females, and society in general?
3. Why do you suppose that an increasing number of women are becoming dissatisfied with their social and work roles? How would you account for the fact that the women's rights movement gained much momentum in the late '60s and the '70s?
4. What do we mean by the terms *sex* and *sex roles*? Why does the "typical" male comport himself differently than the "typical" female?
5. Discuss the role of the family in socializing children into their sex roles. What are some of the processes by which families teach girls "to act like girls" and boys "to act like boys"? Can you recall some of these processes from your own childhood?
6. Cite some examples of sexist advertising. Has the amount of sexist advertising increased, decreased, or remained about the same during the last year? Do you think that sexist advertising has a major impact on people's attitudes and behavior?
7. Betty Friedan suggests that "our own culture does not permit women to accept or gratify their basic needs to grow and fulfill their potentialities as human beings, a need which is not solely defined by their sexual roles." What is meant by her statement? Do you agree with it? Why or why not?
8. In what sense was the civil rights movement a contributing factor to the emergence of the women's rights movement? What similarities and differences do you see between the two movements? Are the goals of the two movements similar? What about the tactics that have been used by participants in the two movements?

9. What will be some of the effects of the Equal Rights Amendment if it is ratified? Why do you suppose that ERA has met with such stiff opposition? What groups seem most opposed to the ratification of this amendment?

10. Statistics seem to indicate that the inequalities between men and women in regard to earnings, educational attainment, and unemployment may actually be increasing. How would you account for this? What impact do you think that the women's movement has had on the self-images of women and on the attitudes that men have toward women?

Glossary

anticipatory socialization Any type of activity that helps, either directly or indirectly, to prepare a child for the role he or she will be expected to assume as an adult.

consciousness-raising groups Informal or semiformal groups which seek to change the self-conceptions of individuals and to increase their understanding of the problems they face in a sexist society.

Equal Rights Amendment (ERA) An amendment to the U.S. Constitution which, if ratified, will strike down hundreds of laws which discriminate against women, and some which discriminate against men. The key section of this amendment simply states that "equality of rights under the law shall not be denied or abridged by the United States or by any State on account of sex."

latent social problem A social problem which represents a very real threat to social order or personal well-being but which is not recognized as a social problem.

manifest social problem A social problem which a significant number of people recognize as a threat to social order or personal well-being and for which they seek some remedy.

molding and canalization Processes by which infants and young children are subtly but clearly taught behaviors deemed "appropriate" to their sex. Both are forms of anticipatory socialization.

sex A term which refers to certain features of a person's anatomy and physiology. More specifically, it refers to what our bodies can or cannot do in the reproduction process.

sexism (*a*) A belief in the superiority of males, or (*b*) the subjugation of women by men. Sexism is rooted in the structure of our society.

sex role A term which refers to how a person is expected to behave by virtue of his or her sex. For example, men are expected to be independent and aggressive; women are expected to be dependent and passive.

sex-role stereotypes Our images of what a "typical" woman should be like and what a "typical" man should be like. If a person fails to conform to these images he or she may be ridiculed, gossiped about, or punished in some other way.

socialization The complex processes of social learning through which we acquire our personalities and learn to internalize cultural and subcultural behavior patterns. Among other things, we are taught our sex roles through the socialization process.

symbol manipulation A process in which a female child is subtly but clearly taught that she belongs to a group (females) which is different from another group (males); a male child, on the other hand, is subtly but clearly taught that he belongs to a group (males) which is different from another group (females).

Suggestions for Further Reading

Bardwick, Judith M., ed., *Readings on the Psychology of Women* (New York: Harper & Row, 1972). A collection of scholarly articles on sex differences, sex roles, and the women's movement. Recommended for the student who wishes to look beyond rhetoric and accusations in trying to understand sex roles in the United States.

Friedan, Betty, *The Feminine Mystique* (New York: Norton, 1963). A highly readable and provocative best-seller which in many ways helped to trigger the contemporary women's movement.

Gornick, Vivian, and Barbara K. Moran, eds., *Women in Sexist Society: Studies in Power and Powerlessness* (New York: Basic, 1971). A widely quoted collection of articles on the women's movement. Many of these articles vividly show how women are degraded and devalued in our society—or placed on an unrealistically high pedestal.

Hecht, Marie B., et al., *The Women, Yes!* (New York: Holt, Rinehart and Winston, 1974). A simple but informative introduction to women and the women's movement in the United States.

Morgan, Robin, ed., *Sisterhood Is Powerful: An Anthology of Writings from the Women's Liberation Movement* (New York: Random House, 1970). A comprehensive collection of articles and writings pertaining to the women's movement. Among other things, this volume gives the reader an excellent insight into how various women feel about themselves and their position in a sexist society.

Oakley, Anne, *Sex, Gender and Society* (New York: Harper & Row, 1973). A top-notch discussion of sex-role differences and how they originate.

Petras, John W., ed., *Sex: Male, Gender: Masculine* (Port Washington, N.Y.: Alfred, 1975). This anthology of readings is similar to some of the others cited in this bibliography except that it focuses on males and the problems that they face in a sexist society.

Social Science Quarterly, 56 (March, 1976), pp. 547–672. This issue of *Social Science Quarterly* examines current patterns of sex stratification in American society. It includes thirteen articles which focus upon such diverse topics as the anti-ERA movement, women in politics, and women and crime.

Stoll, Clarice Stasz, *Female and Male: Socialization, Social Roles, and Social Structure* (Dubuque, Iowa: Wm. C. Brown, 1974). A good examination of sexism in our society and its costs and consequences for both males and females.

Notes

[1]Clarice Stasz Stoll, *Female and Male: Socialization, Social Roles, and Social Structure* (Dubuque, Iowa: Wm. C. Brown, 1974), p. 20.

[2]Vivian Gornick and Barbara K. Moran, eds., *Women in Sexist Society: Studies in Power and Powerlessness* (New York: New American Library, 1972), p. xxv. Kate Millet, a leading writer and feminist, expresses the same idea when she says, "We live in a masculine society owned and operated by a masculine power structure and—just as in a black and white society—the ruling elite will define the reality, even the identity of those whom it rules." Cited in Marie B. Hecht et al., *The Women, Yes!* (New York: Holt, Rinehart and Winston, 1974), p. 6.

[3]U.S. Bureau of the Census, *Statistical Abstract of the United States: 1975*, 96th Ed. (Washington, D.C.: U.S. Government Printing Office, 1975), Table 191.

[4]Ann Sutherland Harris, "The Second Sex in Academe," *Bulletin of the American Association of University Professors*, 56 (September, 1970), p. 284.

[5]Judith M. Bardwick and Elizabeth Douvan, "Ambivalence: The Socialization of Women," in Judith M. Bardwick, ed., *Readings on the Psychology of Women* (New York: Harper & Row, 1972), p. 54.

[6]For example, see Mirra Komarovsky, "Cultural Contradictions and Sex Roles," *American Journal of Sociology*, 52 (November, 1946), pp. 184–89. See also Matina Horner, "The Motive to Avoid Success and Changing Aspirations of College Women," in Bardwick, ed., *Readings on the Psychology of Women*, pp. 62–67.

[7]U.S. Bureau of the Census, *Statistical Abstract of the United States: 1975*, Table 603.

[8]Jonathan H. Turner, *American Society: Problems of Structure*, 2nd Ed. (New York: Harper & Row, 1976), p. 153.

[9]Hecht et al., *The Women, Yes!* pp. 28–30.

[10]See Shana Alexander, *State-by-State Guide to Women's Legal Rights* (Los Angeles: Wollstonecraft, 1975), pp. 215–22.

[11]Stoll, *Female and Male*, p. 196.

[12]Betty Friedan, *The Feminine Mystique* (New York: Dell, 1963), p. 11.

[13]Jack O. Balswick and Charles W. Peek, "The Inexpressive Male: A Tragedy of American Society," *The Family Coordinator*, 20 (October, 1971), p. 366.

[14]For an interesting discussion of fatherhood in our society, see Myron Brenton, "The Paradox of the Contemporary American Father: Every Day Is Mother's Day," in John W. Petras, ed., *Sex: Male, Gender: Masculine* (Port Washington, N.Y.: Alfred, 1975), pp. 179–85.

[15]See Robert J. Trotter, "Sexism Is Depressing," in *Readings in Sociology: 76/77* (Guilford, Conn.: Dushkin, 1976), pp. 123–24.

[16]Bardwick and Douvan, "Ambivalence," p. 52.

[17]Cited in Hecht et al., *The Women, Yes!* p. 5.

[18]See Anne Oakley, *Sex, Gender and Society* (New York: Harper & Row, 1973), pp. 44–47.

[19]*Ibid*., p. 143.

[20]See Stoll, *Female and Male*, p. 7.

[21]*Ibid*., p. 7.

[22]See Margaret Mead, *Sex and Temperament in Three Primitive Societies* (New York: Morrow, 1963), pp. 280–81.

[23]Marvin Harris, *Culture, People, and Nature; An Introduction to General Anthropology*, 2nd Ed. (New York: Crowell, 1975), p. 607.

[24]See Ruth E. Hartley, "A Developmental View of Female Sex-Role Identification," in Bruce J. Biddle and Edwin J. Thomas, *Role Theory: Concepts and Research* (New York: Wiley, 1966), pp. 354–60.

[25]*Ibid*., p. 355.

[26]Cited in Oakley, *Sex, Gender and Society*, p. 177.

[27]Carole Joffe, "Sex Role Socialization and the Nursery School: As the Twig Is Bent," *Journal of Marriage and the Family*, 33 (August, 1971), p. 470.

[28]Marjorie B. U'Ren, "The Image of Women in Textbooks," in Gornick and Moran, eds., *Women in Sexist Society*, pp. 318–19.

[29]*Ibid*., p. 327.

[30]Bardwick and Douvan, "Ambivalence," esp. p. 54.

[31]*Ibid*., p. 54.

[32]Lucy Komisar, "The Image of Woman in Advertising," in Gornick and Moran, eds., *Women in Sexist Society*, p. 310.

[33]*Ibid*., pp. 310–11.

[34]Cited in *Ibid*., p. 309

[35]See Robert K. Merton and Robert Nisbet, eds., *Contemporary Social Problems*, 4th Ed. (New York: Harcourt Brace Jovanovich, 1975), pp. 13–15.

[36]For a history of feminist movements in America see Andrew Sinclair, *The Emancipation of the American Woman* (New York: Harper & Row, 1965).

[37]Friedan, *The Feminine Mystique*, p. 69.

[38]See Robert R. Bell, *Social Deviance: A Substantive Analysis*, Rev. Ed. (Homewood, Ill.: Dorsey, 1976), esp. p. 413.

[39]Cited in *Ibid.*, p. 413.

[40]Ruth E. Hartley, "American Core Culture: Changes and Continuities," in Georgene H. Seward and Robert C. Williamson, eds., *Sex Roles in Changing Society* (New York: Random House, 1970), p. 141.

[41]*Ibid.*, pp. 141–42.

[42]See Valerie Solanis, "Excerpts from the SCUM Manifesto," in Robin Morgan, ed., *Sisterhood Is Powerful: An Anthology of Writings from the Women's Liberation Movement* (New York: Random House, 1970), p. 514.

[43]Bell, *Social Deviance*, p. 415.

[44]For a more complete statement of NOW's goals, see Morgan, ed., *Sisterhood Is Powerful*, p. 512.

[45]Armand L. Mauss, *Social Problems As Social Movements* (Philadelphia: Lippincott, 1975), p. 420.

[46]*Ibid.*, p. 419.

[47]See David W. Brady and Kent L. Tedin, "Ladies in Pink: Religion and Political Ideology in the Anti-ERA Movement," *Social Science Quarterly*, 56 (March, 1976), pp. 564–75.

[48]John R. Howard, *The Cutting Edge: Social Movements and Social Change in America* (Philadelphia: Lippincott, 1974), p. 153.

[49]Computed from U.S. Bureau of the Census, *Statistical Abstract of the United States: 1975*, Table 642.

[50]Computed from *Ibid.*, Table 192 and from U.S. Bureau of the Census, *Statistical Abstract of the United States: 1970*, 91st Ed. (Washington, D.C.: U.S. Government Printing Office, 1970), Table 157.

[51]*Ibid.*, Tables 321 (1970) and 571 (1975).

[52]*Ibid.*, Tables 321 and 571.

Chapter 12
Growing Old

In Philadelphia in the early '70s a new militant equal rights group emerged to protest America's unfair treatment of one of its minorities. Called the "Gray Panthers," this group was organized in order to improve the lot of the millions who are deprived and disadvantaged simply because they are old.

Most of us would agree with the proposition that people who have worked hard for many years, reared families, and contributed in many ways to society deserve the right to enjoy a comfortable retirement and old age. And many older Americans do receive adequate incomes, do enjoy good health, and are socially active with their families, friends, and neighbors. On the average, though, old Americans are less well off than younger Americans. In too many cases, growing old means growing into poverty, poor health, and dependency.

J. S. Clark, former senator ▸ and former mayor of Philadelphia, talks with Maggie Kuhn, founder of the Gray Panthers, at ceremonies starting a drive for a recall referendum to remove Philadelphia's Mayor Frank Rizzo. The Gray Panthers was organized to improve the lot of the millions who are deprived and disadvantaged simply because they are old.

Who Are the Old?

It is not easy to distinguish between the young and the old.[1] A 55-year-old person, for example, is "old" to a 15-year-old but "young" to an 80-year-old. And all of us have known people who are "old" at 40 and others who are still "young" at 75. Chronological age is often a poor criterion for distinguishing between the young and the old. The old are those people society categorizes as old.

Many older Americans receive adequate incomes, enjoy good health, and are socially active with their families, friends, and neighbors.

For practical reasons, we will define persons aged 65 and over as old. Many companies require that their employees retire at 65,

Fresh Up
WITH
7up
SALEM
SUPER KING
OPEN

and this is the age when people become entitled to full Social Security benefits. Many 65-year-olds experience important changes in their lives—they withdraw from the work force, their incomes decline, they must adjust to retirement and assume new social roles. In addition, most statistics refer to people 65 years of age and over as old.

The Demographics of Aging

Old people have not always faced the problems they do today. When this country was predominately rural and most Americans lived on farms, old people were accorded a high status for two reasons: (*a*) they still controlled the purse strings and held the property deeds, and (*b*) despite their declining strength, they still performed many useful tasks around the farm and cared for the children.

In recent years, though, two forces have combined to produce many problems for old people—urbanization and population growth. In our modern, urban, industrial society, younger people usually are not financially dependent on their aging parents and often have neither the room, the money, nor the desire to take their parents into their households. Furthermore, old people rarely wish to live with their children, even though it might help them meet their basic needs.

Our changing birth and death rates have led to a dramatic increase in the percentage of the population aged 65 and over. As Table 12.1 indicates, in 1900, persons aged 65 and over constituted 4.1 percent of the population. Today almost 10 percent of the population is aged 65 and over. In years to come, the old will constitute an even larger percentage of the population. There are

Table 12.1
Total U.S. Population Aged 65 and Over, 1900–1970

Year	Number of People (in Millions) Age 65 and Over	Percent of Total Population Age 65 and Over
1900	3.1	4.1
1910	3.9	4.3
1920	4.9	4.7
1930	6.6	5.5
1940	9.0	6.8
1950	12.3	8.2
1960	16.6	9.2
1970	20.1	9.9

SOURCE: U.S. Bureau of the Census, *Census of Population: 1970*, Vol. I, *Characteristics of the Population*, Part I, *U.S. Summary* (Washington, D.C.: U.S. Government Printing Office, 1973), Table 53.

several reasons for the growing percentage of old people. First, birthrates in the early 1900s were high, and these "youngsters" are now reaching age 65. Second, the decline in the birthrate in recent years has meant proportionately fewer young persons and more old ones. Finally, changes in average life expectancy have had a major impact on the size of our older population. As Table 12.2 indicates, a person born in 1900 could expect to live an average of 47.3 years; a person born in 1970 can expect to live an average of 70.9 years. A larger percentage of today's population survives the rigors of infancy and childhood, so many more people live long enough to become part of the old population.

Table 12.2
Average Length of Life by Race and Sex, United States, 1900–1970

	1900	1970
White		
Male	46.6 Years	68.0 Years
Female	48.7	75.6
All Other		
Male	32.5	61.3
Female	33.5	69.4
Total	47.3	70.9

SOURCE: National Center for Health Statistics, *Vital Statistics of the United States: 1970* (Washington, D.C.: U.S. Government Printing Office, 1974), Table 5–5.

Because old people make up an ever growing portion of the population, some sociologists have specialized in *social gerontology*. Gerontology is the study of aging and the problems of the aged: the social gerontologist is interested in the group behavior of old people, in how they adjust to the demands of society, and in how society reacts to the older individual.[2] We will be drawing on the findings of the social gerontologists throughout this chapter.

Old People: Their Major Problems

Millions of older Americans have adequate incomes, are healthy, and maintain their independence. However, a disproportionately large share of the old are disadvantaged, and almost all old people face certain problems which are disproportionately common to their age group. Among their most serious problems are income, retirement, health, concern about becoming dependent on others, and death. Since many of these latter problems would be much less serious if incomes were adequate, we will begin with a discussion of the economic status of old people.

Income

Old people often receive inadequate incomes. In this section we will examine the extent of poverty among old persons, its causes, and its impact on their lives.

As we pointed out in Chapter 9, "Poverty," it is often difficult to draw a line between the poor and nonpoor in terms of income. However, in 1973, $5,000 was considered adequate to supply a modest budget for a couple.[3] Since about half the population aged 65 and over have incomes of less than $5,000, they are living in poverty according to this criterion.[4] Furthermore, 20.6 percent of the white population and 44.1 percent of the black population aged 65 and over had incomes below the federally defined poverty line (see Table 9.1).[5] Clearly, then, large numbers of old people have little to look forward to but a life of economic deprivation.

Several factors help account for poverty among old persons. In most cases retirement income is simply not enough to keep an individual above the poverty line. For example, in 1970, 48 percent of all nonmarried men and women over the age of 62 had neither a second pension nor other earnings to supplement their Social Security income.[6] The percentage is undoubtedly higher for persons aged 65 and over. Yet, as shown in Table 12.3, Social Security benefits are considerably below the figures needed for a modest, above-the-poverty-line budget.[7] In addition, the few assets that old people have accumulated during their working years are quickly eaten up by inflation and high taxes. A nest egg of $5,000 or $10,000 in a savings account will not go far today, and over half of our old people have less than $1,000 in assets.[8] The idea that people can save enough during their working years to supplement their Social Security payments and realize an adequate retirement income is unrealistic. Furthermore, old

Table 12.3

Social Security Benefits Compared with Income Required to Maintain a Modest Budget

	Approximate Annual Social Security Income in Dollars (1974)[a]	Income in Dollars Required for a Modest Budget (1973)[b]
Married Couples	3,353	5,000
Retired Workers	2,282	NA[c]
Widow or Widower	2,112	NA[c]

[a]Computed from *Social Security Bulletin*, 37 (November, 1974), Table M–13.

[b]Fred Cottrell, *Aging and the Aged* (Dubuque, Iowa: Brown, 1974), p. 24.

[c]These figures are not available. However, in 1974 in order for a single person to be above the federally defined nonfarm poverty line, he or she had to have an income of at least $2,495 per year (see Table 9.1). This is an amount above that paid by Social Security.

people have great difficulty finding jobs, so unemployment adds to their financial problems. Indeed, many old people are forced to retire because they cannot find work.

Lack of adequate income severely limits the choices available to old people. Good income ensures good health care, nutrition, and housing. For the person with good health, good income may also provide the opportunity to travel, entertain, and enjoy recreational activities. However, since many old people do not have adequate incomes, they are deprived not only of the pleasures but also of the necessities of life.[9]

Retirement

Sooner or later most older workers retire from the labor force. Beyond potential financial problems, however, it does not appear that retirement creates serious difficulties: "For people with enough money, the theories which link unhappiness in retirement to the need to work appear ludicrous. In my own studies of retirement, only a minute proportion of those with moderate incomes missed their jobs."[10] It is apparently a myth that all or even most retiring workers face serious problems of adjustment. It is similarly a myth that retirement has an adverse effect on health; many retired persons enjoy as good or better health than they did when they were working.[11]

But because retirement creates severe financial strains for many older people, much attention has centered on the question of whether people should be forced to retire at a certain age. The advocates of compulsory retirement base their argument on several grounds, two of which are particularly important. First, they argue that compulsory retirement is objective, impersonal, and impartial. The employer is not open to charges of bias and discrimination if all older workers are retired when they reach a certain age. Second, they argue that compulsory retirement provides opportunities for younger workers and helps keep channels of upward mobility open.[12] These arguments, however, overlook the fact that old people are often superior workers, that many do not want to retire, and that retirement can cause severe economic deprivation for the individuals involved. The practice of forcing all employees to retire at a certain age, regardless of their capacities, is a form of institutionalized discrimination. As such, it is a practice that is hard to defend.

Health

A person in poor health may suffer from either a chronic or an acute condition. Chronic disorders are marked by long duration or frequent recurrence and include arthritis and rheumatism, heart conditions, and high blood pressure. The common cold, influenza, and measles are examples of short-term acute conditions.

As one might expect, old people suffer from more chronic conditions than younger people do. In fact, 81 percent of persons 65 years of age and over suffer from one or more chronic conditions ranging from poor vision that can be corrected with eyeglasses to total invalidism. Almost 26 percent of these people are limited in their ability to carry out major activities such as holding down a job or keeping house, and another 15.5 percent are totally unable to carry out major activities.[13]

Another index of old people's health status is the number of times per year they visit a physician. Persons aged 45 to 54 visit physicians about five times a year, while persons 65 years of age and over visit physicians about seven times per year.[14]

In general, older women visit physicians more frequently, have more illnesses, and suffer from a slightly higher number of chronic conditions than older men. At the same time, for all age groups, the death rate for men is higher than for women. In other words, "older women predominate among the sick, and older men predominate among the dead."[15] There are only about seventy men per every hundred women in the over-65 age group.

Many factors account for this situation. First, women are more likely to identify themselves as sick and to seek medical care than men. Men are often reluctant to admit they are sick because of the way they have been socialized; in our society men are expected to be "manly"—to carry on with their activities and not seek medical care when they are sick. Because women seek medical care more frequently than men, they appear to be less healthy. But the very fact that women are more likely than men to get medical care when they need it may prolong their lives. There are also other factors, such as differences in constitutional strength, which may help account for women's higher life expectancies.

Although people over age 65 spend much more per year for medical care than younger people do, they are more likely to be poor and unable to afford huge expenditures for health.[16] Among the old, high medical bills mean that income must be diverted away from vitally needed food and shelter. Furthermore, poor health affects a person's interaction with other people; it is one major reason why people retire, and people in poor health may also have to discontinue their participation in organizations such as churches and clubs. Friends, neighbors, and relatives may avoid the sick or disabled person as a social companion because of that person's limited ability to do things. Poor health, then, often cuts old people off from meaningful group ties and may cause loneliness.

Finally, our system of providing health care is not really geared to meeting the medical needs of old people. Our general hospitals are oriented toward treating short-term acute conditions. This means that old people are often dismissed from the hospital before they are fully recuperated and ready to care for themselves. As a result, they often must struggle to recover on their own, impose on relatives, or go to nursing homes. Many nursing homes are of extremely poor quality and do not provide adequate posthospital care. Furthermore, old people often feel that physicians are not interested in them and are reluctant to treat them.[17] Some doctors shy away from treating old people because of the problems involved in collecting Medicare and Medicaid payments and because they may not be able to collect their full fee.

Dependency

Most Americans fear becoming dependent. We are socialized to believe that we should provide for ourselves, pay our own rent, and get around *on our own*. Independence is a virtue, and people who become dependent are called moochers, freeloaders, leeches, and bums. Yet, despite their dread of becoming dependent, about one-third of all old people eventually must ask their children for help.[18] This may involve financial assistance, help in getting around, or asking their children to house them.

Conflicts can easily arise when aging parents must depend on adult children. The role of the dependent person is not a comfort-

Conflicts can easily arise when aging parents must depend upon adult children and grandchildren. The role of the dependent person is not a comfortable one in our society. ▼

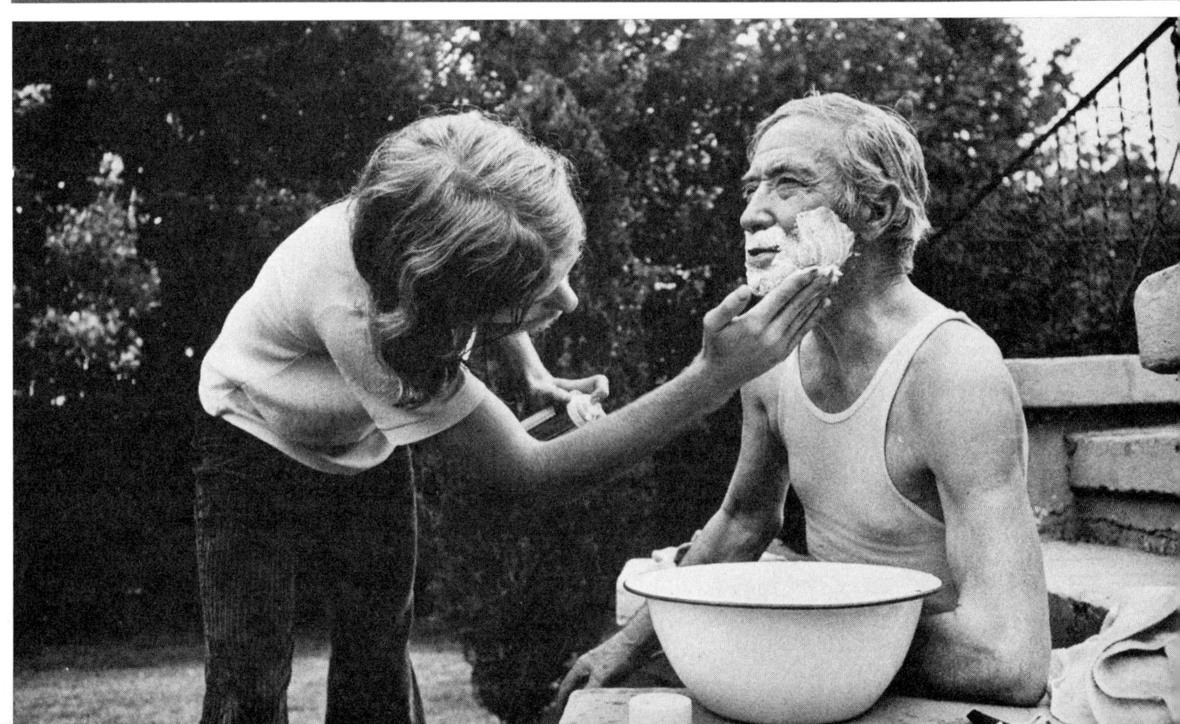

able one. In our society people who are dependent are expected to defer to their benefactors and to be grateful for whatever help is given them. Very often, it is extremely difficult for old people to accept this role and to adjust to the fact that their children now hold the authority and make the important decisions. Furthermore, the adult child often resents taking care of an aging parent and feels guilty about this resentment. Finally, having to take care of or support a dependent parent can put strains on the adult child's marriage. Spouses may resent spending family income on a mother-in-law or father-in-law and making decisions such as whether to send the children to summer camp or to have grandma's teeth fixed. Because of the problems dependency creates for everyone concerned, dependency (financial and/or physical) is the leading source of low morale among old people.[19]

Dependency should not be confused with healthy parent/child relationships. Old people need affection and approval from their children. Three out of four old people have living children, and four out of five of these old people see their children very frequently.[20] Parent/child relationships seem most likely to be rewarding and successful if both parent and child are financially independent and if both are able to care for themselves and to maintain their own households. "[It] would appear that, in our culture, there simply cannot be any happy role reversals between the generations, neither an increasing dependency of parent upon child nor a continuing reliance of child upon parents."[21]

Death

Most of us have experienced the death of someone very close to us. And we're all aware of the possibility of our own deaths through illness or accident. However, for old people death is a special tragedy. As they grow older, more and more of their friends and relatives die. Their spouses also die, and their increasing physical decline is a constant reminder of their own coming deaths.

One of the most difficult transitions in the life of an old person is marked by the death of the spouse. Usually, the wife must cope with the death of her husband. But in any case the bereaved person must face two distinct problems. First, the person must come to grips with feelings of grief, despair, and loneliness. Family and friends may help the person over these feelings. Second, the person must reorganize his or her life and assume new roles. If the bereaved person is a man, he may have to learn to cook, wash clothes, and keep house; if the bereaved person is a woman, she may have to find a job and look after the family's financial affairs. These two problems are even more difficult if there are dependent children.

Social Problems and You

The Shock of Growing Old

It has been said that next to dying, the recognition that we are aging may be the most profound shock we experience in our lifetime. Every day in the United States more than 1000 persons cross the invisible barrier of age 65 and by custom and law are "benched" for the remainder of the game. They are "older persons" or "senior citizens." How these individuals react to their changed status and to the difficult stresses of this age period depends heavily on their personality makeup as well as on the challenges, rewards, and frustrations of their life situation. . . .

Retirement is often the brand that marks a person as a member of the "old age" group. It can be quite demoralizing if it is forced upon the individual. Repeated studies have shown that most persons of 65 are productive workers and that many would prefer to keep on working when they reach retirement age.

Many people depend greatly on their work for status, for self-identity, for satisfying interpersonal relationships, and for meaning in their lives. Retirement often does not meet these needs, and there is a tendency to react with the feeling that one's usefulness and worth are at an end and that one's life is really over . . . .

With aging and physical deterioration, the individual is also confronted with the inescapable fact of his own impending death. Some older people react with equanimity, often stemming from deep religious faith in the meaningfulness of human existence and in the certainty of a life hereafter. Others die as they have lived, with little concern for life or human existence. In fact, they may welcome death as a solution to unsolvable problems and a meaningless life. This is sometimes true also of older people who have lost their friends and loved ones and who feel that they have "outlived their time." However, for many older people the realization that life is drawing to a close is a highly stressful experience.

As the individual grows older, he is faced with the inevitable loss of loved ones, friends, and contemporaries. The death of the mate with whom one may have shared many years of close companionship often poses a particularly difficult adjustment problem. This is especially true for women, who in the U.S. tend to outlive their spouses by some 7 years.

Other factors, too, may contribute to social isolation. Children grow up, marry, and move away; impairment of vision or hearing and various chronic ailments may make social interaction difficult; an attitude of self-pity or an inward centering of interest may alienate family and friends alike. In many instances, the older person also becomes increasingly rigid and intolerant in his outlook and is unable to make effective use of the opportunities for meaningful social interaction that still remain to him.

Of course, retirement, lowered income, impaired health, and loneliness are not just matters of inability to maintain a particular life style or to interact with loved ones. In a larger view, they involve the inability to contribute productively and to feel oneself a vital and needed part of the human enterprise. In essence, they progressively destroy the older person's links with his world and the meaningfulness of his existence as a human being.

SOURCE: James C. Coleman, *Abnormal Psychology and Modern Life* (Glenview, Ill.: Scott, Foresman, 1976).

During the last few years, a number of books and articles have been written on how we deal with death, and two significant conclusions have emerged from this research. First, although we go to great lengths to hide the fact that death is imminent from the dying person, the evidence suggests that the dying person feels much better knowing the truth and will gradually come to accept the reality of the situation.[22] Second, most terminally ill people do come to grips with their impending death, going through five stages, the last of which is acceptance. In this last stage, the patient "shows no more fear, bitterness, anguish, or concern over unfinished business."[23] At this ultimate point the person seems to experience a sense of peace and tranquility.

Many questions remain regarding death and the terminally ill, regardless of age. For example, given our present shortage of health care resources, to what extent is society obligated to keep the terminally ill patient alive? Does a person have the right to request that his or her life be taken? Under what conditions should such a request be honored? These are difficult questions which face all of us, not just old people.

Meeting the Problems

Many of the problems old people face are clearly beyond legal or governmental solution—no law can make up for the loss of a spouse, and no program can restore full independence to a disabled person. However, much can be done to ease the burdens of old people. We can provide every older person with a decent income, adequate health care, sufficient nutrition, and good housing—*if we want to.* In this section we will look at what we are presently doing to ease the problems of old people.

Income-Related Programs

Because many old people lack an adequate income, they cannot afford good food, health care, and housing. And even if they can afford these necessities, old people often lack the money to enjoy retirement through travel or recreational activities. We currently have four programs to help ease old people's financial burdens—Social Security, Supplemental Security Income, private pensions, and food stamps.

Social Security

Beyond the small percentage of old people who work for a living or have other private incomes, the most important source of income for persons 65 years of age and over is Old Age, Survivors, Disability, and Health Insurance (OASDHI)—usually called "Social Security." OASDHI is a federal program managed by the Social Security Administration and funded by contributions from workers and their employers. When employees retire at age 65, or sometimes at age 62, they are entitled to monthly OASDHI benefits. Today most workers are covered by OASDHI and are thus ensured of some economic support when they reach retirement age.

However, OASDHI does not ensure a decent standard of living. As we have already seen, average monthly OASDHI benefits are considerably below the income required to maintain a decent standard of living (Table 12.3). However, the inadequacy of OASDHI benefits is not totally the fault of the system. Rampant inflation is partly to blame, and in 1972 Congress did add an escalator clause to the Social Security Act which provides for automatic increases in OASDHI benefits as the cost of living increases. Unfortunately, the benefits old people were entitled to in 1972 were so low that these automatic increases did almost nothing to improve their financial situations; at best they have been able to hold their own. To pay for OASDHI both the Social Security tax rate and the amount of income that is taxable increases almost every year. There is growing concern that the Social Security system is headed for serious financial difficulties in the years ahead.[24]

Supplemental Security Income

In January, 1974, the federal government terminated the Old Age Assistance program (see Chapter 9) and launched the Supplemental Security Income (SSI) Program. Like OASDHI, this program is administered by the Social Security Administration. In 1975 an individual could receive up to $1,892 per year under SSI and a couple could receive up to $2,938 per year.[25] In order to qualify for SSI the individual must have very limited financial assets. For example, the value of his or her home cannot exceed $25,000 nor can the value of his or her household goods and personal effects exceed $1,500.[26]

SSI is not an insurance program; it is a public assistance program designed to provide financial relief for old people who have very few assets and/or inadequate Social Security benefits. Although SSI is an improvement over the Old Age Assistance program, its payments are unreasonably low. An old person whose only source of income is SSI payments lives below the poverty line.

Private Pensions

The importance of private, company-administered pensions should not be overemphasized. In 1967 only 12 percent of older people received private pensions, totaling only about 5 percent of their aggregate income.[27] More recent data are not available, but one recent source reports that "retired workers receiving private pensions are in the minority."[28] Private pensions are, however, very important to those who receive them. In fact, an old person who receives both a private pension and OASDHI benefits may be able to enjoy a good standard of living.

Because of widespread abuses in many private pension schemes, in 1974 Congress passed the Employee Retirement Income Security Act (ERISA). This act has three important features.[29] First, it specifies that employees are entitled to their pensions even if they leave their company before reaching retirement age. Before the passage of ERISA, companies could, and sometimes did, dismiss employees before they were eligible to retire and therefore deprived them of their pensions. Second, people are allowed to establish individual retirement accounts which are exempt from federal income taxation. This may encourage people who are still working to build up their own nest egg for the future. Third, ERISA established an insurance program that guarantees that a person will receive a pension even if his or her company folds or has insufficient funds to pay the pension which was promised.

Even though ERISA was a much needed piece of legislation, there are still many problems associated with private pensions.[30] For one thing, pensions are usually fixed for life; the benefits are not increased as the cost of living increases due to inflation. Likewise, employers who do have a private pension system may be reluctant to hire older workers because if they work for a company for a short period of time, it costs the company more to provide them with pensions than it does to provide pensions for employees who work for the company for longer periods of time.

Food Stamps

The extent to which old people purchase food stamps is unclear; but it seems likely that many who qualify for food stamps do not take advantage of them. This may be because they are reluctant to accept "charity," they do not know about the program, they have no transportation to get to where the food stamps are sold, or they do not have the money to purchase the stamps.

Health-Related Programs

Any program which increases the income of old people has a direct bearing on the amount and quality of health care they receive. However, benefits under OASDHI and SSI have been so low that old people have little left over for health care after they buy food and pay the rent and utilities. The best-known health-related programs for old people include Medicare, Medicaid, and nursing homes.

Medicare

In 1966, a federal program of hospital insurance, called Medicare, was added to OASDHI. By paying a small extra monthly premium, old people can buy medical insurance to help pay their outpatient medical bills. Although its benefits are very important to old people, Medicare is not an entirely adequate program. In 1971, Medicare paid only 43 percent of old people's medical bills.[31] In addition, Medicare will not pay for such crucial items as eyeglasses, hearing aids, routine dental care, and prescription drugs. So old people must still pay most of their health-care costs, and their bills can have a devastating effect on their budgets.

Medicaid

In contrast to Medicare, Medicaid is a public assistance program which is jointly financed out of the general revenues of federal and state governments. As such, it helps to pay the medical bills for public assistance recipients, including old people. In some states assistance is also provided for people who can meet their daily living expenses but who cannot afford large medical bills. In order to qualify for assistance under the Medicaid program, an individual has to meet a *means test* (the individual's assets must be limited and his or her income must be below a certain level).

Recently, the Medicaid program, and especially the way in which it is administered, has come under severe criticism. The U.S. Department of Health, Education, and Welfare estimates that the annual losses from fraud and abuse of the Medicaid program could exceed $750 million.[32] These losses are not coming from patients. Rather, they can be traced to a few unscrupulous doctors who charge for services that they never actually render, who encourage unnecessary office visits and perform unnecessary operations, and who take extremely high markups on laboratory tests.[33] It must be stressed, of course, that only a small percentage of physicians engage in such practices. According to former senator Frank Moss, only about 4 percent of the 250,000 physicians who participate in the Medicaid program engage in fraudulent practices of the type just described.[34] Presumably, steps are now being taken to deal with those doctors who defraud and abuse the Medicaid program.[35]

Nursing Homes

About 4 percent (1 million) of all persons age 65 and over live in nursing homes.[36] The quality of care most of them receive is a national scandal. One investigator "visited more than two hundred nursing homes around the country. . . . But sad to say, it is the same everywhere. All over the country, nursing homes are similar, and similarly bad. Excellent homes are rare, and most of those that are considered good are good only by comparison to the majority that are worse."[37]

Old people go to nursing homes for many reasons. Some need 24-hour-a-day care for physical or mental conditions, some cannot be cared for any longer by their children or other relatives, and some have no place else to live. But whatever their reasons for going, old people find the adjustment to nursing-home life neither pleasant nor easy. People in nursing homes have little control over their lives. They are told what and when to eat, when to go to bed and when to get up, what TV programs to watch, and who their companions must be. Most nursing homes develop a set of bureaucratic rules and regulations which allow the home to run smoothly but which strip patients of their dignity and independence. Furthermore, to many residents, the nursing home is a warehouse for the dying. Most know they will never leave the nursing home, and the effect on their morale is crushing.

To many residents, the nursing home is a warehouse for the dying. Most know that they will never leave the nursing home, and the effect on their morale is crushing.▶

Problems exist in the very best nursing homes. But most homes are of extremely poor quality and the problems are worse.[38] Physical facilities, for example, are sometimes unsafe. In Marietta, Ohio, thirty-two nursing-home patients died in a fire in 1970 of smoke inhalation. In the three years preceding the fire the home had been cited as deficient in "specifications of alarm signals, frequency of fire drills, and assignment of personnel responsibility in a crisis."[39] Similar incidents have occurred in Missouri, Maryland, and a number of other states.

There have also been numerous, well-documented reports of nursing-home patients who have been practically starved to death, beaten, and forced to bear a number of other indignities. For example, a letter to former congressman David Pryor of Arkansas described a prank in one nursing home:

> It was a prank for revenge for one shift to load the patients with laxatives so the next shift would have to work cleaning up. One of the patients was so weak she was almost dead from laxatives and Fleet enemas.[40]

A particularly widespread practice in nursing homes is the use, or rather the abuse, of tranquilizers to "reduce the demands upon the nursing home staff."[41] One former nursing-home administrator described the situation:

> A layman doesn't know what to look for in a nursing home. He walks in and sees a patient is nice and quiet and he thinks this guy is happy. And the nurse tells him: "This is John. John is one of our best patients. He sits and watches television."
>
> But you just take a look at John's pupils, and you'll see what condition John is in. John is so full of thorazine that it's coming out his ears. Thorazine—that's a tranquilizer they use. It's a brown pill. It looks like an M & M candy.
>
> The nursing home where I worked kept at least 90 percent of the patients on thorazine all the time. They do it for the money. If they can keep John a vegetable, then they don't have to bother with him. They never have to spend anything to rehabilitate him.[42]

Some nursing homes provide excellent care, but the evidence suggests that they are the exceptions. The chief reason for poor health care in nursing homes seems to be that most homes are owned by private individuals or corporations that are in business purely to make a profit. If the cost of patient care is kept low, a nursing home will yield an excellent profit for its owners.

The answer to the nursing-home scandal is not simply to force nursing homes out of business. Nursing homes meet a very important need in our society. But social pressure must be applied and pertinent laws must be enforced so that nursing homes will upgrade their facilities and services. Furthermore, the number of people in nursing homes could be significantly reduced if we made a concerted effort to develop and expand community-based programs to help old people remain in their own homes. These programs include services such as home-delivered health care, community meals programs, cleaning and housekeeping services, and help with grocery and other kinds of shopping.

Other Programs

In most communities of moderate to large size a variety of other programs are available to help ease the problems of old people. These programs may be funded by the federal government, local government, religious or charitable groups, or the United Fund. Some provide modest incomes for old people; others provide services. We cannot possibly review all such programs, but a few of the more important ones should be mentioned.

One federal program, the community meals program, is designed to meet old people's nutritional needs by providing hot meals at least five days a week. If necessary, the meals are delivered to the person's home, but usually they are served in facilities such as senior citizen centers, schools, or churches. Participants are normally asked to pay for their meals, but no one is refused food because of his or her inability to pay. The importance of such a program cannot be overemphasized. For many reasons, old people often do not eat nourishing foods in the right quantity. This, in turn, adversely affects their health and levels of energy. Unfortunately, however, the community meals program has not lived up to its promise. It has not been adequately funded and is not available in many communities.

One of the most successful federal projects is the Foster Grandparent Program. This program pays indigent old people to give personal care and attention to children in institutions such as schools for the retarded, hospitals, and orphanages. In 1970, sixty-eight projects were operating throughout the country.[43] Usually, the old people are not allowed to work more than twenty hours a week each, and they are paid nominal sums for their work. The Foster Grandparent Program has proven highly beneficial for everyone involved.[44] It gives old people an opportunity to serve and to feel they are still needed. The children receive affection and companionship that the employees of child-care institutions usually do not have time to give. In addition, the administrators of child-care institutions have found that old people are a valuable untapped resource for rendering useful and needed services.

Many communities also have senior citizen centers or similar facilities. The typical multipurpose senior citizen center not only

The community meals program is designed to meet old people's nutritional needs by providing hot meals at least five days a week. If necessary, the meals can be delivered to the person's home.

provides a place where old people can find companionship, but it may provide recreational programs, arts and crafts classes, educational programs, and many other services. However, only a small percentage (1 to 5 percent) of the older population use such centers when they are available.[45] This may be because older people are not attuned to participation in group activities, or because they do not like to identify themselves, and be identified by others, as old.

A few colleges and universities now waive tuition for old people. In general, however, education is one area in which old people are almost totally neglected. Our educational system is geared to preparing the young for a career; and many old people, understandably, feel completely out of place in schools, colleges, and universities. But the old too can benefit from education and should be encouraged to use educational facilities. Indeed, old people might well constitute a source of students for the many institutions whose enrollments are currently declining. Both the old person and the school would benefit. Colleges and universities that waive tuition are discovering a small but growing corps of interested and interesting older students.

Depending on the community, there might be a wide variety of other programs for old people—a friendly visitor program, an employment service, a transportation program, and so forth.[46] In most communities one or more agencies or groups can provide old people or their friends and relatives with information about

▲ One of the most successful federal projects is the Foster Grandparent Program. This program pays indigent old people to give personal care and attention to children in institutions such as schools for the retarded, hospitals, and orphanages.

these programs—city, county, regional, or state councils on aging, the local Department of Public Welfare, the clergy and church groups.

A Concluding Note

The facilities and services we provide for old people cover a broad, fairly comprehensive range. We have programs to help meet old people's health, nutritional, and recreational needs. The problem seems to be that these programs do not work well. In many cases they are not adequately funded and provide too little for too few of the people who need them. Rather than creating new programs, then, perhaps we need to focus on improving our present programs so they do the job.

Summary

In this chapter *old people* are defined as those who are aged 65 and over. Growing old in America too often means growing into poverty, poor health, and dependency.

Two forces have combined to produce many of the problems of old age—urbanization and changing patterns of population growth. In our modern, urban, industrial society, neither children nor parents wish to share the same household, as they once did. And high birth rates in the early 1900s coupled with longer life expectancies mean that old people today make up a larger proportion of our population than in the past. *Social gerontologists* study the sociology of this growing segment of our population.

Old people's major problems are income, retirement, health, dependency, and death. About half the population aged 65 and over do not receive an income adequate to maintain a modest budget. Many live below the poverty line.

It is apparently a myth that retiring workers face serious adjustment problems. However, retirement does create severe financial strains for many older people. Much debate has centered on whether retirement should be compulsory. Compulsory retirement is a form of institutionalized discrimination.

Old people have high rates of chronic health problems and many are disabled to some degree. They visit physicians more frequently than young people; and older women make more visits than older men, although older men have higher death rates. However, old people often cannot afford high health-care bills because of their low retirement incomes. Furthermore, our system of providing health care is not geared to old people, and the quality of this care is often deficient.

Despite the American fear of dependency, many old people must ask their adult children for assistance. However, in our society this dependency creates numerous conflicts and resentments.

Death is a special tragedy for old people. The loss of one's spouse is one of the most difficult transitions old people must make. The death of their spouse reminds them of their own coming deaths. Recent studies indicate that dying people feel much better knowing the truth and ultimately accept it with peace.

We could provide every old person with a decent income, adequate health care, sufficient nutrition, and good housing—*if we want to.* There are presently four programs to help ease old people's financial burdens—Social Security (OASDHI), Supplemental Security Income (SSI), private pensions, and food stamps. Medicare, Medicaid, and nursing homes provide health care to old people. In addition, there are numerous other federal and local health programs. Unfortunately, however, both the income-related programs and the health-related programs are inadequate. Indeed, nursing homes are a national scandal. Thus, while we seem to have a good range of programs, the programs do not work well. Rather than create new ones, perhaps we should focus our attention on improving existing programs.

Discussion Questions

1. Why is it difficult to say exactly when a person is old? Why is it convenient to define persons aged 65 and over as old?
2. In 1900, persons aged 65 and over constituted 4.1 percent of the population. Today, almost 10.0 percent of the population is aged 65 and over. This percentage is likely to increase even more in the future. How do you account for this increase?
3. Define *social gerontology*. What contributions can the sociologist make to our understanding of the process of aging and the problems of old people?
4. Where do you stand on the issue of compulsory retirement? What are some of the purported advantages of compulsory retirement? What are some of the disadvantages?
5. What is meant by the statement that "older women predominate among the sick, and older men predominate among the dead"? How do you account for the fact that there are only about seventy men for every hundred women in the over-65 age group?
6. Why do you think that most Americans have an extreme fear of becoming dependent? Why do conflicts so easily arise when aging parents must depend on their adult children? What are some of the forms that this conflict can take?
7. What are your feelings concerning death and the terminally ill patient? Given our present shortage of health-care resources, to what extent is society obligated to keep the terminally ill patient alive? Does a person have the right to request that his or her life be taken? Under what conditions should such a request be honored?
8. What is the difference between the Old Age, Survivors, Disability, and Health Insurance (OASDHI) program and the Supplemental Security Income (SSI) program? Are all older Americans entitled to benefits under the SSI program? Explain.
9. Discuss the role of private pensions in meeting the economic needs of old people. Why was the Employee Retirement Income Security Act (ERISA) passed? What are some of the provisions of this act?
10. Distinguish between Medicare and Medicaid. Does an old person have to meet a means test to qualify for Medicare payments? Does he or she have to meet a means test to qualify for assistance under the Medicaid program?
11. How do you account for the fact that many, if not most, nursing homes are of extremely poor quality? What are some of the steps that might be taken to rectify this situation?

Glossary

acute health disorder A health disorder of short duration. Some examples are the common cold, influenza, and measles.

chronic health disorder A health disorder that is marked by long duration or frequent recurrence. Some examples are arthritis, rheumatism, heart conditions, and high blood pressure.

community meals program A federal program which is designed to meet old people's nutritional needs by providing hot meals at least five days a week. This program has not been adequately funded and is not available in many communities.

compulsory retirement The forced retirement of employees when they reach a certain age, regardless of their capacities. Compulsory retirement is a form of institutionalized discrimination.

Employee Retirement Income Security Act (ERISA) A federal act passed in 1974 which deals with some of the abuses in many private pension schemes. Among other important features, ERISA specifies that employees are entitled to their pensions even if they leave the company before reaching retirement age.

Foster Grandparent Program A federal program which pays indigent old people to give personal care and attention to children in institutions such as schools for the retarded, hospitals, and orphanages. Each old person who participates in this program is usually not allowed to work more than twenty hours a week.

means test A set of tests or criteria which is used to determine a person's eligibility for public assistance, including Medicaid. The person's assets must be limited and his or her income must be below a certain level.

Medicaid A public assistance program which is jointly financed out of the general revenues of federal and state governments. This program helps pay the medical bills of public assistance recipients, including indigent old people.

Medicare A federal program of hospital insurance for old people which is part of OASDHI (see below). By paying a small extra monthly premium, the old person can also buy medical insurance to help pay outpatient medical bills.

Old Age, Survivors, Disability, and Health Insurance (OASDHI) Program A federal program managed by the Social Security Administration and funded by contributions from workers and their employers. When employees retire they are entitled to a retirement income and hospital insurance. Benefits are also available for workers who become disabled and for their immediate survivors should they die.

old people Those people whom society categorizes as old. For practical purposes, it is convenient to define persons aged 65 and over as old, since many companies require their employees to retire at this age and it is at this age that people become entitled to full Social Security benefits.

private pension A fixed sum of money paid (usually monthly) by private, company-administered retirement plans to eligible employees when they reach a specified age.

social gerontology The study of the group behavior of old people, including how they adjust to the demands of society and of how society reacts to them.

Supplemental Security Income (SSI) Program A federally administered public assistance program which provides financial relief for old people who have very few assets and/or inadequate Social Security benefits. One must meet a means test to qualify for SSI; the monthly payments under this program are very low.

Suggestions for Further Reading

Atchley, Robert C., *The Social Forces in Later Life: An Introduction to Social Gerontology* (Belmont, Calif.: Wadsworth, 1972). The most complete introduction to social gerontology that is available today. Contains a wealth of information on old people and the problems that they face.

Brantl, Virginia M., and Sister Marie Raymond Brown, eds., *Readings in Gerontology* (St. Louis: Mosby, 1973). A compact collection of readings which introduces the student to some of the major themes and issues in contemporary gerontology.

Cottrell, Fred, *Aging and the Aged* (Dubuque, Iowa: Brown, 1974). A short introduction to aging, written from the standpoint of a sociologist.

Curtin, Sharon R., *Nobody Ever Died of Old Age* (Boston: Atlantic-Little, Brown, 1972). A best-seller which has much to say about the plight of the aged.

Mendelson, Mary Adelaide, *Tender Loving Greed* (New York: Knopf, 1974). This book has been described by Senator Charles H. Percy as "a lively yet responsible exposé of the incredible financial manipulations that go on in the nursing home industry."

Neugarten, Bernice L., ed., *Middle Age and Aging: A Reader in Social Psychology* (Chicago: University of Chicago, 1968). This is undoubtedly the most complete reader on various aspects of aging that is available today.

"New Outlook for the Aged," *Time*, 105 (June 2, 1975), pp. 44–51. This article gives the reader a good overview of old people in America today.

Percy, Charles H., and Charles Mangel, *Growing Old in the Country of the Young* (New York: McGraw-Hill, 1974). A stirring introduction to the problems faced by old people. This volume also contains a guide to programs and services for older Americans.

Townsend, Claire (Project Director), *Old Age, the Last Segregation: The Report on Nursing Homes* (New York: Grossman, 1971). A passionate indictment of the nursing-home industry, prepared by Ralph Nader's study group on nursing homes.

Notes

[1]See Robert C. Atchley, *The Social Forces in Later Life: An Introduction to Social Gerontology* (Belmont, Calif.: Wadsworth, 1972), pp. 6–8.

[2]For further discussion of the field of social gerontology, see *Ibid*., Ch. 1.

[3]Fred Cottrell, *Aging and the Aged* (Dubuque, Iowa: Brown, 1974), p. 24.

[4]*Ibid*., p. 24.

[5]*The World Almanac and Book of Facts: 1975* (New York: Newspaper Enterprise Association, 1974), p. 156.

[6]U.S. Bureau of the Census, *Statistical Abstract of the United States: 1975*, 96th Ed. (Washington, D.C.: U.S. Government Printing Office, 1975), p. 287.

[7]*Social Security Bulletin*, 38 (June, 1975), Table M–13.

[8]Atchley, *The Social Forces in Later Life*, p. 145.

[9]For a vivid description of the financial plight of millions of older Americans, see Charles H. Percy and Charles Mangel, *Growing Old in the Country of the Young* (New York: McGraw-Hill, 1974), Ch. 3.

[10]Atchley, *The Social Forces in Later Life*, p. 169.

[11]See *Ibid*.; and Wayne E. Thompson and Gordon F. Streib, "Situational Determinants: Health and Economic Deprivation in Retirement," *Journal of Social Issues*, 14 (1958), pp. 18–34.

[12]For a lucid treatment of the case for and against compulsory retirement, see Wilma Donahue, Harold L. Orbach, and Otto Pollak, "Retirement: The Emerging Social Pattern," in Clark Tibbitts, ed., *Handbook of Social Gerontology* (Chicago: University of Chicago, 1960), pp. 355–56.

[13]Atchley, *The Social Forces in Later Life*, p. 122.

[14]Matilda Riley and Ann Foner, *Aging and Society*, Vol. I, *An Inventory of Research Findings* (New York: Russell Sage, 1968), p. 217.

[15]Atchley, *The Social Forces in Later Life*, p. 130.

[16]See Barbara Cooper and Mary McGee, "Medical Care Outlays for Three Age Groups," *Social Security Bulletin*, 34 (May, 1971), pp. 3–14.

[17]Cottrell, *Aging and the Aged*, p. 19.

[18]Riley and Foner, *Aging and Society*, p. 309.

[19]Margaret Clark and Barbara G. Anderson, *Culture and Aging: An Anthropological Study of Older Americans* (Springfield, Ill.: Thomas, 1967), p. 222.

[20]Riley and Foner, *Aging and Society*, p. 541.

[21]Clark and Anderson, *Culture and Aging*, p. 275.

[22]See Barney G. Glaser and Anselm L. Strauss, *Awareness of Dying* (Chicago: Aldine, 1965).

[23]Elisabeth Kubler Ross, "Facing Up to Death," *Today's Education*, 61 (January, 1972), p. 31.

[24]See "Will the Social Security Bubble Burst?" *Nation's Business*, 62 (November, 1974), pp. 28–32; and "Social Security: Promising Too Much to Too Many?" *U.S. News & World Report*, 77 (July 15, 1974), pp. 26–30.

[25]James H. Schultz, *The Economics of Aging* (Belmont, Calif.: Wadsworth, 1976), p. 111.

[26]For a concise summary of the assets that an individual may have, see *Ibid*., p. 111.

[27]Atchley, *The Social Forces in Later Life*, p. 142.

[28]Schultz, *The Economics of Aging*, p. 114.

[29]For a more extended discussion of ERISA, see *Ibid*., pp. 121–22.

[30]See *Ibid*., p. 122.

[31]Cottrell, *Aging and the Aged*, p. 28.

[32]See "HEW Works to Cut Fraud and Abuse in Medicaid," *Aging*, 261 (July, 1976), p. 24.

[33]"Physician, Heal Thyself," *Newsweek*, 88 (August 9, 1976), p. 24.

[34]*Ibid*., p. 24.

[35]"HEW Works to Cut Fraud and Abuse in Medicaid," p. 24.

[36]Atchley, *The Social Forces in Later Life,* p. 261.

[37]Mary Adelaide Mendelson, *Tender Loving Greed* (New York: Knopf, 1974), p. 22.

[38]See *Ibid.* See also Claire Townsend (Project Director), *Old Age, the Last Segregation: The Report on Nursing Homes* (New York: Grossman, 1971).

[39]Townsend, *Old Age, the Last Segregation,* p. 63.

[40]*Ibid.*, p. 102.

[41]*Ibid.*, p. 111.

[42]*Ibid.*, p. 114.

[43]Atchley, *The Social Forces in Later Life,* p. 262.

[44]For further discussion, see "Foster Grandparents Get High Ratings in Five Studies," *Aging, 170* (December, 1968), pp. 14–15.

[45]Atchley, *The Social Forces in Later Life,* p. 261.

[46]For a listing of some of these programs, see *Ibid.*, pp. 264–65.

Chapter 13
Overpopulation

Studying Population Growth
- Population Growth: How Fast?
- The History of World Population Growth
- Population Growth by Region
  - *Asia*
  - *Latin America*
  - *Africa*
  - *United States*

Triggering the Explosion
- Demographic Factors
- Sociological Factors

Rapid Population Growth: Its Costs and Consequences
- Resource Depletion
- Pollution
- Hunger
- Population Growth and International Relations

The Search for Solutions
- Accommodationism
- Antinatalism

Summary

If gigantic spaceships existed, it might be possible to solve our population problems. We could potentially move on to populate new planets, equally comfortable and rich, whenever the earth's resources failed to meet our needs. However, gigantic spaceships do not exist, and there is no guarantee that there are other planets that human beings could inhabit.

On *this* earth, the population cannot continue to increase at high rates for long. Our food stores, natural resources, and international relations can only stand the pressures of population growth up to a certain point. The world population problem is serious already, and the situation is getting worse. It is a problem that simply cannot be ignored.

Paul Ehrlich describes the population problem this way in his book *The Population Bomb:*

> The undeveloped countries of the world face an inevitable population-food crisis. Each year food production in undeveloped countries falls a bit further behind burgeoning population growth, and people go to bed a little bit hungrier. While there are temporary or local reversals of this trend, it now seems inevitable that it will continue to its logical conclusion: mass starvation. The rich are going to get richer, but the more numerous poor are going to get poorer. Of these poor, a minimum of three and one-half million will starve to death this year, mostly children. But this is a mere handful compared to the numbers that will be starving in a decade or so. And it is now too late to take action to save many of those people.[1]

Population has become a problem largely because many societies are operating according to norms and values that are outdated and no longer adaptive. In the past a high death rate made it essential that couples have many children. Today, though, life expectancy is longer, the death rate is much lower, and high fertility rates can only bring on overpopulation. Yet many couples the world over, and especially those in underdeveloped countries, still believe in having large families. Their norms and values are *dysfunctional.* Though their behavior is not deviant, it may nevertheless have disastrous consequences for society.

Studying Population Growth

The growth or decline of a population is determined solely by rates of birth, death, and migration. The study of changes in these rates is called *demography.* On a regional level, when a population's birthrate is high and its death rate low, that population will grow, assuming that few people migrate out of the region in question. On the world level, the demographic equation is even simpler. Since we can't yet migrate from the earth, we need only consider the world birthrate and the world death rate.

Demographers commonly measure levels of fertility in given areas in terms of the number of births per year to a total population of 1,000 people. This figure is called the *crude birthrate.* Thus, if there were 250 births in one year in a population of 10,000, the crude birthrate would be 25.0 per 1,000. The *crude death rate* is calculated in a similar way. If 100 people out of a total population of 10,000 died, the crude death rate would be 10.0 per 1,000.

By examining the birth and death rates of a country, we can determine the country's *rate of natural increase.* This is simply the difference between the crude birthrate and the crude death rate. In 1974, for example, the United States had a birthrate of 15.0 per 1,000 people and a death rate of 9.1 per 1,000 people.[2] The rate of natural increase then was 15.0 births minus 9.1 deaths, or 5.9 per 1,000 people. Clearly, the higher a country's rate of natural increase, the faster its population will grow.

Population Growth: How Fast?

One of the best ways to visualize how fast a population is growing is by establishing its *doubling time,* or the number of years it will take the population to grow to twice its current size. The doubling times for the world as a whole and for the major regions of the world are shown in Table 13.1.

Table 13.1
Doubling Times Under Various Rates of Natural Increase as of 1977

	Crude Birth Rate (per 1,000)	Crude Death Rate (per 1,000)	Rate of Natural Increase (annual, percent)	Number of Years to Double
World	30	12	1.8	38
Major Regions				
Africa	45	19	2.6	27
Asia	32	12	2.0	35
Europe	15	10	0.4	173
Latin America	36	9	2.7	26
North America	15	9	0.6	116
Oceania	22	9	1.3	53

SOURCE: Tabulated from Population Reference Bureau, *1977 World Population Data Sheet* (Washington, D.C.: Population Reference Bureau, 1977.)

As this table shows, the world's population is exploding. At current rates of increase, the populations of the underdeveloped regions will double in about three decades. The world population as a whole will grow to twice its 1977 size within only thirty-eight years. This is in sharp contrast to the ancient past, when it took thousands of years for the world's population to double.

The History of World Population Growth

Nobody knows exactly when people as we know them appeared on the earth, but their numbers grew very slowly until about 1650. At that time about 470 million people inhabited the planet.[3] This may seem to be a large number, but it is really small by today's standards. China alone now has a population of over 850 million and in India there are about 623 million people.

Around 1650, the world's population began to manifest a pattern of slow but steady growth. In two hundred years it more than doubled to about 1.1 billion people. Then between 1850 and 1930 the world's population doubled again to around 2.0 billion people. Today, the world's population is over 4.0 billion.[4]

What are the prospects for the future? Estimates of the world's population in the year 2000 range from a low of 5.4 billion to a high of 7.5 billion.[5] Since our population projections usually tend to be low, the world's population might even double between now and the year 2000. This means the prospects are grim, since untold millions of the world's population already lack adequate food.

Population Growth by Region

Trends in world population growth are the result of growth patterns occurring within individual countries. We don't need to review population trends in every country of the world here, but we should look at some of the more obvious trouble spots and at patterns of population growth in the United States.

Asia

In 1977, Asia's estimated population was 2.3 billion people, or more than half of the world's population. Forecasts of Asia's population in the year 2000 range from a low of 3.0 billion to a high of 4.5 billion. In the year 2000, then, the population of Asia alone may be greater than that of the world today.[6] The problems of providing this many people with a decent standard of living may prove insurmountable.

Latin America

Latin America, including Mexico and the Caribbean Islands, currently has the fastest growing population of any major region in the world. In 1977, the Latin American countries had a rate of natural increase of 2.7 percent. At this rate of natural increase, the population of these countries will double every twenty-six

▲
The male child holds the position of central importance within the Indian family structure. However, demographers have observed that an average Indian family must have 5.4 children before a male child can be expected to survive to maturity.

years. By way of comparison, in 1977 North America had a rate of natural increase of 0.6 percent and its doubling time was one hundred sixteen years. For the world as a whole, the rate of natural increase in 1977 was 1.8 percent. At this rate of increase, the world's population will, as we have already indicated, double every thirty-eight years.[7] In 1977 the total population of Latin America was 336 million; it could reach 550 to 750 million by the year 2000. With so large a population, it is likely that severe food shortages will develop throughout Latin America.

Africa

In 1977, Africa's estimated population was 423 million people, growing at a rate of 2.6 percent per year. The United Nations estimates that by the year 2000 the Africans will number between 700 and 850 million people.[8] Parts of central and western Africa are grim illustrations of the delicate balance between population, food, and climate. During most of the 1960s, the people of this region were able to feed themselves because rain fell in sufficient quantities to nourish their crops. However, the late 1960s brought a period of severe and prolonged drought. Croplands withered, grazing lands turned barren. As a result, untold thousands of Africans died of starvation.[9] If the African countries cannot soon produce more food and reduce their birthrates, their death rates will soar in coming years.

United States

Until very recently, the United States had been a demographic maverick. Despite our level of industrialization, our crude birthrate had been high compared with many developed countries, and our population had grown rapidly, as Figure 13.1 indicates.

Figure 13.1 **United States Population, 1790–1970**

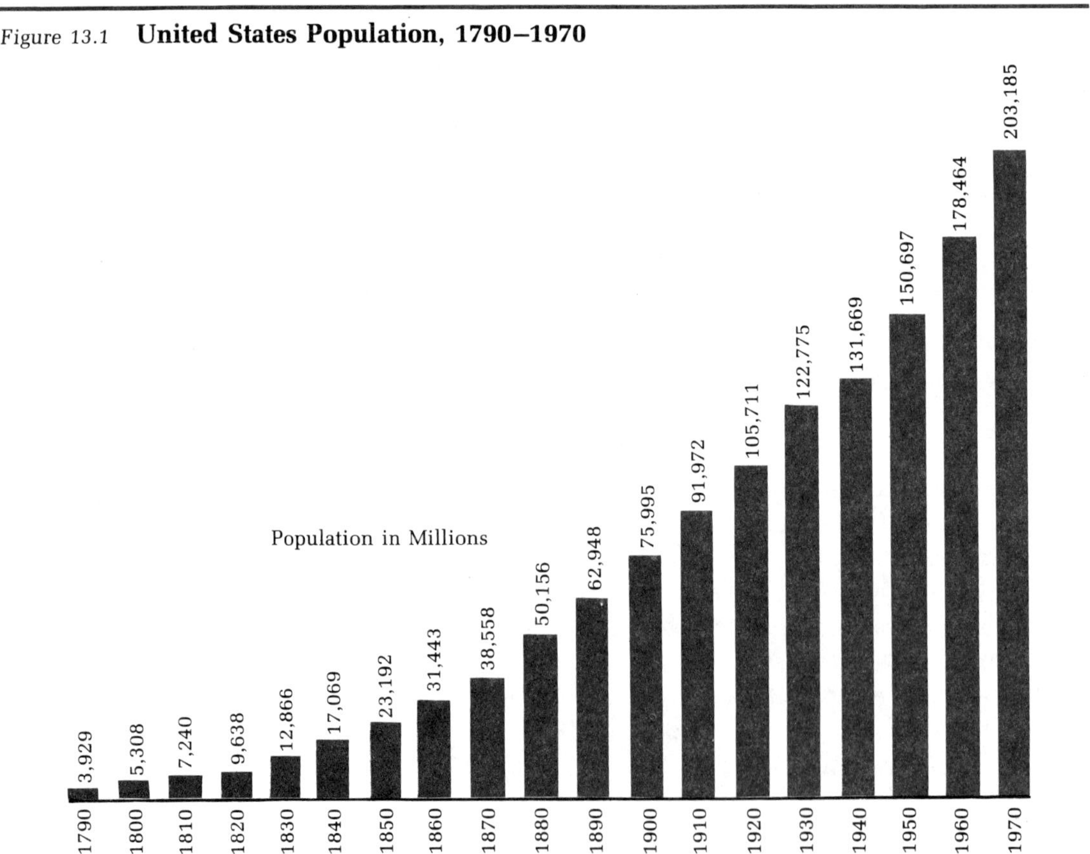

Since the late 1950s, however, this trend has reversed itself. The U.S. crude birthrate has now dropped to levels that could eventually lead to zero population growth.[10] But another baby boom like the one that occurred after World War II is still a possibility. The recent dramatic decline in the birthrate could be interpreted to be merely a temporary reaction to today's unsettled economic conditions, international tensions, and political and social turmoil. On the other hand, the decline in the crude birthrate may mean that rapid population growth in the U.S., as in the other developed countries of the world, has ended.

Several factors are probably contributing to the decline in the U.S. birthrate:[11]

1. Each year we gain greater control over our fertility. The possibility is good that fewer children will be born in the future because of improved methods of birth control and liberalized abortion laws.

2. The cost of rearing children is constantly increasing. It now costs, on the average, $60,000 to rear a child from birth through completion of an education.[12] We don't know for certain that couples are having fewer children because of the cost of providing good food, clothing, shelter, medical care, and education; but it seems likely that cost is a factor.

3. Large segments of the public are now conscious of the dangers of overpopulation.

The United States, however, has traditionally been a child-oriented society, and the birthrate could rise again. As depicted in Figure 13.2, an increase of just one child per family, for example, would have a dramatic impact on U.S. population size.

In December, 1973, the United States population was estimated at 212 million people, or about 57.0 people per square mile. Many other countries are much more densely populated: 852 people per square mile in the Netherlands, 753 per square mile in Japan, and 593 per square mile in the United Kingdom.[13] Compared with these countries, the U.S. cannot be called overpopulated. Yet we contribute greatly to the world's population problem because we consume a disproportionate share of the world's resources. Consider the following, for instance:

> The United States, with less than 6 percent of the world's people, in 1968 accounted for more than one-third of the world's energy consumption; well over a third of its tin consumption; about a fourth of its phosphate, potash, and nitrogenous fertilizer consumption; almost half of its consumption of newsprint and synthetic rubber (produced from a variety of resources); more than a fourth of its steel consumption; and about an eighth of its cotton consumption.[14]

As supplies dwindle and demand around the world increases, U.S. domination of the world's resources will have to give way—either voluntarily or under increasing international pressure.

Figure 13.2 **U.S. Population: Two- vs. Three-Child Family**

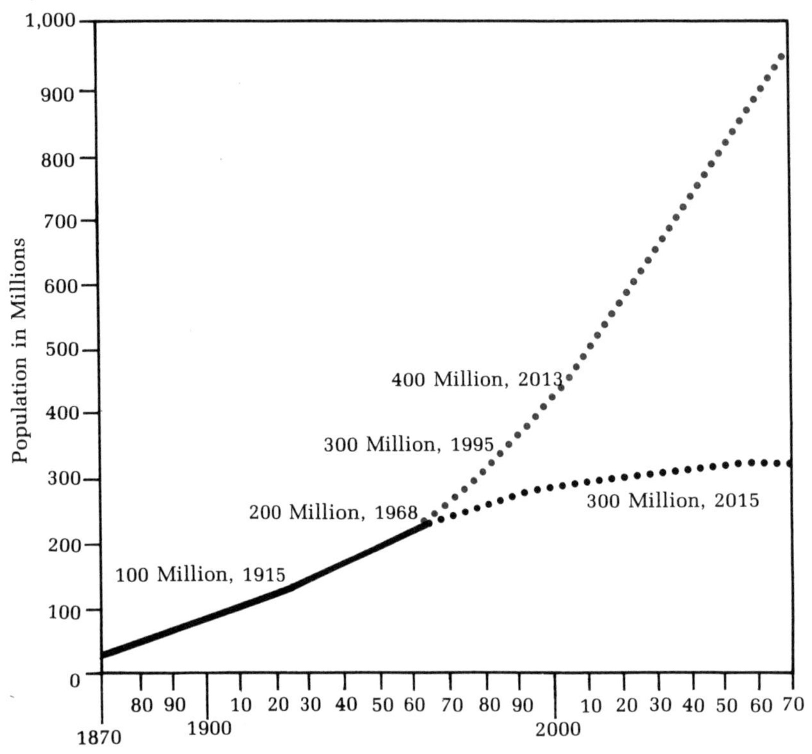

The population of the United States passed the 100-million mark in 1915 and reached 200 million in 1968. If families average two-children in the future, growth rates will slow, and the population will reach 300 million in the year 2015. At the three-child rate, the population would reach 300 million in this century and 400 million in the year 2013. (Projections assume small future reductions in mortality, and assume future immigration at present levels.)

SOURCE: Commission on Population Growth and the American Future, *Population and the American Future* (Washington, D.C.: U.S. Government Printing Office, 1972), p. 23.

Triggering the Explosion

We have briefly looked at the historical trends in population growth in selected areas and at what these trends indicate for the future. Before we can seek solutions to today's problems or find ways to avert tomorrow's catastrophe, we must examine the causes of the population problem.

Demographic Factors

Demographers often use the theory of demographic transition to explain our current population crisis. This theory proposes three stages of population development, depicted in Figure 13.3.

Stage I of the demographic transition is marked by little or no population growth—millions of people are born each year but millions also die. Throughout most of human history, birthrates have been extremely high—higher than they are now in most parts of the world. At the same time, high death rates have tradi-

Social Problems and You

Looking to the ZPGeneration

Worship Cupid, but Don't Be Stupid! advises a press release put out by Zero Population Growth, Inc. A Valentine received by some Americans last [February 14th], inscribed *Love . . . Carefully,* was equipped with a red condom. But few young couples in the U.S. today need antinatalist exhortations or equipment. Since 1957 the fertility rate has dropped from a peak of 3.76 children per woman to a record low of 1.75 last year. Though it may rise in the next thirty years, it is highly improbable that Americans in the foreseeable future will again engage in the great procreational spree of the postwar years. The baby boom has become a bust.

The nation is seemingly on its way to the long-debated goal of Zero Population Growth (ZPG), the theoretical point at which deaths and births balance out. If present fertility and mortality rates remain constant, the U.S. population may stabilize around the year 2025 at between 260 million and 270 million (up from 216 million today). . . .

Americans nowadays are painfully aware that resources may be increasingly short and expensive in coming years. Inflation has already made the cost of rearing a large family (now estimated at more than $250,000 for four children from cradle through college) all but prohibitive. The pleasure principle may be a factor too. Richard Brown, manager of population studies for a General Electric think tank in Washington, observes: "Children are competing with travel, the new house and professional standing. Once the checkbook is balanced and all other desires have been indulged, a couple will think of having a child—or, indeed, that child may have its place in the list of Wants & Goals."

The biggest, if least predictable, element in the fertility rate is the attitude of the American woman. As the economic, social and political status of women has improved, the desirability and mystique of motherhood has declined. Says Princeton's Charles Westoff, a world-renowned demographer: "There is a very pronounced change in the attitude of women toward marriage, childbearing and working, and all these attitudes seem to lead in one direction: they don't want three or four children." As Berkeley Demographer Judith Blake Davis puts it succinctly: "You won't find those sacrificial mothers any more."

Thus—if the U.S. is indeed headed for ZPG—people will for the first time in history be consciously forging their own destiny.

Not all sociologists, demographers and economists agree that a stable population is necessarily desirable. Some worry about the social and cultural implications of a markedly older population. By the year 2020 there will be almost twice as many people over 65 (43 million) as there are today, exerting immense new pressures on the Social Security, pension and Medicare systems. To Columbia University Sociologist Amitai Etzioni, "ZPG spells a decadent society, à la France in the '30s, à la Berlin in the early '30s. This means a less innovative society, a society in which fewer people will have to attend, care, feed, house and pay for a larger number."

Most futurists, however, agree that a better life is in store for a stabilized population. Among those who believe in the beneficial effects is Demographer Westoff: "ZPG will reduce pressures on the environment and on resources. It will probably increase per capita income. It will reduce pressure on governmental services. And it will give society an opportunity to invest more in the quality than the quantity of life."

SOURCE: "Looking to the ZPGeneration," *Time,* 109 (February 28, 1977), p. 71.

Figure 13.3 **Schematic Drawing of the Theory of Demographic Transition**

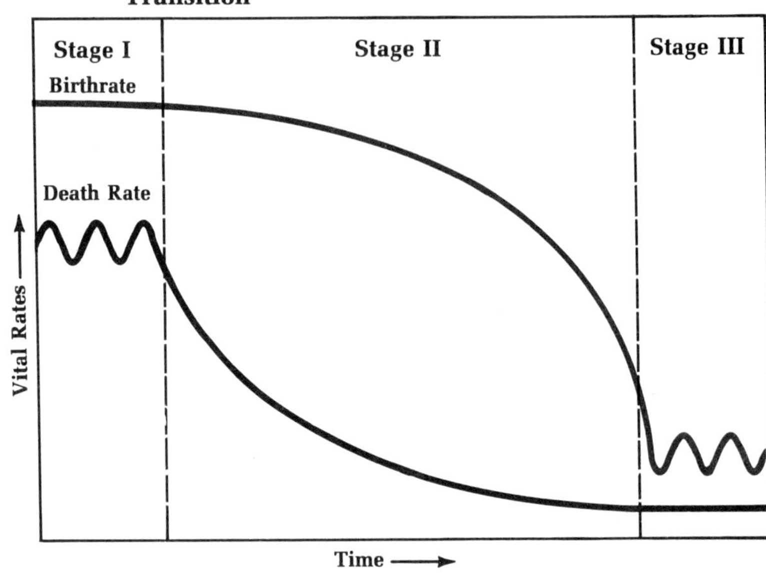

SOURCE: Ansley J. Coale, "The History of the Human Population," *Scientific American*, 231 (September, 1974), p. 49.

tionally offset high birthrates. Thus, in Stage I (before 1650) world population size was nearly static.

In Stage II, birthrates remain high but death rates decline. The result is a huge gap between the two, and a population explosion occurs. Mexico provides an excellent example of a country whose population is well into Stage II of the demographic transition. In 1938 Mexico's crude birthrate was about 44 per 1,000, and the crude death rate was about 23 per 1,000. These rates ensured rapid population growth. In 1977 Mexico's crude birthrate was still about the same at 42 per 1,000, but its crude death rate had dropped to 7 per 1,000.[15] Today Mexico has one of the most rapidly increasing populations in the world and may soon face severe population pressures. Unfortunately, Mexico is not alone in its plight. In 1972, 54 of the world's 158 countries had rates of natural increase greater than 25 people per 1,000.[16] More than a third of the countries in the world, then, are experiencing dramatic population explosions.

Finally, in Stage III of the demographic transition, birthrates decrease until they are in equilibrium with the lowered death rates. Most of the highly industrialized countries in the world have entered this third stage.

Sociological Factors

The theory of demographic transition sheds some light on the immediate causes of the world population explosion—populations explode when death rates decline dramatically and birthrates do not. But we are still left with several questions. What made death rates drop so sharply in underdeveloped countries? Why do birthrates remain high in these areas? And why do birthrates eventually decline in developed countries?

Several factors have contributed to lower death rates in the underdeveloped world. First, innovations in preventive medicine—inoculations and vaccinations—have virtually conquered many fatal diseases, including bubonic plague, smallpox, and cholera. Second, death rates have also been reduced significantly by the widespread use of DDT against malaria-carrying mosquitoes. Before World War II, malaria was a major cause of sickness and death. Today most of the world's people live in areas that are or soon will be free of malaria.[17] Third, all types of medical care have become more widely available, and many sanitary facilities have been improved. In some countries living and working conditions are better. Finally, several major famines have been avoided or curbed because of innovations in agriculture and the development of a global economy. For example, in the early '70s, millions more people might have died in Africa and India had it not been for massive grain shipments from the United States, Russia, Canada, and other developed countries.

Why birthrates persistently remain high in underdeveloped countries is harder to explain. One reason is that, until recently, rates of infant mortality were very high. Couples had to have many children if they wanted a few to survive to adulthood. This is no longer always the case today. However, individual attitudes about family size have not kept pace with overall changes in death rates, particularly in developing countries.

Another reason birthrates stay high is that, in many places, a large family is vital to meeting the individual's needs. In agricultural settings, for example, the labor of each family member is an asset in tilling the soil and harvesting the crop. Where there are no nursing homes, children care for their aged parents—they provide social security. When large families and high birthrates can be a plus for the individual, then a conflict exists between what is good for society and what is good for the individual:

> The peasant who has learned from his culture to depend on his children for labour on the farm, for old-age security, and for other essentials cannot be expected to extrapolate declining mortality with the demographer and to calculate a long-range need for fewer children.[18]

In many places a large family is vital to meeting the individual's needs. In agricultural settings, for example, the labor of each family member is an asset in tilling the soil and harvesting the crop. ▶

Finally, marriage at early ages is typical throughout the underdeveloped world and is associated with high rates of birth. Because families are large and the more mature relatives help care for children, "adolescents can undertake such roles as parenthood while they are still socially immature, for they will not bear the main responsibility for caring for their children."[19]

Sociologists have developed a neat schema for analyzing the interplay between birthrates and social structures in all societies.[20] First, all societies develop social norms that affect the likelihood that a fecund woman will be exposed to intercourse—norms pertaining to age at marriage, celibacy, and frequency of intercourse. Second, the chances that intercourse will result in pregnancy are influenced by social factors, chiefly the use or nonuse of contraceptive techniques, including sterilization. Finally, whether a pregnancy results in a live birth depends upon the degree to which abortions are readily available and on infant mortality rates. On the whole, the social structures of the underdeveloped world tend to promote high rates of fertility.

In more highly developed countries, on the other hand, industrial social structures come into play. Since industrialization makes a high standard of living (entailing a wide variety of goods and services) available, it becomes socially desirable to pursue a high standard of living. But most people cannot afford both a high standard of living *and* a large family. As we noted earlier, children are extremely expensive.

But, perhaps more importantly, modern urban societies make demands on people that tend to discourage high birthrates. People must undergo extended periods of education, training, and competing to become established. Early marriage and a large family are barriers to upward mobility. Furthermore, large numbers of children are no longer needed to work the farm or care for parents in their old age. Children, once economic and social assets, are now considered by some people to be luxuries and economic liabilities. In the developed world, norms favoring high birthrates are highly dysfunctional for both the individual and society.

Rapid Population Growth: Its Costs and Consequences

Growing numbers of people require greater supplies of our finite natural resources; and the faster people multiply, the sooner our supplies will be depleted. In this section, we will examine the high costs of rapid population growth.

Resource Depletion

At current rates of consumption, many of the earth's most valuable—and life-sustaining—resources will soon be used up. Estimating how soon is tricky since there are many unknowns. In the case of petroleum, for example, new reserves may be found, technological improvements may make it economical to extract oil from shale, or future demand might change. If Americans, for instance, learn to rely on small, efficient cars and public transpor-

At current levels of consumption, the world's known reserves of petroleum will last 31 more years.

◀

tation, the world's supply of oil will last much longer. Nonetheless, it is estimated that, at current levels of consumption, the world's known reserves of petroleum will last 31 more years; tungsten, 40 years; manganese, 97 years; and nickel, 150 years. Coal's future is brighter. At current levels of consumption, known reserves of coal should last about 2,300 years.[21]

The quick depletion of the world's natural resources can be attributed to two factors—rapid population growth and people's desire for a higher standard of living. Every year more people worldwide demand electricity for their homes, automobiles to transport them, and appliances to save them time and work.

In the United States, materialistic values have speeded the depletion of rich stores of petroleum, natural gas, iron, timber, and other resources. Because we largely define success in terms of material possessions—expensive homes, cars, and other luxuries—we have carelessly and irresponsibly squandered our natural resources. Look around you. Very likely you are surrounded by furniture, appliances, and ornaments made of steel, wood, glass, and aluminum. The building you may be in—home, dormitory, classroom—is a complex "machine" most likely constructed of wooden planks, structural steel, copper tubing and wiring, and many pounds of nails. Lights burn, motors run, heaters glow, and perhaps a television or stereo plays somewhere. This is the scene across America. At the same time, our factories churn out more and more resource- and energy-consuming goods, and institutions like your school burn tremendous amounts of coal and electricity. Clearly, the American way makes heavy demands on natural resources.

Pollution

Besides depleting resources, large numbers of people cause pollution.[22] Where populations are small and nonindustrialized, the environment can tolerate normal levels of human pollution. But more people and more industry make for a bigger problem—a problem that natural processes cannot eliminate. A prime example is heavily polluted Manhattan Island, the heart of New York City and home of 1.5 million people. Clearly, when this small island was inhabited by a small number of Algonquians before the European settlement of America, pollution was too minimal to pose any threat to the environment.

Unfortunately, in America today environmental pollution is an all too common by-product of large numbers of people, heavy industrial development, and wasteful resource consumption. In 1971, for example, Americans used and discarded 71 billion cans, 38 billion bottles and jars, 35 million tons of wastepaper, 7 million cars, and 100 million tires.[23] Some cities are becoming less and less able to adequately dispose of their solid wastes.

Pollution of our air, water, and soil seriously affects human life.[24] Environmental pollution contributes to respiratory and heart disease, can reduce our stores of good food and water, and can adversely affect our quality of life in many ways. Certain kinds of fish are no longer fit for consumption, and crops are threatened by smog and contaminated soil. In many places, rivers, lakes, and ocean waters are too filthy for even recreational use.

▲ Where populations are small and nonindustrialized, the environment can tolerate normal levels of human pollution. But more people and more industry make for a bigger problem—a problem that natural processes cannot eliminate.

In the United States, our high standard of living and our pollution are interdependent. Our materialistic values demand detergents and disposables, cars and synthetics. Population growth is obviously not the only reason for pollution and resource depletion. Our rapid economic growth, made possible in part by new technology, may be even more to blame. It has been suggested, for instance, that "a reduction in economic growth would reduce pollution emissions by more than would a comparable reduction in population."[25] However, not many of us would favor halting or even slowing down economic growth; it would mean shortages of goods and services and probably higher rates of unemployment. Thus, "direct attacks on pollution problems clearly and easily dominate over reductions in population and economic growth as a strategy for obtaining a cleaner environment."[26]

So far, state and federal efforts to "legislate" a cleaner environment have not been particularly successful.[27] If pollution continues to worsen, however, it may begin to upset our birth, death, and migration rates. Our world population and environmental pollution problems could be compounded many times over.

Hunger

Food, like other natural resources, may be in critically short supply in years to come. In 1975 alone, millions of people starved, and millions more died of diseases stemming from malnutrition. Most of the victims of food shortages are infants and small children in Asia, Africa, and parts of Latin America.[28]

Although floods, droughts, and poor harvests contribute to food shortages, the fundamental cause is rapid population growth. Nearly two hundred years ago, Thomas Robert Malthus, a noted British demographer and economist, predicted that the world's population would grow in geometric progression (2, 4, 8, 16, 32, . . .), whereas food supplies would increase in slower arithmetic progression (1, 2, 3, 4, 5, . . .). Malthus predicted disastrous results from such growth patterns. Even though Malthus failed to anticipate the dramatic increases in agricultural productivity that have occurred during recent years, his theory cannot be dismissed entirely. The basic picture that he painted of a growing imbalance between population and food supplies is increasingly becoming a reality.[29]

The approaching food crisis raises an extremely important question for Americans: Should we make sacrifices in order to help feed hungry people in Asia, Africa, and Latin America? We could alleviate much world hunger if we were willing to modify our eating habits. To produce beef, we feed prodigious quantities of grain to cattle, as shown in Figure 13.4. The same twenty pounds of grain it takes to produce one pound of beef could provide a day's adequate diet for nearly twenty starving people. Our diets need not rely so heavily on beef for nourishment, but we are presently unwilling to reduce our daily meat consumption to lessen world hunger. In the long run, however, we may have no choice.

Population Growth and International Relations

Most of the victims of food shortages are infants and small children in Asia, Africa, and parts of Latin America.

The issue of whether the well-fed are responsible for feeding the hungry leads directly to the issue of population growth and international relations. Today's rapid population growth and develop-

Figure 13.4 **Grain Needed to Produce Other Foods**

Food	Pounds of Grain
1 Lb. Beef	20
1 Lb. Pork	6.3
1 Doz. Eggs	4.25
1 Lb. Poultry	3.0
1 Gal. Milk	2.8
1 Loaf White Bread	0.9

SOURCE: "The World Food Crisis," *Time*, 104 (November 11, 1974), p. 75.

ing food crisis could have the following major implications for international relations.[30]

1. Severe imbalances between rich and poor countries in terms of resources and food can lead to war. World War II, in fact, may have been triggered in part by Japan's inability to acquire food from the western nations, coupled with rapid population growth.[31] If the wealthy nations of the world do not voluntarily share their resources, they may lose them involuntarily through military conquest.

2. In many underdeveloped countries a government which cannot feed its people cannot last. To protect economic interests and maintain international order, wealthier nations may wish to help such countries maintain their political *status quo*. One way to do this is to help the governments of these countries feed their people. Perhaps then, the U.S. will attempt to keep pro-American regimes in power by helping them stabilize or improve their peoples' standards of living—even at the cost of lowering our own. Basically, this means underdeveloped countries could "capitalize on the danger which their political instability poses for the major powers."[32]

3. The underdeveloped countries may also "be the beneficiaries of a gradually developing ethical sense among people and nations."[33] Advocates of this view assume that a "moral imperative" would prompt Americans to sacrifice their luxurious diet simply because it is immoral to allow Africans, Asians, or Latin Americans to starve to death. This premise is debatable, of course. Champions of the moral imperative also maintain that the need to control nuclear weapons will eventually create an effective world governing force. The resulting hypothetical government might serve as an instrument for redistributing the world's wealth of resources, and underdeveloped countries could thereby improve their standards of living.[34]

The Search for Solutions

The world population explosion is potentially the greatest problem to ever threaten humankind. If no solution is found, we may go full circle and find ourselves back at Stage I of the demographic transition. Death rates, due to famine, disease, and lack of life-giving resources, will rise sharply to meet or surpass high birthrates. What, then, can be done?

Accommodationism

Some people hope that the world can continue to accommodate a demanding, ever-growing population. But is it realistic to suppose that we can meet the challenges of rapid population growth by mustering all our resources and technological wizardry?

Accommodationists have some basis for optimism. For example, the world may not have to depend on petroleum as much as the oil suppliers would lead us to believe. There are a number of other potential energy sources. Breakthroughs in nuclear energy may continue, for instance, and safe nuclear power plants may be developed to provide nearly inexhaustible sources of energy. Similarly, we can probably count on always having an adequate water supply. Over 70 percent of the earth's surface is sea water which can be desalinated if other supplies fail.

When we talk about accommodating an ever-increasing world population, we must consider our technological genius. Quite often, only economic and political constraints keep new technologies from doing the next-to-impossible.

More vexing, though, is the problem of adequate food production. Several possible solutions have been proposed—cultivating new lands, harvesting food from the sea, and increasing crop yields per acre. Unfortunately, the first two solutions hold little promise of alleviating food shortages because the costs are too high and the potentialities have been greatly exaggerated.[35] A more promising development is the "green revolution," or the improvement of crops and crop yields per acre through scientific agriculture. Scientists at the International Maize and Wheat Improvement Center near Mexico City have developed a cross between wheat and rye, called triticale. This new grain yields more per acre than durum wheat, requires relatively little fertilizer, and is a protein-rich ingredient for a wholesome meal.

Antinatalism

Not even limitless technological achievement can sustain world population growth forever at the present rate. There are limits to the number of people any area can support.

For this reason, several countries have turned to antinatalist programs designed to lower birthrates and rates of natural increase. Japan is most noteworthy. In the late '40s, the Japanese government passed several laws making low-cost abortions readily available. As a result, the number of induced abortions increased from less than 250,000 per year in 1949 to more than 1,000,000 in 1953 and later years.[36] The government also emphasized the importance of practicing contraception. Japan's crude birthrate dropped from 34 per 1,000 in 1947 to 18 per 1,000 in 1956.[37]

Government policy, however, was only partly responsible for the dramatic decline in Japan's birthrate. Devastated by World War II, Japan suffered a severe shortage of jobs and housing in the late '40s. Furthermore, Japan was a modern industrialized society, and the people could see the dangers in overpopulating their small island nation. When the venerated emperor "let it be known that the control of the size of the family met with his approval,"[38] the Japanese people were already prepared to accept birth control whether or not an antinatalist program were enacted. At most, the government's antinatalist policy merely facilitated, rather than caused, the decline in the birthrate. Probably the most significant factor "was the desire of the average couple to control the number of children they would have. . . . A level of birth limitation would have been attained in the absence of government support for it, though it probably would have taken a somewhat longer period of time."[39]

Unlike the Japanese, people in underdeveloped countries seem unprepared to accept birth control. Antinatalist programs cannot work in these countries until the institutional and social factors that encourage high birthrates change. The people must feel it is practical and important to have fewer children, to marry at older ages, and to use contraceptives. But, as we have already pointed out, the task of changing attitudes is formidable.

In addition, many underdeveloped countries lack the resources to carry out a successful antinatalist program. Even methods of

Table 13.2

Examples of Proposed Measures to Reduce U.S. Fertility

Social Constraints	Economic Deterrents/ Incentives	Social Controls	Measures Predicated on Existing Motivation to Prevent Unwanted Pregnancy
Restructure family: a) Postpone or avoid marriage b) Alter image of ideal family size	Modify tax policies: a) Substantial marriage tax b) Child tax c) Tax married more than single d) Remove parent's tax exemption e) Additional taxes on parents with more than 1 or 2 children	Compulsory abortion of out-of-wedlock pregnancies	Payments to encourage sterilization
Compulsory education of children	Reduce/eliminate paid maternity leave or benefits	Compulsory sterilization of all who have 2 children	Payments to encourage contraception
Encourage increased homosexuality	Reduce/eliminate child or family allowances	Confine childbearing to only a limited number of females	Payments to encourage abortion
Education for family limitation	Bonuses for delayed marriage and greater child-spacing	Stock-certificate-type permits for children	Abortion and sterilization on demand
Fertility control agents in water supply	Pensions for women of 45 with less than N children	Housing policies: a) Discourage private home ownership b) Stop awarding public housing based on family size	Allow certain contraceptives to be distributed nonmedically
Encourage women to work	Eliminate welfare payments after first 2 children		Improve contraceptive technology
	Require women to work and provide few child-care facilities		Make contraception truly available and accessible to all
	Limit/eliminate publicly financed medical care, scholarships, housing, loans, and subsidies to families with more than N children		Improve maternal health care, with family planning as a core element

ADAPTED FROM: Robin Elliot, Lynn C. Landman, Richard Lincoln, and Theodore Tsuoroka, "U.S. Population Growth and Family Planning: A Review of the Literature," *Family Planning Perspectives*, 2 (October, 1970), p. ix.

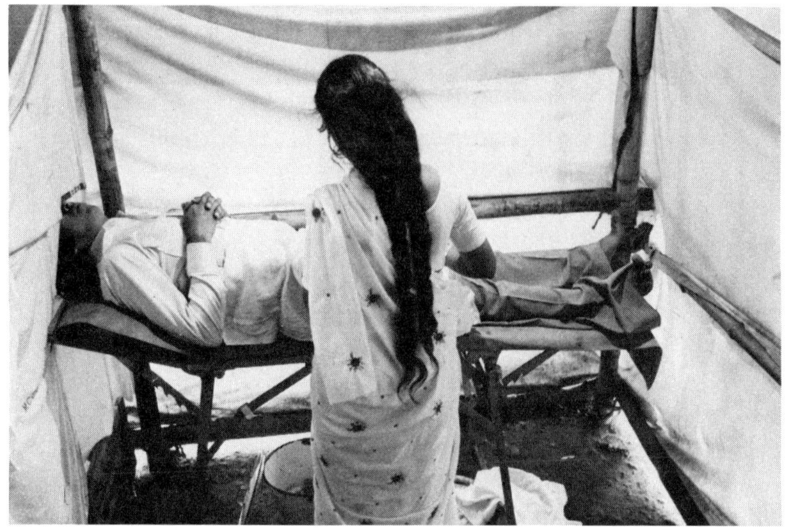

India is one of several countries that have put antinatalist programs into effect. Here a doctor performs a vasectomy in Bombay. ▶

birth control that are relatively inexpensive (oral contraceptives, intrauterine devices, vasectomies) are still too expensive for the underdeveloped countries. The indirect costs associated with a good antinatalist program (training and paying medical personnel and establishing education programs) must also be taken into account. When all these costs are added up, most underdeveloped countries simply cannot afford an effective antinatalist program. Finally, many underdeveloped countries have thousands of inaccessible villages and no effective system of mass communication. The seemingly simple task of bringing contraceptive information and devices to the people in fact presents real difficulties.

For these and other reasons, the overpopulated, underdeveloped countries of the world have made little headway in controlling their birthrates and slowing their population growth. Nonetheless, population growth must be brought under control, or everyone's survival on this limited earth will be jeopardized.

Summary

The statistical study of population is termed demography. Whether a population increases or decreases depends on three factors—its birthrate, its death rate, and its rates of migration. Today, the world population is growing at ever faster and alarming rates.

In terms of the theory of demographic transition, most of the world's population has passed from Stage I, characterized by high birthrates and high death rates, into Stage II, characterized by high birthrates but low death rates. Population explosions result from Stage II conditions. In Stage III, populations are stable with corresponding low birthrates and low death rates. Most modern industrialized countries have reached Stage III.

The low death rates characteristic of Stage II are in large part the result of improvements in health care and agricultural developments. The high birthrates typical of this stage are the result of people's tendency to cling to reproductive norms and values that are dysfunctional and no longer appropriate. Developed countries in Stage III, on the other hand, have adopted norms and values conducive to low birthrates. The world's population growth is reaching dangerous levels primarily because couples around the world, especially in underdeveloped countries, continue to have large families.

Rapid population growth, coupled with people's desire for a high standard of living, costs dearly. At present rates of consumption, many life-sustaining resources could soon be depleted.

One of the by-products of rapid population growth and irresponsible resource consumption is pollution, which adversely affects health and the quality of life. It could also affect world food supplies.

Unquestionably, the world faces critical food shortages in the years to come. In 1975, millions died of starvation and of diseases attributable to malnutrition. Rapid population growth plus widespread hunger could also have serious implications for international relations.

Accommodationists hope that the world can continue to accommodate an ever-growing population. But despite human genius in developing new sources of food, energy, and other life-sustaining resources, the world's population cannot grow indefinitely at its present rate. In response to the problem, several countries have enacted antinatalist programs aimed at reducing birthrates and thereby rates of population growth. For example, at the end of World War II, Japan launched an all-out antinatalist program and by 1954 had halved its crude birthrate. The industrialized Japanese people readily accepted this program.

But the situation is very different in most underdeveloped countries where leaders face the enormous task of changing centuries-old norms, values, and institutions which favor high birthrates. Furthermore, most of these countries are financially unable to carry out a successful antinatalist program. Consequently, little progress has been made toward lowering birthrates in underdeveloped countries.

Discussion Questions

1. What does Paul Ehrlich mean when he refers to a "population bomb"? Do you think that the world population crisis is as serious as Ehrlich makes it out to be? Why or why not?
2. Discuss population trends in the United States. How do you account for the fact that up until recently our crude birthrate has been high compared with most other developed countries? How would you account for the fact that since the late 1950s our crude birthrate has been declining? Do you think that this decline will be permanent? Explain your answer.
3. Compared with the rest of the world, can the United States be considered overpopulated? In what ways do we contribute to the world's population problem?
4. What are some of the reasons why the death rate drops in Stage II of the demographic transition? Why do you suppose that birthrates persistently remain high in underdeveloped countries? How would you account for the fact that in many industrialized countries there has been a third stage to the demographic transition—a stage in which fertility rates have dropped rapidly?
5. At current rates of consumption, many of the earth's most valuable, life-sustaining resources will soon be used up. What proposals do you have to deal with this crucial problem?
6. One expert has suggested that "a reduction in economic growth would reduce pollution emissions by more than would a comparable reduction in population." What is meant by this statement? Is it feasible to try to reduce the rate of economic growth? What proposals do you have for controlling and conquering environmental pollution?
7. Does the United States have any responsibility for helping to feed hungry people in Asia, Africa, and Latin America? Should we reduce our standard of living to help feed these people? In the long run, will we have any choice in this matter?
8. What bearing does rapid population growth have on international relations? Will international relations become even more strained as the world's population continues to grow?
9. Discuss the following statement: "By mustering all our resources and technological wizardry, we can feed, house and otherwise provide for our ever-growing world population for a long time to come." Do you agree with this statement? Why or why not?
10. What is an antinatalist program? Why is it so difficult to launch a successful antinatalist program in underdeveloped countries?

Glossary

accommodationism The view that by mustering all our resources and technological wizardry, we can continue to feed, house, and otherwise provide for our ever-growing world population.

antinatalist programs Governmental programs aimed at lowering birthrates and hence lowering the rate of population growth. Antinatalist programs may include making contraceptives widely available, legalizing abortions, and educating couples to want small families.

crude birthrate The number of births per 1,000 population in a given year. For example, in 1974 the United States had a crude birthrate of 15.0 per 1,000 population.

crude death rate The number of deaths per 1,000 population in a given year. In 1974, the United States had a crude death rate of 9.1 per 1,000 population.

demography The statistical study of populations. The demographer is an expert in analyzing rates of birth, death, and migration.

green revolution A term that refers to the dramatic increases in agricultural productivity that have occurred during recent years. The green revolution has mainly been due to the improvement of crops and crop yields per acre through scientific agriculture.

infant mortality rate The number of deaths of children under age 1 per 1,000 live births in a given year.

rate of natural increase A measure of how rapidly a population is growing. The rate of natural increase is simply the difference between the crude birthrate and the crude death rate.

theory of demographic transition A theory which suggests that populations go through three stages in their development. Stage I is marked by little or no population growth—birthrates and death rates are about equal. Stage II is characterized by high birthrates and low death rates, and hence a population explosion occurs. In Stage III birthrates decrease until they are in equilibrium with lowered death rates.

Suggestions for Further Reading

Armstrong, Terry R., ed., *Why Do We Still Have an Ecological Crisis?* (Englewood Cliffs, N.J.: Prentice-Hall, 1972). A collection of essays which examines the interrelationship between human values, social institutions, and the ecological crisis. Contributors include educators, politicians, economists, lawyers, and philosophers.

Bogue, Donald J., "The End of the Population Explosion," *The Public Interest,* 7 (Spring, 1967), pp. 11–20. Bogue is an optimist who thinks world population control programs are on the verge of succeeding. This article should be read in connection with that written by Kingsley Davis, listed below.

Chamberlain, Neil W., *Beyond Malthus: Population and Power* (Englewood Cliffs, N.J.: Prentice-Hall, 1972). A provocative analysis of how population pressures affect power relationships within and between societies. Of particular interest is the chapter entitled "Population and International Relations."

Commission on Population Growth and the American Future, *Population and the American Future* (Washington, D.C.: U.S. Government Printing Office, 1972). An unsurpassed analysis of the implications of population growth for the United States. The Commission advocates the development and implementation of a rational population policy.

The Crisis of Survival (Compiled by the Editors of *The Progressive* and the College Division of Scott, Foresman and Company) (Glenview, Ill.: Scott, Foresman, 1970). The contributors to this volume, which include a number of noted politicians, statesmen, ecologists, and economists, shed a great deal of light on the environmental crisis facing us today and upon how this crisis might be solved. Highly recommended reading for anyone who is concerned with environmental issues.

Davis, Kingsley, "Population Policy: Will Current Programs Succeed?" *Science*, 158 (November 10, 1967), pp. 730–39. Davis is not particularly optimistic about the outcome of present antinatalist programs. Davis does, however, suggest some helpful changes and improvements.

Detweiler, Robert, Jon N. Sutherland, and Michael S. Werthman, *Environmental Decay in its Historical Context* (Glenview, Ill.: Scott, Foresman, 1973). The selections in this volume provide an excellent overview of the causes and consequences of environmental decay. Included are excerpts from twenty-seven classic writings on population and the environment.

Ehrlich, Paul R., *The Population Bomb* (New York: Ballantine, 1968). Dramatizes the world population crisis and examines some of the things that have been done—and could be done—to cope with it.

Ehrlich, Paul R., Anne H. Ehrlich, and John P. Holdren, *Human Ecology: Problems and Solutions* (San Francisco: Freeman, 1973). Considers the relationship between population growth and resource depletion, pollution, and so on. Solutions to the population problem are also considered. Essential reading for serious students of population, resources, and the environment.

"The Human Population," *Scientific American*, 231 (September, 1974). This issue of *Scientific American* contains eleven articles dealing with the human population. The articles are thorough and complete and written by noted authorities in demography and related fields.

Westoff, Charles F., et al., *Toward the End of Growth: Population in*

America (Englewood Cliffs, N.J.: Prentice-Hall, 1973). A collection of fourteen essays by noted authorities in the field of demography. These articles deal with such diverse topics as "The Increasing Acceptance of Sterilization and Abortion," "The Impact of Population Growth on Resources and the Environment," and "Recent Developments in Population Growth Policy in the United States."

"The World Food Crisis," *Time*, 104 (November 11, 1974), pp. 66–83. A special section of *Time* on the world food crisis. Includes a section on "How Hunger Kills" as well as informative graphs, charts, and maps. Photographs make vivid the tragedy of starvation.

Notes

[1]Paul R. Ehrlich, *The Population Bomb* (New York: Ballantine, 1968), p.17.

[2]U.S. Bureau of the Census, *Statistical Abstract of the United States: 1975*, 96th Ed. (Washington, D.C.: U.S. Government Printing Office, 1975), p. 51.

[3]The historical data that follow are taken from Judah Matras, *Populations and Societies* (Englewood Cliffs, N.J.: Prentice-Hall, 1973), Table 1.2. One of the best reviews of world population history is to be found in Warren S. Thompson and David T. Lewis, *Population Problems*, 5th Ed. (New York: McGraw-Hill, 1965), pp. 382–446.

[4]The 1977 world population estimate was 4.1 billion. In the pages that follow, the data for 1977 are taken from Population Reference Bureau, *1977 World Population Data Sheet* (Washington, D.C.: Population Reference Bureau, 1977).

[5]In the pages that follow, the projections for 2000 are taken from United Nations, *World Population Prospects as Assessed in 1963*, in Paul R. Ehrlich and Anne H. Ehrlich, *Population, Resources, Environment* (San Francisco: Freeman, 1970), pp. 337–40.

[6]See Population Reference Bureau, *1977 World Population Data Sheet;* and Ehrlich and Ehrlich, *Population, Resources, Environment*, pp. 337–40.

[7]*Ibid.*

[8]*Ibid.*

[9]For reports on the food crisis in several African countries, see "Famine: Africa's Quiet Crisis," *Atlas World Press Review*, 21 (June, 1974), pp. 13–21.

[10]For a discussion of various aspects of population growth in the United States, see Charles F. Westoff et al., *Toward the End of Growth: Population in America* (Englewood Cliffs, N.J.: Prentice-Hall, 1973); see also Leslie Aldridge Westoff and Charles F. Westoff, *From Now to Zero: Fertility, Contraception and Abortion in the United States* (Boston: Little, Brown, 1971).

[11]For a more complete discussion of factors affecting fertility in the United States, see Norman B. Ryder, "The Future Growth of the American Population," in Westoff et al., *Toward the End of Growth*, pp. 85–95.

[12]Commission on Population Growth and the American Future, *Population and the American Future* (Washington, D.C.: U.S. Government Printing Office, 1972), p. 81.

[13]Computed from United Nations, *Statistical Yearbook: 1974* (New York: United Nations, 1975), Table 18.

[14]Paul R. Ehrlich, Anne H. Ehrlich, and John P. Holdren, *Human Ecology: Problems and Solutions* (San Francisco: Freeman, 1973), p. 65.

[15]Data for 1938 from *Interamerican Statistical Yearbook: 1940* (New York: Macmillan, 1940), p. 60. Data for 1977 from Population Reference Bureau, *1977 World Population Data Sheet.*

[16]Tabulated by the author from Population Reference Bureau, *1972 World Population Data Sheet.* It should be noted that a rate of natural increase of this magnitude leads to exremely rapid population growth.

[17]See William Petersen, *Population,* 3rd Ed. (New York: Macmillan, 1975), p. 598.

[18]Ronald Freedman, "Norms for Family Size in Underdeveloped Areas," in Michael Micklin, ed., *Population, Environment, and Social Organization: Current Issues in Human Ecology* (Hinsdale, Ill.: Dryden, 1973), p. 179.

[19]Petersen, *Population,* p. 414.

[20]See Kingsley Davis and Judith Blake, "Social Structure and Fertility: An Analytic Framework," *Economic Development and Cultural Change,* 4 (April, 1956), pp. 211–35.

[21]Ehrlich, Ehrlich, and Holdren, *Human Ecology,* p. 64.

[22]For a detailed review of the types and extent of pollution in the United States, see Heinz Kohler, *Economics and Urban Problems* (Lexington, Mass.: D. C. Heath, 1973), pp. 380–401.

[23]*Ibid.*, p. 397.

[24]See Ehrlich, Ehrlich, and Holdren, *Human Ecology,* p. 115.

[25]Ronald Ridker, "The Impact of Population Growth on Resources and the Environment," in Westoff et al., *Toward the End of Growth,* p. 118.

[26]*Ibid.*, p. 115.

[27]See Ralph Nader, "Corporations and Pollution," in *The Crisis of Survival* (Glenview, Ill.: Scott, Foresman, 1970), pp. 151–59.

[28]For a report on world hunger and its victims, see "The World Food Crisis," *Time*, 104 (November 11, 1974), pp. 66–83.

[29]Thomas Robert Malthus, *Population: The First Essay* (Ann Arbor, Mich.: University of Michigan, 1959).

[30]See Neil W. Chamberlain, *Beyond Malthus: Population and Power* (Englewood Cliffs, N.J.: Prentice-Hall, 1972), esp. pp. 173–92.

[31]See Warren S. Thompson, *Population Problems* (New York: McGraw-Hill, 1953), pp. 355–359.

[32]Chamberlain, *Beyond Malthus*, p. 183.

[33]*Ibid*., p. 186

[34]*Ibid*., p. 188.

[35]Ehrlich, Ehrlich, and Holdren, *Human Ecology*, p. 97.

[36]David M. Heer, *Society and Population*, 2nd Ed. (Englewood Cliffs, N.J.: Prentice-Hall, 1975), p. 134.

[37]Ralph Thomlinson, *Population Dynamics: Causes and Consequences of World Demographic Change* (New York: Random House, 1965), p. 414.

[38]Thompson and Lewis, *Population Problems*, p. 544.

[39]Cited in William Petersen, *Population* (New York: Macmillan, 1961), pp. 488–89.

PART IV

INSTITUTIONAL CRISES

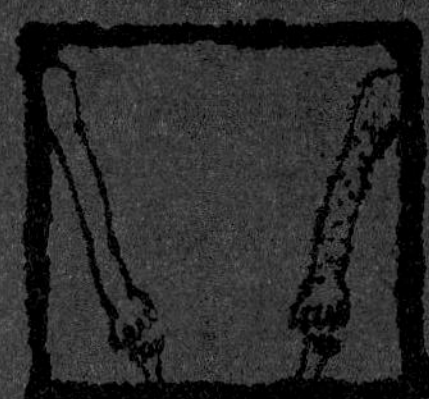

The Family

Education

Criminal Justice

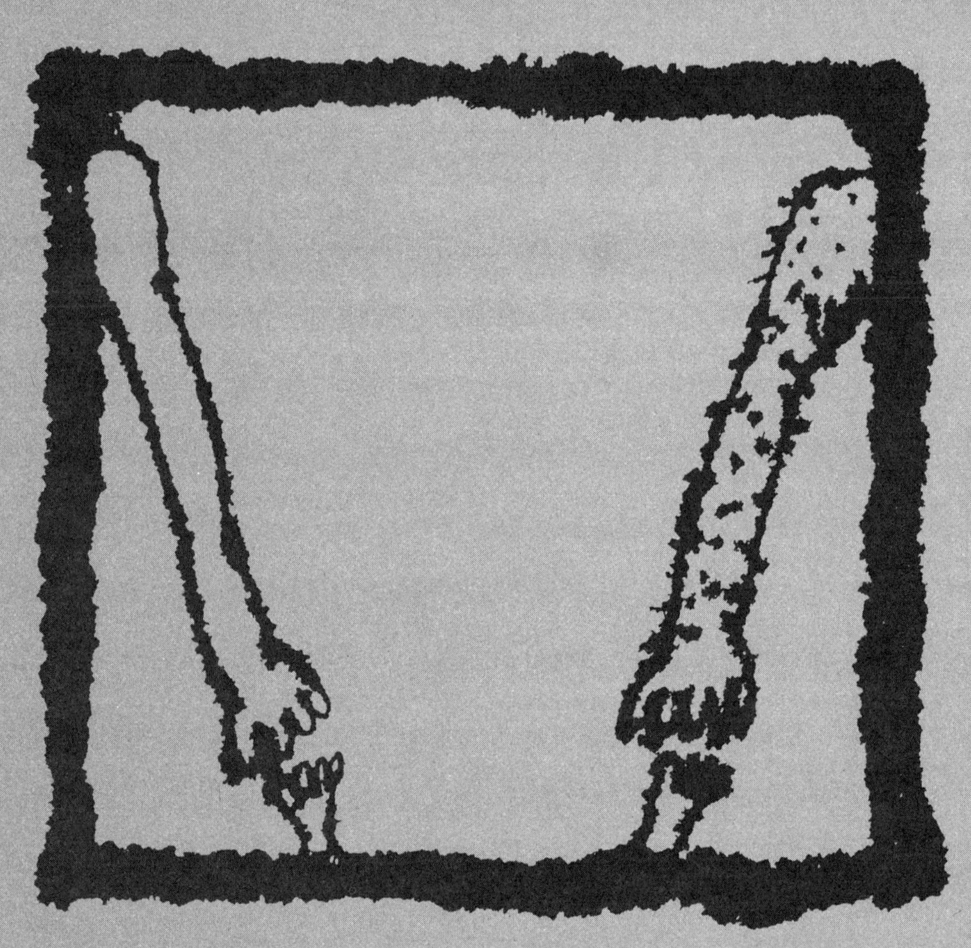

Chapter 14

The Family

Social critics who predict doom for American society frequently point to our divorce rates and the breakdown of the American family to support their dire forecasts. At the same time, the society columns of our Sunday newspapers are filled with engagement, wedding, and birth announcements. Marriage and family are still a very prominent part of our life.

Certain basic social institutions enable every society to survive and endure. Of all these basic institutions, the family is probably the oldest and most enduring. Yet, in the United States, many difficult problems are associated with marriage and family life. As we examine family problems in this chapter, we should keep in mind that what one social critic calls a "problem" is what another calls a "healthy development."

Despite many problems and changes and the growing concern of social critics, marriage and the family are basic social institutions and remain very prominent parts of our lives. A wedding is almost always regarded as a very special occasion. ▶

Social Change and the Family

The problems of the contemporary American family are partly the result of other changes that have occurred in our society. As our society has grown more complex, the family has lost many of its external supports. In our rural past, the responsibilities heaped on married couples were so great that they were hardly able to divorce and go their separate ways. They had to educate their children, make a success of their farm or business, and care for infirm members of their family.[1] Romantic love was only one of many bonds that held marriage together; in fact, a couple's subjective feelings about each other were probably not very important in determining the success or failure of their marriage. If the husband satisfactorily played his role as breadwinner and the wife satisfactorily played her role as homemaker and mother, the marriage endured.

Today, however, we have institutions to educate children and care for the infirm, and most people work for huge corporate or government bureaucracies. Since most men do not necessarily need women and most women do not necessarily need men to earn a living, meet health needs, or educate children, it is not surprising that the family faces many problems.

Although the family has lost many of its external supports, it has emerged as an extremely important source of primary relationships. The quality of the emotional relationship between a couple now determines the success or failure of their marriage. Today, a spouse is expected to provide friendship, erotic experience, romantic love, ego support, and even continuous lay psychotherapy.[2] In short, an individual may depend almost entirely on his or her spouse for emotional well-being. It is to the credit of the institution of marriage that it has been as successful as it has in meeting these diverse emotional needs. Yet, it is unrealistic for one person to depend on another to such a large extent over an extended period of time. That many people become so dependent on their spouses helps explain why an unhappy marriage or a divorce can be such a painful experience.

Over the years, then, the family has lost many of the external supports that once helped to hold it together. In this sense, it has become a much more vulnerable, fragile institution. But at the same time, it has become increasingly important as a source of primary relationships. Bearing these points in mind, we now turn to definitions of modern family problems.

Defining Family Problems

There is little consensus on how to define family problems; sociologist Armand L. Mauss, however, suggests that those who identify family problems can be divided into two groups—the *traditionalists* and the *challengers*.[3]

Traditionalists believe that much is wrong with modern family life. They deplore the loss of family unity that is supposed to have existed in the past, and they find increasing rates of divorce extremely disturbing. To them, high divorce rates signal the breakdown and perhaps even the eventual disappearance of the family as we know it. Traditionalists are equally shocked by increasing rates of illegitimacy and abortion and the declining birthrate. They are baffled by women who would rather work than be full-time wives and mothers, and they have a hard time accepting the sexual freedom of today's young and unmarried. To them, all these more or less recent developments symbolize the breakdown of marriage and family life.

The *challengers* agree that much is wrong with the family, but they define the problem quite differently.[4] To them, the notions that people should get married primarily to rear children and should stay married for better or for worse are outmoded. They deplore the custom of lifelong marriages that are sometimes miserably unhappy, and they disapprove of divorce procedures that are frequently difficult, expensive, and embittering. Most importantly, they see marriage (especially for women) as an instrument of oppression. Some challengers say that we are forced to marry whether we want to or not, and they see motherhood as a way of keeping women out of socially productive roles. To the challengers, then, the problem is not that the family is breaking down, but that it is not breaking down fast enough.

In this chapter, we will look at some types of marital breakdown, such as divorce, desertion, and illegitimacy, as problems. In this sense, we will be traditionalists. However, at times, we will try to look at these problems in a new light, asking ourselves such questions as: Is the traditional nuclear family worth salvaging? Should marriage be forever? Are increasing divorce rates necessarily bad? Should unwed mothers be encouraged to keep their children?

The Unhappy Unbroken Marriage

Probably the most common type of marital breakdown is the *empty-shell* family.[5] In an empty-shell family a couple continue to live together and to play their roles as breadwinner and housekeeper respectively. But their marriage is empty of affection and respect; the interaction that occurs is only instrumental—that is, it has to do with getting the bills paid, getting the children off to school, getting dinner on the table, and so forth. The couple rarely share their joys and sorrows with each other and they do not look to each other for companionship. Bickering, quarreling, and fighting are common but are usually over trivial, insignificant issues. To deal with the real issues would be very painful and might well lead to divorce. There is no sure way to assess the number of empty-shell marriages, but they must number in the millions.

Although the partners in an empty-shell marriage would seem likely to divorce, they often do not.[6] They may belong to a religious group which frowns on divorce, or they may be reluctant to admit publicly that their marriage has failed. A couple may avoid divorce because the alternatives to their unhappy marriage seem even more unpleasant. After all, the marriage meets their instrumental needs, and they may feel that they will have little chance to remarry. An unhappily married couple may also continue their marriage because they do not know how to file for divorce, because they lack grounds for divorce under their state's divorce law, or because they cannot afford one. Getting a divorce may seem to be a bigger hassle than continuing the marriage. The husband may avoid divorce because he fears heavy alimony and/or child-support payments.

Many couples avoid divorce "for the sake of the children"; it is a popular notion in our society that children are irreparably hurt when their parents divorce. However, divorce may do less damage to the child than the experience of living in an unhappy unbroken home. "Adolescents in broken homes show less psychosomatic illness, less delinquent behavior, and better adjustment to parents than do children in unhappy unbroken homes."[7] So parents who stay together only because of their children may actually be doing their children a disservice.

Almost nothing is known about how an unhappy unbroken marriage affects the marriage partners themselves. Certainly, the partners in this type of marriage might well exhibit high rates of alcoholism, mental illness, and other disorders.

Divorce

The existence of so many empty-shell families forces us to question whether an increasing divorce rate is necessarily bad. What is to be gained by preserving a totally miserable and unrewarding marriage? Are we helping or hurting children by subjecting them to constant bickering and quarreling in an unhappy unbroken home? Many, perhaps most, Americans, however, see divorce as a serious social problem.

Extent

There is really no good measure of the extent of divorce. One measure is to compare the number of divorces in a given year with the number of marriages in the same year. This method yields the prediction that approximately one out of four marriages will end in divorce.[8] However, this measure can be very misleading.[9] For example, just because 100,000 divorces occur during the same year that 400,000 marriages occur does not mean that one in four of these marriages will end in divorce. It means simply that in the year in question 100,000 couples decided to divorce and 400,000 decided to marry. In measuring the extent of divorce, one should take into account the total number of people who are married and who could therefore potentially get divorced and not just the number of people who get married during a particular year. The number of people who get married during a given year has no bearing on the number of people who get divorced during that same year. In the future, rates of marriage may go up and rates of divorce down, or vice versa.

Another measure of the extent of divorce is to compute the number of divorces in a given year per 1,000 total population. This gives us a picture of trends in the divorce rate over time, as shown in Table 14.1. However, in many ways this table raises more questions than it answers. We have a good idea why the divorce rate soared in 1945: apparently many couples who were separated during World War II were unable to rebuild their marriages after the war. But why did the divorce rate decline steadily between 1950 and 1960? Why has it increased rapidly since 1965? Does the divorce rate of 4.6 per 1,000 in 1974 mean that marriages are still reasonably stable or that our divorce rate has reached crisis proportions? These questions are almost impossible to answer. Perhaps one of the best measurements of divorce is the simple statement that "considerably more than 10 million living Americans have been divorced at one time or another."[10]

Table 14.1

Estimated Number of Divorces and Estimated Divorce Rate per 1,000 Population, United States, 1920–1974

Year	Number of Divorces	Divorce Rate per 1,000 Population
1920	170,505	1.6
1925	175,449	1.5
1930	195,961	1.6
1935	218,000	1.7
1940	264,000	2.0
1945	610,000	4.3
1950	385,144	2.6
1955	377,000	2.3
1960	393,000	2.2
1965	479,000	2.5
1970	708,000	3.5
1974	970,000	4.6

SOURCES: U.S. Public Health Service, *Vital Statistics of the United States: 1970*, Vol. III, *Marriage and Divorce* (Washington, D.C.: U.S. Government Printing Office, 1974), Table 2-1; and U.S. Bureau of the Census, *Statistical Abstract of the United States: 1975*, 96th Ed. (Washington, D.C.: U.S. Government Printing Office, 1975), Table 94.

On the basis of statistics alone, then, we cannot automatically conclude that marriage is a highly vulnerable, unstable institution. However, as Table 14.1 indicates, a tremendous number of people are involved in divorce each year. While this may not necessarily be bad, divorce does often create problems for both the individual and for society.[11] It calls for painful emotional readjustments and may produce economic difficulties. Sometimes the wife and children must apply for public assistance, thus making society responsible for supporting the broken family.

Compared with other countries, our divorce rate is high.[12] This may mean that we take a more realistic approach to divorce, or a less realistic approach to marriage. In either case, given the large number of divorces in America coupled with the high costs and mental anguish of divorce, we can legitimately consider divorce a social problem. But is the problem that too many marriages end in divorce, or is the problem that society makes divorce a wrenching, degrading experience?

Causes

One way to analyze the causes of divorce is to look at the complaints husbands and wives voice against each other when they seek divorce. One of the most thorough of such analyses was conducted by George Levinger.[13] As Table 14.2 shows, he found that wives have considerably different complaints than husbands do. When asked why they wished to end their marriages, wives most frequently cited neglect of home or children by the husband, physical abuse, financial problems, and mental cruelty. Husbands, on the other hand, most often complained of cruelty, neglect of home and children, sexual incompatibility (reluctance or refusal of coitus, inconsiderateness, etc.), and infidelity. Only 22.8 percent of the wives and 13.5 percent of the husbands identified "lack of love" as a major problem in their marriage. There are also systematic differences in the types of complaints voiced by middle-class and lower-class couples: "Spouses in the middle-class marriages were more concerned with psychological and emotional interaction, while the lower-class partners saw as most salient in their lives financial problems and unsubtle physical actions of their partners."[14]

Even though Levinger's findings are interesting, they do not necessarily explain why some couples seek divorce and others do not. If we conducted a survey, we might well find that couples who never contemplate divorce have about the same number and types of complaints as those who do. What we need, then, is a more general theory of divorce. Such a theory has also been developed by Levinger and suggests that all marriages are subject to certain forces that tend to keep the marriage intact and to certain forces that tend to tear the marriage apart. His theory can be summarized as follows:

1. *There are forces within all marriages which can lead to marital success or failure.* Some couples genuinely enjoy each

Table 14.2

Marital Complaints Among 600 Couples Applying for Divorce

	Proportion of Complaints by Respondent Groups					
	Wives	Husbands	Social Position of Wives		Social Position of Husbands	
Complaint	Total	Total	Middle	Lower	Middle	Lower
Physical Abuse	.368	.033	.228	.401	.029	.035
Verbal Abuse	.238	.075	.200	.245	.048	.082
Financial Problems	.368	.087	.219	.402	.124	.079
Drinking	.265	.050	.143	.294	.048	.051
Neglect of Home or Children	.390	.262	.457	.374	.200	.276
Mental Cruelty	.403	.297	.372	.408	.267	.306
In-Law Trouble	.067	.162	.038	.074	.200	.153
Excessive Demands	.025	.040	.057	.018	.057	.035
Infidelity	.240	.200	.324	.223	.114	.198
Sexual Incompatibility	.138	.200	.124	.141	.267	.188
Lack of Love	.228	.135	.324	.206	.200	.120

SOURCE: George Levinger, "Sources of Marital Dissatisfaction Among Applicants for Divorce," in Paul H. Glasser and Lois N. Glasser, eds., *Families in Crisis* (New York: Harper & Row, 1971), p. 129.

other's companionship, find sexual fulfillment in marriage, and share similar religious and intellectual interests. Their relationship is a resource which helps keep the marriage alive. On the other hand, some couples eventually grow away from each other. Their marriage becomes sexually unfulfilling, and they develop diverse religious, recreational, and intellectual interests. For these people, their relationship becomes a liability which may eventually lead them to divorce.

2. *Surrounding all marriages there are forces which influence whether a couple whose marriage has failed will stay married or get divorced.* Some couples are reluctant to divorce because they fear their children will be harmed, divorce is frowned on by their church, they believe that breaking the marriage bond is morally wrong, or they do not want the stigma associated with divorce. In addition, the couple may not be able to afford a divorce or know how to obtain one. For all these people, social and cultural forces surrounding the marriage serve as a barrier against divorce. On the other hand, some couples either have no children or feel that divorce will not unduly harm them. In addition, their church may be permissive toward divorce, they may feel that it is silly to continue an unhappy marriage, and they may have friends and relatives who encourage them to divorce. These couples are obviously more likely to seek divorce than those couples whose marriages are surrounded by barriers to divorce.

3. Still, many couples do not get divorced even though their marriage is neither gratifying nor surrounded by barriers to divorce. *Rather, whether they divorce may depend on whether the alternatives to the marriage are attractive.*[15] Unhappily married persons who have alternative sexual or marital partners are more likely to divorce than those who believe divorce will bring their sexual and marital lives to an end. Similarly, men and women who can improve their economic and occupational status by getting a divorce are more likely to do so than those for whom the alternative to remaining married is to go on public welfare. In some cases, "the marital relationship itself may be so unattractive that any alternative condition—with or without another partner—is preferred."[16]

In summary, we can analyze any marriage in terms of the relationship between the spouses, the potential barriers to divorce, and the alternatives to continuing the marriage. If the marriage is characterized by a good relationship between the spouses, if it has strong social and cultural supports, and if the couple see no attractive alternatives to their present marriage, the chances are good that the marriage will endure.

Other general theories of divorce suggest a link between our increasing divorce rate and the increasing industrialization and urbanization of our society in recent years.[17] Urbanization and industrialization imply that young people leave the farm for the city. In the city there is a much greater chance that a person will marry someone from a different social, religious, or ethnic background. Such marriages have higher rates of failure than marriages between people of similar backgrounds.[18] Furthermore, in a large city there are fewer economic or social barriers between a couple and divorce. Spouses depend less on each other professionally and economically. In rural areas, there are few jobs for unmarried women; and, at the same time, a wife is needed to help run the farm. In urban areas, by contrast, a businessman does not need a wife to ensure his occupational success, and a professional woman does not need a husband for financial security. Finally, divorce is more readily accepted in urban areas than in rural areas where even today a divorced person may be stigmatized.

Consequences

Divorce is a means of escape from an unhappy, unrewarding marital relationship. However, our current system of divorce creates a great deal of unhappiness as well.

In most cases, divorce is a wrenching psychological experience for all concerned. This is largely because of our expectations for marriage: "If we are encouraged in the dating years to search for a special partner who will match our personal dreams and expectations, won't we experience a great deal of frustration and disappointment if we discover that this love has vanished a few years after marriage?"[19] Divorce also often leads to economic difficulties for the divorced couple. A man may simply not have enough money to meet his financial obligations to his ex-wife and his children; a woman may have difficulty finding a job that pays adequately and covers the cost of day care for children. If the woman must turn to welfare as a result, society ends up bearing the economic costs of divorce. Finally, the children of divorced couples experience problems in making social and emotional adjustments, although perhaps not to as great a degree as children who live in unhappy unbroken homes.[20] And again, society must often pay the price.

Despite the numerous unhappy consequences of divorce, it is cruel and inhumane to force a couple to continue a totally miserable marital relationship. Indeed, because marital conflict and disillusionment are seemingly inevitable in a complex society such as our own, some students of family life have suggested alternatives, such as contract marriages in which, after a period of time, a couple would be free to renew the contract or not.[21] However, Americans have traditionally favored and supported the permanent, monogamous marriage. Until this norm changes, as some think it will, divorce will continue to be a difficult and perhaps destructive experience.

Remarriage

Most people who get divorced usually remarry within a rather short period of time.[22] "[S]tep by step, we are reshaping the rules—legal, religious, and conventional—in order to institutionalize not only the dissolution of marriages but also the creation of second marriages."[23] Indeed, someday something akin to a system of serial marriages may become institutionalized in this country. Such a system would recognize that, first, there are certain human needs that can be met only through marriage and that, second, marriage today is a very fragile institution. Love between two people can easily be lost. Under a system of serial marriages, both partners would be free to find new loves and new marriages if their old marriage wears out.

What is the success rate of remarriages? A 1956 study indicated that remarriages are usually more successful than first marriages.[24] However, more recent research has not borne this finding out.[25] Divorced people actually appear to be poorer marital risks than people who have not been married previously. For a divorced man, for example, alimony or child-support payments can put a financial strain on the new marriage.

Furthermore, divorce does not completely terminate a marital relationship; rather, the relationship continues under different conditions, particularly when children are involved.[26] Even though the courts usually grant custody of the children to one parent, they usually insist that the other parent be given visitation rights. The details of visitation must be worked out as must the relationship between the new stepparent and the stepchildren. All of these special challenges reduce the chances of successful remarriage. However, most remarriages, like most first marriages, do endure.

Even though the courts usually grant custody of the children to only one parent in a divorce, they usually insist that the other parent be given visitation rights. Beaches and amusement parks are popular spots where divorced parents can spend some time with their children on visiting days. ◀

Desertion

In a divorce action the court terminates a marriage that was once legally valid; and most, though not all, segments of society recognize this action. But while neither the courts nor society in general defines desertion as a valid way to terminate a marriage, the results of divorce and desertion are the same—the bonds of marriage and family life are broken.

Desertion occurs when a spouse abandons his or her family, perhaps never to be seen again. Although few statistics are available, "rates of desertion are probably about as high as divorce, but the very ambiguity of the practice seems to arouse less public alarm."[27] This contention is supported by a study in Philadelphia that indicated that the ratio of desertions to divorces is at least one-to-one.[28] If this is the case, desertion deserves more attention from sociologists. Although we know a great deal about divorce, its correlates, and its dynamics, we know very little about desertion.

We do know that desertion is, to a great extent, a lower-class phenomenon.[29] Lower-class men, regardless of race, are more likely to abandon their families than middle- or upper-class men. Lower-class men who have low incomes and who are underemployed or irregularly employed have more difficulty assuming the role of husband and father; they are also more likely to believe that caring for and rearing children is "women's work." Many of them have never experienced a happy, healthy family life. For them, desertion is a way out of yet another unhappy experience in family living.

Desertion may have an even greater impact on the family than divorce. Because desertion tends to be a lower-class phenomenon and because the rates of fertility are higher among lower-class than among middle- or upper-class people, "desertion . . . is likely to involve minor children to an even greater extent than divorce."[30] Desertion is also likely to occur later in the marriage than divorce so a couple has a longer period in which to have children before one of the partners deserts.

The children of desertion may well suffer even more than the children of divorce. What does a child say, for example, when his or her father has deserted the family and schoolmates ask, "Where is your daddy? What does your daddy do?" Furthermore, a lower-class child in particular needs a stable, mature adult male to identify with.

Desertion can also have a devastating psychological impact on the abandoned partner. Even though the family's financial status and overall well-being may improve after the deserting spouse leaves, the experience of being deserted is both degrading and humiliating.

Marital Conflict and Strain

All marriages are marked by a certain amount of conflict and strain. This conflict and strain may be rooted within the marital relationship itself or in outside social pressures. When a marriage does become conflict-ridden, one of three things may happen. First, after quarreling, bickering, and fighting, the couple may eventually resolve the conflict. If the conflicts are squarely faced and resolved, all members of the family may experience considerable growth and development. Second, if the conflict is never faced and hangs over the marriage unresolved, an empty-shell marriage may eventually emerge as a result. Finally, if the conflict becomes so intense that the marriage can no longer be continued, divorce or desertion ensues. In this section we will examine some of the different sources of marital conflict and strain.

Interfaith Marriages

In a certain sense, all marriages are intermarriages.[31] We marry persons of the opposite sex and we marry outside our own families. Generally, however, we frown on marriages in which one of the partners is a member of a group towards which we feel prejudicial. Many writers stress the dangers of interfaith marriages between Catholics and Protestants, Protestants and Jews, and so forth. However, the data presented in Table 14.3 suggest that interfaith marriages are not extremely unstable.[32] As a matter of fact, about 85 percent of those Catholics and Protestants who marry one another make a go of their marriage.

Table 14.3
Percentage of Marriages Ending in Divorce or Separation, by Religion

Religion	Percent Ending in Divorce or Separation
Both Catholic	5
Both Jewish	5
Both Protestant	8
Mixed, Catholic-Protestant	15
Both None	18

SOURCE: Clarke E. Vincent, "Interfaith Marriages: Problem or Symptom?" in Ruth E. Albrecht and E. Wilbur Bock, eds., *Encounter: Love, Marriage, and Family* (Boston: Holbrook, 1972), p. 222.

Yet, Table 14.3 does indicate that interfaith marriages are somewhat more unstable than intrafaith marriages. Interfaith marriages, however, do not necessarily fail solely because of religious differences. For example, a study of a sample of Catholic-Protestant marriages revealed that 7 percent of the marriages involving a Catholic wife and a Protestant husband ended in divorce or separation whereas 21 percent of the marriages involving a Catholic husband and a Protestant wife were so ended.[33] This disparity may be partly due to social factors. In our society the mother is primarily responsible for the child's upbringing, including religious training; a Protestant mother may resent having to bring her children up in the Catholic faith.

In addition, interfaith marriages frequently involve people of diverse cultural and ethnic backgrounds, for example, an Italian Catholic marrying a German Lutheran. Thus, when conflict enters interfaith marriages, we cannot be sure whether it is primarily religious, social, cultural, or ethnic.

Interracial Marriages

Many Americans strongly disapprove of interracial marriage—some even consider it a separate social problem in itself. In the past some states passed miscegenation laws forbidding marriage or cohabitation between persons of different races. Such laws no longer exist, but interracial marriage remains an issue that receives considerable attention.

Interracial marriage has never been particularly common in this country. No recent data are available on its extent, but a 1959 study found that only one out of every 1,200 marriages is interracial.[34] And although interracial marriage may be more common today than in 1959, we can safely assume that even today only a fraction of 1 percent of all marriages are interracial.

Most writers give interracial marriages little chance of succeeding: "When individuals cross the lines of race in mate selection, they often encounter extreme difficulties in developing a satisfactory marriage relationship."[35] Because there are no statistics on how many interracial marriages end in divorce or desertion, we cannot tell whether they are more likely to fail than other marriages. An in-depth study of twenty-two black-white marriages in metropolitan New York, however, suggests that the couples had achieved satisfactory levels of marital adjustment.[36]

Nonetheless, interracial marriage is not easy. Indeed, the couples in the New York study reported having special difficulties in two areas. First, many had to face parental rejection: "Negative reactions from parents were described as the most difficult for the couples emotionally—especially for the white partner. In a number of cases, breaches developed between the white partner and his parents around the time of marriage which were not mended for years after the marriage, if at all."[37] Apparently the black parents were more accepting of their child's marital partner.

The second area of difficulty was the reactions of other people to the marriage: "The couples interviewed considered staring to be the most difficult reaction from others to which interracial couples must become accustomed."[38] Further, several of the couples had been attacked on the streets, almost all had been targets of discrimination, and many had even been harassed by police officers.

The same study also suggested two factors that can contribute to the success of an interracial marriage. First, the couple must be open with each other, willing to learn about each other, and ready to discuss their problems frankly and honestly. Good communication is essential in any marriage, particularly in an interracial one. Second, the couple must be determined to make a success of their marriage. In a way, prejudice may serve to strengthen the marriage. As one black woman said, "We didn't want to give society the satisfaction of our marriage breaking up, so we worked at it harder."[39]

Unemployment, Subemployment, and the Family

During the Great Depression of the 1930s, several studies explored the impact of unemployment on family life.[40] At times during the depression, nearly 25 percent of the total civilian labor force was unemployed. Unemployment rates since then have been much lower, and social analysts have tended to ignore the impact of unemployment and subemployment on family life. This is unfortunate for two reasons. First, our total unemployment rates may well increase gradually during the remainder of this century (see Chapter 9). If this happens, we will want research on the impact of unemployment on the family so that we can cope with the problem. Second, many of our urban slums and ghettos have for all practical purposes never really gotten out of the depression—their rates of unemployment and subemployment are still extremely high. This may help explain the instability of the urban, lower-class, nonwhite family.

The few studies that have been conducted since the depression indicate that unemployment may have a devastating effect on workers and their families. Workers feel threatened when they can no longer provide for their families, and they often vent their frustration on them. As the wife of an unemployed factory worker stated, "My husband never used to get upset at anything, but since the shutdown he's been hell on me and on the kids."[41]

In its study of ghetto conditions during the late '60s, the National Commission on Civil Disorders found that unemployment and subemployment are closely associated with divorce and desertion.[42] The questions here are: (1) Do unemployment and subemployment contribute to divorce and desertion? (2) Are people who divorce or desert their families less likely to look diligently for jobs? The evidence seems to indicate that unemployment and subemployment contribute to family breakdown. When men are unemployed and unable to support their families, they define themselves as failures in their roles as husbands and fathers. The wife may become the primary breadwinner, and conflict and tension can easily develop among husband, wife, and children. What happens, for example, if the wife deeply resents having to support her husband? Under such conditions the temptation to leave family obligations behind must be great: "It is not surprising that many of the [unemployed] men flee their responsibilities as husbands and fathers, leaving home, and drifting from city to city, or adopting the style of 'street corner men.' "[43]

The National Commission on Civil Disorders also found that unemployment and subemployment have a negative effect on ghetto children. Ghetto children observe that men who hustle and exploit others seem to enjoy more financial success and personal prestige than men who marry and work to support their families in legitimate ways. As a result, these children not only become cynical about marriage and fatherhood, they also become cynical about society and its institutions.[44]

Parent-Youth Conflict

Conflict between parents and their children—particularly adolescent children—is an age-old problem. Parents and children have always fought over dress and hairstyles, bedtime, chores, allowances, and so on endlessly. However, in recent years the generation gap has widened because of rapid social change in general and sexual permissiveness and drug use in particular.

The incidence of premarital sex has steadily increased since the last generation (see Chapter 6). Many of today's parents grew up in the '50s when a "heavy date" meant holding hands and "petting." It is understandable then why these same people, as parents, climb the walls when they find birth-control pills in their daughter's purse or when their teenage son spends the night with his girl friend.

The increasing involvement of young people, particularly middle-class youth, in the drug culture is also a relatively new development. During the '60s, in fact, marijuana became one of the great symbols of the widening generation gap (see Chapter 5).

We should point out, however, that most young people are not heavily involved with drugs and most differ little from their parents' generation in their sexual behavior. Nonetheless, most parents today, because of the way in which they were socialized, are particularly sensitive to the issues of drugs and sex. And most young people today are particularly vehement in demanding their right to lead their own lives. Thus, the issues of drugs and sex can become the sources of bitter parent-child conflicts, even though the child may never actually engage in the controversial behavior.

The impact of parent-youth conflict on family life should not be minimized. It can rupture family ties and can create great bitterness and hostility. Very often, cordial relationships between parents and their offspring are not re-established until the children marry and begin rearing their own children. Furthermore, parent-youth conflict can also produce conflict between husband and wife: "A high percentage of parents fight with each other when a youngster rebels, if only in the process of trying to place the blame."[45] Most parents, however, work through their conflict over rearing children; it is rarely the major complaint in a divorce suit.

What is the future of parent-youth conflict? The issues of drugs and sexual behavior may well diminish in importance when today's young people become parents. But much will depend on whether they look back on their experiences in a drug-oriented, sexually permissive culture as good or bad. And even if these two issues do subside, new ones will certainly take their place.

Women's Rights and Family Life

Many women today are demanding a change in their status, and some of them categorize marriage and family life as oppressive institutions. Women are often the losers in the sexual division of labor between husband and wife. Even though we claim that being a housewife is a respectable role, many women find that maintaining a household is, in fact, not particularly rewarding. Many women undergo an abrupt change of status when they marry:

> From being a secretary, sales girl, teacher or nurse in her own right she becomes a housekeeper, an occupation that is classified in the labor market and in her own mind as menial and of low status. The apologetic "I'm just a housewife" that she tenders in reply to what she does illustrates how low her self-evaluation of her occupation is, no matter how loudly and defensively she proclaims her pleasure in it.[46]

Even when a woman continues to work after marriage, her career is often considered secondary to her husband's. For example, if the husband can further his career by moving to another city, his wife is expected to follow him, even though her own career might suffer. Family life can become even more oppressive when children enter the picture. Washing diapers, wiping noses, and otherwise tending children are not necessarily rich and rewarding experiences. But they are considered "women's work" and are almost inevitably performed by the wife.

Modern family life is often sexually repressive for women. Many people still assume that women do not take much pleasure in sex, and that a married woman should engage in sex only to please her husband and to have children.[47] The fact is, of course, that women have the same need for and right to sexual fulfillment in marriage as men do.

▲
Family life can become even more oppressive when children enter the picture. Washing diapers, wiping noses, and otherwise tending children are not necessarily rich and rewarding experiences.

Although it is not surprising that some women consider the contemporary American family repressive, we do not know how much family conflict and strain can be attributed to the women's rights movement. But we do know that married couples are reacting to it. Some couples are satisfied with their current life-style and are untouched by the movement. At least one feminist believes that "the wiser female militants should not tamper with the happiness of home-bound females by suggesting that they are unhappy."[48] Other couples recognize that they are exploiting each other and seek to do something about it. They might, for example, draw up a marriage contract specifying who is to care for the children at what times, who is responsible for various household tasks, whose career takes priority in case of conflict, and so on.[49] For still other couples, the women's rights movement may lead to open and intense conflict. This conflict may eventually subside, lead to an empty-shell marriage, or lead to divorce.

Illegitimacy

Our social norms regarding the complete family unit dictate, first, marriage by a civil or religious official and, second, childbirth after a certain amount of time (preferably at least nine months). Illegitimacy is a form of family breakdown because the first step in the traditional sequence is omitted.[50] Further, of all the different types of family disorganization that occur in the United States, illegitimacy is perhaps the most frowned on. Yet it occurs fairly frequently. In 1970 there were 3,731,386 live births in the United States, 398,700 of which were illegitimate.[51] In other words, slightly more than one out of every ten births in the United States is illegitimate.

Why do so many Americans frown on illegitimacy? A small part of the answer is that illegitimacy is evidence of premarital sex. However, a larger part of the answer is that illegitimacy is considered evidence of promiscuity. Since the likelihood that pregnancy will occur after an occasional sexual episode is small, the popular image of the unwed mother is that of a young girl who "sleeps around." This stereotype may be incorrect, but the unwed mother is almost always viewed as a person who flaunts basic social norms.

In addition, illegitimate children are often a burden to society. For example, the public may have to pay for maternity homes, placement and counseling services, and financial assistance for the unwed mother and her child. In fact, one of the complaints most frequently voiced against the Aid to Families with Dependent Children (AFDC; see Chapter 9) program is that it subsidizes the unwed mother. Preconceptions about promiscuity and welfare mothers, then, seem to cause the hostility society expresses toward unwed mothers. The possibility that illegitimacy could threaten the social institutions of marriage and the family rarely crosses the public's mind.

The unwed mother has four alternatives. First, if the child's father is willing, she can get married. This is probably the alternative most commonly chosen. As early as 1958, about 20 percent of all American marriages were preceded by conception.[52] The unwed mother is frequently discouraged from getting married on the grounds that it might give the child a name but not a wholesome family life. This type of discouragement may not be entirely warranted, however, given the large number of marriages that are preceded by conception and that apparently do work out.

Second, if she does not marry, the unwed mother may place her baby with an adoption agency. This alternative meets the need of the child for a family and the need of couples who want a family but cannot have their own. Putting the child up for adoption was a common solution in the past but is being done less frequently today.

Although some authorities question whether or not it is really a satisfactory answer, a third and increasingly common solution to the problem of illegitimacy is abortion.[53] A 1971 study reported that "abortion is defined as deviant behavior by a large majority of Americans—at least under most circumstances."[54] Being labeled a deviant for having an abortion may have as many negative consequences for the unwed mother as the pregnancy itself.

Finally, the unwed mother may keep and rear her child herself. Many people disapprove of this alternative presumably because of the immaturity of the unwed mother and because they feel that the child should have both a mother *and* a father. However, "we may have to begin encouraging and supporting unwed mothers to keep their children."[55] Some illegitimate children, and especially those who are racially mixed or handicapped, are extremely difficult to place with adoptive parents. As a result, these children grow up in orphanages or they are shuffled from foster home to foster home. With help and encouragement, many unwed mothers could keep their babies and eventually marry and meet their personal needs and those of their children.

Violence and the Family

The types of family conflict we have previously discussed do not involve physical violence. However, violent conflict does occur with some frequency. A particularly destructive type of family violence is the *battered child syndrome* in which children are physically abused by their parents or guardians. Its most common clinical manifestations are broken bones, multiple bruises, and malnutrition. Usually, the battered child is under 3 years old; and although it is impossible to determine how many children are battered, there is evidence that the number is substantial.[56]

As this picture attests, the battered child syndrome is a particularly destructive type of family violence. ▶

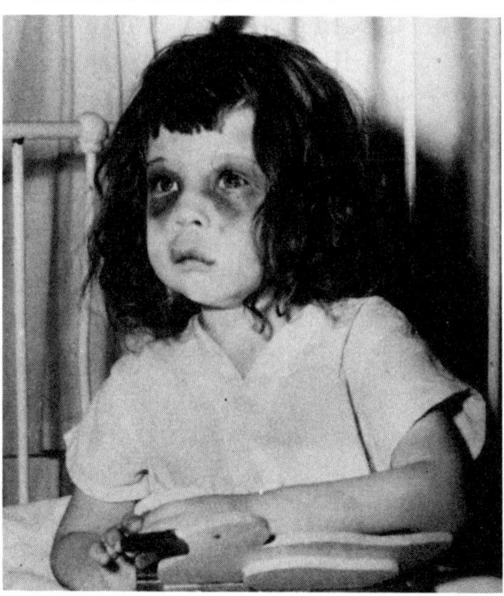

The causes of the battered child syndrome, of course, lie with the parents. An analysis of 115 battered child cases found that most abusive families had tenuous ties with their communities and that 90 percent were having serious problems such as marital and financial difficulties.[57] In addition, many of the children had been conceived before their parents' marriage. In short, "problems had existed at the time of the marriage and had intensified rather than abated by the date the abuse of the child took place."[58]

Most analysts attribute the behavior of parents who physically batter their children to personality disorders; these parents are often seen as sick people who suffer from unmet personality needs. However, we must not forget that the battered child syndrome is the product of a culture which often views violence as the answer to problems. Thus, in trying to understand parents who batter their children, we must realize that they not only suffer from personality disorders but that they also function in a culture that tolerates and permits high levels of violence (see Chapter 2).

The Future of the Family

Writers who predict the demise of monogamous marriage and the nuclear family base their predictions on our increasing divorce rate, declining birthrate, and some contemporary developments that run counter to traditional family life. Monogamous marriage, however, remains extremely popular, and there are certain contemporary developments that may, in fact, strengthen monogamous marriage and the nuclear family. In this section, we will try to place the future of the American family in some perspective.

Marriage in Perspective

Nearly 90 percent of today's U.S. population gets married at some time.[59] This figure is really impressive when we recall that there will always be some people who never marry because they don't want to, have severe physical or mental defects, or are exclusively homosexual. The high rate of remarriage among divorced persons also suggests that we strongly prefer a viable marital relationship. Furthermore, the nuclear family may well become stronger, not weaker, as our society becomes increasingly complex and bureaucratized. Because we are only numbers—student numbers, social security numbers, credit card numbers—in so many situations, we may increasingly turn to the family as the institution that meets our basic needs for affection, security, and approval.

One modern trend that may strengthen the family is the development of birth-control technology. Couples can now control the size of their families. They can choose whether to have chil-

Social Problems and You

Parents and Children: Yesterday and Today

What bound the family together in the past and made it such a marvelously successful institution was that parents and children provided each other with security, in the down-to-earth sense. . . . Throughout the ages children were the family's greatest economic asset. . . .

But the children who used to contribute so much to the economic well-being of the family have now become its greatest economic liability. Witness the expenses involved in raising a child. And although social conditions force children to accept these expenditures, they do feel guilty about it. Often a child's belittling his parents is due to nothing but his ineffective efforts to deny his feelings of guilt for the way they make sacrifices for him. . . .

Not so long ago, the daily round of work and after-work was common to parents and children. Working together taught parent and child the art of living together. Life was hard, labor backbreaking. But, as exhausting as the work was, children knew from an early age that their labor was needed, that they were needed. It is simply not enough for a child to feel that he provides emotional satisfaction for his parents. If this is all the value he has, then his security is tenuous. Any change in his parents' feelings can destroy it. Any new arrival, not just another child, may easily replace him, and who will need him then? "Nobody needs me" is the desperate complaint of many an alienated adolescent today. But long before children reach this age, quite a few begin to feel this way much to their dismay. As long as the strength of a person's arms powered the economic process, it was clear that as parents grew old and weak—which happened at a much earlier age than it now does, usually as soon as children reached maturity—the children would take over, for everybody's benefit.

Not only did children feel needed from an early age, but because people worked together day in and day out, no one was ever alone. Whether one remained with one's family, or was apprenticed out, or entered domestic service, individuals were members of a closely knit unit. Loneliness, the feeling that one has no roots, these are the curses of modern man, while blood, sweat and tears were those of our ancestors. But our ancestors did not have to carry these hardships without the support of those working close along them. The modern family usually enjoys its togetherness only on weekends, on vacations or around the dinner table—that is, when no activities essential for its support occur. Pleasant as these times may be, they are lacking in meaning compared to doing what must be done. We all know that we have an easy time getting along when all is well. What we need for our security is to feel that somebody will stick with us, share our sorrows and difficulties, labor hard alongside us when things do not go well.

Most of all, people need a feeling of belonging. But what child today truly feels he has a rightful place within his family, earned through his own efforts? To have a place because one's parents have granted it is to be on a shaky basis. We all like to please when we feel like it, but we resist it if we think we have to ingratiate ourselves, or be grateful, which many a modern child feels and resents. . . .

Since neither ties of work nor ties of place any longer bind us, the only bond that can now hold families together is an emotional one. It is essential, therefore, when difficulties arise, that we refrain from blaming each other. We must instead accept problems as challenges to be met together, because it is only through trying to cope with these by our combined best efforts, that we can regain the feeling that we truly belong to each other.

SOURCE: Bruno Bettelheim, "Recreating Family Life: The Means Are In Our Hands," *Parents' Magazine*, 51 (October, 1976), pp. 64, 72.

▲
Because it meets our basic needs for affection, security, and approval, the nuclear family may well become stronger as our society becomes increasingly bureaucratized.

dren and how many children they want; they can pursue separate careers if they want to and use their resources to meet their unique needs.

The nationwide trend toward higher education also bears on the future of the family. Well-educated couples may be better equipped to deal with marital and family crises, and an increasing percentage of the population will be well educated in the future. In addition, more and more schools and colleges are offering preparation-for-marriage courses which may help people realistically adjust to marriage and family life.

Finally, the women's rights movement will probably have an effect on the family of the future. One of the goals of the women's movement is to alter role relationships within the family so that they are more rewarding to both partners in the marriage and to the children.

We should not lose sight of the fact that there will always be people who encounter difficulties in family living and in their marriages. We are slowly beginning to recognize the need to make effective counseling services available to those couples who have problems and who want to save their marriages. But, for the most part, marriage counseling services are still not widely used. They are not available in many communities, and, if they are available, they are sometimes very expensive. Further, many people are reluctant to use marriage counseling services either because they think that these services will not help or because they believe it is not their fault that their marriage is failing.[60] In fact, most husbands and wives are more than willing to have their partners seek counseling when marital problems arise, but they are not willing to do so themselves. However, "there is every reason to believe that the [marriage counseling] profession will take a giant step forward in the decade ahead. This is about the best hope for couples in trouble."[61]

Recent Innovations

The future may also bring some dramatic innovations in marriage and family life. We hear much talk today, for example, about trial marriages and about marriage contracts. In a trial marriage a couple agree to live together for a certain period of time, usually two to five years. At the end of the specified period, they are free to renew the marriage or not, depending upon their desires:

> If a couple grew disenchanted with their life together, they would not feel trapped for life. They would not have to anticipate and then go through the destructive agonies of divorce. They would not have to carry about the stigma of marital failure. . . . Instead of a declaration of war, they could simply let their contracts lapse, and while still friendly, be free to continue their romantic quests.[62]

At first glance, trial marriage seems to make a great deal of sense. However, what would happen if one marital partner wanted to let the marriage lapse and the other did not? Would they then go to court the same way couples seeking divorce do? Furthermore, trial marriages do not eliminate the problems of distributing joint property or awarding child custody.

Marriage contracts, on the other hand, might avoid child and property disputes. Basically, marriage contracts are designed to ensure smooth, orderly interaction within a marriage by making clear the rights, duties, and obligations of each partner. A marriage contract might, for example, specify which days the wife has off, which partner cooks and cleans, whose career takes priority when a move might enhance one career but damage the other, and so on. It might also specify the grounds under which the marriage can be terminated and how disputes over property and the custody of minor children are to be settled if the marriage is dissolved. Marriage contracts are not yet legally binding and are not recognized by the courts. They are merely good-faith agreements between marriage partners.

In the decades ahead, there will no doubt be further experimentation with alternative forms of family life. We have already heard much about communal living, for example, where married couples, perhaps along with a few singles, normally share common dining, living, and sleeping quarters. In another communal living arrangement, couples may rent adjoining apartments or buy homes close to one another. Participants in communal living arrangements generally hope to cope with modern society more effectively than they could as isolated couples or individuals.[63]

▲ Participants in communal living arrangements generally hope to cope with modern society more effectively than they could as isolated couples or individuals.

People enter into communal living arrangements for a wide variety of reasons. Some couples band together simply to increase their buying power and improve their economic status. A good deal of money can be saved by buying groceries at caselot prices or by sharing a car with two or three families. In other instances, couples share household tasks and child-rearing responsibilities. In this type of commune, those who wish to are free to pursue a career, while those who are happy rearing children and homemaking perform a valuable service for the commune. Finally, some communes take on the characteristics of a group marriage; that is, every adult member is free to have sexual relations with every other adult member. But whatever its form, communal living is appealing to some people because it represents, in part, a return to the extended family system of the past—a type of family system that had certain advantages over the modern nuclear family. Indeed, "many, many communes refer to themselves not by name, but simply as 'the family.' "[64]

Summary

The family is probably our oldest and most enduring social institution. Yet there are many difficult problems associated with American marriage and family life. Many of these problems are the result of social change.

Those who identify family problems can be divided into two groups—traditionalists and challengers. Traditionalists deplore the breakdown of the family. Challengers agree that the family is breaking down but argue that this is a healthy development.

The most common type of marital breakdown is to be found in the unhappy unbroken home, or the empty-shell family. In such families, interaction is usually only instrumental. For a number of reasons, many such marriages do not end in divorce. Those couples who stay together "for the sake of the children" usually do their children more harm than good.

Although there is no really accurate way to measure the extent of divorce, we know that the number of divorces is very large and appears to be increasing.

One way to analyze the causes of divorce is to look at people's complaints about their spouses when they seek divorce. The complaints voiced by husbands against their wives differ markedly from wives' complaints against their husbands.

A general theory of divorce suggests that any marriage can be analyzed in terms of the forces for success and for failure within the marriage, the forces for success and for failure outside the marriage, and the alternatives to continuing the marriage.

Divorce can create emotional and economic problems for a couple, and adjustment problems if there are children. It is, however, cruel and inhumane to force a couple to continue a miserable marriage.

Most people who get divorced soon remarry. Although divorced people are poorer marriage risks than people who have not been divorced, most remarriages do endure.

While neither the courts nor society considers desertion to be a valid way to terminate a marriage, desertion rates are probably as high as divorce rates. Desertion is largely a lower-class phenomenon, and it may have a greater negative impact on a family than divorce.

When a marriage becomes conflict-ridden, one of three things may happen: the conflict may be resolved; the conflict may hang over the marriage unresolved, resulting in an empty-shell marriage; or the conflict may become so intense that the marriage can no longer be continued, resulting in divorce or desertion. Some of the sources of marital conflict include interfaith and interracial marriages, unemployment and subemployment, parent-youth conflicts, the women's rights movement, illegitimacy, and violence.

Despite dire predictions concerning the demise of monogamous marriage and the nuclear family, we must try to place the future of the American family in some perspective. Monogamous marriage is clearly still extremely popular, and a number of contemporary trends may serve to strengthen it—bureaucratization, birth control, education, the women's rights movement, and marriage counseling.

The future may also bring some dramatic innovations in marriage and family life—trial marriages, contract marriages, and communal living arrangements. Communes may take many forms and appeal to some people because they represent, in part, a return to the extended family of the past.

Discussion Questions

1. What is meant by the statement, "The problems of the contemporary family are partly the result of other changes that have occurred in our society"? In what sense is the family a more vulnerable, fragile institution than it was in our rural past?

2. How would you define the problems surrounding family life in the United States today? Are you nearer to the traditionalists or the challengers in terms of the way in which you define family problems?

3. What do we mean when we refer to an "empty-shell" family? What are some of the characteristics of empty-shell families? Why do some people choose not to get divorced, even though their marriage is totally miserable?

4. Carefully review the section of this chapter which deals with the extent of divorce as well as Table 14.1. Taking everything into account, would you say that our divorce rate is high, low, or about what might be expected?

5. All marriages are subject to certain forces that tend to keep the marriage intact and to certain forces that tend to tear the marriage apart. What are some of the forces that tend to keep marriages intact? What are some of the forces that tend to tear marriages apart?

6. Discuss desertion. Why is desertion, to a great extent, a lower-class phenomenon? What impact does desertion seem to have on the abandoned spouse and his or her children?

7. Are interfaith marriages extremely unstable? What are some of the factors that can contribute to the success of an interracial marriage? What are some of the most difficult problems that the partners in an interracial marriage must face?
8. Why do we need more research on the impact of unemployment and subemployment on family life? The National Commission on Civil Disorders found that under ghetto conditions, unemployment and subemployment are closely associated with divorce and desertion. Why do you think that this is the case?
9. Discuss the impact of the women's rights movement on marriage and family life. Do you agree with one feminist who believes that wiser female militants should not tamper with the happiness of homebound females by suggesting that they are unhappy?
10. Why do so many Americans frown on illegitimacy? What are the alternatives open to the unwed mother? What do you think of the suggestion that more unwed mothers should be encouraged and helped to keep their children?
11. Discuss the battered child syndrome. In what sense is the battered child syndrome at least partly a product of the culture in which we live?
12. Do you think that American society will eventually see the demise of monogamous marriage and the nuclear family? What do you see as the future of marriage contracts, trial marriages, and communal living arrangements? Do you approve of these alternative forms of marriage? Why or why not?

Glossary

battered child syndrome The physical abuse of children by their parents or guardians. Its most common clinical manifestations are broken bones, multiple bruises, and malnutrition. The battered child syndrome is in part a function of American culture and the high level of violence that it tolerates.

communal living Living arrangements in which several married couples — and perhaps a few singles —pool their resources in order to cope with modern society more effectively than they could as isolated couples or individuals.

desertion A form of marital breakdown in which a spouse abandons his or her family, perhaps never to be seen again. Neither the courts nor society views desertion as a valid way to terminate a marriage.

divorce A court action that terminates a legally valid marriage. Divorce represents society's way of allowing people out of an unhappy marriage.

empty-shell marriage A marriage in which the couple continue to live together and play their instrumental roles. The marriage is, however, devoid of affection and respect.

extended family system A family system which includes not only a married couple and their children, but grandparents, aunts and uncles, and so on. Very often all of these people live under the same roof.

group marriage A form of communal living in which every adult member of the "family" is free to have sexual relations with every other adult member.

marriage contract Contracts designed to ensure smooth, orderly interaction within a marriage by making clear the rights, duties, and obligations of each partner. Marriage contracts are merely good-faith agreements between marriage partners and are not recognized by the courts.

miscegenation laws Laws which forbid marriage or cohabitation between persons of different races. The Supreme Court has found such laws to be unconstitutional.

nuclear family A family system which includes only a married couple and their children.

primary relationships Relationships between two or more people which are marked by deep emotional commitments, close and continuous interaction, and so on.

serial marriages (system of) A phrase which is sometimes used to refer to the practice of remarrying—perhaps several times—when the preceding marriage does not work out.

trial marriage In a "marriage" of this type a couple agree to live together for a certain period of time. At the end of the specified period, they are free to renew the marriage or not. Trial marriages are not recognized as legally valid by the courts.

Suggestions for Further Reading

Albrecht, Ruth E., and E. Wilbur Bock, eds., *Encounter: Love, Marriage, and Family* (Boston: Holbrook, 1972). A wide-ranging and stimulating collection of articles on marriage and family life. Most of these articles are pertinent to day-to-day realities of marriage and family living.

Bell, Robert R., *Marriage and Family Interaction*, 3rd Ed. (Homewood, Ill.: Dorsey, 1971). A basic textbook on marriage and family life in the United States. This book is exceptionally well documented and contains a wealth of statistical data.

Benson, Leonard, *The Family Bond: Marriage, Love, and Sex in America* (New York: Random House, 1971). Like Bell's book, this is a basic introduction to marriage and family life. Benson covers his material in a thorough and interesting manner.

Cadwallader, Mervyn, "Marriage as a Wretched Institution," *Atlantic Monthly,* 218 (November, 1966), pp. 62–66. A provocative article which maintains that today we expect more of marriage than it can possibly deliver. Because divorce is such a painful experience, Cadwallader suggests a system of marriage contracts in which, after the contract has elapsed, both partners would be free to pursue a new love and a new marriage.

Davids, Leo, "North American Marriage: 1990," in Judson R. Landis, ed., *Current Perspectives on Social Problems,* 3rd Ed. (Belmont, Calif.: Wadsworth, 1973), pp. 174–84. Davids makes some interesting predictions about the future of marriage and family life in America. Among other things, he hypothesizes that new forms of marriage will evolve and that only certain people will be allowed to reproduce and rear children.

Glasser, Paul H., and Lois N. Glasser, eds., *Families in Crisis* (New York: Harper & Row, 1970). A carefully selected collection of articles that deal with a wide range of crises that can potentially beset families.

Perrucci, Carolyn C., and Dena B. Targ, eds., *Marriage and Family: A Critical Analysis and Proposals for Change* (New York: McKay, 1974). An interesting and provocative collection of articles which attempts "to combine feminist values with the sociological perspective of marriage and the family in the present-day United States."

Sussman, Marvin B., ed., *Sourcebook in Marriage and the Family,* 4th Ed. (Boston: Houghton Mifflin, 1974). Although some of the articles contained in this anthology are somewhat staid, Sussman's book nonetheless is the best collection of articles on the sociology of family life available today.

Notes

[1]For further discussion of the family in the rural past, see Otto Pollak, "The Outlook for the American Family," *Journal of Marriage and the Family,* 29 (February, 1967), pp. 193–205.

[2]See Mervyn Cadwallader, "Marriage as a Wretched Institution," *Atlantic Monthly,* 218 (November, 1966), p. 62.

[3]See Armand L. Mauss, *Social Problems and Social Movements* (Philadelphia: Lippincott, 1975), p. 478.

[4]For a rather pointed critique of American marriage and family life, see Cadwallader, "Marriage as a Wretched Institution," pp. 62–66; see also Richard Sennett, "The Brutality of Modern Families," in John W. Kinch, ed., *Social Problems in the World Today* (Reading, Mass.: Addison-Wesley, 1974), pp. 56–68.

[5]William J. Goode, "Marital Satisfaction and Instability: A Cross-Cultural Analysis of Divorce Rates," in Paul H. Glasser and Lois N. Glasser, eds., *Families in Crisis* (New York: Harper & Row, 1970), p. 137.

[6]See Leonard Benson, *The Family Bond: Marriage, Love, and Sex in America* (New York: Random House, 1971), pp. 266–72.

[7]F. Ivan Nye, "Child Adjustment in Broken and in Unhappy Unbroken Homes," in Marvin B. Sussman, ed., *Sourcebook in Marriage and the Family,* 3rd Ed. (Boston: Houghton Mifflin, 1968), pp. 437–38.

[8]For example, see David Popenoe, *Sociology*, 2nd Ed. (New York: Prentice-Hall, 1974), p. 230. One source even suggests that one in every three marriages will end in divorce, see *Encyclopedia of Sociology* (Guilford, Conn: Dushkin, 1974), p. 83.

[9]Benson, *The Family Bond*, p. 284.

[10]*Ibid.*, p. 384.

[11]See Robert K. Kelley, *Courtship, Marriage, and the Family* (New York: Harcourt Brace Jovanovich, 1969), esp. 580–81.

[12]See William J. Goode, *World Revolution and Family Patterns* (New York: Free Press, 1963), p. 82.

[13]See George Levinger, "Sources of Marital Dissatisfaction Among Applicants for Divorce," in Glasser and Glasser, eds., *Families in Crisis*, pp. 126–32.

[14]*Ibid.*, p. 130.

[15]See George Levinger, "Marital Cohesiveness and Dissolution: An Integrative Review," *Journal of Marriage and the Family*, 27 (February, 1965), pp. 25–27.

[16]*Ibid.*, p. 25.

[17]For a statement of this thesis, see Ernest W. Burgess and Harvey J. Locke, *The Family: From Institution to Companionship* (New York: American Book, 1945).

[18]For further discussion of the factors associated with success and failure in marriage, see Lloyd Saxton, *The Individual, Marriage, and the Family*, 2nd Ed. (Belmont, Calif.: Wadsworth, 1972), pp. 158–71.

[19]Kelley, *Courtship, Marriage, and the Family*, p. 580.

[20]See F. Ivan Nye, "Child Adjustment in Broken and in Unhappy Unbroken Homes," pp. 434–40.

[21]See Cadwallader, "Marriage as a Wretched Institution," pp. 65–66. Another interesting discussion of trial marriages can be found in Miriam E. Berger, "Trial Marriage: Harnessing the Trend Constructively," *The Family Coordinator*, 20 (January, 1971), pp. 38–43.

[22]Recent data on rates of remarriage are almost nonexistent, but in 1949 Glick reported that about three-fourths of those people who had divorced during the previous five years were remarried. The rate of remarriage among divorcées is undoubtedly as high or higher today than it was in the 1940s, since remarriage has become increasingly accepted. See Paul C. Glick, "First Marriages and Remarriages," *American Sociological Review*, 14 (December, 1949), pp. 726–34.

[23]Jessie Bernard, "The Institutionalization of Remarriage," in Sussman, ed., *Sourcebook in Marriage and the Family*, p. 560.

[24]See William J. Goode, *Women in Divorce* (New York: Free Press, 1956), esp. pp. 334–35.

[25]See Benjamin Schlesinger, "Remarriage: An Inventory of Findings," *The Family Coordinator*, 17 (October, 1968), pp. 248–49.

[26]See Bernard Farber, *Family and Kinship in Modern Society* (Glenview, Ill.: Scott, Foresman, 1973), p. 50.

[27]Benson, *The Family Bond*, p. 275.

[28]See William M. Kephart, "Occupational Level and Marital Disruption," *American Sociological Review*, 20 (August, 1955), esp. p. 460.

[29]Benson, *The Family Bond*, pp. 277–78.

[30]*Ibid.*, p. 279.

[31]Robert K. Merton, "Intermarriage and the Social Structure: Fact and Theory," *Psychiatry*, 4 (August, 1941), p. 361.

[32]See Clark E. Vincent, "Interfaith Marriages: Problem or Symptom?" in Ruth E. Albrecht and E. Wilbur Bock, eds., *Encounter: Love, Marriage, and Family* (Boston: Holbrook, 1972), p. 222.

[33]Judson T. Landis, "Marriages of Mixed and Non-Mixed Religious Faith," *American Sociological Review*, 14 (June, 1949), p. 403.

[34]Paul H. Jacobson, *American Marriage and Divorce* (New York: Holt, Rinehart, and Winston, 1959), p. 62.

[35]Robert R. Bell, *Marriage and Family Interaction*, 3rd Ed. (Homewood, Ill.: Dorsey, 1971), p. 143.

[36]Charles U. Smith, "Negro-White Intermarriage: Forbidden Sexual Union," in Albrecht and Bock, eds., *Encounter*, pp. 231–40.

[37]*Ibid.*, p. 236.

[38]*Ibid.*, p. 238.

[39]*Ibid.*, p. 237.

[40]For example, see Mirra Komarovsky, *The Unemployed Man and His Family* (New York: Dryden, 1940); and Robert C. Angell, *The Family Encounters the Depression* (New York: Scribner's, 1936).

[41]Cited in William J. Goode, "Family Disorganization," in Robert K. Merton and Robert Nisbet, eds., *Contemporary Social Problems*, 3rd Ed. (New York: Harcourt Brace Jovanovich, 1971), p. 531.

[42]National Advisory Commission on Civil Disorders, *Report of the National Advisory Commission on Civil Disorders* (Washington, D.C.: U.S. Government Printing Office, 1968), p. 128.

[43]*Ibid.*, p. 128.

[44]*Ibid.*, p. 129–30.

[45]Goode, "Family Disorganization," p. 531.

[46]Jessie Bernard, "The Paradox of the Happy Marriage," in Vivian Gornick and Barbara K. Moran, eds., *Women in Sexist Society: Studies in Power and Powerlessness* (New York: Signet, 1972), p. 154.

[47]Carolyn C. Perrucci and Dena B. Targ, eds., *Marriage and Family: A Critical Analysis and Proposals for Change* (New York: McKay, 1974), p. 11.

[48]Marya Mannes, "How Men Will Benefit from the Women's Power Revolution," *PTA Magazine*, 65 (January, 1971), p. 7.

[49]For a sample of a marriage contract see Alix Shulman, "A Marriage Agreement," in Perrucci and Targ, eds., *Marriage and Family*, pp. 296–301.

[50]For a widely cited and insightful study of unwed mothers, see Clark E. Vincent, *Unmarried Mothers* (New York: Free Press, 1961).

[51]U.S. Public Health Service, *Vital Statistics of the U.S.*, Vol I, *Natality* (Washington, D.C.: U.S. Government Printing Office, 1975), Tables 1–1, 1–32.

[52]Harold T. Christensen, "The Method of Record Linkage Applied to Family Data," *Marriage and Family Living*, 20 (February, 1958), p. 42.

[53]In an interview with the director of a large maternity home, the author was told that a large percentage of the unwed mothers in the home were recidivists, i.e., they had been pregnant before. Furthermore, the director reported that most of the girls had aborted their previous pregnancies and found this not to be a satisfactory solution to the problem. Whether this is the case or whether the director was expressing a personal judgment is unclear. Certainly this point merits further investigation.

[54]Robert R. Bell, *Social Deviance: A Substantive Analysis* (Homewood, Ill.: Dorsey, 1971), p. 117.

[55]Benjamin Schlesinger, "The One Parent Family: An Overview," in Albrecht and Bock, eds., *Encounter*, p. 367.

[56]Henri Christian Raffalli, "The Battered Child: An Overview of a Medical, Legal, and Social Problem," in Frank R. Scarpitti and Paul T. McFarlane, eds., *Deviance: Action, Reaction, Interaction* (Reading, Mass.: Addison-Wesley, 1975), p. 63.

[57]*Ibid.*, p. 65.

[58]*Ibid.*

[59]U.S. Bureau of the Census, *Census of Population: 1970*, Vol. I, *Characteristics of the Population*, Part I, *U.S. Summary* (Washington, D.C.: U.S. Government Printing Office, 1973), Table 203.

[60]Benson, *The Family Bond*, p. 296.

[61]*Ibid.*, p. 300.

[62]Cadwallader, "Marriage as a Wretched Institution," p. 65.

[63]James W. Ramey, "Emerging Patterns of Behavior in Marriage: Deviations or Innovations?" in Perrucci and Targ, eds., *Marriage and Family*, p. 359.

[64]*Ibid.*, p. 358.

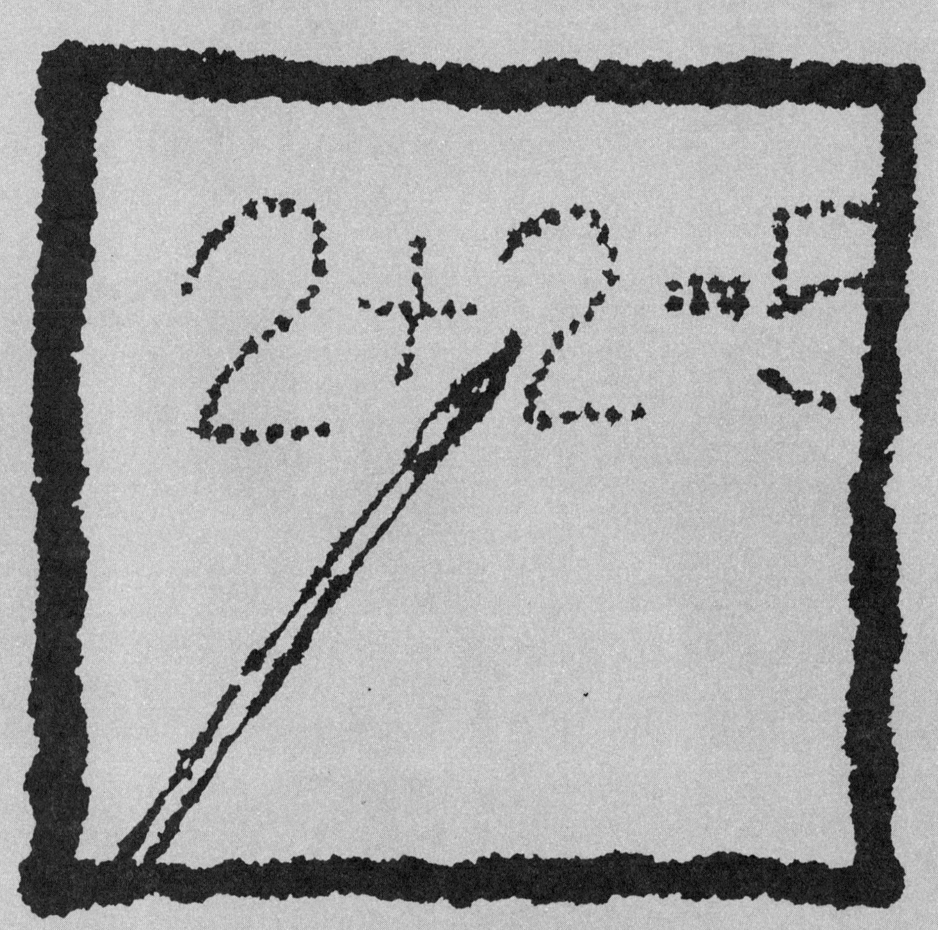
2+2=5

Chapter 15

Education

In a school just outside of San Francisco, a grade-school teacher uses *McGuffey's Eclectic Readers,* textbooks that attained great popularity in the one-room schoolhouses of mid-nineteenth-century America, to teach his students reading. Surprisingly, his students are reading *above* the national averages for their grades.

Across our nation, parents and teachers are desperately trying to answer the troublesome question, "Why can't Johnny read?" Unfortunately, there is no ready and simple answer to their question. Parents, teachers, and students agree on at least one point—our schools are not functioning as well as we would like them to.

Unfortunately, Johnny's problem is not confined to reading. A recent survey revealed that less than half of our adult population is proficient in everyday language and math. About 29 percent cannot compute a week's paycheck if it includes overtime, and 14 percent cannot write out a check properly. About 20 percent—23,000,000 people—cannot fill out Medicare or Social Security forms, pick the best buy on a grocery-store shelf, or correctly apply for a driver's license.[1] How productive then, we must ask, is the time we spend in school?

Not surprisingly, many Americans cut their schooling short; one in four do not complete high school.[2] Dropouts are severely limited in their job opportunities and, regardless of their economic success, generally are intellectually limited, fatalistic, and poorly adjusted.[3] Even more depressing are the "mental dropouts": "Numerically far more important than these overt dropouts at 16, however, are the children who conform to schooling between the ages of 6 to 16 or 20, but who drop out internally and daydream, their days wasted, their liberty caged and scheduled."[4]

Compulsory education has long been considered both basic and necessary to the American system. And as our society has grown more complex, we have looked increasingly to our educational institutions to (1) prepare people for life in a highly technological society, (2) help promote racial and sexual equality, (3) instill in young people a belief in our most cherished values, and (4) contribute to the scientific and economic development of our country. Certainly one reason why our schools are not working well is that we expect our schools to do too much for too many with too little.

In this chapter we will explore the many problems of American education.

The Goals and Problems of Education

Because our educational system is so large and because we expect it to do so much, its goals are often unclear, diffuse, and conflicting. What are some of these goals? What are some of the problems our schools face in pursuing them?

Preparation for Adulthood

One of the foremost goals of our educational system is to provide people with the skills required for survival in a highly competitive, highly technological society. Our educational system must prepare people, first, for careers that will ensure economic self-sufficiency and, second, for understanding and coping with life in modern society.

Education for Economic Self-Sufficiency

There is reason to think that our schools are not fully succeeding in preparing people for careers that will give them economic self-sufficiency. For example, it is well known that a college education no longer has the economic value it once had. College graduates no longer earn a great deal more money than high-school graduates, and many college graduates are plagued by long-term unemployment.[5] Our schools and colleges are increasingly producing people who are overeducated and underemployed. In 1974, for example, one-third of all male college graduates and two-thirds of female graduates had to accept positions unrelated to their college majors.[6] The Bureau of Labor Statistics estimates that only 20 percent of the jobs available in the '70s will require an education beyond high school, but that perhaps 50 percent or more of high-school students will go to college.[7]

Not only do we call upon our educational system to prepare people for today's jobs, we also ask that it prepare them for future jobs; it must attempt to forecast the future economic and technological climate, and it must project future needs for personnel. We need only recall, for example, the extreme cutbacks in the aerospace industry in the late '60s which left hundreds of highly trained engineers driving cabs, pumping gas, and sweeping floors. Such cutbacks will become more common in the future as profession after profession becomes glutted with excess personnel. The problem of matching people with jobs will be further compounded by expected fluctuations in economic and social conditions.

At least two factors have contributed to the problems our schools and colleges face in preparing people for economic self-sufficiency. First, high schools emphasize college preparatory education, and the students who do not go to college are often left without practical job skills. Although many public schools now have vocational and technical programs, this training is often of inferior quality and given without regard to whether there is actually a demand for the skill being taught.

▲ Phillips Academy in Andover, Massachusetts, is one of many schools whose administrators strongly believe in the value of a traditional, college preparatory education.

Second, in many cases, the educational qualifications for jobs are set too high. Many jobs which now require college degrees could be competently performed by high-school graduates. Requiring four years of college when less would do obviously handicaps lower-class and minority-group students who are ill prepared for college or who cannot afford it. This practice effectively restricts the competition for jobs to the middle and upper classes.[8]

Education for Life in Modern Society

We also expect our schools and colleges to help prepare people for life in modern society; the future demands that people be able to quickly adjust and readjust to a constantly changing world.

An increasing number of public and private high schools are offering vocational and technical programs which often lead to high-paying jobs immediately upon graduation.

The complexity of modern life is to some extent responsible for the charge of irrelevance that is frequently aimed at our educational curricula. A large number of people believe that many courses taught in our schools and colleges are outdated and of little real immediate value to the average person. For example, these critics think that most of the traditional disciplines such as history, mathematics, and literature could explore the future and

the challenges it will pose. These disciplines presently do not do so, however, because such speculation is considered unscholarly. Even current events sometimes suffer from unrealistic classroom treatment. The government or economics course which describes how democracy or capitalism really works is rare, and students are left with a one-sided view of our economic and political institutions.

In general, then, irrelevance in education amounts to a failure to teach about many important aspects of the world coupled with a tendency to teach other aspects in a way that few students can directly use in later life.[9] The belief that much of what our schools and colleges teach is irrelevant is a major factor contributing to public discontent with our educational system.

Preparation for Citizenship

The nineteenth century handed down to us both the idea that education should support our political institutions and that, to survive, democracy requires a literate and informed public. We thus expect our schools and colleges to teach students about our political principles and heritage and to instill in them the desire to become good citizens.

Once again, the evidence suggests that our schools and colleges are not fully succeeding in this task. In a series of experiments, both school-age children and adults were asked to sign petitions which bore the opening section of the Declaration of Independence, the First Amendment to the Constitution, or some other key political principle (although unlabeled as such). Repeatedly, large percentages—sometimes majorities—refused to sign, often denouncing the petitioners as troublemakers and Communists.[10]

The failure of the schools to teach citizenship is also illustrated every year by the low voter turnout for elections. In recent national elections only about 60 percent of the eligible voters have balloted, a figure far below European standards. Most disturbing of all is the fact that by 1973 more than 60 percent of our college students felt that America was democratic in name only.[11]

The failure of our schools to teach good citizenship may partly be due to the mixed reaction the public has toward student participation in the political process. The student-led protests and youthful political activism of the '60s demonstrated that students can have considerable enthusiasm for politics. Yet much of the public views student political activism with hostility. Furthermore, many student governments are dominated by school administrators who tend to reduce students to second-class citizens.[12]

In general, the public refuses to acknowledge that mass demonstrations and minor violence are among our political traditions. Our schools are often criticized for not teaching a belief in law and order, respect for person and property, and deference to authority. But they are rarely criticized for failing to teach the rights of citizenship or for failing to give students a realistic view of our political heritage and process.

As a result, students learn little about effective participation in a representative democracy. They are left with the vague impression that the ballot box and letters to their congressmen and senators are the only legitimate means of political expression.

Promoting Equality

Traditionally, our schools have been expected to play a major role in promoting equality and in integrating diverse peoples into our society. In some respects, our schools have been enormously successful in this regard. Certainly, free public education has provided millions of immigrants with the skills and values that they needed to become full participants in our society.

But our schools have, to a great extent, failed in their efforts to promote equality. Many people today stubbornly oppose the integration of blacks, Mexican Americans, Indians, and other minorities into our schools and our society. Many people also object to the suggestion that girls as well as boys should be trained as engineers or mathematicians, or that athletic facilities for girls should be of comparable quality to those for boys. Can our schools help people overcome their prejudices and help create an equal society? Where do we stand in terms of creating a society in which achievement is not limited by race or sex?

In 1954, the U.S. Supreme Court's landmark decision in the case of *Brown* v. *The Board of Education of Topeka* declared segregated schooling unconstitutional. A year later the Court ordered schools across the country to desegregate "with all deliberate speed" (see also Chapter 10). Although considerable progress has been made since that time, blacks still lag behind whites. In 1972, for example, 39.1 percent of all blacks age 25 and over had completed high school and 6.9 percent had completed four or more years of college; the comparable figures for whites were 60.4 percent and 12.6 percent.[13] In terms of grades, rates of learning, reading levels, and dropout rates, blacks trail white students.[14] Only in school athletics have blacks begun to excel recently, and this offends radical critics who feel that black athletes are being exploited.

Proponents of school integration are distressed because black students are not showing the hoped-for gains in integrated schools. Large jumps in I.Q. and achievement, which would constitute proof that school integration yields benefits, often do not occur. The failure of integrated schools to equalize abilities and opportunities is often traced to the deprived cultural environment into which black children are often born, to the fact that teachers often expect little of black students, and to the poor self-images that black children have of themselves. Still another reason why school integration has not lived up to its promise is due to the fact that lower-class blacks are often integrated with lower-class whites. Integration would undoubtedly yield more benefits if disadvantaged youths, regardless of race, were exposed to a middle-class educational environment.

▲ Not all classrooms are as well integrated as this one. Despite Supreme Court decisions and much progress, true equal educational opportunity still seems a long way off.

Two other minority groups that encounter barriers to educational success are Mexican Americans and American Indians. Because English is often a second language for the Mexican American, the communication gap between teachers and students may be wide. Similarly, schools run by the Bureau of Indian Affairs on Indian reservations are frequently staffed by teachers who cannot communicate with their students and who have little understanding of Indian culture. In addition, Indian schools often take children from their homes and families to live in a strange and forbidding environment. In urban areas, Indian children face essentially the same school problems as other disadvantaged children.

Social class also hampers academic success.[15] Children from lower-class homes, regardless of race, are usually poorly prepared for academic work. Their parents often do not encourage them to be academically successful, and there is frequently a lack of intellectual stimulation in the home. High schools often fail to provide them with good teachers and a curriculum that is relevant to their needs and aspirations. Lower-class students frequently do not go to college because of insufficient funds, inadequate admission scores, or because they believe that college attendance will not benefit them. Whether our educational system can be redesigned so that lower-class youths can overcome the handicaps imposed upon them is an open question.

Schools today have the added task of promoting equality between the sexes. In the past, parents socialized their children to believe that girls needed less education than boys. Despite the widespread myth that girls are favored in the classroom, as early as age nine they fall behind boys in math, science, social studies, and citizenship.[16] Textbooks, fellow students, and teachers all tend to reinforce sexist stereotypes—math and auto mechanics are "not for girls," sports are "unfeminine." Again, whether the schools can help overcome long-standing patterns of sexual inequality is an open question.

Whether based on race, sex, or social class, inequality in education is a problem for which there are no clear solutions. Historically, schools have been structured to keep lower-class children locked into their disadvantaged social and economic positions.[17] In effect, schools help perpetuate the lower class, just as they do the middle class. Even James Coleman, the chief architect of integration-for-equality, has come to see forced school busing as furthering segregation because busing simply drives white middle-class children into private schools or farther out into the suburbs.[18] Many scholars now doubt that education alone can ensure the good life for everyone regardless of race, sex, or social class.[19]

Serving Larger Interests

In addition to preparing children for adulthood, teaching them to be good citizens, and promoting equality, the educational system is also expected to perform a variety of other functions for the larger society.

One such function, performed mainly by large universities, is doing research for government, defense, and private industry.

Critics charge that this function has produced a military-industrial-education complex. Well-to-do, conservative businessmen tend to dominate state university boards of regents, and university administrators in turn are invited to sit on many corporate boards. Similarly, faculty members may find more profit and prestige in doing research for business and the Pentagon than in teaching or pursuing knowledge for its own sake. Indeed, our universities devote so much effort to improving the technology of capitalism and militarism that some scientists fear that they are not paying enough attention to environmental problems such as overpopulation, resource depletion, and pollution.[20]

Education also helps to maintain social order. At the elementary and secondary levels, the child learns to obey hundreds of different social norms. Some of these norms allow the child, and later the adult, to function in society. Other norms, however, have no rationale and must be obeyed only because "they are there." In addition, our society has few clearly defined economic and social roles for the adolescent. As a result, college becomes a place to control and detain the adolescent: "The neatest way to get rid of a superfluous 18-year-old is to amuse him all day long at a community college while his family feeds and houses him. This is not only cheaper than a residential college but cheaper than supporting him on welfare, a make-work job, in prison or in the armed forces."[21]

Education as a Bureaucratic Enterprise

Most Americans would probably resent the idea that our educational system has become thoroughly bureaucratized. We like to think of our schools as learning centers staffed by dedicated, inspired teachers and administrators who treat each and every student as an individual. However, numbers alone dictate that our educational system be bureaucratized. In 1974 an estimated 33.5 million students were enrolled in elementary schools and another 15.6 million in secondary schools. Over 9 million students were enrolled in public colleges and universities, including community colleges.[22] Education then is, of necessity, a bureaucratic enterprise. What are some of the characteristics of this bureaucracy? What are some of its shortcomings?

Conveying Information

Clearly, one of the principal goals of our educational system is to convey information to students. We have already alluded to the fact that elementary and secondary schools are only partly successful in meeting this goal. Even though the vast majority of

Americans have completed elementary school and at least some secondary school, millions have not acquired many of the skills which are basic for survival in modern society. One reason for this may be that only part of the typical school day is devoted to learning. Much of a teacher's time is devoted to essentially non-teaching activities such as maintaining discipline and doing paperwork.

In major universities, research and scholarly writing have long been the yardsticks of success for professors, and they are becoming more so as jobs and raises become scarcer. The professor who is a top-notch researcher or writer is often highly rewarded in both money and prestige. The professor who is a top-notch classroom teacher is often only nominally rewarded. Although much lip service is paid to excellence in teaching, many scholars prefer to avoid the classroom. The most widely used method of conveying information at the university level is through lectures, sometimes delivered to several hundred students at a time. This method discourages dialogue, and potential professor-student contact is sometimes further reduced by having graduate assistants grade exams and coach students who are having problems. For the students, the well-done or even entertaining lecture is uncommon.[23]

Students are also turned off by the constant use of quizzes and grades to motivate them and to measure their progress. They complain about the inconsistency in grading practices from teacher to teacher. Other critics of American education find deeper faults in our obsession with quizzes and grades. The importance attached to quizzes and grades encourages cheating and rote learning in which the student simply parrots the teacher's views. It also stigmatizes the students who do not receive As and Bs and takes much of the joy out of learning. Instead of stimulating significant learning, quizzes and grades may actually prevent it.[24]

Grades are, in fact, highly unreliable as measures of learning and ability. In one experiment, high-school English teachers were each given a copy of the same student theme to grade, and their evaluations ranged from A to D.[25] Nonetheless, grades and quizzes are the foundation of the educational bureaucracy. Through grades, students are primarily motivated to conform to the demands of the educational system. If students do not play the educational game successfully, low grades punish and stigmatize them.

The Hidden Curriculum

Although schools are expected to prepare students for adulthood, citizenship, and life in our complex, technologically oriented culture, what students sometimes learn best is the hidden curriculum of the classroom, hallway, and playground. Sometimes this curriculum is at odds with our ideals.

Beginning in kindergarten, students are encouraged to distrust their senses and accept authority as the test of truth. It is the teacher's viewpoint, not the student's, that counts on quizzes and in the principal's office. Students often learn to suppress their own ideas and feelings and replace them with strategies of faking, conning, and groupthink. Finally, learning may cease to be the aim of school attendance; getting to class on time, taking quizzes, and pursuing grades become ends in themselves. Students who are unable to master these bureaucratic routines may eventually come to see themselves as failures and drop out of school. Some scholars believe that this hidden curriculum fosters undesirable personality traits in almost all students.[26]

Controlling Students

For any bureaucracy to function, its members must obey certain rules and regulations and possess a certain amount of self-discipline. Our educational system is no exception. If students were completely free to act on their spur-of-the-moment impulses, schools would become "blackboard jungles." However, there is some evidence that schools may have gone overboard in attempting to control student behavior.

Authoritarianism seems to be the rule at all levels of the educational bureaucracy and particularly in secondary schools: "Because adolescents are harder to 'control' than younger children, secondary schools tend to be even more authoritarian and repressive than elementary schools."[27] Faced with too many students, many of whom would rather be elsewhere, and too much paperwork, many school teachers become preoccupied with order and discipline which, in turn, often stifles student creativity and curiosity. But it is not only job pressure that encourages teachers to adopt a warden mentality; they also acquire it in education courses with titles like "Classroom Control" and "Maintaining Discipline."

Despite the best efforts of teachers, our schools have largely failed to control student behavior. Students who are turned off by book learning are particularly likely to vent their discontent violently. A 1975 Senate subcommittee study, for example, estimated that public schools are spending as much as $500,000,000 annually to repair vandalism.[28] This is almost as much as they spend on textbooks. Serious assaults on teachers number about 70,000 each year; and between 1970 and 1973, assaults on students rose 85 percent, robberies 37 percent, and confiscation of weapons 54 percent.[29] Much of this violence is confined to inner-city schools, but maintaining order and discipline is also a problem in rural and suburban schools: "What is most shocking and horrifying about public education today is that in almost all schools the children are treated, most of the time, like convicts in a jail."[30] As long as students feel locked up, constant disciplinary problems and occasional violence can be expected.

The Joyless Bureaucracy

As in most bureaucracies, there is a division of labor in education which encourages teachers to specialize. As a result, many teachers lose sight of where and how their subject matter fits into the larger educational scheme. This, in turn, leads students to see a math or language course as an obstacle, not as an opportunity to acquire a valuable skill.

As the educational bureaucracy grows more complex, the rules and regulations governing learning proliferate. The chronic drive for efficiency and economy in the educational enterprise can lead to impersonality and mass processing of students. Educational bureaucracies too often become more concerned with their own survival than with meeting the changing needs of students. When all of these bureaucratic traits and pressures are added together the result is simple—there is no joy in the classroom.

Most students and teachers are aware of the bureaucratic pressures against learning. Students complain about poorly trained teachers, excessive rules, computerized registration. And teachers complain about their powerlessness and the busywork heaped on them. Yet, the impact that the absence of joy in the classroom has on students, and ultimately on society, is still not understood.

Financing Education

Any bureaucracy as vast as our education system requires huge amounts of money to function effectively. Yet, lack of sufficient funds may be precipitating a crisis in education. Because education seems at times to yield so few tangible results, taxpayers are beginning to wonder where their school-tax dollar goes. They are also wondering where the money for education will come from in the future.

Using and Misusing Educational Dollars

Since the mid-1960s, educational costs have risen rapidly. In the 1974-75 school year, the total cost of public education was $107.7 billion. Of this amount, $68.2 billion was spent by elementary and secondary schools, and $39.5 billion was spent by colleges and universities. This represents an increase of 172 percent over

1965.[31] These sums break down to an average of $1,255 spent per elementary- and high-school student and $3,045 per college student.[32] These dollars provide almost one American in three with some type of formal schooling.

These expenditures seem huge, but they must be kept in perspective. Since 1950 the nation has spent more on defense than on education. Another interesting comparison reveals that we spend more each year on automobiles, liquor, or cosmetics than we do on education.[33] Relative to other national expenditures, in fact, education is given low priority.

We should point out that what we do spend on each student differs from state to state. Each state varies in terms of the importance it attaches to education relative to other government activities. For example, in 1974-75, New York spent an average of $2,005 per student whereas Mississippi spent $834 per student.[34] In general, the northeastern states have the highest per-pupil expenditures, the south and southwestern states have the lowest.[35] Thus, where we live has a profound impact on the quality of education we receive.

Since property taxes are the chief source of revenue for most school districts, there is a wide disparity in the amounts of money spent per student from school district to school district even within the same state.[36] During the 1969-70 school year, for example, Beverly Hills, California, spent nearly $1,232 per student whereas nearby Baldwin Park spent only $577 per student.[37] This disparity arose largely because the assessed value of property in Beverly Hills was $50,885 per student while the assessed value of property in Baldwin Park was only $3,706 per student.[38] Similar inequities can be found in every state. Even within school districts, there may be inequities in financing from school to school. Although some critics have concluded that money alone does not have great bearing on the quality of education, there are many other critics who disagree with them.[39]

Per-pupil expenditures also vary widely between elementary and secondary schools and institutions of higher learning. In 1974-75, as we pointed out above, public colleges and universities spent an average of $3,045 per student whereas elementary and secondary schools spent an average of $1,255 per student.[40] While it is true that teaching students is only one of the activities of higher education (it is also actively engaged in research and community service), this gross inequity is nonetheless troubling when we realize that by the time children reach the third grade perhaps two-thirds of their intellectual potential is fixed. The first few years in school are crucial to future academic success. Yet, we spend far less on these beginning students than we do on students who have already cultivated the skills to succeed in school.

Educational Financing in the Near Future

In the near future, the cost of education will continue to rise. While the numbers of young people in school may level off and, in some cases, decrease, new programs will be required to serve the growing number of adults who are returning to school. The federal government is also likely to continue its drive to improve and equalize educational opportunities. New educational technology and more aid for the educationally disadvantaged will further increase costs.

At the same time, taxpayers will be reluctant to spend more on education. Today, school bond issues often fail at the polls, and proposed increases in property tax rates are fought vigorously. In some areas, school administrators are bargaining hard with striking teachers to try to keep the costs of education down. Some state legislatures have cut back on the amount of money appropriated to education, and the federal contribution to education has slowed down during recent years. Unless these present trends are reversed, the educational bureaucracy may be faced with severe financial problems in coming years.

Reforming and Changing Education

Despite the many problems of our educational system, few proposals have been put forth for reforming it. Most of the proposals that have been made deal with specifics such as changing the content of curricula, improving teaching methods, and finding new sources of revenue. Fewer in number are the proposals which would bring about sweeping changes in the way in which Americans are educated.

Curriculum Changes

The problem of making education more relevant to student needs has been attacked in many different ways. A few elementary schools are now putting much more emphasis on the three Rs. A more typical response has been to add new courses to the curriculum. There are many sound reasons for this response. The knowledge explosion dictates that new courses be constantly added to the curriculum. And, as new social concerns arise, schools are pressured to offer such courses as drug abuse, ecology, marriage and family living. Special interest groups have also demanded new courses with subject matter ranging from Chicano history and women's studies to driver education and Frisbee.

It would be difficult to argue that the curricula of our schools and colleges should not be changed and expanded to meet new needs. However, our educational system runs the risk of spreading itself too thin. It may simply be attempting to do too many things—with the end result of doing none of them well.

One curriculum-related development of considerable interest is the Head Start program. Begun in 1965, this program seeks to enrich the preschool environment of disadvantaged children. It is based on the premise that, by the first grade, many children have already lost the educational race. Typically, children in a Head Start program are given physical exams, good meals each day, and some of the learning stimuli which middle-class children receive from their families.

In this Head Start classroom in Dallas, Texas, Mexican-American and Anglo children are being given a Spanish language lesson. ▶

Another attempt to increase the academic potential of disadvantaged slum children was conducted in Milwaukee.[41] In this project a team of highly qualified educators began working intensively with infants from intellectually deprived environments almost from the time they were born. Between infancy and about the time they reached age 5, the subjects' I.Q.s jumped an average of more than 50 percent. The same improvement was not observed in a comparable group of children who were not included in the program. However, programs of this type are extremely expensive and probably cannot be carried out on a widespread basis.

Social Problems and You

How Much Must a Student Master?

"Reeling and Writhing, of course, to begin with," the Mock Turtle replied; "and then the different branches of Arithmetic—Ambition, Distraction, Uglification and Derison."
—Alice's Adventures in Wonderland

To many worried parents, the new math–new methods teaching that swept public schools in the '60s made about as much sense as Lewis Carroll's Turtle. When they complained that children were no longer learning basic reading, writing and arithmetic, however, no one listened. Until, that is, test scores began plunging, and legislators and officials discovered that the supposed mess in public education could be a dangerous political issue.

The result: in the past year, "minimal competency testing" has become the hottest new catch phrase in public education. Described by educators as a "man on the street" effort to halt the devaluation of a high school diploma, minimal competency requires students to pass proficiency exams, in addition to course work, in order to graduate. . . . Colleges, too, have caught the fever, and are increasingly requiring students to pass a writing exam before graduating.

Politicians have been quick to recognize a test whose time has come. Says California State Assemblyman Leroy Greene: "When a youngster gets out of high school, I expect him to be able to read a newspaper article, tell me what it said, and write me a couple hundred words on it in proper English." Adds Alabama State Senator Bill King, who has just introduced a minimal competency bill: "Taxpayers see so much money going into education yet producing students without basic skills. Legislators want to account for all of that money."

Once a state has ratified minimal competency testing, however, the rhetoric ends and the problems begin. Foremost among them: What constitutes "functional literacy"? Should only reading and math be tested? Or should the exams include such "survival skills" as how to balance a checkbook or read a road map? Should standard statewide exams, which might be biased against, say, inner-city children, be used? Or should individual tests be developed by local school districts? . . .

Nor do the problems stop there. When should students be tested? Many states, realizing that students must have time for remedial work if they fail a competency exam, are studying programs that would test students from early elementary grades upward. Extended remedial programs, however, would clearly cost additional tax dollars which may not be available. . . .

Perhaps the most outspoken opponent of minimal competency is Educator Arthur Wise, whose influential 1968 treatise, *Rich Schools, Poor Schools,* argued that children in both affluent and underprivileged school districts had the right to an equal education. Wise is currently working on another book, tentatively titled *Hyper-Rationalization,* which condemns competency testing for "narrowing the goals of education and prompting teachers to teach the test." Wise fears that minimal competency entails the extension to education of such business-school concepts as cost effectiveness and accountability. Says he of minimal competency advocates: "It is as if they want to set goals and objectives by numbers. There is little room for the excellent teacher." Or, perhaps, for the excellent student.

SOURCE: "How Much Must a Student Master?" *Time,* 109 (February 28, 1977), p. 74.

Changes in Teaching Methods

The reform of teaching methods is often plagued by superficial changes, such as the employment of a gag writer by the University of Southern California to add spice to dry lectures. The widespread adoption of pass-fail grading to replace conventional letter grading is an unsophisticated attempt to deemphasize grades. In addition, classrooms have been brightened, textbooks made more attractive, and modern media incorporated into the classroom. However, these basically decorative changes have not yielded dramatic results; and, in general, teaching reform continues to be characterized by attempts to improve old, timeworn methods rather than by developing new, innovative approaches to education.

Further, the innovations that have been developed have not been highly successful in many cases. For example, the tracking system, devised to promote greater learning and equal opportunity in school, sorts students into groups on a continuum from low to high academic potential. The purpose of sorting students into tracks is to prevent slow learners from becoming discouraged by adverse competition and to ensure that fast learners are not held back. Tracking also makes it easier for the teacher to work with the special learning needs of each group. The ultimate goal of tracking is to create conditions that permit slow learners to experience academic success and begin to catch up with their peers.

To date, however, tracking has achieved only mixed results.[42] Slow learners feel stigmatized by being confined to the low track and having to take courses in remedial math and reading, often called dummy courses. As a result, these students frequently accept the verdict of society, lower their goals, and define themselves as failures. Their self-definition is often reinforced by teachers who stereotype students in the lower track as incapable of learning and then put forth only a halfhearted effort to teach them. Since students who are labeled "slow learners" are especially likely to come from culturally deprived, lower-class backgrounds, the tracking system helps perpetuate some of the gross inequalities that exist in our society.

At colleges and universities, the systems approach to instruction has received wide attention. One example of this approach is self-paced learning. Self-paced learning de-emphasizes lectures as the primary means of conveying knowledge. Students proceed instead through a fixed sequence of reading and other learning activities at their own pace. Frequent quizzes and some tutorial aid enable students to check their progress and ensure that they are following the proper sequence. Self-paced instruction is more personalized than lectures; it also yields a higher percentage of As and Bs than conventional instruction. However, it is not particularly popular with students, many of whom quickly drop out of such programs. And, as with other methods of instruction, the emphasis in self-paced learning is on acquiring facts in order to pass quizzes and earn good grades.

Financial Reform

As we have already pointed out, our schools face two financial problems—inadequate funds and inequitable distribution of the funds they do have. What is being done to rectify these problems?

Despite dislike of growing federal control, many people hope the federal government will fund larger shares of school budgets. However, with so many other federal expenditures, local school districts are unlikely to receive greater federal aid. In the meantime, many schools have tightened their budgets by reducing teachers' raises, spending less on expensive educational hardware, making do with older buildings, and cutting back on athletic programs. But the public sometimes will not tolerate cutbacks. In 1975, for example, the San Francisco school board's threat to reduce or eliminate athletic programs raised such a storm of protest and promises of donations that the board capitulated.

A much more important issue concerning school financing arose in 1971 when the California Supreme Court ruled that the use of property taxes to finance schools denies children the equal protection of the law guaranteed under the Fourteenth Amendment: "It makes the quality of a child's education a function of the wealth of his parents and neighbors."[43] With the lower courts divided, in 1973 the U.S. Supreme Court overturned a Texas federal court ruling which was similar to that reached by the California Supreme Court.[44] But the Supreme Court could reverse itself on this issue; it all depends on how much longer we will continue to tolerate the inequalities built into our educational system by our reliance on property taxes as the chief source of revenue for local school districts.

Within their own borders, some states are attempting to equalize educational expenditures.[45] This raises the problem of finding alternative sources of revenue. One proposal under consideration in several states is to put all property tax revenue in a common state fund and distribute dollars to schools on the basis of enrollment. This proposal is not likely to be too popular, however, since it would work to the detriment of wealthy school districts. Other potential revenue sources are also being examined, including sales taxes, income taxes, and corporation taxes.

Under another proposal, the voucher plan, parents would receive state tuition vouchers to be used to send their children to the schools of their choice. As with most of the reform proposals, one aim of the voucher plan is to equalize per-pupil expenditures. It would also force schools to compete with each other for students. This competition, in turn, should motivate school administrators to improve the range and quality of educational programs. The first large-scale experiment with the voucher plan at Alum Rock, California, yielded encouraging results.[46] However, the voucher plan could lead to increased segregation in our schools and deprive disadvantaged youth of contact with middle-class students. Most affluent white parents would undoubtedly send their children to suburban schools which are inaccessible to ghetto youths.

Changing the System

The programs and proposals we have discussed so far have been concerned with improving traditional methods of educating students. However, there have also been some new, innovative programs and proposals that would radically change the way people are educated.

The Open Classroom

In primary grades the open classroom concept has generated considerable enthusiasm.[47] The open classroom attempts to overcome assembly-line instruction by encouraging children to follow their curiosity from project to project with a minimum of teacher supervision. In a single room, students may work on projects as varied as weaving, reading, Indian culture, and modern math. The

The open classroom attempts to overcome assembly-line instruction by encouraging children to follow their curiosity from project to project with a minimum of teacher supervision.
▼

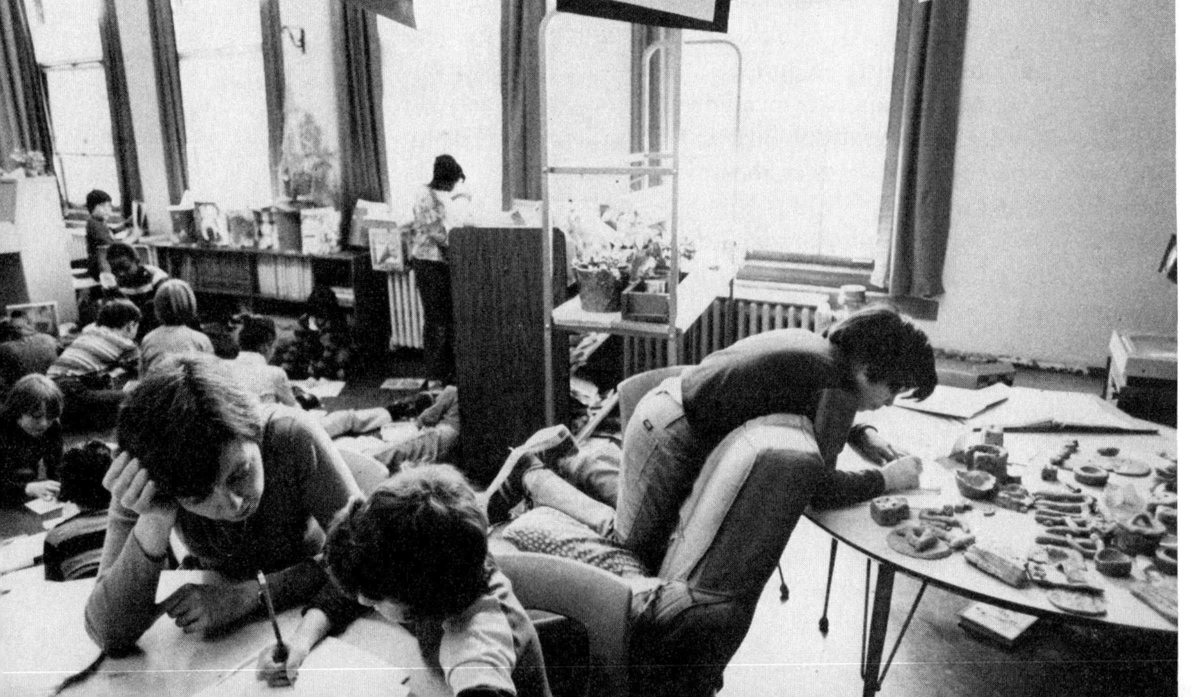

proponents of the open classroom hope that, by starting with what interests the student and allowing that interest to develop into other areas, the child's educational experience will be more pleasurable and productive. Critics, however, point out that this approach to education could lead to expertise in such subjects as weaving, astrology, and photography and ignorance in such subjects as reading, writing, and arithmetic. There is also some evidence to suggest that lower-class students do not perform as well in the open classroom as do middle- and upper-class students.[48]

Deschooling Society

An even more dramatic approach to changing education has been suggested by Ivan Illich.[49] Illich has a profound distaste for our present educational system because it perpetuates the inequities that pervade our society, it costs too much, and it denies knowledge to people who are unwilling or unable to proceed through a predetermined curriculum in lockstep fashion (for example, "you cannot study 12th grade history until you pass 11th grade math"). Illich thus proposes to deschool society and, in effect, to do away with our present educational bureaucracy. Learning opportunities would instead be made available throughout society—for example, in libraries, factories, museums, on farms. In addition, means would be provided by which people could contact other people who desire to learn the same thing. These people, in turn, would locate yet other people who could teach them what they want to know. Everybody would be free to learn what they want when they want to learn it.

Illich's proposal to deschool society is appealing to those who are displeased with our present educational system. Indeed, education and learning have probably become, in the public's mind, too closely equated with formal schooling; the importance of learning activities outside the classroom is often overlooked. However, the feasibility of Illich's proposals is questionable. Certain basic skills are indispensable in our society, such as being able to read or add a column of figures. Would most people, particularly children, be sufficiently self-motivated to seek out this knowledge voluntarily? Without several years of formal schooling, could people acquire the basic skills needed for the study of medicine, law, the professions, and so forth?

The Future of Education

During recent years, a major struggle over education has developed. Many students, parents, teachers, and alumni are dissatisfied with the way our schools and colleges are run and with the way our educational system is structured and organized.

By 1970, protesting college students had won the right to choose their own life-styles and living arrangements. Their struggle for a voice in the direction and operation of their colleges and universities met with less success, however. Although the student protest movement has abated on college campuses, a somewhat different type of unrest has emerged in the public schools. Today, many public school students are calling for the elimination of dress codes, closed hallways, and restricted campuses. And increasing rates of vandalism and terrorism are one sure sign that many students are becoming increasingly discontented with our educational system.[50]

A growing number of parents are also protesting. In West Virginia, California, Texas, and North Dakota, parents have demanded censorship of books which they do not want their children to read.[51] By 1970, school busing to achieve racial balance came under fire from parents who responded with court injunctions, boycotts, and violence. Minorities also began to raise their voices as they saw inner-city schools functioning poorly under the supervision of unresponsive, white-dominated bureaucracies. The demand for neighborhood control of schools can be seen as another form of pressure to make the massive educational structure more responsive to public will.

Out of this struggle to shape and form the educational system, several fundamental questions emerge: Is the school responsible for preparing students to be good citizens as well as good workers? Should the school be a substitute parent and an instrument of social control? Should the school simply parrot old norms and values or should it suggest new norms and values for students? Is the school to mold the individual to fit society, or should it try to change society itself? These are difficult questions which cannot be answered by simply plugging in a computer or conducting a research project.

Even if we provide answers to the foregoing questions about the ends of education (*what* questions), we must still answer means questions (*how* questions): Should we use more technology or less? Is self-paced instruction a solution or a problem? To what extent should schools control their students, and to what extent should students control their schools? Must we build bigger educational bureaucracies or should we deschool society?

Some critics are also troubled by the failure of schools to tackle some of the major challenges that face us in the future. They argue that our universities should devote more attention to the pressing problems of our time and less attention to designing more sophisticated military hardware and consumer gadgetry. They fear that the rising tempo of change will drive many people into "future shock," an emotional state in which they cannot cope with the world. They feel that we might avoid future shock if our schools helped people learn to cope with life in a fast-paced, ever-changing society.[52] They suggest that schools should help people develop a built-in "crap detector" which will enable them to separate truth from the flood of modern propaganda.[53] In looking at education and the future it is easy to become pessimistic and hopeless, but most critics are still confident that education can provide the technological and moral leadership necessary for a safe future.

Summary

Many people—teachers, parents, students—are becoming increasingly concerned that our schools are not functioning as well as we would like them to.

One problem with American education is that its goals are often unclear, diffuse, and confusing. We expect schools to prepare children for adulthood by (1) providing them with skills for careers that will ensure economic self-sufficiency, and (2) educating them to meet the anticipated demands of our rapidly changing society. In most cases, however, schools do not provide students with realistic career orientations nor do they prepare students to meet the challenges of the future.

Another goal of the educational system is to promote good citizenship. However, consistently poor voter turnouts and widespread public ignorance about our political heritage and processes denote failure in this area as well.

Schools are expected to promote equality, but many minority groups receive inferior educations because of race, sex, or social class.

Finally, the goals of our educational system include research and maintenance of social order.

Education is thoroughly bureaucratized. Teachers must devote much of their time to nonteaching activities, and colleges rely on lectures, quizzes, and grades. The hidden curriculum of bureaucratic routines is what students often learn best. Authoritarian discipline characterizes most schools; however, rates of vandalism and assaults in schools are rising. Because teachers are often narrow specialists, rules and regulations proliferate, and the system is impersonal, there is no joy in the classroom.

We are approaching a crisis in financing education. Although expenditures for schooling are high, education is given low priority relative to other national expenditures. Furthermore, the distribution of funds among schools is highly inequitable largely because we rely on property taxes as the chief source of revenue for schools.

While the costs of education are likely to continue to increase, taxpayers are becoming reluctant to spend more on schools and much state and federal government funding has been cut back.

Efforts to improve the educational system can take two forms—reform and change. Proposals to reform the system include curriculum changes to meet the knowledge explosion and changes in teaching methods such as pass-fail grading, tracking, and self-paced learning. A few attempts have been made to reform school funding to more equitably distribute revenue, including common state funds and voucher plans.

Proposals to radically change the system include the open classroom and deschooling society. So far, neither reform nor change has had much success.

The growing dissatisfaction with our educational system has raised many difficult and basic questions about the aims of education and the means to achieve these aims.

Discussion Questions

1. In the United States, everyone has access to free public education through high school. Yet one in four Americans does not complete high school. How can you account for this fact? What happens to those people who do not complete high school?
2. Discuss the goals of our educational system. Are schools succeeding in achieving these goals? Why or why not? Do we expect too much of our educational system? Explain your answer.
3. As of 1973, more than 60 percent of our college students felt that America was democratic in name only. How would you account for this rather disturbing fact? Do you feel that our country is democratic in name only?
4. How would you account for the fact that integrated schools have, to a great extent, failed to bring about equality between blacks and whites in terms of academic achievement? How would you rectify this situation?
5. What is meant by the phrase "military-industrial-education complex"? Some of our larger universities in particular have been accused of devoting too much effort to improving the technology of capitalism and militarism. Is this a valid criticism? Explain your answer.
6. How has our educational system become thoroughly bureaucratized? Explain your answer.

7. What is meant by "the hidden curriculum"? Was there a hidden curriculum in the elementary and high schools that you attended? If so, what were some of the lessons that you learned from this curriculum?
8. How would you account for the high rates of violence in many public school systems? What would you do to curb this violence?
9. Discuss some of the problems involved in financing public education. What, in your opinion, might be done to equalize per-pupil school expenditures between one school district and another? In your discussion, comment specifically on the voucher plan and on the proposal to lump all property tax revenue into a common state fund with the result that schools would be funded strictly on the basis of their enrollments.
10. Discuss the tracking system. What are some of the advantages and disadvantages of placing students into different groups in terms of their academic abilities? In what sense does tracking help perpetuate some of the inequalities that are already built into our society?
11. Ivan Illich has suggested that we should "deschool" society. What does Illich mean when he talks about deschooling society? Do you think that Illich's proposals are practical and workable? Why or why not?
12. What do you see as the future of education? Is our public school system on the brink of collapse? Explain your answer.

Glossary

deschooling society A proposal put forth by Ivan Illich which would do away with our present educational bureaucracy. Learning opportunities would instead be made available throughout society.

future shock A concept which suggests that the rising tempo of change in our society will drive many people into an emotional state in which they cannot cope with the world.

Head Start program A federally financed program for disadvantaged children that provides them with some of the learning stimuli which middle-class children receive from their parents.

hidden curriculum A concept which infers that what children really learn in school is to suppress their own ideas and feelings and to replace them with strategies of faking, conning, and so on.

military-industrial-education complex A phrase which suggests that some universities devote too much effort to improving the technology of capitalism and militarism. This phrase is used by critics who argue that universities should spend more time educating students and that they should pay more attention to such problems as overpopulation, resource depletion, and pollution.

open classroom An approach to primary education in which children follow their curiosity from project to project with a minimum of teacher supervision. The hope is that by starting with what interests the student and allowing that interest to spread into other areas, the child's educational experience will be both more pleasurable and productive.

tracking system A controversial approach to education which sorts students into groups according to their academic abilities. The goal of tracking is to permit slow learners to experience academic success and to begin to catch up with their peers.

voucher plan A plan under which parents would receive state tuition vouchers to be used to send their children to the schools of their choice. The aims of the voucher plan are to (1) equalize per-pupil expenditures, and (2) improve the quality of schools by forcing them to compete with each other for students.

Suggestions for Further Reading

"Crisis in the Schools," *U.S. News and World Report,* 79 (September 1, 1975), pp. 42–59. An informative overview of many of the problems facing the American educational system today.

Freeman, Richard, and J. Herbert Hollomon, "The Declining Value of College Going," *Change,* 7 (September, 1975), pp. 24–31. A sobering article which suggests (1) that the amount of money earned by college graduates is declining relative to that earned by noncollege graduates, and (2) that college graduates suffer more than their fair share of long-term unemployment.

Ianni, Francis A. J., ed., *Conflict and Change in Education* (Glenview, Ill.: Scott, Foresman, 1975). An exhaustive and provocative collection of articles on various facets of American education. Most of these articles are written from a social problems perspective.

Kirschenbaum, Howard, Rodney Napier, and Sidney B. Simon, *Wad-Ja-Get? The Grading Game in American Education* (New York: Hart, 1971). This book, written in the form of a novel, provides the reader with a great deal of insight into the grading game—a game which pervades our educational system and gives rise to endless controversy.

Pearl, Arthur, *The Atrocity of Education* (New York: Dutton, 1972). An insightful critique of American public education which calls for sweeping changes in our educational system.

Postman, Neil, and Charles Weingartner, *Teaching as a Subversive Activity* (New York: Delacorte, 1969). The authors argue that education is not adequately preparing people for life in modern society. It also contains a host of ideas about how education can be made more relevant to the needs of those whom it serves.

Swift, David W., ed., *American Education: A Sociological View* (Boston: Houghton Mifflin, 1976). An excellent introduction to the sociology of education. Of particular interest is Part III, which deals with the education of minorities.

Notes

[1]"The Incompetent Society," *Science News*, 108 (November 8, 1975), p. 294.

[2]"Big Shifts Ahead in Classrooms: Less Laxity, More Stress on Job Skills," *U.S. News & World Report*, 79 (September 1, 1975), p. 51.

[3]See Joffre T. Whisenton and M. Ray Loree, "A Comparison of the Values, Needs, and Aspirations of School Leavers with Those of Non-School Leavers," *Journal of Negro Education*, 39 (Fall, 1970), pp. 325–32.

[4]Paul Goodman, *Compulsory Mis-Education* (New York: Horizon, 1964), p. 87.

[5]See Richard Freeman and J. Herbert Hollomon, "The Declining Value of College Going," *Change*, 7 (September, 1975), pp. 24–31.

[6]*Ibid*., p. 25.

[7]Cited in "What the Schools Cannot Do," *Time*, 101 (April 16, 1973), p. 80.

[8]Ivar E. Berg, *Education for Jobs: The Great Training Robbery* (New York: Praeger, 1970); and Randall Collins, "Functional and Conflict Theories of Educational Stratification," *American Sociological Review*, 36 (December, 1971), pp. 1002–1016.

[9]See Neil Postman and Charles Weingartner, *Teaching as a Subversive Activity* (New York: Delacorte, 1969), esp. pp. 39–58.

[10]Cited in Thomas Ford Hoult, *Sociology for a New Day* (New York: Random House, 1974), p. 240.

[11]Daniel Yankelovich, *The New Morality: A Profile of American Youth in the 70's* (New York: McGraw-Hill, 1974), p. 116.

[12]See Arthur Pearl, *The Atrocity of Education* (New York: Dutton, 1972), pp. 124–31.

[13]See Sar A. Levitan, William B. Johnston, and Robert Taggart, *Still a Dream: The Changing Status of Blacks Since 1960* (Cambridge, Mass.: Harvard, 1975), Table 4–1.

[14]James S. Coleman et al., *Equality of Educational Opportunity* (Washington, D.C.: U.S. Government Printing Office, 1966), esp. pp. 218–90, 447–59.

[15]See Arthur Pearl, "Educational Change: Why, How, for Whom?" in Glen Gaviglio and David Raye, eds., *Society as It Is* (New York: Macmillan, 1971), pp. 298–310.

[16]"Girls Lag on Tests: Unequal Education?" *U.S. News & World Report*, 79 (October 20, 1975), p. 54.

[17]This thesis is explored by Colin Greer, *The Great School Legend* (New York: Basic, 1972).

[18]"New Coleman Report," *Time*, 105 (June 23, 1975), p. 60.

[19]For example, see Christopher Jencks et al., *Inequality* (New York: Basic, 1972); and Fred Mosteller and Daniel P. Moynihan, eds., *On Equality of Educational Opportunity* (New York: Random House, 1972).

[20]See James Ridgeway, "Of Corporate Bondage," *Change*, 7 (October, 1975), pp. 25–29.

[21]Cited in "Case Against College," *Time*, 105 (April 21, 1975), p. 64.

[22]"A Lean Year Begins," *U.S. News & World Report*, 79 (September 1, 1975), p. 45.

[23]For an interesting discussion of how college students feel about their professors, see James A. Foley and Robert K. Foley, *The College Scene* (New York: McGraw-Hill, 1971), pp.78–90.

[24]See Howard Kirschenbaum, Rodney Napier, and Sidney B. Simon, *Wad-Ja-Get? The Grading Game in American Education* (New York: Hart, 1971), pp. 136–40.

[25]*Ibid.*, pp. 157–60.

[26]For example, see John Holt, *Instead of Education: Ways to Help People Do Things Better* (New York: Dutton, 1976).

[27]Charles E. Silberman, *Crisis in the Classroom* (New York: Random House, 1970), pp. 323–24.

[28]Cited in John P. DeCecco and Arlene K. Richards, "Civil War in the High Schools," *Psychology Today*, 9 (November, 1975), p. 51.

[29]*Ibid.*, p. 51.

[30]John Holt, "Education for the Future," in Robert Theobald, ed., *Social Policies for America in the Seventies* (Garden City, N.Y.: Doubleday, 1968), p. 190.

[31]"A Lean Year Begins," p. 44.

[32]*Ibid.*

[33]J. Victor Baldridge, *Sociology: A Critical Approach to Power, Conflict, and Change* (New York: Wiley, 1975), pp. 355–56.

[34]U.S. Bureau of the Census, *Statistical Abstract of the United States: 1975* (Washington, D.C.: U.S. Government Printing Office, 1975), Table 220.

[35]*Ibid.*

[36]For an excellent discussion of the problems involved in using property taxes to finance schools, see Jerome Zukosky, "Taxes and Schools: Equalizing Educational Opportunity," in Francis A. J. Ianni, ed., *Conflict and Change in Education* (Glenview, Ill.: Scott, Foresman, 1975), pp. 274–80.

[37]Robert Lekachman, "Schools, Money, and Politics," in Ianni, ed., *Conflict and Change in Education*, p. 354.

[38]*Ibid.*

[39]See Godfrey Hodgson, "Do Schools Make a Difference?" *Atlantic,* 231 (March, 1973), pp. 35–46.

[40]"A Lean Year Begins," p. 44.

[41]See Stephen P. Strickland, "Can Slum Children Learn?" *American Education,* 7 (July, 1971), pp. 3–7.

[42]See Walter E. Schafer, Carol Olexa, and Kenneth Polk, "Programmed for Social Class: Tracking in High School," *Transaction,* 7 (October, 1970), pp. 39–46.

[43]Cited in Lekachman, "Schools, Money, and Politics," p. 354.

[44]See "The Public School: Assaults on a Great Idea," *The Nation,* 216 (April 30, 1973), pp. 555–57.

[45]Zukosky, "Taxes and Schools," pp. 277–78.

[46]David Selden, "Vouchers: A Critic Changes His Mind," *Nation's Schools and Colleges,* 2 (June, 1975), pp. 44–46.

[47]For further information on the open classroom approach to education, see Charles E. Silberman, ed., *The Open Classroom Reader* (New York: Random House, 1973).

[48]See "The Mixed Results of Open Classrooms," *Human Behavior* (April, 1975), p. 29.

[49]See Ivan Illich, *Deschooling Society* (New York: Harper & Row, 1970). For a briefer presentation, see Ivan Illich, "The Alternative to Schooling," *Saturday Review* (June 19, 1971), pp. 44–48, 59–60.

[50]DeCecco and Richards, "Civil War in the High Schools," pp. 51–56; and "Terror in Schools," *U.S. News & World Report,* 80 (January 26, 1976), pp. 52–55.

[51]"Parents vs. Educators," *U.S. News & World Report,* 78 (January 27, 1975), pp. 30–32.

[52]See Alvin Toffler, *Future Shock* (New York: Random House, 1970), esp. Ch. 18.

[53]Postman and Weingartner, *Teaching as a Subversive Activity,* esp. pp. 3–5.

Chapter 16
Criminal Justice

Outline of the Criminal Justice System
The Suspect and the Police
Police Discretion
Police Brutality and Abuse
Understanding Police Behavior
Processing the Defendant
Setting Bail
Arraignment
On Trial
Sentencing
The Juvenile in Court
Juvenile Justice
Juvenile Justice Reform
The Criminal in Prison
Imprisonment
Rethinking the Prison System
Summary

The American symbol of justice is the figure of a blindfolded woman with balanced scales in her right hand and a sword in her left hand. She fairly weighs the evidence on her scales and then administers punishment to the guilty with her sword. She is blindfolded because, in theory, we believe in equal justice for all. In practice, however, justice is not always fair. Sometimes justice peeks through her blindfold and tips her scales on the basis of age, race, sex, and class.

As we discussed in Chapters 7 and 8, crime and juvenile delinquency are two of our gravest social problems. Very much related to these two problems is our highly controversial and crisis ridden system of criminal justice. We have so many problems with our system of criminal justice because it is not always just; the decisions of police officers, judges and juries, and penal officials are sometimes arbitrary and discriminatory. Because we all seek to solve the problems of crime and criminal justice, we are all advocates of "law and order."[1]

In this chapter, we will examine the problematic aspects of criminal justice; that is, we will look at our criminal justice system from a social problems perspective as a social institution in crisis.

Outline of the Criminal Justice System

Perhaps the best way to understand the problems of criminal justice in our country is to follow a fictitious individual through the criminal justice system. As we saw in Chapter 8, the typical criminal is a white, lower-class male in his 20s. In the following sections of this chapter, we will look at what happens to this young man as he comes into contact with the police, the courts, and the penal system.

As Figure 16.1 (pp. 456–457) indicates, progress through the criminal justice system is not a series of totally unrelated steps. Rather, the decisions made by the police will determine whether our typical criminal will go to court and what offense he will be charged with. In turn, decisions made by prosecutors, defense attorneys, and the court will determine whether he will go free, be placed on probation, or be incarcerated. Finally, the decisions made by the court will influence how prison officials treat him and whether he will be paroled.

The criminal justice system is extremely complex and we cannot possibly cover all the things that can happen to our typical criminal between the time he becomes a suspect through the time that he is either found not guilty and released or found guilty and punished. But we will attempt to give a general impression of how the system operates, and at times we will digress to consider what might happen to our typical criminal if he happened to be a woman, a black, a minor, or rich.[2]

The Suspect and the Police

Our typical criminal's first contact with the system is with the police. The police may actually see him commit a crime or they may suspect him of committing a crime which someone else has reported. He may also come into contact with the police because his local police department has a policy of aggressive, preventive patrol (stopping people on the streets to gather information, to confiscate weapons or drugs, or even to harass them). This policy often leads to arrests for investigation or suspicion. Aggressive, preventive patrol tactics also include roadblocks designed to catch drunk drivers.[3]

A criminal's first contact with the criminal justice system is with the police. The police may actually see him commit a crime or they may suspect him of committing a crime which someone else has reported.

Police Discretion

Even though it is clear that a law has been violated, our young criminal might not be arrested. The police exercise tremendous discretion in deciding who to arrest and who not to arrest.[4] There are many reasons why the police might decide not to arrest a

Figure 16.1 **Outline of the Criminal Justice System**

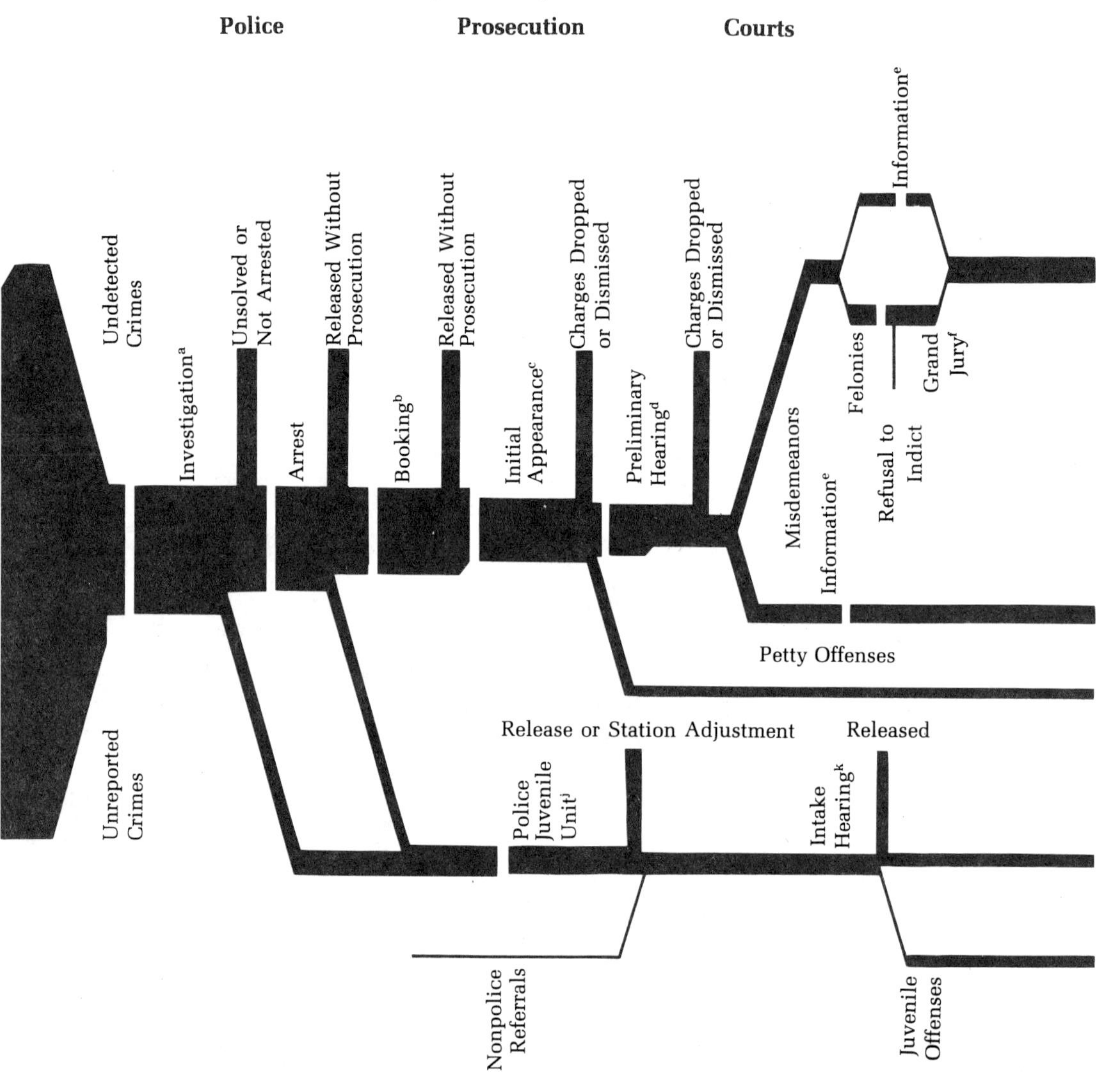

[a]May continue until trial.

[b]Administrative record of arrest. First step at which temporary release on bail may be available.

[c]Before magistrate, commissioner, or justice of peace. Formal notice of charge, advice of rights. Bail set. Summary trials for petty offenses usually conducted here without further processing.

[d]Preliminary testing of evidence against defendant. Charge may be reduced. No separate preliminary hearing for misdemeanors in some systems.

[e]Charge filed by prosecution on basis of information supplied by police or citizens. Alternative to grand jury indictment; often used in felonies, almost always in misdemeanors.

[f]Reviews whether government evidence sufficient to justify trial. Some states have no grand jury system; others seldom use it.

SOURCE: President's Commission on Law Enforcement and Administration of Justice, *The Challenge of Crime in a Free Society* (Washington, D.C.: U.S. Government Printing Office, 1967), pp. 8–9.

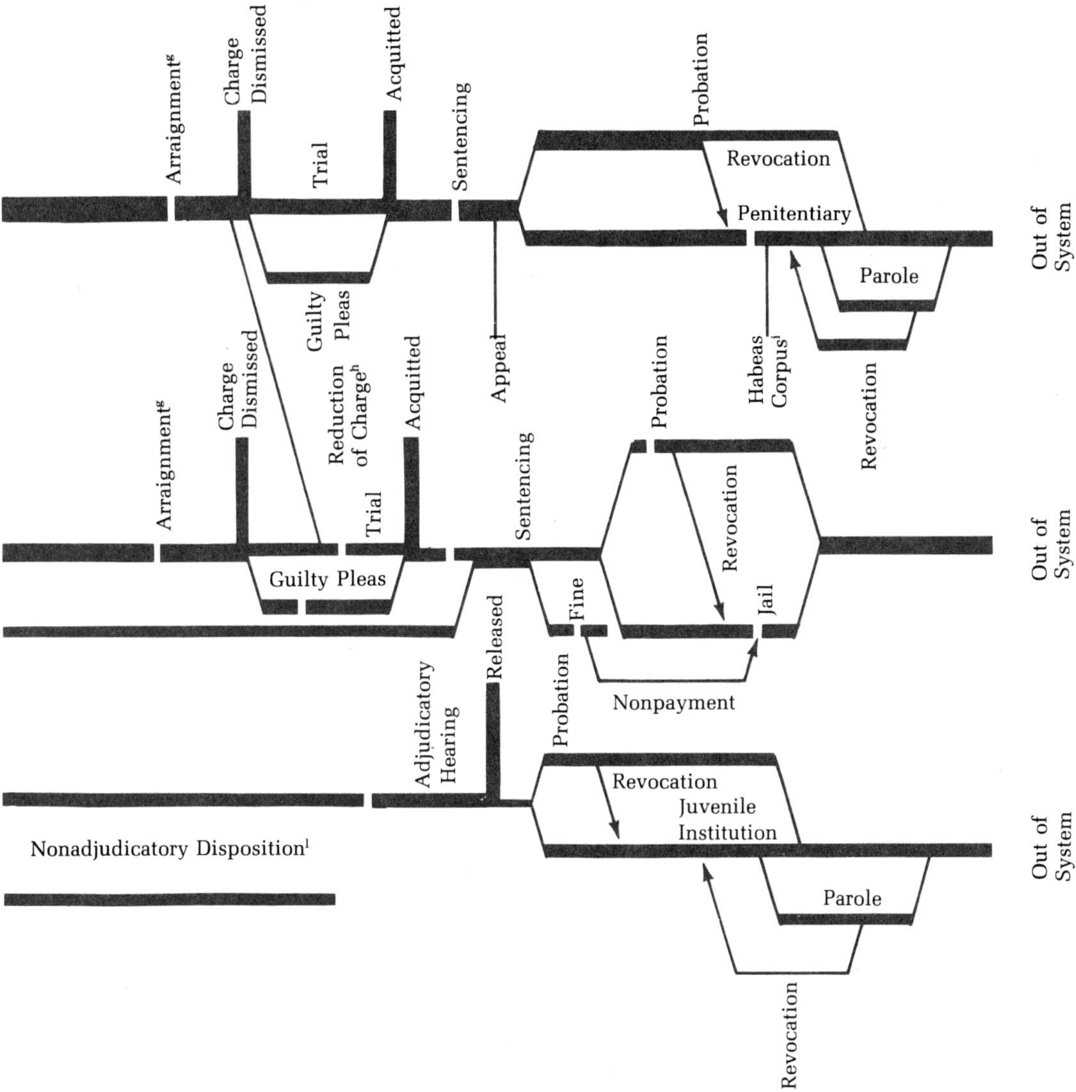

[g]Appearance for plea; defendant elects trial by judge or jury (if available); counsel for indigent usually appointed here in felonies. Often not at all in other cases.

[h]Charge may be reduced at any time prior to trial in return for plea of guilty or for other reasons.

[i]Challenge on constitutional grounds to legality of detention. May be sought at any point in process.

[j]Police often hold informal hearings, dismiss or adjust many cases without further processing.

[k]Probation officer decides desirability of further court action.

[l]Welfare agency, social services, counseling, medical care, etc., for cases where adjudicatory handling not needed.

person, even one who has clearly broken the law. In deciding whether to make an arrest, the officer may ask:

> Has anyone been hurt or deprived? Will anyone be hurt or deprived if I do nothing? Will an arrest improve the situation or only make matters worse? Is a complaint more likely if there is no arrest, or if there is an arrest? What does the sergeant expect of me? Am I getting near the end of my tour of duty? Will I have to go to court on my day off? If I do appear in court, will the charge stand up or will it be withdrawn or dismissed by the prosecutor? Will my partner think that an arrest shows I can handle things or that I can't handle things? What will the guy do if I let him go?[5]

The officer may also feel that the law is not worth enforcing or that the costs of enforcement are greater than the costs of nonenforcement. For example, our typical criminal might not be arrested for a relatively minor offense if he is a physician, professor, or teacher because the officer recognizes the tremendous damage that arrest would do to his reputation. Or, the officer may not make an arrest in the hope that our criminal will become an informer. Informers are often used to lead the police to big-time criminals or to obtain information.[6]

Finally, our criminal's demeanor may influence whether he is arrested or not, particularly if he is a juvenile. Several studies have shown that the police are less likely to take a juvenile into custody if the youth is polite and cooperative rather than surly and impudent.[7]

Technically, the police do not have the authority to decide who to arrest and who not to arrest—it is their duty to enforce all laws regardless of their personal feelings about the law or about the violator. This, however, is clearly not always feasible. Some laws are unenforceable. For example, it would be absurd for the police to suddenly arrest everyone caught selling or buying merchandise on Sunday in a city or state with Sunday blue laws. In many cases, the costs of making an arrest may simply be too high. For example, although most states outlaw gambling, penny-ante poker games are a common form of Friday-night recreation. A great deal of damage could be done if the otherwise law-abiding citizens who participate in these games were arrested and turned into criminals; and the costs and time involved in processing their cases would be tremendous.

At times, however, police discretion can be used as a tool of discrimination. Because of police discretion, the black and the poor are more likely to be arrested than the white and the rich, the uncooperative person is more likely to be taken in than the cooperative person. Thus, although a certain amount of police discretion is inevitable, the conditions under which an officer can exercise discretion should be spelled out precisely.[8]

Police Brutality and Abuse

Sometimes a police officer must use force to restrain a suspect or to protect himself or innocent citizens. However, most of us would agree that the police should never use physical brutality to teach suspects a lesson, to harass them, or in the hope of gaining their "respect." Brutality for the sake of brutality is a gross misuse of the authority society delegates to the police.

There is little agreement in the literature as to the extent of police brutality. One author reports that "there is little, if any, police brutality in an enlightened police agency today."[9] But another found that "in major metropolitan areas the sort of behavior commonly called police brutality is far from rare."[10] The latter also found that blacks are apparently no more likely to be the victims of police brutality than whites.[11]

Verbal abuse of suspects is probably much more common than physical brutality. Most often, verbal abuse is aimed at minority groups or at individuals whom officers consider deviant. A drunken person may be addressed as a bum, a woman walking alone may be called a whore. Even when officers do not use obscene or derogatory language, they may treat the suspect in a degrading manner.[12] In any case, our typical criminal might well be abused in some way by the police.

Wherever they occur, physical brutality and verbal abuse place tremendous strains on police-community relations. They also make police officers' jobs much more difficult: citizens can hardly be expected to respect the police if they suspect that the police do not respect them.

Understanding Police Behavior

Not all police officers, of course, are arbitrary, brutal, and abusive. In fact, most police officers perform their duties efficiently, courteously, and according to the ethics of their profession. And when the police do resort to brutality or abuse their discretionary powers, their behavior can often be understood within the context of the occupational role they play. To understand brutality, however, is not to excuse or justify it.

One key to understanding police behavior is to appreciate the fact that the police are constantly in the public eye. This is undoubtedly the basis for some of their discretionary practices. For example, if the police arrest a surly black youth or a skid row drunk, nobody is likely to complain; in fact, the police may even be praised for their diligence in enforcing the law. But if they arrest a surly graduate student or the drunken daughter of a prominent local businessman, they may incur the wrath of the entire community and be pressured to "use some discretion."

Furthermore, the police often encounter considerable hostility in their work. Certainly, the inhabitants of ghettos and slum neighborhoods tend to be extremely hostile toward the police, and even middle-class citizens may deeply resent police officers for writing out parking or traffic tickets.[13] Greeted with hostility, most of us tend to react with hostility. This is as true of the police officer as it is of anyone else.

The police are also under constant pressure to be efficient.[14] For example, the victims of our young criminal's actions may feel that it is more efficient for the police to knock him senseless than to courteously read him his rights and take him to the station for booking.

In large cities, the police are socialized to be suspicious. They are taught to be suspicious of persons who are in places where they do not seem to belong, who are inexplicably at the scene of a crime, who loiter around school yards or shopping centers, and so forth.[15] As a result, some officers may approach people with hostility and contempt.

Finally, police work is dangerous. Many officers function in a climate of violence—muggings, aggravated assaults, rapes, and murders. Thus, it should not be surprising that a few officers become cynical and violent themselves.

After his arrest, our typical criminal is fingerprinted and booked. ▶

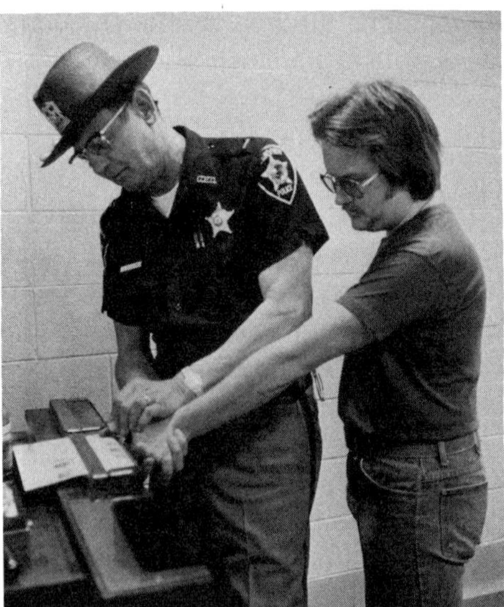

Processing the Defendant

Let us assume that our typical criminal has been arrested and is about to be processed through the court system; his troubles have just begun. Depending upon how far his case proceeds and the seriousness of his offense, he may face an extremely complicated judicial process that includes setting bail, several preliminary court appearances, a grand jury indictment, a trial, and one or more appearances for sentencing. Although difficulties and inequities can appear at any point in this complicated judicial process, they are most likely to occur at the time bail is set, in the legal maneuverings which precede the trial, in the trial itself, and during sentencing.

Setting Bail

Unless he has committed a very serious crime such as kidnapping or murder, our typical criminal is entitled to be released on bail shortly after he is arrested. The primary purpose of bail is to motivate the defendant to appear at later court proceedings. If our criminal fails to appear, he forfeits his bail and, therefore, loses his money. His bail can be set at almost any sum the judge feels is sufficient to motivate him to appear in court; in our case let us say that bail is set at $1,000.

But our defendant, like most defendants, does not have money for bail. Here the bail bondsman enters the picture. For a nonrefundable fee of at least 10 to 15 percent, the bail bondsman guarantees that our defendant's bail will be paid if he fails to appear in court. So our defendant owes the bail bondsman at least $100 to $150 in return for guaranteeing that his bail will be paid—if he fails to appear in court.

The practice of setting bail can be used as a form of preventive detention—as a means of keeping the defendant in confinement until the case is decided in court. Within limits, judges can set bail as high as they see fit. So, if the judge decides that our criminal should be held in confinement, the judge can set bail so high that he cannot possibly bail himself out or afford to pay a bail bondsman.

The judge may use bail to detain a defendant for several reasons. In some cases, the judge may have reason to think that the person must be kept in confinement to ensure appearance in court or to protect the community. In other cases, however, the judge may set excessively high bails to detain people who offend his conception of morality or against whom he and his community are prejudiced. In these latter cases, using bail for preventive detention is clearly discriminatory.

Posting bail and remaining free while awaiting trial has several obvious advantages for any individual. But our defendant is poor and may not be able to afford even $100 to $150 for the bail bond; thus, the practice of requiring a monetary deposit as a condition for pretrial release can be grossly discriminatory. If he cannot bail himself out, our defendant may be held in jail and treated as a prisoner even though innocent of the crime in question. This is a serious problem because sometimes weeks or even months elapse between the time a person is arrested and guilt or innocence is established. A study of seventy-one persons who were not released on bail and were eventually found not guilty revealed that twenty were detained in jail for two months or less, thirteen for over three months, and "five of those not convicted . . . served jail terms of six months or more although found guilty of nothing."[16]

Furthermore, defendants who are unable to afford bail are more likely to be found guilty than those who can afford bail. Often imprisoned defendants cannot help to prepare their defense.

> Tracking down ordinary defense witnesses in the slums to support the defendant's alibi or to act as character witnesses often has a Runyonesque aspect to it. The defendant in jail tells his counsel he has known the witnesses for years but only by the names of "Toothpick," "Malachi Joe," or "Jet." He does not know where they live or if they have a phone. If he could get out and look himself, he is sure he could find them at the old haunts, but his descriptive facilities leave something to be desired.[17]

In addition, people who cannot afford bail are usually from the social classes and racial groups that are most likely to experience discrimination throughout their processing by the judicial system. Our typical criminal may well not be able to afford counsel of his own choosing and may not be able to coherently testify on his own behalf.

Since bail procedures can discriminate against the poor, the disadvantaged, and the unpopular, other methods of ensuring the defendant's appearance in court have been tried. For example, the Manhattan Bail Project has amply demonstrated that people can be safely released on their own recognizance.[18] This means that defendants are not required to post monetary bail; rather, they sign a promissory note guaranteeing that they will appear in court at the appropriate time. In the Bail Project, defendants were released on the basis of interviews concerning their family ties and involvement in the community. The Manhattan experiment concluded that the "available evidence at least suggests that the financial deterrent to flight has been overrated and that other factors—ties to the community—are really the effective deterrents."[19] In fact, it was found that persons released on their own recognizance are *more* likely to appear in court than persons released on bail.[20] These results suggest that many defendants who are now being held in jail because they cannot afford bail could be safely released if the courts would take the time to find out whether they are committed to jobs, families, and communities. Persons with these kinds of commitments are not likely to fail to appear in court.

Arraignment

Our typical criminal's next big step in the criminal justice process is the arraignment, when he enters his plea. He has several options, but his most important choice is whether to plead guilty or not guilty.

▲
Our typical criminal's next big step in the criminal justice process is the arraignment, when he enters his plea. He has several options, but his most important choice is whether to plead guilty or not guilty.

About 90 percent of those persons accused of committing a crime plead guilty.[21] Some plead guilty because, guilty or not, they know the prosecution has a strong case against them and because they know that they have little or no chance of being acquitted. However, in many cases the guilty plea is the result of a bargaining process between the prosecutor, the defendant, and the defense attorney. This process is often termed plea bargaining, copping a plea, or bargain-basement justice.

Plea bargaining can take at least four forms.[22] First, the defendant may agree to plead guilty if the prosecutor agrees to reduce the charges. For example, a defendant might plead guilty if the prosecutor reduces the charge from murder to involuntary manslaughter. Second, the defendant may enter a guilty plea in exchange for a promise of leniency in sentencing. Third, the defendant may enter a guilty plea if the prosecutor promises to recommend that the defendant be allowed to serve sentences concurrently. If, for example, the defendant is charged with robbery, auto theft, and possession of a deadly weapon, the prosecutor might recommend that the defendant be allowed to serve one sentence for all three crimes. Finally, the defendant may agree to plead guilty if the prosecutor agrees to charge the defendant only with the most serious offense and to drop the other charges. For example, if the defendant committed auto theft in the course of an armed robbery, the prosecutor might agree to drop the charge of auto theft in exchange for a guilty plea.

Plea bargaining is tolerated because it can work to the advantage of everybody—the prosecuting attorney, the defense attorney, the defendant, and the court. Plea bargaining may enable the prosecuting attorney to get convictions that might not otherwise be possible. It can also work to the advantage of the defense attorney, especially a court-appointed defense attorney who receives only a small fee for representing the defendant. Plea bargaining allows the defense attorney to dispose of the case in a minimum amount of time and to return to a more lucrative private practice.

Plea bargaining can work to our defendant's advantage if he is obviously guilty and has little or no chance of being acquitted. Through plea bargaining he can negotiate a lighter sentence than if he were prosecuted to the fullest extent of the law and found guilty.

Plea bargaining can also definitely work to the advantage of the court. Our court system is so understaffed and poorly financed that it would collapse if every defendant demanded a jury trial. There would not be enough judges, prosecutors, and other court staff to handle the load. The judge "also has a vested interest in a high rate of negotiated pleas. . . . He sees an impossible backlog of cases, with their mounting delays, as possible public evidence of his 'inefficiency' and failure."[23]

Plea bargaining may have its benefits, but it nonetheless mocks the idea of equal justice for all. For example, how many innocent people are conned into pleading guilty by prosecuting or defense attorneys who use plea bargaining unethically? Plea bargaining also works as a form of discrimination against the unseasoned, first offender. The seasoned criminal knows how to use plea bargaining to get a light sentence. But the first offender does not know how to bargain or may refuse to bargain at all and may "get the book thrown at him."[24]

Finally, plea bargaining may encourage a general disrespect for the law. In theory, under our criminal justice system, a person is found guilty and punished only after a thorough and rigorous court trial—a person is presumed innocent until proven guilty. In practice, however, the person is often found guilty as the result of negotiations conducted in the prosecutor's office or a back room of the courthouse.

On Trial

If our defendant pleads not guilty, his next major step in the criminal justice process is the trial. Many factors will influence the outcome of his trial, including his demeanor, the nature of his offense, and the attitude of the presiding judge. However, two of the most important factors are the quality of his legal representation and whether he chooses to have a trial by jury.

Many factors will influence the outcome of our criminal's trial, including whether or not he chooses to have a trial by jury.
◀

The cornerstone of our trial system is the *adversary process.* Every major criminal trial has two attorneys—the prosecuting attorney and the defense attorney. The prosecuting attorney's job is to present all the evidence that tends to incriminate the defendant, while the defense attorney's job is to present all the evidence that supports the defendant's claim of innocence. The idea is that through the process of calling and cross-examining witnesses, through the defense attorney's attempts to discredit the evidence and arguments of the prosecuting attorney, and vice versa, the truth will emerge.

For the adversary system to work well, the defense attorney must be at least as competent, if not more competent, than the prosecuting attorney. Thus, our young, impoverished defendant is less likely to be acquitted than an affluent defendant is. Poor

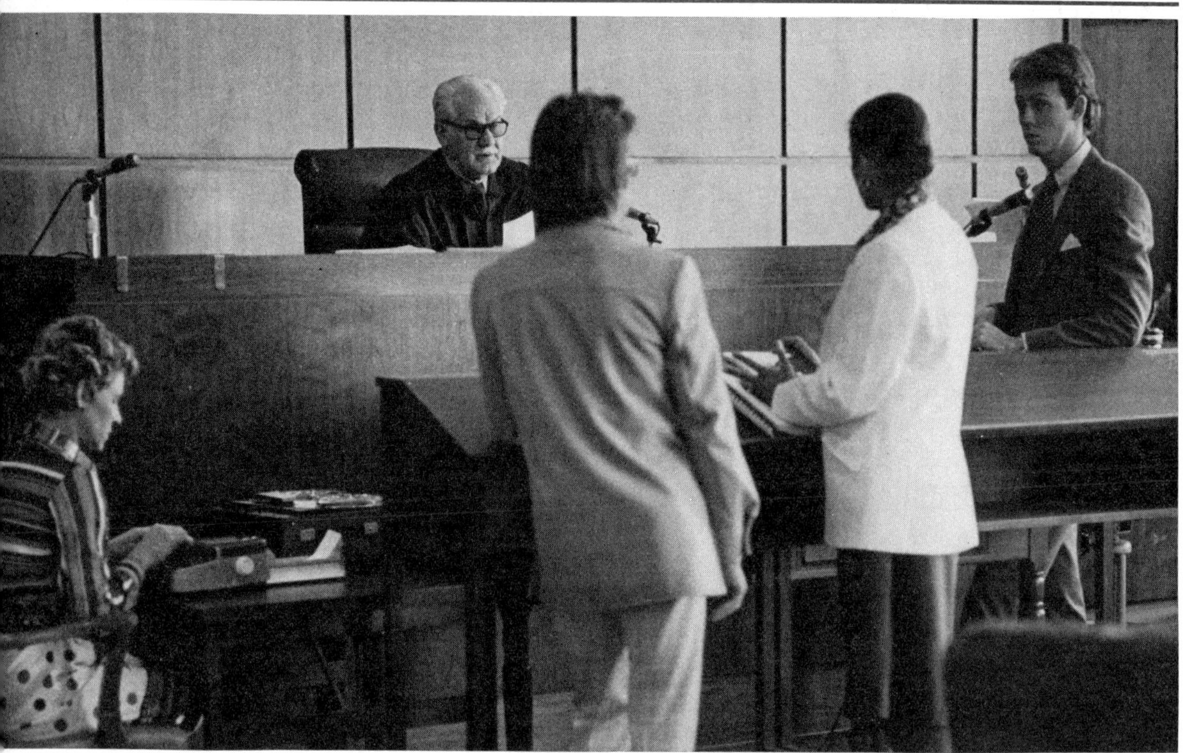

▲
The cornerstone of our trial system is the adversary process. Every major criminal trial has two attorneys—the prosecuting attorney *(right)* and the defense attorney *(second from right)*.

people cannot afford to retain private counsel and the counsel assigned to them by the court may be inexperienced, overworked, underpaid, and not motivated to give the case the best effort.[25]

However, a study of all felony cases (5,579 indictments) processed in Cook County, Illinois, in 1964 found that the relationship between type of counsel and the likelihood of conviction is rather complicated.[26] In bench trials (before a judge only), 55 percent of the defendants represented by public defenders and 48 percent of the defendants represented by volunteers from the Bar Association were acquitted of the charges against them, contrasted with only 20 percent of the defendants represented by private attorneys. In jury trials, the picture changed dramatically—18 percent of the defendants represented by public defenders were acquitted but 30 percent of the defendants represented by private counsel were acquitted.

At first glance, this study suggests that poverty does not have much to do with whether a defendant is found guilty or innocent. However, one reason why the public defenders have reasonably high rates of acquittal is because they only take safe cases to court. In fact, 75.4 percent of the cases handled by the public defender were disposed of through guilty pleas, but only 53.0 percent of the cases handled by private attorneys were disposed of in this manner. In other words, the public defender who was not fairly certain of winning the case advised the defendant to plead guilty. But even though the relationship between type of counsel and the likelihood of acquittal is a complicated one, we would have to agree with the assertion that "there is considerable evidence to suggest that neither the assigned counsel nor public defender system as now constituted is capable of providing adequate service to the indigent accused." [27] The defendant who is represented by assigned counsel or a public defender is more likely to be pushed into pleading guilty. At the same time, he or she is less likely to benefit from exercising his or her right to a trial by jury because the assigned counsel or public defender does not have a great deal to gain by presenting a vigorous defense.

If our defendant is charged with a felony, he is entitled to a trial by jury. However, as indicated above, it might be to his advantage to waive this right in favor of a bench trial. For example, in Cook County, Illinois, defendants represented by public defenders had much higher rates of acquittal in bench trials than in jury trials; and, by contrast, defendants represented by private counsel did better in jury trials than bench trials. There are two possible reasons for this disparity. First, privately retained attorneys may be more experienced in manipulating juries and may know how to play on their sympathies. Second, and more important, the public defender usually represents people the typical juror might be prejudiced against; that is, the poor, the black, and other disadvantaged minority groups. One unwritten rule among trial lawyers is to demand a trial by jury if the client is white, well educated, and affluent; a person who is black, illiterate, poor, and shabby usually fares better before a judge alone.

The jury system has been the target of endless controversy, and one of its most vocal critics was the late Jerome Frank.[28] In a careful, well-reasoned argument, Frank contended that juries can neither comprehend the facts involved in a complicated court case nor apply the appropriate legal rules and reasoning to those facts. As a result, jury decisions are sometimes arbitrary and capricious.

However, studies have found that in most cases the jury hands down the same decision that the presiding judge would hand down trying the case alone in a bench trial.[29] For example, in 95 percent of the cases in which the judge would acquit the defendant, the jury actually did acquit. In cases where a major difference was found between the decision which the judge would render in a bench trial and the decision actually reached by the jury, the judge would have convicted the defendant, but the juries acquitted the defendant 46 percent of the time. In cases where the facts and legal issues were fuzzy, the juries appeared to be more lenient than the judges.

Jerome Frank was undoubtedly correct when he argued that juries are ill suited either to determine the facts of a case or to apply the appropriate legal rules and reasoning to these facts. At the same time, juries do not appear to perpetrate gross injustices. We could have a sound judicial system without having juries, but juries do not prevent the defendant from receiving a fair trial. It is true that juries are probably more likely to convict the poor and individuals from disadvantaged minority groups than they are to convict white middle- or upper-class citizens, but the same may be true of judges.

Sentencing

If our typical defendant pleads or is found guilty and does not appeal his case, his final contact with the court is for sentencing. Very few crimes carry a mandatory, fixed sentence. Rather, the judge usually has the discretion to suspend the sentence, place the defendant on probation, impose a fine, or order an indeterminate sentence (for example, one to five years). The last, in effect, relieves the judge of determining the exact length of time to be served and assigns this responsibility instead to a parole board. Given all these options, gross discrimination could easily enter

If our typical defendant is found guilty and does not appeal his case, his final contact with the court is for sentencing. ▼

into the sentencing process, particularly if our typical defendant were black.

But it is difficult to prove that gross discrimination does exist. One widely quoted study concluded that there is "no warrant for the charge of racial discrimination in sentencing."[30] Another study of assault and larceny cases found that "of those actually imprisoned, the Negro defendants (particularly in larceny cases) tend to receive lighter sentences."[31] However, these findings and conclusions must be interpreted with extreme caution, and in light of the following three other findings.

First, the stiffest sentences are meted out to blacks who commit crimes against whites; less severe sentences are meted out to blacks who commit crimes against other blacks.[32] The court apparently often adopts the attitude that how blacks treat other blacks is their own business. These findings pertain only to the crimes of burglary and robbery, and for various reasons blacks are perhaps more likely to rob or burglarize other blacks than they are whites. Thus, blacks may appear to receive lighter sentences than whites if the court "adopts an indulgent attitude toward the Negro who robs a Negro."[33]

Second, black persons are more likely to be prosecuted for relatively minor offenses than white persons. When the alleged offense is a relatively minor one, the white person is often able to have the charges dropped. So it is possible that whites who are processed through the court system are charged, on the whole, with more serious crimes than blacks. This too would contribute to the illusion that blacks receive lighter sentences than whites.

Third, blacks and the poor in general are more likely to enter into or be forced into plea bargaining, and defendants who do bargain are more likely to receive relatively light sentences than defendants who refuse to plead guilty. One obvious reason for entering into plea bargaining is to receive a light sentence, and judges tend to be lenient with those who plead guilty. "Many judges give a less severe sentence to a defendant who has negotiated a plea than to one who has been convicted of the same offense after a trial."[34] In addition, "sometimes the judge throws his weight behind the effort to induce a defendant to plead guilty by suggesting that more severe punishment may be imposed if the accused insists on his right to a trial."[35] The fact that blacks and the poor in general engage more frequently in plea bargaining again contributes to the illusion that they are not discriminated against in length of sentence.

Even though blacks do not appear to receive particularly long sentences, they have been grossly discriminated against in one area of sentencing—the death penalty. When the death sentence was widely used, it was much more likely to be imposed on the black than on the white offender. "A close examination of statistics seems to confirm another argument of abolitionists: that the death penalty operates primarily against the poor, the lower classes, and the socially deprived ethnic and racial groups."[36] This is why the Supreme Court ruled in 1972 that the death penalty is unconstitutional unless it is mandatory for the crime in question. In other words, if a state has the death penalty for kidnapping, it must apply to all persons convicted of kidnapping, regardless of their age, race, sex, and socioeconomic status.

Discrimination can be interpreted in many ways. For example, as we have seen, blacks who commit crimes against other blacks receive lighter sentences than blacks who commit crimes against whites. This could be interpreted as discrimination against the black victim. A study of grand larceny and felonious assault cases found that female defendants are considerably more likely than male defendants to have their cases dismissed or acquitted, or to receive suspended or probated sentences: "To the extent that male and female larceny and assault cases are comparable, the data suggest that the difference in treatment may be explained by a judicial attitude which assumes women . . . to be weaker, and therefore more likely to be harmed by pretrial and postconviction jailing."[37] Does this judicial attitude imply that women are discriminated against because they are not treated as harshly as men, or that men are discriminated against because they are not treated as leniently as women?

In summary, the length and type of sentence our typical defendant receives depends on his own race and sex and on the race of his victim. However, discrimination can occur at any point in the judicial process—arrest, bail, arraignment; and it just may be that less discrimination occurs in sentencing than at other points in the criminal justice process.

The Juvenile in Court

So far, this chapter has followed an adult offender through the criminal justice system. However, every year large numbers of juveniles are also processed through the court system. How would things differ if our typical defendant were a juvenile?

The juvenile court operates much differently than the adult criminal court. But it does have at least one characteristic in common with the criminal court—it too is riddled with crisis and controversy.

Juvenile Justice

The practice of treating juvenile offenders differently from adult offenders dates back only to the turn of this century.[38] By 1900, juvenile courts had been established in several states; and it was widely believed that they should deal with the needs of children. The goal of the juvenile courts was to rehabilitate children and not simply punish them.

To achieve rehabilitation, juvenile court judges were given two powers never extended to judges in adult criminal court. First, judges were authorized to conduct the juvenile hearing in an informal, noncriminal manner. The goal of rehabilitating the child was thought to be best served in an atmosphere free of haggling lawyers, gaping spectators, and scrutinizing jurors. Second, juvenile court judges were given a great deal of freedom in deciding how to dispose of cases. Juvenile justice is individualized in the sense that the judge can tailor treatment programs to meet the particular needs of each child. The result of these two changes was to convert the juvenile court into a combination legal institution and social service agency, with emphasis on the latter.

Although the idea that juvenile offenders should be treated rather than punished is laudable, the accompanying flexibility built into the juvenile court system led to tremendous abuses as many juvenile court judges completely lost sight of the basic constitutional rights and liberties of juveniles.

These constitutional abuses eventually led to the case of *Gault v. Arizona*, decided by the Supreme Court in May 1967.[39] In this case, 16-year-old Gerald Gault was sentenced to six years in an Arizona state industrial school for allegedly making an obscene telephone call to a neighbor. Young Gault was not fully informed of the charges against him, was not allowed to cross-examine the woman he had supposedly called, and was not represented by an attorney. But young Gault and his parents had one advantage—they were able to appeal Gerald's case to the Supreme Court.

In ruling on this case, " the U.S. Supreme Court found that the juvenile court in Arizona—and by implication the great majority of courts—were procedurally unfair."[40] In short, Gerald Gault had been denied due process of law. The Court ruled that children and their parents have a right to written notice of the charges against them, that children have a right to counsel, that children or their attorneys have the right to confront and cross-examine accusers, and that children cannot be forced to make any statements that might incriminate them.[41] It is still rather early to determine the full impact of the Gault decision on juvenile cases. But one writer indicates that his "research has shown that cases with attorneys are more likely to be dismissed, less likely to result in wardship, and more likely to end in a suspended sentence than cases without an attorney."[42]

The Gault decision, however, dealt only with juvenile court procedures, not with the substantive aspects of juvenile justice. For example, the justice system has much more latitude to intervene in a defendant's life if he or she is a child rather than an adult. As we saw in Chapter 7, juveniles can be declared delinquent if they commit a misdemeanor or felony or if they engage in patterns of behavior which, even though not technically illegal, constitute a threat to themselves or to other people. The latter are often referred to as *juvenile status offenses* and include, for example, incorrigibility, sexual misconduct or experimentation, and running away. "Most Americans are probably unaware that juveniles are subject to stricter laws than adults, and to more severe penalties for noncriminal acts than are many adults who commit misdemeanors and felonies."[43]

Furthermore, the juvenile court judge has exceptionally wide latitude in deciding how to dispose of juvenile cases. Gerald Gault, for example, almost spent six years in an industrial school for making an obscene telephone call. In most states, the maximum penalty an adult could receive for making such a call would be one year in jail and/or a relatively small fine.

The juvenile court judge is also empowered, even on relatively minor offenses, to remove our typical juvenile delinquent from the custody of his parents and to place him in a foster home. This power is important because our society considers the parent-child relationship a very special one—we believe that children have a basic right to be with their parents. Certainly judges should exercise this power with great discretion.

Juvenile Justice Reform

At least one major proposal has been made for reforming juvenile justice. This proposal grows out of the realization that being labeled delinquent is tremendously stigmatizing for a child. Even though it is not on the public record that a court finds a child delinquent, the word gets out nonetheless and can have an adverse affect on his or her relationship with parents, teachers, and peers. He or she is also likely to be under constant police scrutiny. Employability might be affected as might eligibility to join the armed forces. Perhaps most importantly, our youth may begin to perceive himself as a "bad egg" and start to associate with other children who are seriously delinquent.

Because labeling has so many bad effects, it has been suggested that many children who are now being processed through the juvenile court, especially juvenile status offenders, could be diverted into other treatment programs. Surely well-staffed school and child guidance centers, child welfare agencies, and even juvenile divisions within police departments could develop programs to deal effectively with youthful offenses such as incorrigibility, sexual experimentation, truancy, and running away. The youth would thus not be saddled with the stigma of having been found delinquent. As one writer puts it. "Since the powers of the juvenile court are extraordinary, properly it should deal with extraordinary cases."[44] He goes on to point out that "law operates by punishment, injunction against specific acts, specific redress, and substitutional redress. It cannot by such means make a father good, a mother moral, or a youth respectful of authority."[45]

In addition, more limits should be placed on the discretionary authority of juvenile court judges. These limits should probably be reasonably broad—judges do need flexible treatment options. But it is grossly unreasonable that a young person could be incarcerated for six years for an offense for which an adult might be sentenced to only a small fine or a year in jail. Even more questionable is whether children should be incarcerated for offenses for which adults cannot even be tried. Age-related discriminatory treatment of this type can only make young offenders hostile toward the law.

Finally, the conditions under which a juvenile court judge can remove children from the custody of their parents should be clearly specified. This decision has serious implications for both the child and the family. It also raises a profound legal question: To what extent does the legal system have a right to inquire into and interfere with individual families?

The Criminal in Prison

Over half of all convicted offenders are placed on probation.[46] However, next to the death penalty, imprisonment is our society's harshest form of criminal punishment. It is at the core of our approach to dealing with crime and the criminal.

Imprisonment

Our typical criminal is sent to prison for several reasons. First, we imprison him to take him out of circulation for a while; while he is in prison, he cannot commit new crimes. Second, we imprison him to gain revenge and retribution. The idea that criminals must pay for their offenses is still strong in our society; and, unquestionably, prison is painful. "The physical deprivations in prison are overwhelming, and having all the everyday freedoms with-

Social Problems and You

Let the Punishment Fit the Crime

When a thief in Chicago stole a motorcycle, the press reported, the victim, who knew the thief, was not particularly interested in seeing the thief punished, just in getting his motorcycle back. By the time the police caught the thief, he had sold the motorcycle. He received a suspended sentence. The victim was told he would have to sue the thief if he wanted his money back.

What is wrong with this story? It does not satisfy our sense of justice because justice means that everyone gets what he deserves. Justice should mean helping victims as well as punishing offenders. This story and our criminal justice system ignore the problem of restoring fairness for victims as a principle of justice.

We set two primary goals for our criminal penalties. We want them to deter crime and we want them to rehabilitate criminals. In theory these two goals should go together, since they amount to saying that we want to keep crime from happening in the first place, through deterrence, and to keep crime from happening again, through rehabilitation.

In practice these two goals seem incompatible, since the harsh penalties that might work as deterrence offer little hope for rehabilitation, while the supportive treatments that might work as rehabilitation seem inadequate as deterrents.

Curiously, however, neither deterring crime nor rehabilitating offenders are principles of justice. Our sense of justice requires that penalties be proportionate to their crimes.

Suppose we took restoring fairness as the first principle of our criminal justice system instead of either deterrence or rehabilitation. What would such a system look like?

Simply put, offenders would be given sentences whose purpose, in the end, was to restore both the loss that the victims had suffered and the loss that society suffered through its investment in preventing, detecting, and punishing crimes. Where possible, this could involve labor directly related to recovering property, repairing damage, or making streets safer. More generally, it might involve contributing earnings from specified tasks to a general fund whose purpose was to compensate victims.

In informal systems, where victims and offenders are known to one another, restoring fairness is the common penalty that satisfies all concerned and preserves the social bond. It is typical of penalties that are meted out in healthy families. . . .

Although not widely known, laws for victim compensation have been enacted in a number of countries (including England and New Zealand) and a growing number of states (including New York and California), while experimental programs for offender restitution are underway in Georgia, Iowa, and Minnesota. Preliminary results are encouraging, but they represent only a beginning. Much remains to be learned about tailoring sentences to both society's needs and offenders' capacities, and we have yet to work out how to allow prisoners to work without threatening jobs for anyone outside prison. These are reasonable tasks for social science and social policy. It is unreasonable to leave the field of criminal justice to the bankrupt debate between deterrence and rehabilitation.

SOURCE: Philip Brickman, "Let the Punishment Fit the Crime," *Psychology Today*, 10 (May, 1977), p. 29.

drawn is also an attack against the foundations of one's sense of being."[47] Third, we imprison him to deter others; if other people see criminals suffering severe deprivations, we hope that they may be discouraged from committing crimes. Finally, we imprison him to reform him; we hope prison can turn him into a law-abiding citizen.

There is much disagreement about the extent to which prisons succeed in reforming criminals. One study indicates that most police chiefs, judges, wardens, and criminologists think that "between 60 and 70 percent of the men who leave prison come back for new crimes."[48] However, this same study actually found lower rates of recidivism, concluding that about 35 percent of offenders come back.[49] Another study argues that imprisonment is not very effective as a rehabilitative device and cites statistics that 80 to 85 percent of offenders admitted to prison have been in prison before.[50] Despite these conflicting figures, one fact is clear—at least one-third, and probably nearer two-thirds or more, of the individuals released from prison commit further crimes.

There are many reasons why imprisonment is not a very effective method of reforming our typical criminal. One is that our prisons are not conducive to rehabilitation. For example, most of our prisons are severely overcrowded and understaffed. This means that individual treatment programs must be sacrificed in the interest of maintaining order and keeping the prison system going on a day-to-day basis. If our prisons were truly designed to change the lawbreaker, a tailor-made program of treatment would have to be developed for every inmate. For example, a treatment program that would benefit our typical criminal might be no help to the man in the next cell. As things stand today, however, most prisons can operate only if every prisoner follows the same daily routine and if work assignments and other potentially constructive activities are devised and assigned on the basis of the needs of the system rather than the needs of the individual.

Another important reason why prison fails to rehabilitate is the prison subculture that is part of every prison.[51] This subculture helps our typical criminal cope with prison life but it also instills values in him which could prevent him from becoming a law-abiding citizen after his release. Like most subcultures, the prison subculture is extremely complex. It emphasizes manipulation and the use of other people to achieve personal goals—prison bywords are "be shrewd" and "play it cool." The prison subculture also fosters a disdain for authority. Prison personnel are the targets of suspicion and distrust and in a conflict situation are automatically considered to be in the wrong.[52] Finally, the prison subculture views society as an army of hypocrites who cannot be trusted. Clearly, if our typical criminal carries these values with him when he leaves prison, he may well be unable to readjust to the law-abiding community; he will most likely wind up back in prison.

Rethinking the Prison System

Few people are satisfied with our current methods of dealing with convicted criminals. Our current prison system inflicts punishment on them and gets them off the streets—at least for a while. Beyond this, it seems to achieve little. Although there is some consensus that the present system does not work, there is little consensus on what should be done to rectify the situation.

On the one hand, a large number of authorities have argued for a more liberal, rehabilitative approach. These people feel that rehabilitation can best be achieved through community-based treatment programs.[53] Some supporters advocate effective probation and parole programs: "Records of probationers and parolees universally demonstrate a high 'success' rate, showing that the majority of probationers and parolees complete their sentences without committing further crimes."[54] These same people also urge the establishment of community-based halfway houses which would supervise convicted offenders but would, at the same time, allow them to go to school, to work to support their families, and so on.

Large segments of the public, however, are in no mood to support these liberal proposals. Rather the general public seems to have given up on the idea that criminals can be reformed. For example, there is a trend underway to abandon indeterminate sentences in favor of fixed, or flat-time, sentences.[55] This type of sentencing procedure does not allow for probation or parole. If fixed sentences become a reality, as they have in Maine, persons convicted of a crime will, on the average, spend more time in prison; if the sentence calls for thirty years, they will serve thirty years (with the possible exception that they may be given some time off for good behavior). The fixed sentence approach reflects the belief that the only answer to the crime problem is to "lock 'em up and throw the keys away."

There is no way to predict whether or not we will eventually develop effective programs to rehabilitate criminals. At the present time, however, we do know that large segments of the public regard crime as one of our most pressing domestic problems.[56] People are sick and tired of crime and of the people who commit crimes. This is the type of environment which fosters a repressive, rather than a rehabilitative, approach to the problem of crime.

Imprisonment is at the core of our approach to dealing with crime and the criminal.

Summary

Our criminal justice system is not always just; police officers, judges and juries, and penal officials are sometimes arbitrary and discriminatory.

The suspect's first contact with the criminal justice system is with the police. The police exercise tremendous discretion in deciding who to arrest and who not to arrest.. Sometimes police discretion is necessary, but at other times it is used as a tool of discrimination.

Police sometimes resort to physical and/or verbal abuse of suspects. This behavior can be explained, although it cannot be justified, by the inherent pressures and tensions of police work.

Once arrested, the suspect (now the defendant) faces an extremely complicated judicial process. First, unless the crime is very serious, bail is set. Although the main purpose of bail is to motivate the defendant to appear at later court proceedings, it can also be used to effect preventive detention and as a tool of discrimination.

At the arraignment, the defendant pleads guilty or not guilty. Many plead guilty as a result of *plea bargaining*. Plea bargaining can be advantageous to everyone involved in the case, but it nonetheless mocks the idea of equal justice for all.

If the defendant pleads not guilty, the next step is the trial. Two of the most important factors in the outcome of the trial are the quality of the defense attorney and whether the defendant chooses to have a jury trial or a bench trial.

At the time of sentencing, judges have a great deal of discretionary power. Although discrimination in sentencing is difficult to prove, length of sentence may well depend on the defendant's race and sex, and the race of the victim.

Juvenile court is much different from adult criminal court. Since juvenile justice is aimed at rehabilitation, judges can conduct hearings in an informal, noncriminal manner and have a great deal of freedom in disposing of cases. This freedom has led to tremendous abuses.

In addition, juveniles are subject to harsher laws and, sometimes, more stringent penalties than adults. Juvenile courts can also take children away from their parents.

Imprisonment is at the core of our approach to dealing with crime and the criminal. Although one purpose of prison is reform, there is much evidence that prisons are not effective in reforming criminals.

There is no way to predict whether or not we will eventually revamp our criminal justice system in order to truly rehabilitate criminals. Although punishing criminals does not seem to decrease or stabilize our high crime rates, the general public is not presently in the mood to act upon proposals for reform.

Discussion Questions

1. Do you think that the police should have discretionary power? Under what conditions should the police exercise their discretionary powers? What are some of the disadvantages of allowing the police to exercise discretion?
2. What are some forms that police brutality and abuse can take? Why do some police officers abuse their powers?
3. What were the findings of the Manhattan Bail Project? Why are persons released on their own recognizance actually more likely to appear in court than persons released on bail?
4. What is meant by the term *plea bargaining*? What are some of the forms that plea bargaining can take? What are the pros and cons of allowing people to "cop a plea"?
5. What is involved in the adversary process? What is the basic idea or theory behind the adversary process?
6. Discuss our jury system. Do juries perpetrate gross injustices and prevent defendants from receiving fair trials? Could we have a sound judicial system without having juries? Explain your answer.
7. How can you account for the fact that some studies have found that black defendants actually seem to receive lighter sentences than white defendants? Does the evidence suggest to you that there is gross discrimination in sentencing? Why or why not?
8. Discuss the *Gault* v. *Arizona* decision. What rights did this decision extend to the juvenile offender? What impact might the Gault decision have on the operation of the juvenile court?
9. What are some of the characteristics of the prison subculture? In what ways does the prison subculture help the criminal adjust to prison life? In what ways might the prison subculture hamper ex-convicts in their later efforts to adjust to the law-abiding community?
10. Few people are satisfied with our current methods of dealing with convicted criminals. What suggestions can you make for dealing with criminals? Do you think that the general public would agree with your suggestions? Why or why not?

Glossary

adversary process The cornerstone of our trial system. Two attorneys (one for the defense and one for the prosecution) attempt to discredit each other's evidence and arguments. Through this adversary (opposing) interaction, the truth should emerge.

arraignment That step in the criminal justice process at which the defendant enters a plea. The two most important options are to plead guilty or not guilty.

bail A monetary deposit which is intended to motivate the defendant to appear at later court proceedings. If the defendant posts bail and fails to appear, his or her bail is forfeited.

bail bondsman A person who guarantees (for at least a 10 or 15 percent nonrefundable fee) that the defendant's bail will be paid if he or she fails to appear in court.

bench trial A trial before a judge only. A bench trial occurs when the defendant waives his or her right to a trial by jury.

community-based treatment programs Programs designed to rehabilitate and reform criminals while keeping them in the community. Some examples include probation, parole, and halfway houses.

criminal justice system A complex series of steps by which we process the suspected criminal offender. Contact with the criminal justice system begins at the moment of arrest (or even before) and, assuming that the defendant is found guilty, ends when sentencing has been carried out.

fixed (or flat-time) sentences Sentencing which does not allow for probation or parole. If the sentence is for thirty years, then the person would actually serve thirty years (with the possible exception that he or she may be given some time off for good behavior).

Gault* v. *Arizona A 1967 Supreme Court decision which gave the juvenile offender many of the same rights given to the adult offender—including the right to counsel and the right to cross-examine accusers.

indeterminate sentences Sentences with very broad limits, for example, two to ten years. Primary responsibility is placed on the parole board to determine when the defendant is ready for release.

juvenile status offenses Offenses for which a child, but not an adult, can be processed through the court system. Examples include incorrigibility, truancy, and running away from home.

plea bargaining Bargaining in which the defendant agrees to plead guilty if the prosecuting attorney agrees to reduce the charges against him, to recommend leniency in sentencing, or to allow him to serve his sentences concurrently.

police discretion A phrase which reminds us that the police have great latitude in deciding whether or not to arrest an individual, even though he or she has clearly committed a crime.

preventive detention The practice of setting bail so high that the defendant cannot possibly pay it. This keeps the defendant in confinement until the case is decided in court.

prison subculture A system of norms and values which helps criminals adjust to prison life but which may hamper them in their efforts to become law-abiding citizens after their release.

Suggestions for Further Reading

Blumberg, Abraham S., ed., *Law and Order: The Scales of Justice*, Rev. 2nd Ed. (New Brunswick, N.J.: Transaction, 1973). A fascinating, easily read collection of articles on justice in America. The central theme is that the wealthy receive the substance of justice whereas the black, the young, the poor, and the deviant receive only the form of justice.

Frank, Jerome, *Courts on Trial: Myth and Reality in American Justice* (New York: Atheneum,1963). A detailed look at our court system, written with clarity, wit, and candor. Frank looks at our trial courts, how they operate, and at reforms that are needed in our court system.

Neigher, Alan, "The Gault Decision: Due Process and the Juvenile Courts," in John P. Reed and Fuad Baali, eds., *Faces of Delinquency* (Englewood Cliffs, N.J.: Prentice-Hall, 1972), pp. 345-59. An in-depth analysis of a Supreme Court decision that may eventually revolutionize our entire system of juvenile justice.

Neubauer, David W., *Criminal Justice in Middle America* (Morristown, N.J.: General Learning, 1974). A case study of how criminal justice is administered in one medium-sized town. This study constitutes an excellent introduction to the criminal justice system and how it works.

Newman, Donald J., *Introduction to Criminal Justice* (Philadelphia: Lippincott, 1975). As the title indicates, this is a basic textbook that introduces the student to the entire field of criminal justice in America. This book is highly recommended for anyone who wishes to acquire a factual understanding of our criminal justice system.

Quinney, Richard, *Criminology: Analysis and Critique of Crime in America* (Boston: Little, Brown, 1975), esp. Part IV. Although some readers will find Quinney's treatment of "Enforcing and Administering Criminal Law" to be slanted and even somewhat biased, he nonetheless provides the reader with a perceptive look at criminal justice.

Radzinowicz, Leon, and Marvin E. Wolfgang, *Crime and Justice*, Vol. II, *The Criminal in the Arms of the Law* (New York: Basic, 1971). An extremely well-chosen selection of articles that examine the purposes of penal sanctions, the police, and judicial decision-making processes. One would be hard pressed to find a better anthology of articles dealing with various facets of criminal justice.

Skolnick, Jerome H., *Justice Without Trial: Law Enforcement in Democratic Society* (New York: Wiley, 1966). An insightful case study and analysis of the police and how they function on a day-by-day basis as perceived by an authority in the sociology of the law. Of particular interest is Skolnick's sketch of the policeman's working personality.

Notes

[1]During recent years the phrase "law and order" has, of course, taken on a somewhat different meaning than that implied here. For further discussion, see Abraham S. Blumberg, "Law and Order: The Counterfeit Crusade," in Abraham S. Blumberg, ed., *Law and Order: The Scales of Justice*, Rev. 2nd Ed. (New Brunswick, N.J: Transaction, 1973), pp. 1-45.

[2]For an excellent overview of the entire criminal justice system, see Donald J. Newman, *Introduction to Criminal Justice* (Philadelphia: Lippincott, 1975).

[3]For further discussion of aggressive, preventive patrol and the problems that it creates, see *Ibid.*, pp. 173-78.

[4]For example, see Joseph Goldstein, "Police Discretion Not to Invoke the Criminal Process: Low-Visibility Decisions in the Administration of Justice," in Abraham S. Goldstein and Joseph Goldstein, eds., *Crime, Law, and Society* (New York: Free Press, 1971), pp. 145-72; and James Q. Wilson, *Varieties of Police Behavior* (Cambridge: Harvard, 1968), pp. 83-139.

[5]Wilson, *Varieties of Police Behavior*, p. 84.

[6]See Goldstein, "Police Discretion Not to Invoke the Criminal Process," pp. 152-60.

[7]For example, see U.S. President's Commission on Law Enforcement and Administration of Justice, "Police Practices," in Leon Radzinowicz and Marvin E. Wolfgang, eds., *Crime and Justice*, Vol. II, *The Criminal in the Arms of the Law* (New York: Basic, 1971), pp. 270-73; and Irving Piliavin and Scott Briar, "Police Encounters with Juveniles," *American Journal of Sociology*, 70 (September, 1964), pp. 206-14.

[8]See Newman, *Introduction to Criminal Justice*, pp. 169-73.

[9]A. C. Germann et al., *Introduction to Law Enforcement and Criminal Justice* (Springfield, Ill.: Thomas, 1973), p. 345.

[10]See Albert J. Reiss, Jr., "Police Brutality," in Radzinowicz and Wolfgang, eds., *Crime and Justice*, Vol. II, p. 303.

[11]*Ibid.*, pp. 303-4.

[12]*Ibid.*, p. 295.

[13]Jerome H. Skolnick, *Justice Without Trial: Law Enforcement in Democratic Society* (New York: Wiley, 1966), p. 56.

[14]*Ibid.*, p. 44.

[15]*Ibid.*, pp. 45–46.

[16]Stuart S. Nagel, "The Tipped Scales of American Justice," in Blumberg, ed., *Law and Order*, pp. 52–53.

[17]Patricia M. Wald, "Poverty and Criminal Justice," in U.S. President's Commission on Law Enforcement and Administration of Justice, *Task Force Report: The Courts* (Washington, D.C.: U.S. Government Printing Office, 1967), p. 145.

[18]See Charles E. Ares, Anne Rankin, and Herbert Sturz, "The Manhattan Bail Project," in Radzinowicz and Wolfgang, eds., *Crime and Justice*, Vol II, pp. 396-410.

[19]*Ibid.*, p. 407.

[20]*Ibid.*, p. 405.

[21]Richard Quinney, *Criminology: Analysis and Critique of Crime in America* (Boston: Little, Brown, 1975), p. 204.

[22]For a more thorough discussion of the forms that plea bargaining can take, see Donald J. Newman, "Informal Bargaining," in Radzinowicz and Wolfgang, eds., *Crime and Justice*, Vol. II, pp. 430-33.

[23]Abraham S. Blumberg, *Criminal Justice* (Chicago: Quadrangle, 1967), p. 65.

[24]Newman, "Informal Bargaining," in Radzinowicz and Wolfgang, eds., *Crime and Justice*, Vol. II, p. 436.

[25]There are several major ways in which indigent defendants are provided with counsel. In some jurisdictions the judge assigns cases to local attorneys on a rotational basis. These attorneys are usually paid a nominal fee plus expenses. Other jurisdictions have a public defender who is hired by the court. In still other jurisdictions the local bar association provides free counsel.

[26] See Dallin H. Oaks and Warren Lehman, "Lawyers for the Poor," in Blumberg, ed., *Law and Order*, pp. 159-72.

[27]Cited in Quinney, *Criminology*, p. 211.

[28]See Jerome Frank, *Courts on Trial: Myth and Reality in American Justice* (New York: Atheneum, 1963), esp. pp. 108-45.

[29]Harry Kalven, Jr., and Hans Zeisel, *The American Jury* (Boston: Little, Brown, 1966), Table 51.

[30]See Edward Green, "Inter-and Intra-Racial Crime Relative to Sentencing," *Journal of Criminal Law, Criminology, and Police Science*, 55 (September, 1964), p. 358.

[31]Nagel, "The Tipped Scales of American Justice," p. 58.

[32]Green, "Inter- and Intra-Racial Crime Relative to Sentencing," pp. 350-56.

[33]*Ibid*., p. 351.

[34]Blumberg, *Criminal Justice*, p. 65.

[35]See Arthur Rosett, "The Negotiated Guilty Plea," *The Annals of the American Academy of Political and Social Science*, 374 (November, 1967), p. 72.

[36]See Leonard Savitz, *Dilemmas in Criminology* (New York: McGraw-Hill, 1967), p. 111.

[37]See Stuart S. Nagel and Lenore J. Weitzman, "Double Standard of American Justice," in Blumberg, ed., *Law and Order*, esp. p. 110.

[38]For an interesting history of the juvenile court movement, see Anthony M. Platt, *The Child Savers: The Invention of Delinquency* (Chicago: University of Chicago, 1969).

[39]For an in-depth analysis of the Gault case, see Alan Neigher, "The Gault Decision: Due Process and the Juvenile Courts," in John P. Reed and Fuad Baali, eds., *Faces of Delinquency* (Englewood Cliffs, N.J.: Prentice-Hall, 1972), pp. 345–59.

[40]Paul Lerman, "Delinquents Without Crimes," in Blumberg, ed., *Law and Order*, p. 255.

[41]Neigher, "The Gault Decision," pp. 353-57.

[42]Edwin M. Lemert, "The Juvenile Court—Quest and Realities," in Blumberg, ed., *Law and Order*, p. 238.

[43]Lerman, "Delinquents Without Crimes," p. 242.

[44]Lemert, "The Juvenile Court," p. 230.

[45]*Ibid*.

[46]Newman, *Introduction to Criminal Justice*, p. 291.

[47]Quinney, *Criminology*, p. 229.

[48]See Daniel Glaser, "How Many Prisoners Return?" in Radzinowicz and Wolfgang, eds., *Crime and Justice*, Vol. III, *The Criminal in Confinement*, p. 202.

[49]*Ibid.*, p. 205.

[50]See Edwin H. Sutherland and Donald R. Cressey, *Criminology*, 9th Ed., (Philadelphia: Lippincott, 1974), esp. pp. 517, 608.

[51]There have been several excellent studies of the prison community and prison subcultures. For example, see Gresham M. Sykes and Sheldon L. Messinger, "The Inmate Social System," in Radzinowicz and Wolfgang, eds., *Crime and Justice*, Vol. III, *The Criminal in Confinement*, pp. 77-85; Donald Clemmer, *The Prison Community* (New York: Rinehart, 1958); Peter G. Garabedian, "Social Roles and Processes of Socialization in the Prison Community," *Social*

Problems, 11 (Fall, 1963), pp. 139-52; and Gresham M. Sykes, *The Society of Captives: A Study of a Maximum Security Prison* (Princeton, N.J.: Princeton, 1958).

[52]Sykes and Messinger, "The Inmate Social System," p. 78.

[53]Newman, *Introduction to Criminal Justice*, pp. 291-96.

[54]*Ibid.*, p. 294.

[55]"Fixed Sentences: New Step in U.S. Prison Reform," *Pittsburgh Post-Gazette* (October 2, 1976), p. 1f.

[56]See Gwynn Nettler, *Explaining Crime* (New York: McGraw-Hill, 1974), p. 3.

Picture Credits

5 U.P.I.
10 International Correspondence School
11 Richard Stromberg
15 Charles Gatewood
24 Stephen Frish/Photo Researchers
27 David Powers/Jereboam
31 Cary Wolinsky/Stock, Boston
34 George Gardner
42 Nicholas Sapieha/Stock, Boston
60 Alfred Eisenstadt © 1964, Time Inc.
65 Bruce Davidson/Magnum
75 Paul Fusco/Magnum
78 National Institute of Mental Health
89 Jean-Claude LeJuene/Black Star
92 Charles Gatewood
94 Werner Wolff/Black Star
108 Scott, Foresman staff
109 Curt Gunther/Camera 5
121 The Smithsonian Institution
123 Ian Berry/Magnum
128 Scott, Foresman staff
131 Foothorap/Jereboam
133 Peter Martens/Nancy Palmer
138 Lee Chaplin/Black Star
158 Virginia Hamilton
161 Bob Adelman
165 Paul Sequira
169 Wide World
179 Sepp Seitz/Magnum
180 Donald Dietz/Stock, Boston
181 Larry Keenan/Nest
186 Jack Spratt/Black Star
197 Burt Glinn/Magnum
199 Charles Harbutt/Magnum
209 Larry Keenan/Nest
213 Timothy Carlson/Stock, Boston
216 Owen Franken/Stock, Boston
223 U.P.I.
227 Danny Lyon/Magnum
244 *(top)* Constantine Manos/Magnum
(bottom) Bruce Davidson/Magnum
246 Lisa Ebright
248 Richard Stromberg
252 George Gardner
259 O.E.O.
277 Library of Congress
281 Norris McNamara/Nancy Palmer
285 U.P.I.
286 U.P.I.
289 Ellis Herwig/Stock, Boston
300 *(left)* Ellis Herwig/Stock, Boston
(center) U.P.I.
(right) Peter Vandermark/Stock, Boston
301 James Motlow/Jereboam
312 Abigail Heyman/Magnum
314 Peter Bradshaw
318 Bettye Lane/Nancy Palmer
330 U.P.I.
331 *(top left)* by courtesy of the Colonial Penn Group
(top right) Jay King
(bottom) Mark Jury Communications
337 Mark Jury Communications
344 Peter Amft
347 Richard Stromberg
348 Paul Sequira
361 Bhupendra Karia/Magnum
368 Roger Malloch/Magnum
369 Patricia Hollander Gross/Stock, Boston
371 Ellis Herwig/Stock, Boston
373 Henri Bureau/Sygma
378 Gazdar/Woodfin Camp
390 Scott, Foresman staff
399 E. Hamton/Stock, Boston
406 Patricia Hollander Gross/Stock, Boston
408 Wide World
411 Bill Owens
413 H. Kubota/Magnum
426 Constantine Manos/Magnum
427 Scott, Foresman staff
430 Michael Mauney
438 Cary Wolinsky/Stock, Boston
442 Michael Mauney
455–477 Scott, Foresman staff

Name Index

Subject Index

In this subject index an asterisk (*) is used to indicate the page on which the Glossary definition of the term is found.